THEOLOGY AND THE PHILOSOPHY OF SCIENCE

WOLFHART PANNENBERG

THEOLOGY
AND THE PHILOSOPHY
OF SCIENCE

Translated by
FRANCIS McDONAGH

Darton, Longman & Todd
London

First published in Great Britain in 1976 by
Darton, Longman & Todd Ltd
85 Gloucester Road, London SW7 4SU

Copyright © 1976 Darton, Longman & Todd Ltd

Printed in Great Britain by The Anchor Press Ltd,
and bound by Wm. Brendon & Son Ltd, both of Tiptree, Essex

ISBN 0 232 51290 6

CONTENTS

INTRODUCTION

Philosophy of Science and Theology

PHILOSOPHY OF SCIENCE AND THEOLOGY

1. University Reform, Philosophy of Science, Theology

IT CANNOT be a mere accident that a period of worldwide uncertainty in institutions of higher education should coincide with a breakthrough in discussion within philosophy of science to an intensity and influence it has not enjoyed in Germany since before the founding of the Berlin University. Not that the movement for university reform and the activity in philosophy of science are completely parallel. University reform is today surrounded by the ruin of the deceptive hopes which had been fastened on the power of institutional changes, and on the abolition of the professorial privileges which were claimed to be an obstacle to the free development of knowledge. These hopes were the modern embodiment of the idea of the republic of scholars, though the original idea had already lost most of its impetus through the demands of mass academic training and the trend to autonomy among specialist disciplines. In the meantime the institutional forms of Wilhelm von Humboldt's republic of scholars have been abolished or fundamentally changed, but it cannot be claimed that academic life has shown a notable increase in energy as a result of this liberation from professorial privileges. The result has more often been a dramatic worsening of the conditions and atmosphere in which academic work is carried on, as a result of the greatly increased load of administrative work and the intergroup fighting which has grown up in universities. This is yet another area in which it has been shown to be a misguided optimism which looked to the abolition of traditional institutional structures to produce by itself conditions in which life could expand freely, as though the only restrictions were these external ones. The difficulties it is desired to eliminate usually have deeper roots, as in this case in the question of the proper objects of study of the sciences.

The unsatisfactoriness of so many previous attempts to reform universities through institutional change has given additional importance to the discussion in philosophy of science. In spite of a sometimes strong air of the esoteric, philosophy of science is in no sense an attempt to escape from the primary professional responsibilities of science into an unproductive narcissism. Its object is, rather, to reach a new self-understanding of science in general which will provide the basis for a new ordering of scientific disciplines and their methods. An important part of this process is the questioning of the claims of established specialisms whose introduction is no longer remembered. The individual areas of study are being forced to consider the reasons for their existence within a wider context and to justify themselves afresh. If it is possible at all, a renewal of the sciences can be hoped for only as the result of such a consideration, which, since it derives from a common concentration on the fundamental questions of what constitutes the characteristic attitude of science as such, may for that reason be able to help the university as the universe of sciences eventually to discover a new structure, something it will never get as long as the word 'reform' is mainly a cover for power-struggles between various groups.

If the aim of this discussion is to produce a new version of the concept of a scientific discipline and of the system of the sciences, and also to provide the basis for a later careful renewal of the institutions of scientific research and education, theology cannot afford to ignore it. The institutional base of theology in the university is extremely precarious when it rests on no more than existing practice. This institutional position is derived ultimately from the medieval view of the university and the system of the sciences. Even then the existence of theology in the university depended on the fact that it could be shown to have a place in the totality of the sciences. Since the medieval arguments for that position have since become obsolete, the continued existence of theological faculties in the universities of secular states has become a mere matter of fact. It is due to a certain respect on the part of society for the origins of the western university and to society's awareness of the social power of the main religious denominations. This is particularly clear in cases where denominational pluralism has led to a duplication of theological faculties in a single university. This situation so clearly displays the influence of non-academic factors on the institutional structure of the university that its potential as a threat to the continuance of theological faculties in universities cannot be underestimated. The denominational connections and divisions of university theology make attempts by theology to find its place, or any place, among the totality of disciplines in the university more difficult. Nevertheless these efforts, and theology's participation in the discussion in philosophy of science, ought to be seen as vital to theology as part of the university, since it can find its unity and inner articulation only through a rethinking of the nature of science and the range of its own responsibilities. By taking part in this discussion theology is not contributing to the ideological legitimation of the status quo. Instead it is beginning a process of self-criticism of its present condition which it hopes will be the source of its renewal as a scientific discipline, just as the university as a whole can renew itself only through reflection on the nature of science within a multiplicity of specialised disciplines. Theology's membership of the class of scientific disciplines cannot, of course, be assumed without discussion. But equally a negative answer to this question, if it is to be more than mere prejudice, cannot, given the long history of the subject, simply be taken for granted.

A discipline's self-appraisal in terms of philosophy of science must always have two aspects. On the one hand it seeks to establish an external relation to other disciplines on the common basis of their scientific character. On the other, it must consider its own internal organisation. Here too the examination starts from the existing state of affairs. The plurality of subsidiary disciplines within theology makes it necessary to ask what is the specifically theological feature which links these disciplines. Conversely a conception of theology in general ought to be able to show to what extent its internal organisation into the disciplines of exegesis, church history, dogmatics and practical theology can be defended as necessary or at least rational, or to what extent the existing divisions of theology should be critically re-examined in the light of the concept of theology, particularly as regards their mutual relations and their understanding of method. This second aspect of the self-appraisal of theology within the framework of philosophy of science is the subject-matter of the theological encyclopedia. Through its content it is closely related to the first, the question of the sense in which theology is a science, since the plurality of theological disciplines means — as the word *disciplina* indicates — a plurality of scientific methods and areas of investigation. The mutual relations and unity of these disciplines and areas can be determined only by means of a concept of theology as a science.

This is much more than a matter of 'science for science's sake', both in the general philosophical aspect of the concept of theology and in that of an encylopedia of theological disciplines. The questions involved have far-reaching implications and go far beyond theoretical discussion. The encyclopedic question of the relation of the theological disciplines to the single science of theology has direct implications for the composition of theological faculties and for the structure of theological studies. Any rational reform of the theology course must be guided by a decision about what theology in fact is and what knowledge and skills a person must acquire to become competent in theology. The crucial question here is what specific subjects make up the essential area of theological enquiry. Individual theological disciplines are not in the theological faculty for their own sake, but are practised and taught in the belief that, say, church history or biblical exegesis are necessary parts of theology. It would be conceivable for the interpretation of biblical texts to be taught as a part of a general course in literature, or as a branch of classical philology or semitic studies, and church history could be catered for within general history. What makes these disciplines theological disciplines once they are inside the theology faculty? Is it only the practical requirements arising out of the Church's need for a training process for its personnel? Or is there some essential unifying factor, one deriving from the nature of theology? For that matter, what is theology? All the questions about the internal structure of theology lead back to the question of how theology sees itself, and in particular how it sees itself as a scientific discipline.

2. The Origin of Theology's Claim to be a Science

It is noteworthy that the question of theology's scientific character first becomes prominent in the discussions about its self-understanding in the thirteenth century – that is, in the century in which the first universities came into being, starting with Paris about 1200. The word 'theology' itself came into common use as a comprehensive description for the investigation and presentation of Christian teaching only a short time before. The dialectician Abelard had used it in the early twelfth century in the titles of successive versions of his major work (*Theologia christiana, Theologia, Theologia scholarum*) to describe sacred learning as a whole.[1] This usage then spread in the work of Gilbert de la Porrée and his school. The term 'theology' had also been in common use long before, however, but in a narrower sense, the influence of which can still be seen in the twelfth century. 'Theology' was used as the name of one part of Christian teaching, the doctrine of God and the Trinity, and in the early church, especially in the east, it had a companion term, 'economy', to describe the saving activity of God in human history. This use of 'theology' in the narrower sense to refer to the doctrine of God itself goes back only to the beginning of the third century. In his *Stromata*, Clement of Alexandria[2] contrasted Christian *theologia* with the *mythologia* of the pagan poets: just as the maenads in the story of Dionysus tore the god in pieces, so the truth of the imperishable Logos (= *theologia*) had been

[1] On the history of the term theology in early scholasticism see B. Geyer, 'Facultas theologica. Eine bedeuntungsgeschichtliche Untersuchung', *ZKG* 75 (1964), pp. 133–45, on Abelard esp. pp. 140–1. Radulphus Ardens' *Speculum universale*, mentioned by J. Wallmann (*Der Theologiebegriff bei Johann Gerhard und Georg Calixt*, 1961, pp. 12–13) is not older than Abelard's work, as Wallman believed. Wallmann still accepts the incorrect dating of the work by M. Grabmann (*Die Geschichte der scholastichen Methode* I, 1909, reprinted 1956, pp. 246ff.) to the end of the eleventh century, whereas modern work has shown that it cannot have been written much before 1200 and belongs to the school of Gilbert of Poitiers (J. Gründel, *LThK*, 2nd ed. 8, 967–8).

[2] The basic treatment of the earlier history of the concept of theology is still F. Kattenbusch, 'Die Entstehung einer christlichen Theologie (zur Geschichte der Ausdrücke theologia, theologein, theologos) ', *ZThK* (NF) 11 (1930), pp. 161–205, published separately 1962. On Clement, Kattenbusch 39. Additional bibliography in B. Geyer, 'Facultas theologica', p. 138, n. 32.

fragmented by the philosophers. For Clement theology concerned not myths but true knowledge of God, which was first revealed in its fullness in the revelation of Christ. The concept of theology used here derives, as will be explained later, from philosophy, and in particular from Aristotle. For the Latin Fathers the word still had a foreign flavour, and they used it sparingly.[3] It was first brought into common use by the twelfth-century scholastics, who had learned it from Pseudo-Denis and especially from Boethius,[4] and it was the scholastics who extended its meaning to cover the whole of Christian teaching. This happened as part of the activity of the medieval schools, which were anxious to separate sacred learning from the profane disciplines or faculties: 'The word *theologia* first became established in general use in association with the university term *facultas theologica.*'[5] The term also raised the question of the scientific status of theology.

In the thirteenth century the question was 'a new element which was bound to have a strong influence on the method of teaching'.[6] Previously Christian teaching, under the influence of Augustine, had been regarded as *sapientia,* in sharp distinction from *scientia.*[7] Sciences, Augustine argued in his book on the Trinity, dealt with temporal things, whereas wisdom was devoted to the Eternal, that is to God as the highest good. But

[3] B. Geyer, p. 139. As an illustration Geyer cites Augustine, *De civ, Dei* VIII, 1 (*CSEL* 40, 1, 354, 2), where Augustine comments that his immediate concern is to refute not all the views of the philosophers 'sed eas tantum quae ad theologiam pertinent, quo verbo Graeco significari intelligimus de divinitate rationem sive sermonem.

[4] Geyer, pp. 139–40.

[5] Geyer, p. 143. On Gilbert of Poitiers see also M. A. Schmidt, *Gottheit und Trinität nach dem Kommentar des Gilbert Porreta zu Boethius, De Trinitate, 1956,* pp. 24–49.

[6] Geyer, p. 144. The history of the concept of theology in the thirteenth century and the controversies over the scientific status of theology in the period have been described by M.-D. Chenu, 'La théologie comme science au XIIIe siècle', *Archives d'Histoire doctrinale et littéraire du Moyen Age* 2 (1927), pp. 31–71.

[7] On Augustine's doctrine of science see R. Lorenz, 'Die Wissenschaftslehre Augustins', *ZKG* 67 (1955/56), pp. 29–60 and 213–51. The concept of wisdom in Augustine is discussed at length by R. Holte, *Béatitude et sagesse. Saint Augustin et le problème de la fin de l'homme dans la philosophie ancienne,* 1962.

this did not mean that knowledge and wisdom excluded each other. The various branches of knowledge could lead to wisdom.[8] For this to happen, however, the aspects of knowledge which the sciences acquired from transitory, temporal things must be ordered in relation to the highest good. Knowledge and science must serve wisdom, which was also the goal of philosophy, the pursuit of wisdom. Augustine found the perfection of philosophy in the teaching of Christianity, which he called 'true philosophy'.[9]

The view of Christian teaching as wisdom appeared earlier in Clement of Alexandria, though with a different emphasis from Augustine's. Like him, Clement took up the idea of philosophy as 'love of wisdom' but used it to bring out the superiority of Christian teaching to philosophy, claiming that it was the wisdom towards which the philosophers could only strive. According to Clement, the instructed Christian was therefore the possessor of true knowledge, the true Gnostic (Strom. I, 5, 30, 1). Clement did not regard Paul's attack on the 'wisdom' of which the Corinthians boasted as an obstacle to his view,[10] claiming that Paul's criticisms were directed only against Epicurean (and Stoic) philosophy (Strom. I, 11, 50, 6). It is not necessary to accept this exegesis in order to agree with Clement at least in saying that Paul was not trying to reject the wisdom which classical philosophy sought. His immediate quarrel was with a quite specific Corinthian 'wisdom', which he opposed because it had no room for the cross of Christ. Paul could still say that God made Christ our wisdom (1 Co 1:30), and when Clement described Christian teaching as wisdom he meant this wisdom of

[8] H.-I. Marrou, Saint Augustin et la fin de la culture antique, 1949. Augustine's unfavourable view of scientific curiosity, stressed by H. Blumenberg (Revue des Etudes augustiniennes 7 (1961), pp. 35–70, and Die Legitimität der Neuzeit, 1966, pp. 295–314) is most marked towards the end of his life (Lorenz, 'Die Wissenschaftslehre Augustins', pp. 244ff) and even then is directed at a pedantry absorbed in trivialities rather than interested in attaining wisdom. It does not imply an unfavourable view of the sciences as such.

[9] Augustine, Contra Julianum IV, 14, 72 (PL 44, col. 775): 'Obsecro te, non sit honestior philosophia gentium quam nostra christiana, quae una est vera philosophia, quando quidem studuim vel amor sapientiae significatur hoc nomine.'

[10] 1 Co 1.18; cf. U. Wilckens, TDNT, VII, 517–22.

God which is revealed in Christ.

While Clement was the first to use the medieval image of philosophy as the handmaid of theology (*ancilla theologiae*), which was given its classical form in Peter Damian's allegorical interpretation of Dt 21:10ff,[11] Augustine contrasted Christian teaching not so much with philosophy as with knowledge. In Augustine, Christian teaching, as the true philosophy, was associated with philosophy in opposition to the sciences, which dealt with temporal things rather than the eternal. However, Christian teaching had also to deal not only with the eternal God but also with temporal phenomena. This followed from the incarnation of the eternal divine Word.[12] By the incarnation, said Augustine, appealing to Paul (Col 2:3), Christ was the essence not only of wisdom but also of knowledge.[13]

The conception of Christian teaching as wisdom, which, thanks to Augustine's influence, remained active until well into the middle ages, is an illuminating combination of both Platonic and Aristotelian themes. Plato had the idea that philosophy was not wisdom itself but a striving after wisdom, 'love of wisdom', as the literal meaning of the word implies, an intermediate state between complete ignorance and the perfect wisdom possessed by the gods (*Symp.* 204b).[14] But if even philosophy did not reach the full status of wisdom, Plato could obviously not permit any other learning to be regarded as wisdom. Least of all would he have given that title to what in his time was called theology, namely the myths of the poets.

Unlike Plato, Aristotle regarded wisdom as attainable by

---

[11] Peter Damian, *De divina omnipotentia,* chap. 5 (*PL* 145, 603D).

[12] Augustine, *De Trinitate,* XIII, 19 (n. 24): 'Quod autem Verbum est sine tempore et sine loco, est Patri coaeternum et ubique totum; de quo si quisquam potest, quantum potest, veracem proferre sermonem, sermo ille erit sapientiae; ac per hoc Verbum caro factum, quod est Christus Jesus, et sapientiae Thesauros habet et scientiae (1033).'

[13] *De Trin.,* XIII, 19: 'Scientia nostra ergo Christus est, sapientia quoque nostra idem Christus est. Ipse nobis fidem de rebus temporalibus inserit, ipse de sempiternis exhibit veritatem. Per ipsum pergimus ad ipsum, tendimus per scientiam ad sapientiam: ab uno eodemque Christo non recedimus, in quo sunt omnes thesauri sapientiae et scientiae absconditi (1034).'

[14] Augustine traced the origin of this interpretation of philosophy beyond Plato to Pythagoras (*De Trin.,* XIV, 1 (1037)).

philosophy, and in this he was followed by the Stoics. Aristotle also made a remark about the relations of knowledge and wisdom (*epistēmē* and *sophia, Nic. Eth.* VI, 6–7, 1141a) which was to be important for the later development of theology. For him wisdom was the highest branch of knowledge, because the wise man not only knows what can be deduced from first principles but also has in himself a firm intuitive knowledge of the sources (*archai*) of knowledge. Wisdom therefore includes both intuitive insight (*nous*) and knowledge derived from deduction (*epistēmē*, 1141a 17-20). It is the science of the highest forms of being (1141b 5f), the divine things, and of the sources of all existence and all knowledge. The transmitters of this knowledge, according to Aristotle, are the philosophers, and in the same passage (1141b 6f) he gives as examples Anaxagoras and Thales.

Clement of Alexandria followed Plato in distinguishing philosophy as love of wisdom from wisdom itself, but did not regard wisdom as unattainable; he believed it to be embodied in Christian teaching, which he held to be divine teaching and therefore distinct not only from the sciences but also from philosophy as something unique. Augustine also described Christian teaching as wisdom, though not so much in opposition as analogous to philosophy. Even knowledge is not excluded from Christian teaching, which has to consider God not only in his eternity but also in his incarnation. Nevertheless, in contrast to Aristotle, Augustine maintained a distinction between knowledge and wisdom, corresponding to the distinction between the temporal and the eternal.[15] By this characteristic distinction, close to Plato in spirit but contradicting his words, Augustine brought the sciences and philosophy into harmony: he reduced the latter 'to the knowledge of God and the soul and then made the sciences a means to reaching this goal, thus including philosophy'.[16]

---

[15] In *De Trin.* XIV, 3 Augustine mentions a definition of the *disputantes de sapientia* which makes 'wisdom' cover knowledge of both divine and human things. He himself, however, quotes 1 Co 12: 8 ('To one is given . . . the utterance of wisdom, and to another the utterance of knowledge') to justify a distinction in which 'strictly speaking, "wisdom" refers to knowledge of divine things and "knowledge" to knowledge of human things' (1037).

[16] Lorenz, 'Die Wissenschaftslehre Augustins', p. 44.

In the thirteenth century, theology's view of itself as a wisdom distinct from and superior to the sciences (including philosophy) could no longer be maintained. Aristotle, the philosophical authority who increasingly determined the contemporary understanding of science, had regarded wisdom as the highest science and had identified it with philosophy. Sacred learning had therefore also to produce its legitimation as a science, which at that time meant as a science by the criteria worked out by Aristotle in his *Posterior Analytics*, i.e. a system of logical deductions from first principles. In theology the place of these principles had to be filled by the articles of faith.

The history of the discussions about the scientific status of theology from the thirteenth century to the present will be dealt with in more detail later. For the present it is enough to say that the question of the extent to which theology is a science has been in the forefront of all efforts to state what Christian teaching believes itself to be since the thirteenth century. Since that time the effort to clarify the relation of theology to the dominant concept of science has also involved the question of the position of theology in the university.

Part of the background to this activity is a still more general concern of Christian thought: from the very beginning of anything that could be called Christian theology, Christian teachers linked the Christian tradition with the ideas of the philosophers, and in particular identified the God of faith with the God of philosophy, in an attempt to demonstrate the general truth of Christian doctrines. Gerhard Ebeling has shown that this connection of a religious tradition with the general outlook of philosophy as it had developed in Greece constitutes the uniqueness of what Christianity has become familiar with as 'theology'.[17] Characteristic of this approach is the initial suspicion shown by Christian thinkers towards the expression *theologia*, which was used to describe the mythical 'theology' of the poets. In the face of this Christian thought felt an affinity with the criticism of the myths by the philosophers, and regarded itself as 'true philosophy'. The concept 'theology' was accepted in Christianity only in the specific sense it had acquired in

---

[17] *RGG*, 3rd ed. VI, 754–69 (s.v. 'Theologie').

philosophy, and in particular in Aristotle, of the science of divine, that is, incorporeal things (Aristotle, *Met.* 1026a 19; 1064b 3), one of the three theoretical sciences, mathematics, physics and theology. In this use theology covers what was called metaphysics, and this, as well as meaning the science of supra-physical entities, could also be described as the science of being in itself. This sense of theology was limited in Christian thought to the doctrine of God, as distinguished from that of the divine economy or saving history. In this way the history of the meaning of the term 'theology' in Christianity is itself an example of the close connection between Christian thought and philosophy. This connection was developed by Christian thinkers from as early as the second century in an attempt to demonstrate the general truth of the Christian message, and this attempt was fundamental for the development of Christianity as a Jewish sect spreading in a non-Jewish world.

The same concern, to defend the truth of Christianity by generally accepted criteria, has been present since the thirteenth century in the argument about the scientific status of theology and its right to be included among the sciences taught in a university. If theology were now forced to disappear from universities on the ground, maintained by many people, that it is essentially tied to authority and therefore unscientific, this would be a severe setback for the Christian understanding of truth, even if theology were taken over by educational establishments belonging to the Church and continued to be studied there. But such a change could also contain dangers for the sciences, in particular because without the critical collaboration of theology and philosophy[18] the unity of knowledge, which prevents the sciences from totally disintegrating into a set of completely separate disciplines and ossifying, would no longer be appreciated. Collaboration between theology and philosophy is necessary because philosophy alone cannot provide a basis for the understanding of the unity of the perception of meaning, the historical roots of intellectual life. Why is this so?

It has become apparent that the question of how far theology is a science is presupposed in the question of the relation of

[18] For a fuller discussion see W. Pannenberg, 'Christliche Theologie und philosophische Kritik', *Gottesgedanke und menschliche Freiheit*, 1972, pp. 48ff.

theology to the university and the set of sciences taught there. This is why the subject came into prominence only in the thirteenth century, as a direct result of the Aristotelian concept of science. Since then theology as a whole has been regarded no longer as merely *sapientia,* but as *scientia* as well.[19] Part of the background to this development was the fundamental concern of Christian thought to prove its truth to itself by generally acceptable philosophical criteria. Since the thirteenth century one expression of this concern has been the importance of the scientific status of theology in theology's own view of itself.

3. Theological Encyclopedia as a Question about the Internal Organisation of Theology

For a long time the importance of the concept of theology as the unifying principle of the various theological disciplines has been treated under the heading of 'theological encyclopedia', a traditional title of books and courses. The practical connection between this subject and the question of whether theology is a science has already been mentioned. Only a concept of theology as a science makes it possible to determine which theological disciplines are necessary for theology to be practised methodically, that is, with scientific validity. In fact, however, the theological disciplines were not the result of such systematic consideration. The practical needs and interests which led to their

[19] In early Protestant theology the view of theology as *sapientia* rather than *scientia* had a temporary revival under the influence of the dichotomy between revelation and reason (or philosophy). In 1610 Johann Gerhard, in the foreword to the first volume of his *Loci theologici,* rejected the scholastic view of theology as a science, mainly on account of the distinction between *scire* and *credere*: 'scientiae enim certitudo ab internis et inhaerentibus principiis, fidei vero ab externis, vid. ab auctoritate revelantis pendet' (1885 ed. by Frank, p. 2 no. 8). On Gerhard, see also the book by Wallmann mentioned in note 1 above. But as early as 1623 Johann Heinrich Alsted, in his *Methodus sacrosanctae theologiae,* while rejecting the view that theology was a branch of knowledge in the strict sense for similar reasons to Gerhard (I, 9, p. 38), nevertheless allowed the application of 'knowledge' in a more general sense to theology because scripture referred to 'knowledge' of divine things. In support of his view

establishment and development will have to be discussed in detail later. Demonstrations of the systematic connection between theological disciplines have an overwhelmingly a posteriori character; they are the result of subsequent critical reflection on existing theological disciplines and their methods in terms of the current conception of theology and its purposes.

In the sense mentioned above, theological encyclopedia is a modern discipline. It grew out of the multiplicity of attempts to produce a survey of theology as a whole and an introduction for students, and was placed on a firm basis for the first time by Schleiermacher's *Brief Outline of the Study of Theology* (1811, 2nd edition 1830). Schleiermacher made it a theory of theology which justified its internal structure by appealing to its concept. His book has remained the classical work in the field. [20]

The term 'encyclopedia' goes back to the Greek expression *enkyklios paideia,* which was used from the time of Aristotle to describe the round of sciences and arts through which the young Greek had to pass before taking up a specialised study or entering public life. 'General education' is perhaps the corresponding term in English. The rhetorician Quintilian described the disciplines making up this group as the 'round of learning' (*orbis doctrinae, Inst.* I. 10, 101), and listed them as grammar, rhetoric, music, geometry and astronomy. This led to the idea of the 'liberal arts' (*artes liberales*), i.e. those regarded by the classical world as suitable for a free man, as opposed to manual activities. The seven liberal arts, which were fixed by the end of the classical period and formed the basic education of orators, were the 'trivium' of

Alsted could quote Augustine, *De Trin.* XIII, 19. Later the prevailing attitude in early Protestant theology was to regard theology as a *scientia practica,* a corollary of the preference for the so-called analytical method. (For a short account see C. H. Ratschow, *Lutherische Dogmatik zwischen Orthodoxie und Aufklärung* I, 1964, pp. 41ff).

[20] On this topic generally, see G. Heinrici's article 'Theologische Enzyklopädie' in *Realencyklopädie für protestantische Theologie und Kirche* (RE), 3rd ed. 1898, 351–64; also G. Ebeling, 'Erwägungen zu einer evangelischen Fundamentaltheologie', *ZThK* 67 (1970), 484–9; on the history of the general concept of 'encyclopedia' see also the articles by H. Fuchs, 'Enkyklios Paideia' and 'Enzyklopädie', *RAC* V, 365–98, 504–15, and J. Henningsen, ' "Enzyklopädie". Zur Sprach- und Bedeutungsgeschichte eines pädagogischen Begriffs', *Archiv für Begriffsgeschichte* 10 (1966), pp. 271–362.

grammar, rhetoric and dialectic, and the 'quadrivium' of arithmetic, geometry, music and astronomy. These remained the basis of the course in the medieval 'arts faculties', in which students prepared for the study of theology, medicine or law.

In the modern period the term 'encyclopedia' began to be used to describe introductory surveys of all knowledge, and no longer elementary, preparatory knowledge as opposed to philosophy. 'Encyclopedia' is occasionally used in this wider sense as early as the thirteenth century, as by the Dominican Vincent of Beauvais (d. *c* 1264) in his *Speculum doctrinale,* in which he envisages a work which would constitute '*omnium scientiarum encyclopaediam, temporum et actionum humanarum theatrum amplissimum*'. Numerous encyclopedias of this sort were written from the seventeenth century onwards, mostly in the form of dictionaries. The culmination of this movement was the famous French *Encyclopédie ou dictionnaire raisonné des sciences, des arts et des métiers,* published from 1751 onwards by Diderot and D'Alembert with the assistance of over 200 collaborators. The twenty-eight volumes and seven supplementary volumes of this work were a representative synthesis of the anti-religious and materialistic intellectual world of the French Enlightenment.

In philosophy and theology too 'encyclopedia' came to be used as a title for general surveys of the material dealt with by the two disciplines. It occurs first in the title of the work by the Reformed theologian S. Mursinna, *Primae lineae encylopaediae theologicae* (Halle 1784), though in theology too such comprehensive encyclopedias finally came to be the joint work of many authors presented in dictionary form. One such was the *Realenzyklopädie für protestantische Theologie und Kirche* (1854–66). The third edition of this work (1896–1913, 24 volumes) was the last comprehensive survey of this sort in Protestant theology.

As well as these material encylopedias, with their aim of complete coverage of subject matter, works of a more formal and methodological nature were produced. From the Renaissance onwards they were often called introductions to the science concerned. The genre begins with Erasmus's *Ratio seu methodus compendio perveniendi ad veram theologiam, paraclesis i.e. exhortatio ad sanctissimum et saluberrimum Christianae philosophiae studium,* of 1520. Schleiermacher's previously mentioned *Brief Outline* of

1811 also falls into this category. For Erasmus an introduction to the study of theology had a predominantly pedagogical and didactic character, but this was soon turned into a more methodological and systematic direction by Andreas Hyperius (*De theologo seu de ratione studii theologici,* 1562). This interest can also be seen from the tendency evident in his work to divide theology into exegetical, dogmatic, historical and practical. Nevertheless Schleiermacher was the first to attempt to derive the internal divisions of theology from the concept of theology as such.

This attempt is the first sign of a new idea of encyclopedia as a formal theory of science. This has its origin in German idealism, particularly in Fichte's *Deduzierter Plan einer zu Berlin zu errichtenden höheren Lehranstalt* (1807), which called for 'a philosophical encylopedia of all science as a permanent guide to the treatment of all particular sciences' (§ 19). With his *Encyclopädie der philosophischen Wissenschaften im Grundrisse* (1817) Hegel later carried out in his own way Fichte's demand that the totality of the subject-matter of science should be seen and explored in its 'organic unity'. The Hegelian Karl Rosenkranz planned his *Encyclopädie der theologischen Wissenschaften* of 1831 as a specialised encyclopedia, but with a similar purpose.

Among later works in the field of theological encyclopedia the book by the Basle church historian Karl Rudolf Hagenbach, *Encyclopädie und Methodologie der theologischen Wissenschaften* (1833) was particularly successful. The popularity of this book, which went through twelve editions and was translated into several languages, was due not only to the versatility of its theological approach, but also to the fact that it offered the beginner a pedagogically oriented introduction to the study of theology and to the contemporary stage of discussion in individual branches of theology.

Quite different was Georg Heinrici's *Theologische Enzyklopädie* of 1893. This book, close in outlook to the school of Albrecht Ritschl, is interesting mainly as an example of theological historicism. Heinrici agreed with Hagenbach in seeing biblical exegesis as the first of the theological disciplines and the foundation of all theology. But where Hagenbach, against Schleiermacher, still vigorously defended the special position of

scriptural interpretation as the authoritative charter of revelation
which distinguished Christianity from historical theology, for the
New Testament scholar Heinrici exegesis was absorbed into
historical theology, and history had become 'the content of
theology' (10). This theological historicism regarded itself as
pure scientific theology. In C. A. Bernoulli's *Die wissenschaftliche
und die kirckliche Methode in der Theologie* (1897) the historical
branches of theology, which are based on scientific principles, are
contrasted with the 'ecclesial' branches of dogmatic and practical
theology. The purpose of Bernoulli's distinction was to free
theology from all practical connection with the interests of the
Church by giving it a new basis as a science investigating the
history of religion.

   These tendencies were opposed at every point by dialectical
theology, which identified itself emphatically as ecclesiastical
theology. This is true not only of Karl Barth's *Church Dogmatics*
(1932–62), but also of the work in theological encyclopedia
produced by this school. The position from which Hermann
Diem wrote his three-volume *Theologie als kirchliche Wissenschaft*
(1951–63) is summed up not so much by the definition of the
object of theology as the 'event' of the 'revelation of God in Jesus
Christ' (I,21) as by the statement that this object is 'an event
which eludes both evaluation by means of enquiry into historical
fact and theoretical philosophical enquiry into truth' (I,35).
Following this premise through, Diem attacked the 'assumption
that theology is linked to the rest of science by a shared concept
of truth, which makes it appear possible . . . to establish a relation
with the science of natural man' (I,35). Diem regarded such an
attempt as characteristically 'catholic', where 'catholic' stood for
what has no place in theology. Theology becomes unfaithful to
its task when it 'uses a concept of truth which is shared by
philosophy' (I,41). Nevertheless Diem regarded it as important
that theology should be a science, but it must be an 'ecclesial'
science, as the title of his book said (I, 24f). Diem saw theology as
a function of the Church in precisely the same sense as Karl
Barth. In his view, theology could form part of a 'cosmos of
sciences' only if 'all science were inspired by faith in the
revelation of God in Jesus Christ' (I,25). But since this was not
the actual situation, theology must regard itself as a 'particular

science'. This too, however, would be possible only if a general concept of science could be assumed which would transcend such particularity and unite theology and the other sciences – a possibility Diem rejected. Theologians may envisage such a general concept of science in a different way from other philosophers of science, but these very differences must rest on an assumption of the unity of truth which Diem rejected, for without this assumption all discussion would inevitably cease. It is not true, however, that the assumption of the unity of truth, which was so suspect to Diem, must mean that theology has to take over a ready-made concept of truth from somewhere else, say from philosophy. What is true is that it is possible to argue about truth only where the unity of truth is presupposed. This means that theology must be able to defend its claim to be a science in argument with other views of science, and to do this it must accept a common basis for the argument about what science is. It is only through argument of this sort that it is possible to discover the meaning of the claim made by Diem, following Barth, namely that science should really be 'inspired by faith in the revelation of God in Jesus Christ'. On Diem's presuppositions it could be objected to this that such an argument would have no meaning because the other sciences accept the assumptions of 'natural', i.e. sinful, man. But this objection also applies to theology. What means has theology of justifying its claim to be automatically in a different and privileged position when the truth of its statements is challenged? Any such claim can be no more than an empty assertion. Even if claims of this sort are made on the theological side with disarming innocence, it is understandable, to say no more, if in other quarters they give an impression of immense arrogance on the part of a discipline which can ultimately, as a discipline, be no more than human.

Our criticism of Diem's view has brought us back to the importance for theology's present view of itself of the question of whether theology is a science. The answer to this question will also decide the questions of the scope of the historical method within theology as a whole, of the relation of theology to the non-theological sciences and philosophy, and of the ecclesial nature of theology. Both Bernoulli and Diem, though with opposite intentions, set this characteristic of theology in sharp contrast to any attempt by theologians to understand theology as a science in terms of a general concept of science.

4. Plan of the Work

The questioning of the scientific character of theology within theology itself is paralleled in recent discussion in philosophy of science by influential tendencies which seek to deny Christian theology any claim to scientific validity. As a reaction to the efforts of many theologians to provide theology with general immunity from rational criticism, these tendencies are largely understandable. They have, however, the additional effect of helping to tie theology to a justification of its thematic which is irrationalist and based on an appeal to authority, even though this in turn constitutes another ground for criticism of theology. This association, though it is the joint product of specific movements within theology and of specific attitudes critical of theology within general philosophy of science, nevertheless contradicts theology's claim to be rational and scientific, a claim which theology has gradually formulated during the history of its reflection on its own nature. Even today this claim deserves a hearing and an unprejudiced examination, if only because it draws attention to the curious nature of this convergence in views of theology between particular movements within theology and theology's radical critics.

To take account of this situation the following enquiry will devote much more attention to philosophy of science and the place of theology within science than is usual within the framework of theological encyclopedia. The whole first part of the book will deal with this set of questions. The second part will deal with the internal division of theology into its various disciplines. It will examine the disciplines at present distinguished and given institutional acknowledgement in the teaching of theology, and the relations between them, in an attempt to determine how far they can be justified by the task of theology and how far they may require correction in the light of that task.

Before considering theology's traditional claims to scientific status it is necessary to examine the most important views represented in the current discussion within philosophy of science. The most important sources of this discussion are the models for a philosophy of science proposed by analytical philosophy (logical positivism and critical rationalism). These models rely on a unitary concept of science which contrasts with the approach of the 'moral' or 'human' sciences (*Geisteswissenschaften*), which have built methodological foundations of their own on hermeneutic and on a distinction between the methods of historical and natural science. The two concepts of science conflict most strongly in the social sciences, which may explain why in recent decades it has been representatives of the social sciences who have been particularly active in seeking a solution to the problems of philosophy of science.

The analytical theories take their model from the natural sciences, but hermeneutic and dialectical social science, on the other hand, are based on a distinction between the natural or physical sciences and what they call the 'human' sciences, the sciences of culture and society, for which they claim methodological autonomy. For this reason the problems raised by the distinction between 'natural' and 'human' sciences are treated in this book immediately after analytical theories of science. This forms a transition to the consideration of the hermeneutical and dialectical accounts of the human or social sciences, and of attempts to analyse them in terms of systems theory.

The discussion of each of the various positions in philosophy of science will be followed by a consideration of their relevance to theology's understanding of itself. The second part of the book will then draw the various threads together and try to answer the general question of whether theology can be regarded as a science, and if so in what sense. The first stage will be an attempt to clarify the sense in which theology has been regarded as a science in the past, starting from the problems raised by the medieval scholastic accounts and using these as a background for a consideration of post-Enlightenment views of theology as a positive science. The internal difficulties of these attempts to describe theology's understanding of itself will lead logically to a consideration of how theology can be practised as a science, what fundamental features it shares with other sciences, and what features distinguish it from them. This will show that it is the systematic task of theology which is the key to an understanding of the theological disciplines. (Schleiermacher saw this long ago, but his insight was thrust back into obscurity by the combined pressure of denominational divisions and historicism.) Only an understanding of the task laid on theology as a whole enables us to say how far the historical disciplines included in theological faculties have a theological character. Again, only a systematic concept of theology as such enables us to answer the question, disputed throughout the whole course of theology's attempts to define its place among the sciences, of whether practical theology is a genuinely scientific discipline, an essential part of the definition of theology as a science, or is to be understood merely pragmatically as the preparation of students for the work of the Church's ministry.

PART ONE

Theology Between the Unity and Multiplicity of the Sciences

THEOLOGY BETWEEN THE UNITY AND
MULTIPLICITY OF SCIENCES

DOES all knowledge constitute a unity, at least in its form, i.e. inasmuch as it is knowledge, irrespective of the variety of content? The assumption seems reasonable, since all knowledge seems to share the characteristic of being known and so being distinct from what is not known. But human knowledge is always incomplete, which means never completely known. For this reason science is not only the essence of knowledge, but always at the same time the road to a knowledge which has not yet been reached. This is taken into account when the unity of science is understood as a unity not of known content but of the means or method which progressively enlarges the circle of the known. But can the way to knowledge be described independently of the variety of the contents of which knowledge is to be obtained? If human science has not already arrived at the goal of total knowledge, we cannot ignore the multiplicity of the objects of knowledge and treat the unity of the form of knowledge as such as proof of the unity of the way. For such incomplete knowledge the form is not independent of its contents.[21] All the more in such a case is the way to knowledge distinct from complete knowledge as such, nor can we exclude in advance the possibility of a plurality of ways to final knowledge

---

[21] The nature of this dependence could be described more precisely by saying that the form represents 'an anticipation of the totality of possible contents' (N. Luhmann, 'Sinn als Grundbegriff der Soziologie', in Habermas-Luhmann, *Theorie der Gesellschaft oder Sozialtechnologie?* (*Theorie-Diskussion* 3), 1971, 68. In other words, the category distinction between form and content is to be understood in temporal terms. 'Form and content are ... guides to a progressive grasp of meaning which appear in meaning itself' (69).

in contrast to the universality of knowledge itself. On the other hand, it would be impossible to start out on the road to knowledge without a provisional knowledge of its goal, and the various sciences cannot therefore remain indifferent to the idea of knowledge as a unity and the criteria for testing claims to knowledge which that idea includes. Moreover the multiplicity of the sciences cannot be defended simply on the ground of the multiplicity of their objects, since that would require present possession of a final knowledge of these objects and areas of investigation which the sciences are only now obtaining or which they only hope to obtain. Alternatively, the multiplicity of the sciences may be seen as the result of the variety of cognitive interests, as simply the different sorts of questions they ask about their objects. This approach may show that certain sorts of questions are pressed in relation to certain sorts of objects and neglected in relation to others, which would indicate that even cognitive interests are fundamentally dependent on objects. Nevertheless, as such, cognitive interests would still be rooted in a prior unity of the idea of knowledge. This brings us back to the search for a road to knowledge which transcends all the differences between the sciences and is based on the idea of knowledge as such. It is a search for a single scientific method which only afterwards separates into different particular sciences.

Idealist theories of science tried to answer these questions by deriving the particular sciences from an idea of knowledge already given in self-awareness or acquired from the experience of self-awareness. An attempt to work with the procedures of transcendental philosophy of science would not be adequate to the present stage of discussion within philosophy of science, however. This stage is determined by the historical experience of the developing unity of actual science, which exists in spite of the conflicting attempts to account for it in transcendental philosophies of science and has established itself in common thinking. The paradigm of such science today is natural science, which no longer needs epistemological justification but instead, as a result of its overwhelming successes, now itself lays down where and in what sense we shall talk of knowledge.[22] A

[22] Jürgen Habermas, *Knowledge and Human Interests*, Boston, Mass. 1971, London 1972, p. 67.

corollary of this has been the 'replacement of epistemology by the philosophy of science' in positivism.[23] The thirst for knowledge and the evaluation of claims to knowledge no longer have to be guided by an idea of knowledge hidden in consciousness, but have a public standard in the 'paradigmatic' givenness of the knowledge of natural science.[24] This is the reason for the immense importance of positivism and its efforts to produce a unitary concept of science which would take the modern natural sciences as its model and have unrestricted validity for all areas of study. Because of its tremendous importance in this century, positivism, as Habermas has said, 'can no longer be effectively overcome from without, from the position of a renovated epistemology, but only by a methodology which transcends its own limitations'.[25] This applies not only to the positivist objectivism which Habermas was immediately attacking, but equally to the monopolisation of the concept of science as such by methods simply generalised from the procedures of the natural sciences. The claim of this concept of science to sole validity can be meaningfully disputed only if it is essentially connected with internal difficulties which, when followed up, force us to go outside the original concept of science. Habermas has tried to demonstrate the existence of such difficulties in Ernst Mach's theory of the elements of experience, which was an attempt to prove the intersubjective givenness of facts in sense-experience without becoming involved in the problems of a genetic, psychological derivation of knowledge from sense-experience,[26] which would have led back to the position of transcendental epistemology. But demonstrating that Mach's theory of the elements of experience given in sense-perception in practice claims more than it can justify — namely a view of 'reality as the totality of facts'[27] is no threat to

---

[23] Habermas, *Knowledge and Human Interests*, pp. 67–8.

[24] On the paradigmatic function of particular theories in the history of science, see Thomas S. Kuhn, *The Structure of Scientific Revolutions*, Chicago and London 1962, 2nd ed. 1970. The attitude which emerged in positivism seems to have given classical natural sciences as a whole such a paradigmatic function.

[25] *Knowledge and Human Interests*, p. 69.

[26] Habermas, pp. 81ff.

[27] Habermas, p. 86.

the operations of positivist techniques of investigation. These have no need to bother about such implications and can leave them to speculative discussion. Such demonstrations can, however, reassure the transcendental philosopher, by showing him, from the positivists' own arguments, that the problem of the transcendental constitution of objects cannot be avoided, although this does not mean that positivism has to extend its principles, even to a pragmatic logic of enquiry such as that proposed by Charles S. Peirce. The operation of positivist investigation procedures could be threatened only if either the clarity of facts in their independence of the subject could not be proved or the scope for testing knowledge provided by the givenness of facts were cast in doubt. These two points are also the focuses of all the problems which have led to the development of logical positivism out of the older empiricism and positivism and are now also leading beyond logical positivism.

Chapter One

FROM POSITIVISM TO CRITICAL RATIONALISM

1. Logical Positivism

EVERY form of positivism takes some fact or institution as the ultimate basis of its arguments. In the case of legal positivism it is existing laws, which are not open to question. In the case of the positivism of revelation which Dietrich Bonhoeffer detected in Karl Barth, it is the fact of the word of God or of his revelation in Christ. Barth took this as the basis of all his arguments, without considering what grounds he had for such an assumption. Empiricist positivism takes experience, or, more accurately, sense-perception, as the ultimate fact upon which all knowledge builds or by reference to which it must be justified. This is the sense given to the term positivism by Auguste Comte in 1830.

But in modern, 'logical' positivism the role of the given has changed.[28] It is no longer, as it was for Ernst Mach, the starting-point of knowledge or its only object, but simply the paradigm for all possible assertions. By this move, logical positivism, the form which starts from the analysis of the meaning of assertions, rids itself of many of the problems which

[28] Moritz Schlick was particularly active in attacking not only the misleading associations which so easily cluster round the idea of the 'given' – such as that there must be a 'giver' who 'gives' them – but also the claim that only the given is real. Schlick argues that the true importance of the given is that all assertions have to be verified with reference to it ('Positivismus und Realismus', *Erkenntnis* 3 (1932/33), pp. 1–31). In contrast, Rudolf Carnap, in 1928 (in *The Logical Structure of the World*) and for a long time afterwards, pursued the ideal of a 'constitution' of all objects by reducing them to 'the given' in the form of elementary experiences (§§ 64ff). But even Carnap was trying to *reduce* propositions to the given, not to derive them from the given as

have burdened the older empiricist tradition since Locke and Hume. In particular it abandons the claim to offer a theory of the origin of knowledge from sense-impressions. By making this claim, older forms of empiricism had laid themselves open to the criticisms of transcedental philosophy, culminating in the proof of the subjectivity of even forms of perception. Logical positivism avoids these problems by regarding the given as no more than a yardstick for the validity of assertions.[29] It thereby accepts, somewhat reluctantly, that language constantly uses expressions whose origin in sense-impressions is difficult to prove. All the more stress is therefore laid on the principle that assertions must show in their logical structure a correspondence to states of affairs whose existence can be determined by observation. The central question of logical positivism has in this way come to be whether, and if so how, propositions which make assertions about states of affairs are open to verification, falsification or testing of any sort.

Logical positivism originated in the 'Vienna Circle' founded in 1922 by Moritz Schlick, Ernst Mach's successor as professor at Vienna.[30] The circle was composed of philosophers sympathetic to empiricism and natural scientists, and in its early days was strongly influenced by Ludwig Wittgenstein's Tractatus Logico-philosophicus (1922).

In this early work Wittgenstein developed an analysis of the logical structure of language as revealed in assertive propositions. On this view the connection of words in a proposition reproduces the connection of objects in a situation, the 'logical form' of reality itself. The proposition in which we assert something is therefore a picture of facts (cf. 2.1), and 'in a picture the elements of the picture are the representatives of objects'

---

a source. On the problem of the 'given' in modern empiricism see W. Stegmüller, Hauptströmungen der Gegenwartsphilosophie, 3rd ed. 1965, pp. 361, 362ff, and his essay 'Der Phänomenalismus und seine Probleme', Archiv für Philosophie 8, pp. 36–100.

[29] But the older empiricism can run into similar problems here, as in the case of Carnap's doctrine of constitution which tried for a long time to make it a requirement that all scientifically meaningful propositions should be reducible to observation reports.

[30] For details see V. Kraft, Der Wiener Kreis. Der Ursprung des Neopositivismus (1950).

(2.131). In contrast to older forms of empiricism and positivism, in this view it is not the individual word, the individual concept, which is the image of reality, but the proposition as a whole. Only the proposition, therefore, can be true or false, and the truth or falsity of the proposition consists in its agreement or disagreement with the state of affairs with which it is concerned (2.222) The 'sense' of a proposition lies in its showing 'how things stand if it is true' (4.022). This means that false propositions can have 'a sense' (4.064), but not propositions in which it is impossible to say what the state of affairs is if they are true.

The philosophers of the Vienna Circle, especially Moritz Schlick and Rudolf Carnap, understood these theses to mean that a proposition can be recognised as having meaning only when it is possible to say what *state of affairs* must hold if the proposition is true. This means that a proposition is meaningful only if it is possible to say what observations (of states of affairs) would verify it.[31] Wittgenstein himself also seems to have held this view until the early 'thirties, although it has been correctly pointed out that the *Tractatus* does not explicitly mention verification by sense-perceptions.[32] In 1929–30, however, Wittgenstein wrote in his posthumously published *Philosophische Bemerkungen*: 'Every proposition is an instruction to look for verification.'[33] Only this assumption makes sense of the view expressed in the *Tractatus* that only 'propositions of natural science' can be uttered, i.e., are meaningful, whereas metaphysical propositions are nonsensical because 'certain signs' in them, certain words 'lack meaning', i.e. correspond to nothing which is empirically identifiable (6.53).

It was the philosophers of the Vienna Circle who first developed Wittgenstein's ideas about meaningful and meaningless propositions into a systematic theory of the way in which

[31] This is more or less the position of M. Schlick, 'Meaning and Verification', *Philosophical Review* 45 (1936), 339–69. See also R. Carnap; 'Pseudoproblems in Philosophy', *Logical Structure*, Berkeley and London, 1967, pp. 327–8. In this book Carnap distinguishes between the possibility of proving a proposition and its coherence, which may still exist even if at a particular time no proof can be given, though one is at least conceivable (p.46).

[32] G. E. M. Anscombe, *An Introduction to Wittgenstein's Tractatus*, 2nd ed. 1963, p. 150.

[33] *Philosophische Bemerkungen* Oxford, 1964, § 150, (p. 174). See Kurt Wuchterl, *Struktur und Sprachspiel bei Wittgenstein*, 1969, p. 100.

statements could be checked and into a model of a general scientific language. In doing this they ignored Wittgenstein's own mystical remarks, which occur particularly at the end of the *Tractatus*. In the German-speaking countries the main contributor to this process, besides Schlick, was Rudolf Carnap,[34] and in England the leading figures were A. J. Ayer[35] and Bertrand Russell.[36] An important result of the work was that the appeal to sensation or sense-perceptions to provide a logically unassailable procedure for testing assertions proved unsuitable, because propositions can be tested only in respect of their relation to other propositions. Interest therefore concentrated on the question of whether so-called 'protocol statements' or 'basic propositions' which report the content of observations and to which all other propositions must in some way or other be reducible, are susceptible of clear intersubjective formulation. The difficulties connected with this point are only one aspect of the problems raised by the verification principle, and in the further development of logical positivism this principle has been more and more heavily modified. Only the early, radical formulation, however, produced what the positivists wanted it to produce, i.e. a clear rejection of metaphysical propositions as meaningless assertions.

2. The Application of Logical Positivism to Theology

For the author of the *Tractatus* the word 'God' was certainly not finished. The assertion of the early Wittgenstein that it is impossible to make meaningful statements about God becomes in the *Tractatus* merely that 'God does not reveal himself *in* the world' (6.432). In a dualism which may be compared with the crisis theology of the early Barth, the idea of God belongs with the 'mystical' view that the 'sense' of the world must lie 'outside the world' (6.41), and that the solution of the riddle of life in

---

[34] *The Logical Structure of the World*, Berkeley, Calif. 1967 (original 1928).
[35] *Language, Truth and Logic*, London 1936.
[36] *An Inquiry into Meaning and Truth*, London 1940, 2nd ed. 1966, esp. pp. 289ff. On the various theories of verification see W. Stegmüller, *Das Wahrheitsproblem und die Idee der Semantik* (1957), 2nd. ed. 1968, pp. 262–82.

space and time must lie 'outside space and time' (6.4312).

For Carnap, on the other hand, the word 'God' once had a sense or a meaning, in a previous historical period, the age of mythical thought, when people believed in gods as physical beings who lived on Olympus, in heaven or in the underworld. But since metaphysics had deliberately removed the word 'God' from all connection with physical reality the word had lost its original meaning without acquiring any new meaningful reference. According to Carnap, the language of theologians alternates between myth and its metaphysical demolition. Their mythical talk about God – which describes him as having a connection with the empirical world – has been made untenable by the criticism of science, so that theology has constantly to resort to the metaphysical exclusion of God from empirical reality.[37]

Carnap's idea that the word 'God' lost its original strong sense as a result of the qualifications of metaphysicians who wanted to immunise it against the attacks of experimental science was put into a famous parable by Antony Flew. 'Once upon a time two explorers came upon a clearing in the jungle. In the clearing were growing many flowers and many weeds. One explorer says, "Some gardener must tend this plot". The other disagrees, "There is no gardener". So they pitch their tents and set a watch.' But the gardener proves to be invisible, intangible and undetectable by any test, and the sceptical explorer finally asks his companion what is left of his hypothesis: 'Just how does what you call an invisible, intangible, eternally elusive gardener differ from an imaginary gardener or even from no gardener at all?' He has, it seems, died 'the death of a thousand qualifications'.[38] By being made immune to any empirical test, the assertion of the existence of God loses all statable meaning.

It is no way out of this dilemma to base theological assertions

[37] Carnap, 'Uberwindung der Metaphysik durch logische Analyse der Sprache', *Erkenntnis* 2 (1932/3). In his *The Logical Structure of the World*, pp. 292–5, Carnap still went no further than denying belief in revelation the status of knowledge and emphasising its 'complete heterogeneity' from it (p. 295).

[38] Antony Flew, 'Theology and Falsification', A. Flew and A. MacIntyre (ed.) *New Essays in Philosophical Theology*, London 1955, pp. 96–7. Flew's parable was based in turn on John Wisdom's article 'Gods'. See also Flew, *God and Philosophy*, 2nd ed. 1968, esp. pp. 25–57.

on a particular sort of experience distinct from sense-experience.[39] An intuitive religious experience can offer no basis for predictions which can be tested (A. J. Ayer). Allegedly supernatural events must be explained by natural causes, if they are to be explained at all (P. Nowell-Smith), and the same is true of claims of visionary experiences (A. MacIntyre). Nor is D. Cox's thesis that statements about God are based on the experience of encounters with God any more tenable, since such encounters are not experiences which can be proved to a third party to have taken place and only such experiences can be distinguished from illusions and serve to verify assertions.[40] Theological statements can therefore not be based on a special sort of experience available in no other way. Nor, for those who accept the arguments of logical positivism, can they be defended as necessary implications of generally available experience, since the only necessary propositions are analytical ones, which contain no implication of the existence of anything (J. N. Findlay). Even the logical coherence of the idea of God has been challenged with reference to the old problem of theodicy: the alleged impossibility of reconciling the evil in the world with the existence of a good and omnipotent God (J. L. Mackie).

In this situation two escape routes are open to theology, if it is not willing to stop talking about God at all.

The first route starts from the claim that religious and theological propositions are not meant to make any assertions about a reality denoted by the word 'God'. Ayer recommended this way out as long ago as 1936.[41] Many writers have attempted to interpret religious propositions as not making assertions, but merely expressing something. R. B. Braithewaite tried to show that religious assertions about God in fact do no more than express the ethical commitment of the speaker.[42] Similarly, R. Hepburn has claimed that religious propositions are no more than parables used to reinforce morality.[43] In a slightly different

---

[39] For what follows see F. Ferré, *Language, Logic and God*, London 1961, New York 1969, pp. 18ff.

[40] Ferré, p. 40.

[41] *Language, Truth and Logic*, 2nd ed., pp. 115ff.

[42] *An Empiricist View of the Nature of Religious Belief*, Cambridge 1955.

[43] *Christianity and Paradox*, London 1958.

approach, R. M. Hare has interpreted religious statements as the expression of a 'blik', a particular way of looking at ordinary empirical reality, rather than as a reference towards a particular reality denoted by the statements.[44] Following Hare, Paul van Buren has denied that the language of faith has any cognitive meaning, appealing, interestingly, to Karl Barth's critique of the natural knowledge of God. Van Buren interpreted the language of faith as a mere form of expression for a particular attitude to life.[45]

The second way out of the dilemma created for theology by logical positivism involves a critique of the empiricist criterion of meaning as the verification of propositions by reference to sense-perceptions or observations or to basic propositions embodying such observations. This critique is based largely on the work of Karl Popper.

3. Popper's Attack on Logical Positivism

In his *Logic of Scientific Discovery*, first published in German in 1934, Karl Popper attacked both Carnap's attempt to base a theory of empirical knowledge on protocol sentences and the claim that our knowledge of the laws of natural science was derived from the process of induction, that is by generalisation from observations. His main attack, however, was directed against the positivist principle of verification, which he rejected as untenable, and beyond that against tying the question of the meaning or meaninglessness of statements in with the problem of their openness to empirical determination.

There is a fundamental connection between Popper's rejection of the positivist principle of verification and his criticism of the principle of induction. His criticism of induction is concerned not so much with the heuristic value of generalisation as with its

[44] R. M. Hare, 'Religion and Morals', in B. Mitchell (ed.), *Faith and Logic*, London 1957, pp. 176–93. See also his answer to Flew's arguments, *New Essays in Philosophical Theology*, pp. 99–103.

[45] Paul M. van Buren, *The Secular Meaning of the Gospel*, London 1963, Harmondsworth 1968, pp. 88–111, 140–59.

status as a claim to knowledge. Here Popper is taking up Hume's argument that no number of identical observations, however large, permits the formulation of a strictly general law valid for all similar cases. There remains a gap between the limited number of the observations and the generality of the law derived from them. This reasoning had already encouraged Kant to argue that the universality of scientific laws must have a different basis. Kant suggested the a priori structure of experience. Popper argued, however, that with this theory Kant 'proved too much', since by postulating a basis for Newton's laws in the a priori structure of experience he made them necessarily valid, whereas, according to Popper, scientific laws can never be more than hypotheses.[46]

Popper regards the inductive method as an expression of the attempt to base science on ultimate certainties. Both the idealist and the empiricist line of modern thought started from the premise that truth is self-evident, in other words evident at its source. Empiricists and idealists, however, went to different sources. For Bacon it was sense-impressions, for Descartes and his idealist successors it was the ultimate indisputable certainties of reason, the implications of the Cogito. The two opposed tendencies nevertheless agreed that the only way to obtain knowledge of any sort from a given source was by logically impeccable reasoning. Descartes' method was deduction; that of Bacon and his empiricist successors was induction. But Popper says of them both that their epistemology 'remains essentially a religious doctrine in which the source of all knowledge is divine

---

[46] Karl Popper, *Conjectures and Refutations,* London, 1963, 3rd ed, 1969, p. 48. On Popper's criticisms of Kant see also A. Wellmer, *Methodologie als Erkenntnistheorie. Zur Wissenschaftslehre Karl Poppers,* 1967, pp. 61–7. Wellmer both denies that Kant's a priori combines logical and psychological apriority (p. 62) and at the same time describes it as characteristic of Kant 'not to distinguish between the actually transcendental and transcendental validity' (ibid.), which is precisely what Popper accuses him of. Contrary to what Wellmer thinks, Popper's point is not that Kant 'confuses origin and validity in the case of particular *empirical* hypotheses' (p. 63), but that the forms of knowledge which Kant claims to be 'transcendental' are to be assessed in the same way as other hypotheses. Popper cannot therefore be said not to have taken 'transcendental reflection' far enough (p. 65), but simply to have maintained a critical distance from Kant's transcendental philosophy.

authority . . . They could only replace one authority – that of Aristotle and the Bible – by another.' [47] In fact, says Popper, there are many sources from which we derive ideas and knowledge, but none of them is infallible, none has authority (24). We cannot derive sure knowledge from ultimate certainties; all claims to have found ultimate certainties have as a matter of fact always been disputed. The idealists reject the certainties of the empiricists and vice versa. In Popper's view we can learn only by trial and error. Our knowledge always begins with conjectures, models, hypotheses. Even immediate sense-perception contains interpretation: 'all observation involves interpretation' (21–2). The crucial step is to put the hypothetical models of our minds to the proof. This means confronting their implications with actual situations:

> From a new idea, put up tentatively, and not yet justified in any way – an anticipation, a hypothesis, a theoretical system, or what you will – conclusions are drawn by means of logical deduction. These conclusions are then compared with one another and with other relevant statements . . .
>
> We may . . . distinguish four different lines along which the testing of the theory could be carried out. First there is the logical comparison of the conclusions among themselves, by which the internal consistency of the system is tested. Secondly there is the investigation of the logical form of the theory, with the object of determining whether it has the character of an empirical or scientific theory, or whether it is, for example, tautological. Thirdly, there is the comparison with other theories, chiefly with the aim of determining whether the theory would constitute a scientific advance . . . And finally, there is the testing of the theory by way of empirical applications of the conclusions which can be derived from it. [48]

Popper's criticisms of the principle of induction were not new,

[47] *Conjectures and Refutations*, p. 15. This reference and the following ones are to the essay 'On the Sources of Knowledge and Ignorance'.

[48] K. Popper, *The Logic of Scientific Discovery*, 2nd ed. London and New York 1968, pp. 32–3 (1st English edition 1959).

but the argument he based on it against the principle of verification was. Popper said that if any general rule or law corresponds to an infinite number of instances, a general statement can never be verified by observation. The result is that the positivist demand for verification is much more rigorous than its originators had imagined. It excludes not just metaphysical assertions, but also all attempts to formulate scientific laws: 'This criterion excludes from the realm of meaning all scientific theories (or "laws of nature"); for these are no more reducible to observation reports than so-called metaphysical pseudo-propositions.' [49] The positivist criterion of meaning has thus proved itself 'just as destructive of science as it was of metaphysics' (264).

Carnap has accepted Popper's criticisms in his writings published after 1934. Since then he has limited the criterion of verification to the requirement that scientific statements must have a relation to possible observations, and in this way be open to examination. Popper comments rightly on this that a 'weakened verification' of this sort no longer provides any basis for discriminating between scientific and metaphysical statements,[50] since metaphysical statements also have, inevitably, some relation to observations. A. J. Ayer also admits, in the introduction to the 1946 edition of his Language, Truth and Logic, that the simple requirement of a relation to possible observation provides no clear criterion for rejecting metaphysical propositions.

Popper himself has abandoned the claim that metaphysical sentences are meaningless. His view is that if a theory is untestable in the scientific sense, as, for example, psychoanalytic or metaphysical systems are, it is not therefore necessarily unimportant, insignificant or nonsensical.[51] Nevertheless, he is still anxious to find a principle of demarcation between scientific and non-scientific statements.[52]

Popper finds this principle of demarcation in falsifiability. Assertions of scientific laws are not verifiable, since they can

[49] Conjectures, p. 261.
[50] Conjectures, pp. 280–1.
[51] Conjectures, pp. 37–8.
[52] Logic, pp. 34ff.

never be tested in all the cases to which they apply. They are, however, falsifiable, since the assertion of a general rule fails immediately a single case is found which contradicts the alleged rule. In this situation the rule cannot have the strict generality of a law, but can at most be an approximation to the actual state of affairs.

If an assertion stands up to attempts to falsify it, it can be regarded provisionally as 'established'. Popper lays down a number of conditions for this. A hypothesis or theory is not established merely by being able to explain the present situation; we can begin to describe it as empirically established only when it gives rise to predictions which turn out to be accurate.[53] A theory or hypothesis is therefore the more fruitful the more it forbids, since in this way it offers all the more possibilities for testing.[54] Popper makes a connection here with the natural scientist's preference for simple laws. This preference is based not merely on aesthetic but also on technical reasons, since the simpler a proposed law or theory is the more it excludes, and therefore the more possibilities there are for checking it.[55] Conversely, Popper rejects attempts to 'save' a theory which has been refuted in its original form by the introduction of auxiliary assumptions and changes in definitions. He regards such attempts as an immunisation technique which, as in the case of Flew's parable of the invisible gardener, robs the theory of empirical relevance.[56]

With his principle of falsification Popper believes he has formulated a principle which metaphysical propositions cannot satisfy, and that he has therefore produced a criterion for distinguishing between scientific and metaphysical statements. But if Popper allows that metaphysical statements are not simply meaningless, what positive function do they have?

Firstly, they help to 'organise the picture of the world' in areas where no scientifically testable theories are yet available.[57] In this function, Popper says, criteria can be laid down for

---

[53] *Logic*, pp. 40–1.
[54] *Conjectures*, p. 117.
[55] *Logic*, pp. 41–2.
[56] *Conjectures*, p. 37.
[57] *The Logic of Scientific Discovery*, p. 277.

distinguishing between 'true' and 'false' philosophical theories: a philosophical theory is rational and intelligible to the extent that it relates to a specific problem situations and suggests solution for it.[58] Unfortunately Popper does not say very precisely at this point what sort of situations he has in mind; in his view, once a philosophical theory succeeds in making contact with a scientific problematic it is no longer 'metaphysical', but automatically becomes 'scientific'.[59] It remains unclear from Popper's discussion how far metaphysical theories can have a truth value even without such a relation to scientific problem situations.

Popper also recognises a second function of metaphysical ideas. In his view metaphysical, i.e. scientifically unwarranted, assumptions are involved in all scientific enquiry. According to Popper, the principle, 'We do not know; we can only guess', also applies to science:[60] 'and our guesses are guided by the unscientific, the metaphysical . . . faith in laws, in regularities which we can uncover – discover' (278). He suggests, quite generally: 'From the psychological angle . . . scientific discovery is impossible without faith in ideas which are of a purely speculative kind, and sometimes even quite hazy; a faith which is completely unwarranted from the point of view of science, and which, to that extent, is "metaphysical" '(38). Popper's view can thus accommodate the many cases in which 'metaphysical' and even 'religious' assumptions have been shown to have played a part in the history of modern scientific thought.[61] Popper would also perhaps not deny that such assumptions also play a part in the history of philosophy of science.

[58] Conjectures and Refutations, pp. 184ff: 'On the Status of Science and of Metaphysics'.

[59] Logic, p. 277. Hans Albert similarly regards it as possible to 'develop even metaphysical ideas into theories which are in principle refutable' (Traktat über kritische Vernunft, 1968, p. 48). Albert too regards this as a transformation of metaphysical theories into 'scientific' ones, as is shown by his subsequent remark that when thus recast the former metaphysical ideas 'can begin to compete with existing scientific theories' (ibid.).

[60] Logic, p. 278. In other words the form of scientific propositions is that which Bacon rejected as the source of all error: anticipation.

[61] On this, see esp. C. F. von Weizsäcker, Die Tragweite der Wissenschaft, vol. I, 1964; E. A. Burtt, The Metaphysical Foundations of Modern Science, 1924; and the works of A. Koyré.

The question now arises whether these assumptions were merely external, historical conditions of the origin of scientific knowledge, or whether the validity claimed by scientific statements, and their structure, themselves contain 'metaphysical' implications. This is clearest in connection with their claim to truth. It is fundamental to the semantic structure of assertions that they claim to be true in the sense of agreeing with the state of affairs to which they relate.[62] Without this element the idea of assertion, and also of science, is meaningless. As Popper rightly says of science: 'The system called "empirical science" is intended to represent only *one* world: the "real world" or the "world of our experience".'[63] In other words, Popper regards the idea of truth as correspondence as semantically indispensable, and he maintains it in the form given to it by the Polish logician Tarski to secure it against logical paradoxes.[64] But Popper's own analysis of structural theories of science leads to the conclusion that these theories never satisfy the idea of truth as correspondence definitively or without qualification, but are at best only provisionally established. 'We have,' says Popper

[62] It is undeniable that truth as correspondence depends on (at least the presumption of) an intersubjective consensus about the state of affairs which is an essential part of its objectivity. But it does not follow from this that the correspondence theory of truth can be reduced to a consensus theory of truth, as proposed by Habermas ('Vorbereitende Bemerkungen zu einer Theorie der kommunikativen Kompetenz', in Habermas-Luhmann, *Theorie der Gesellschaft oder Sozialtechnologie*, 1971, pp. 101ff, esp. 123ff). A pure consensus theory of truth, as Habermas' discussion shows very illuminatingly, is incapable of accounting for the distinction between a consensus in truth and a prevailing convention. Habermas' assumption that convention always involves constraint and can therefore always be exposed as mere convention by a utopian anticipation of unconstrained communication seems to depend on an unhistorical and naturalistic idea of human rationality. This takes the form of a projection of an ideally successful convention, ignoring the fact that even in 'non-dominative dialogue' this would remain convention with an uncertain relation to actual fact. The two factors of correspondence to objects and consensus each require the other, and neither can ultimately be subordinated to the other. To set up a correspondence theory and a consensus theory of truth as alternatives is therefore self-defeating. Just as consensus about truth and factual correspondence can only be anticipated in any case, the unity between the two can also be achieved only in anticipation.

[63] *Logic*, p. 39.
[64] *Conjectures*, pp. 215–50.

therefore, 'no criterion of truth, but are nevertheless guided by the idea of truth as a *regulative principle.*' [65] Here, however, the idea of a regulative principle is no more than a vague analogy with Kant's terminology. Unlike Kant's, Popper's idea is not securely set in the framework of a transcendental analysis of constitutive principles of understanding, the full application of which is described in Kant's account of regulative ideas. Moreover truth as correspondence with objects as revealed by a semantic analysis of assertions cannot be regarded as a merely regulative principle, since it is already constitutive of the idea of statement or assertion. Popper's description of the idea of truth as a regulative principle relocates the truth of statements at the imaginary end of an infinite process, whereas every assertion in fact makes a claim to truth here and now. This immediate claim to a truth which is nevertheless still open to dispute, so that the most that can be done is to 'approximate' to it, might be described as anticipation. The resulting situation with regard to the object aspect of the problem of truth is analogous to that which Jürgen Habermas has analysed in connection with the consensus aspect of truth and which imposes itself as characteristic of the immediate accessibility of truth through knowledge in general. [66] Popper himself stressed the anticipatory character of hypotheses, [67] and since in his view all knowledge is hypothetical it would have been logical for him to have carried over this structural feature into his consideration of the problem of truth. Yet another question arises here. Can the anticipatory character of human knowledge be merely subjective and external to the objects known when that knowledge should at least potentially correspond to its object if it is to be genuine knowledge? Implied

---

[65] *Conjectures*, p. 226.

[66] J. Habermas, 'Die Universalitätsanspruch der Hermeneutik', *Hermeneutik und Dialektik* I, 1970, pp. 73–103, esp. 99–100. See also the essay referred to in note 62 above, pp. 136ff. Habermas emphasises, interestingly, that the ideal dialogue situation would not be 'simply a regulative principle in Kant's sense' since it is already implied as a premise in every act of linguistic communication (p. 140).

[67] See note 60 above. In *Conjectures*, pp. 13–14, Popper shows at greater length that the method of forming hypotheses or framing conjectures is precisely the *anticipatio mentis* which Bacon contrasted, as the false method, with the true *interpretatio naturae*.

in this question is a new form of the old 'metaphysical' distinction between substance and accidents, since the way in which the object of knowledge is presented in present hypotheses must be distinguished from what it will ultimately prove to be. The distinction between substance and accidents contained in the concept of anticipation naturally has an effect on the status of the observations and observation reports by which empirical hypotheses have to be tested. Many of the difficulties connected with such basic propositions which will be discussed later may become intelligible with the help of this distinction. What has certainly become clear is that the question of truth cannot be separated from that of essence, of the ultimate nature of things. This means, however, that 'metaphysical' ideas are not just among the accidental historical conditions of the growth of scientific knowledge but are constitutive of its meaning and validity. If this is so, these questions cannot be left for later consideration when the validity and truth of scientific statements are being discussed.

4. The Application of Critical Rationalism to Criticism of Theology

In giving the falsifiability of theories a central place in his study of the logic of scientific enquiry, Popper's immediate aim was to separate science from 'metaphysics', but he also regarded his basic idea as having much wider relevance. The social sciences too, to the extent that they were sciences, were expected to put forward hypotheses and theories and test them for falsifiability.[68] In his book *The Open Society and its Enemies* (1937/1958), Popper developed his view of science into an explicit basis for an alternative outlook for the whole of social life; as an alternative to the effects on social life on philosophical dogmatism he proposed a combination of the 'open society' with the tradition of 'critical thought' in which all views were put forward as hypotheses and kept open to criticism.

[68] Popper has explicitly stated that the unity of scientific method applies to all theoretical sciences, whether natural sciences or social sciences: see *The Poverty of Historicism* (1957), New York 1964, pp. 130ff.

This would seem to be a suitable context for a discussion of the
social role of religion and theology, but no work was done on
this until Popper's pupil W. W. Bartley published a study of the
relation of theology to the tradition of critical thought. Bartley
diagnoses contemporary Protestant theology of all tendencies as
suffering from a 'retreat to commitment'.[69] Bartley sees this as a
reaction to the collapse of nineteenth-century liberal theology's
attempts to base the Christian faith on historical knowledge of
Jesus. Bartley tries to show that the disintegration of the liberal
picture of Jesus led theology into a retreat to an irrational
commitment based on 'faith'; his main examples are Karl Barth
and Paul Tillich, but his argument applies to other leading
figures in the Protestant theology of this period.[70] The central
theme of Barth's theology, according to Bartley, is commitment
to the Word of God revealed in Christ (63–4), which as such
cannot be criticised (128), while all theological conjectures about
the Word of God are ruled out by the same principle (64).
Bartley discovers a similar underlying irrationalism behind Paul
Tillich's symbolic interpretation of Christian teaching (73–4) and
behind his 'Protestant principle' (75ff). Tillich, he says, claims
explicitly that the power of new being which makes itself known
in Jesus Christ is 'the bedrock' which is not subject to criticism.[71]

[69] W. W. Bartley, *The Retreat to Commitment*, New York 1962, London
1964.
[70] A difficulty for this view of the causal relationships is the fact that liberal
theology itself usually required a commitment of faith in addition to a picture
of Jesus based on historical research. Attempts to base theology purely on
history have been even rarer than Bartley believes, the most far-reaching
being that of Ernst Troeltsch. Troeltsch's work, however, was not invalidated
by the crisis in the search for the historical Jesus; it was not followed up for
other reasons. Bartley's detailed discussion is weakest in the section to which
he gives the abstract title 'Gestalt Theology' (pp. 67–72). In it Bartley assesses
attempts to reduce the multiplicity of biblical statements about man, history,
the world and knowledge to a general common feature ('Gestalt') in order to
compare them with contemporary thought, and declares them to have been
'fundamentally unsuccessful' (p. 69). Unfortunately he does not say why.
Bartley's detailed discussion is limited to the two poles of Barth and Tillich, of
whom he evidently prefers Barth for the greater rigour of his thought (pp.
65–6). This partiality makes his account of Barth fairer than his account of
Tillich.
[71] Bartley, *Retreat to Commitment*, p. 82, quoting Tillich, *The Protestant Era*,
pp. xxiiff and 234.

Bartley also accuses Tillich of relativising theological discussion by making it depend on a previous act of faith. The charge does not seem unjustified when Bartley can quote from Tillich a sentence such as this: 'All speaking about divine matters which is not done in the state of ultimate concern is meaningless . . . That which is meant by the act of faith cannot be approached in any other way than through an act of faith.' [72] Tillich does seem here to be claiming that an irrational commitment is a necessary preliminary to any theological statement, whatever striving for rationality is evident in his apologetic theology. The efforts in Tillich's theology to produce a universally acceptable description of the human situation, which set it apart from the approach of Karl Barth, do not interest Bartley. However, when Tillich says: 'There is no criterion by which faith can be judged from outside the correlation of faith,' [73] he not only withdraws the Christian position from the possibility of criticism by any critic who is not himself willing to accept the position, but also deprives himself of the right to make judgments on those who hold different beliefs from him, a right which Tillich is, however, unwilling to forgo. It is impossible not to agree with Bartley's comment: 'One gains the right to be irrational at the expense of losing the right to criticise' (103).

But if we ignore these contradictions, Bartley argues, the theological 'retreat to commitment' has always previously been able to rely on one argument to defend its intellectual integrity (90). This is the claim that any position, and any scientific procedure, rests on premises which have to be assumed without proof, on a set of basic postulates or axioms which are the basis of all subsequent reasoning. If this were true, there would be no fundamental methodological difference between a theologian and a mathematician or physicist: all three start from basic axioms which cannot themselves be proved. Bartley calls this the 'tu quoque argument'. Its function in theology, he says, is to provide 'a rational excuse for irrational commitment' (89–90). Bartley says that this tu quoque argument is a perfectly adequate answer to the rationalist positions of the past, which formed the outlook of the natural sciences. It is true, he says, that the two

---

[72] Tillich, *Dynamics of Faith*, p. 72 (quoted Bartley, p. 100).
[73] Tillich, *Dynamics*, pp. 58ff (quoted, Bartley, p. 101).

main forms of modern rationalism, empiricism and idealism, have precisely this structure. They try to derive all knowledge from ultimate certainties which themselves need no justification, either sense-perceptions or indisputable intellectual proofs. According to Bartley, these two traditions within the rationalist approach have a starting-point which is no less irrational than that of modern Protestant theology (109ff).

Bartley's argument here is clearly based on Popper's essay 'On the Sources of Knowledge and of Ignorance', of 1960.[74] Popper's idea was that in the structure of their reasoning both empiricism and idealism are tied to a model of knowledge as revelation, in that they presuppose a source of knowledge which is certain in itself, with the difference that this source is now not the authority of the bible but sense-perception or mental certainties, regarded as 'clear and certain'. Bartley simply goes a step further. He shows that this analogy between the traditional varieties of rationalism and theology still exists and is the basis of modern theology's apologetic defence of the Christian position. This defence relies on the analogy between its own methods and those of other disciplines to demonstrate its intellectual integrity.

Bartley, like Popper, is convinced that empiricism and idealism must be superseded, and can be superseded by Popper's method of critical examination, understood as the formalisation of everyday learning processes of 'trial and error'. The setting up and testing of hypotheses presupposes no ultimate certainties, either empirical or ideal. Here Bartley has taken what Popper worked out as a theory of knowledge in the natural sciences and extended it to produce a universally applicable programme of 'pancritical rationalism'.[75]

Popper's 'pancritical rationalism' is no longer exposed to the *tu quoque* argument. It is not a valid objection to his position to assert that even a rationalist assumes an irrationally adopted

---

[74] As admitted by several references (Bartley, pp. xi, 19, 135).

[75] Bartley's list (pp. 158–9) of the four criteria by which hypotheses are to be tested, logic, sense observation, relation to other scientific theories, relation to the general problematic, corresponds to statements made in *The Logic of Scientific Discovery*, pp. 32–3, but Bartley has replaced the criterion of 'empirical character' by that of appropriateness to the problematic which was proposed by Popper specifically for philosophical statements.

starting-point in all his arguments, unless one is willing to describe even taking part in argument and criticism and accepting the logical rules of understanding implied by this as irrational. But since this has always been the basis for any argument or dispute whatever, 'it is no longer possible to avoid facing these criticisms by citing the *tu quoque*' (175). This position also entails that if theology continues to retreat to an irrational fideist commitment as the ultimate basis and invariably accepted premise of all its arguments, it can no longer claim intellectual integrity for such an approach.

Bartley's attack on the '*tu quoque* argument' in theological apologetics, and his demonstration of the irrational commitment it involves, has influenced other critics of theology and Christianity.[76] Hans Albert, in his critical remarks about theology, follows Bartley as well as W. Kaufmann,[76a] but his discussion of 'Faith and Knowledge' (*Traktat über kritische Vernunft* 1968, 104–30), goes further on two points. First, he stresses that theology is 'in no sense a critical enterprise, but predominantly a hermeneutical one' (109). In other words, for Albert hermeneutic is opposed to criticism. He also describes Bultmann's theology of demythologisation as 'a hermeneutical enterprise with an apologetic purpose'. Albert regards this as proved by the fact that it starts from the concepts of kerygma and the obedience of faith (109–10). He describes Bultmann's distinction between the primitive Christian world-view, which is now outmoded, and the self-understanding of the New Testament writers, which can still be accepted, as 'a hermeneutical immunisation technique for that part of the Christian faith which modern theologians want at all costs to save from current criticism' (113).

It is not just in the hands of theologians, but in themselves, that Albert regards hermeneutical methods as theological whenever they attempt to interpret a given 'text' rather than risk destroying it by criticism. This makes him suspect even non-theological supporters of hermeneutical theory in the human or social sciences as being all crypto-theologians. Here again the background is what Popper called the revelation model which he

---

[76] E.g. J. B. Kahl, *The Misery of Christianity*, London 1971, pp. 143, 146.
[76a] W. Kaufmann, *Religion und Philosophie*, 1966.

regarded as forming the common basis of the two views of knowledge which have become standard in modern times, empiricism and idealism. Albert, however, regards this model of knowledge as particularly influential in the hermeneutical treatment of traditions, and therefore attacks the hermeneutical method in general and hermeneutical theology in particular, against both of which he maintains Popper's principle of critical examination (35ff). Occasionally the blade of his polemic cuts down not only opponents but also the rules of fair play, as when he accuses Bultmann of requiring his readers to adopt 'the' critical method, 'solely because the tradition of our faith contains elements which would otherwise have to be jettisoned, though we may have grown very attached to them' (114). There was really no need to be so cheap as this, particularly since Albert in fact has strong substantial arguments, for example, about Bultmann's separation of world-view and personal consciousness, which is far from convincing.[77] But in making this distinction Bultmann need not have been aware of any infringement of the critical-historical method, which was the only 'critical method' he was bound by. There are no grounds for Albert's insinuation that he was willing to 'abandon the rules because his cherished views were being demolished' (115). It should be possible to admit that Bultmann's integrity as a scholar is beyond the reach of such accusations even if one judges his methods to be inadequate.

Albert's second argument against theology concerns the debate on the idea of God. Albert accuses theology of trying to save the idea of God by means of a technique of 'immunisation'. At the beginning of the modern period, he says, the idea of God 'as a part of cosmology had an explanatory function' (116); it has now been made redundant in this function by natural science. But instead of giving up 'belief in the existence of essences which were important only in unsuccessful and abandoned theories' (117), theology, Albert claims, has tried to alter the concept of God so as to leave it unaffected by this change in our understanding of the world. This is particularly true of the 'thesis

---

[77] On this see the criticism of Bultmann in my essay, 'On Historical and Theological Hermeneutic', W. Pannenberg, *Basic Questions in Theology,* vol. 1, London 1970, pp. 137–81.

of the non-objectifiability of God', which restricts the idea of God in practice to 'moral and rhetorical functions' (119), since questions of truth or falsity are excluded from the concept of faith. It seems to me that this particular argument of Albert's is largely unanswerable, although the general assumption that the idea of God must be abandoned with the theologically based cosmology of the middle ages is unjustified. Albert is here using Popper's argument that a theory which has once been falsified may not be modified ad hoc to allow it to escape refutation (Popper calls this the 'conventional stratagem' or 'conventional twist'). We shall see that even in the natural sciences this principle is not applied as rigorously as Popper proposed, and that in any case it cannot be transferred without examination to historical studies. But even in Popper's formulation this principle does not prevent elements of the old theory, the idea of God, in Albert's example, from forming part of a new theory, provided that the new theory is in turn exposed to the risk of falsification and not simply devised to achieve immunity from all criticism. In the case of the thesis of the non-objectifiability of God, it is a reasonable supposition that the desire to secure the idea of God against criticism played an important part, although the thesis has a different and purely theoretical basis in ideas connected with philosophical Kantianism. Nevertheless this does not entail, even on Popper's theory of science, that the idea of God is totally useless, and Albert's insistence that it should be completely abandoned makes sense only as an expression of hostility to theology. It cannot be justified by the principles of his critical rationalism.[77a]

But should theology in fact be judged by the standards worked out in the *Logic of Scientific Discovery*? Does this provide us with valid criteria for any sort of scientific statement? The 'logic of discovery' was originally elaborated with reference to the natural sciences. Do the procedures of the natural sciences completely match this description of their principles? And if they do match it sufficiently, does this show that the requirement of critical examination by falsification can be simply transferred to other

[77a] A theological contribution to the discussion with Hans Albert which appeared while this book was in the press is G. Ebeling, *Kritischer Rationalismus? Zu Hans Alberts 'Traktat über kritischer Vernunft'*, Tübingen 1973.

disciplines in the name of an ideal of the unity of scientific method in all disciplines? Popper himself certainly seems to have taken this view of his proposal, and, following him, Bartley and especially Albert have tried to use his criterion of falsifiability to develop a unitary theory of knowledge as such? If this procedure is justified, it would also apply to theology. The question of whether or not theological statements are scientific would then have to be decided by whether or not they met the criteria laid down by Popper, for example, whether they allowed predictions which could be falsified by testing. But should Popper's postulates in fact be accepted as binding criteria for all knowledge? Does such a claim itself stand up to examination?

5. The Possibility of Falsification

Karl Popper tried to answer the question of how postulated general rules, such as are put forward by the natural sciences and other systematic sciences, can be proved or at least given adequate solidity. Inductive reasoning provides no solution, since a general rule always applies to an infinte number of cases, of which only a few are known at any time. As a result, generalisations can never claim absolute certainty. For the same reason strict verification of postulated general laws by experience is not possible. On the other hand, it is possible to refute such alleged general rules; this requires no more than a single instance of a deviation from the alleged rule.

Carnap, who accepted Popper's criticisms of the verification principle as early as 1934,[78] nevertheless rejected his criterion of falsification as also inadequate on the ground that it allowed the critic to disregard the observation reports (protocol statements) which refuted a hypothesis. For this reason he accepted as a substitute the broadly conceived principle (which he later elaborated with greater precision) of 'testing' and 'confirmation'. On Carnap's view, the confirmation of a proposed law by observations could gradually grow stronger as the number of observations increased, but it could never be final.[79]

[78] R. Carnap, *The Logical Syntax of Language,* London 1937, p. 321.
[79] Carnap, pp. 317–18.

The value of the criterion of falsification depends on the possibility of a proposed law's being refuted by observation reports which are clear and irrefutable. The epistemological status of such reports is, however, still disputed. Carnap, following Neurath, described them as 'protocol sentences', i.e. sentences which protocol the content of observations. Popper insists, however, that such statements always contain more than the bare content of perception. There is no such statement, he says, 'that does not go far beyond what can be known with certainty "on the basis of immediate experience" '.[80] The reason for this is that every statement makes use of general terms or symbols, universals. Even a protocol sentence like 'This table here is white' must use general expressions to describe the observation it reports. Every statement therefore inherently possesses 'the character of a theory, of a hypothesis'.[81] But whereas hypotheses can usually, at least in theory, be decided by recourse to observations, with the mere linguistic description of observations this is not possible in any simple way because the observations themselves can be recorded only in statements. Carnap therefore assumes such observation reports as the ultimate basis for the foundation of scientific theories and incapable of derivation from anything else. Popper will not allow this to hold of *particular* observation reports, since these can be corrected by other observations, but the *class* of observation reports has a similar function in his theory vis-à-vis more general hypotheses. Popper uses the term 'basic propositions' instead of 'protocol sentences' in his formulation, to avoid getting involved in the problems of the psychology of perception. Basic propositions concern only the 'physical bodies' given in perception.[82] They 'have the form of singular existential statements, "there-is" statements',[83] and 'must be testable, intersubjectively, by "observation" '.[84] But how can a basic proposition be

[80] *The Logic of Scientific Discovery*, p. 94,

[81] Ibid.

[82] *Conjectures and Refutations*, p. 267.

[83] *Logic*, p. 102. This distinguishes basic propositions not only from general statements, but also from 'singular "there-is-not" statements, whose logical form is different' (p. 101).

[84] *Logic*, p. 102. A. Wellmer (*Methodologie als Erkenntnistheorie. Zur Wissenschaftslehre Karl Poppers*, 1967) rightly remarks that Popper's 'ultimate

'intersubjectively testable' by observations when the observations in turn become scientifically relevant only when they too are formulated in basic propositions, of which the same requirement can be made? Clearly, no intersubjectively acceptable test can go behind basic propositions, except to other basic propositions, and the end of the process is always more basic propositions. Here Popper and Carnap both admit that 'basic propositions are accepted as the result of a decision or agreement; and to that extent they are conventions'.[85] Popper describes the 'dogmatism' involved in this agreement as 'innocuous', but this is surely an underestimate of the problems the point raises. The problems have given rise to serious objections against the falsification principle for not excluding the possibility of rejecting a basic proposition which contradicts a hypothesis. It has already been mentioned that this was Carnap's first and fundamental criticism of the criterion of falsification, and the importance of this objection for the practice of scientific work will be a subject for discussion later in this book.

From a different point of view, C. F. von Weizsäcker has recently questioned the assumption that there is 'a radical distinction in certainty' between verification and falsification.[87] The problems of basic propositions are also at the centre of Weizsäcker's criticisms, but in a slightly different way. Popper himself admitted that any basic proposition which expresses a singular observable state of affairs must make use of general concepts. Weizäcker says that this also implies general propositions. In other words, in Popper's example, 'This table here is white,' the quality 'white' presupposes the concept of colour, either as a predication, giving the proposition: 'white is a colour', or as the negation of a predication, giving the proposition: 'white is not a colour, but something else (perhaps a general quality of light)'.[88] Further, says Weizsäcker, 'no

---

aim, like that of the positivists, was to prove the exclusive validity of the concept of experience and empirical testability embodied in the experimental method' (p. 29).

[85] Popper, *Logic*, p. 106.

[86] ibid. p. 70.

[87] C. F. von Weizsäcker, *Die Einheit der Natur*, 1971, p. 124.

[88] See also the argument in Wellmer, pp. 133–4, that the principle of

falsification can be more credible than the general propositions which the falsification assumes as unfalsified'.[89] Weizsäcker accepts Popper's claim as a 'description' of empirical procedure. 'In practice,' he says, 'we work with hypotheses until they are falsified.'[90] A theoretical justification of this procedure is not possible, however, because 'the appearance of a radical distinction in the type and degree of certitude afforded by verification and falsification' is invalidated by the fact that further general propositions are constantly assumed.[91] Weizsäcker therefore attempts to prove the unity of science and the validity of its propositions by a different method, namely by going back to Kant and adopting a theory of conditions of

repeatability contained in the principle that the content of 'singular there-is statements' must be observable involves 'a general hypothesis, a causal interpretation', which means that the formulation of a relevant basic proposition always presupposes such a general hypothesis and 'is itself only the rudiment of a general hypothesis' (p. 134). Nevertheless the claim Wellmer bases on this, that the control function attributed to individual events is 'incompatible' with the principle of reproduceability (pp. 134–5), is not convincing, since the latter can be fulfilled only by producing (and identifying) 'individual events'. Popper could rightly point out in reply to Wellmer that in individual events the individual and the general are always intertwined. This also invalidates Wellmer's further claim that ' "singular" propositions . . . are not suitable as "basic propositions" ', because if they are so used 'as little as a few moments after the end of an experiment it would be generally impossible to test a basic proposition by experiment' (p. 137). It could rightly be objected to this view that by his principle of observability Popper can so far neglect the implications of the individuality of basic propositions as to call the question of 'whether events which are in principle unrepeatable and unique ever do occur' 'metaphysical', and one which cannot be decided by science (*Logic*, p. 46), instead of relying on the combination of unique and typical elements in the phenomenon of what is individual. Popper's failure to see that even the generalising sciences, through their basic propositions, depend on singulars and thus implicitly on the unique and unrepeatable aspects of singulars, may have contributed to his restriction of the concept of science to the recognition of laws. This is a subject to which we will have to return.

[89] Weizsäcker, p. 124; cf. p. 218.

[90] Weizsäcker, p. 123.

[91] On this point compare Weizsäcker's more general views on the 'circle' involved in any act of knowing, as set out in, e.g., his essay 'Das Verhältnis der Quantenmechanik zur Philosophie Kants', *Zum Weltbild der Physik*, 1963, pp. 80ff, esp. 111.

experience.[92] Weizsäcker's criticisms of Popper, however, are not completely convincing. That falsification and verification provide different types of certainty in the testing of hypothetical laws can be justified independently of the fact that the basic propositions on which the falsification is based themselves presuppose other, general, propositions. This relative character of basic propositions makes it more difficult to agree whether a particular observation falsifies a given hypothesis or not, but does not alter the fact that if agreement is reached on this point a single clear counterexample to a hypothetical law destroys that law's claim to validity, whereas in the converse procedure all positive confirmations can be no more than provisional.[93] The significance of Weizsäcker's point that basic propositions presuppose not only general concepts but also general propositions should certainly not be underestimated, although Popper did recognise this in principle in the element of convention incorporated into the theory of basic propositions. In this sense, Weizsäcker's point is fundamentally no more than that the general propositions implied in basic propositions are to be understood as developments of the implications of the general concepts used in them. Popper described the choice of these general concepts as a matter of convention, of agreement between competent judges. This acceptance of convention probably takes more account of the historical nature of the formation of natural science concepts than Weizsäcker's return to

[92] *Einheit der Natur*, pp. 219ff; cf. also p. 217: 'Anyone who could analyse the conditions under which experience is possible at all would have to be able to show that all the general laws of physics could be derived from these conditions.'

[93] This 'asymmetry' between falsification and verification in the testing of hypotheses on which Popper constantly insists is also recognised by Carnap, in spite of his rejection of the possibility of falsification 'in the strict sense' (*Logical Syntax of Language*, p. 318). In his *Philosophical Foundations of Physics* (New York and London 1966), Carnap stresses the simplicity of falsification: 'One need find only a single counterinstance. The knowledge of a counterinstance may, in itself, be uncertain. You may have made an error of observation or have been deceived in some way. But, if we assume that the counterinstance is a fact, then the negation of the law follows immediately . . . A million positive instances are insufficient to verify the law; one counterinstance is sufficient to falsify it. The situation is strongly asymmetric' (p. 21).

transcendental conditions of experience in general. It may be doubted, however, whether Popper has realised the full extent of the uncertainty this produces. If basic propositions, with their general concepts, automatically presuppose general propositions, this means that their formulation in itself implies developed theoretical perspectives. In a similar situation Lavoisier saw oxygen 'where Priestley had seen dephlogisticated air and where others had seen nothing at all'.[94]

Considerations such as these create difficulties for attempts to separate scientific assertions from 'metaphysical' ones by reliance on observation. If the concepts, the language, in which an experience is described are a matter of convention, there is no longer any conclusive reason for excluding the concept of God in advance from the range of permissible utterances. And for the Israelites the proposition that God saved them from their Egyptian pursuers at the crossing of the sea of reeds must certainly have been a description of a situation from their immediate experience and not a secondary interpretation separable from the experience. In this context the word 'God' would therefore have to be regarded as part of a 'singular there-is statement', and at this point Popper's efforts to separate scientific and 'metaphysical' statements lose their force. Not only does the language required for the formulation of basic propositions root natural science in the psychology of the individual investigator, but the logic of its statements fixes it firmly in general attitudes which are ultimately philosophical or religious in character. This statement does not exclude the possibility that these statements may be open to correction by experience; indeed it should be stressed that this openness must be a property of philosophical and religious views as long as they remain living and have not solidified into dogma.

The dependence of the linguistic form of basic propositions on a general perspective of experience expressed in their formulation strengthens the view that the objects of scientific controversy are

[94] T. S. Kuhn, *The Structure of Scientific Revolutions*, Chicago and London, 1962, p. 117. In this connection it is also interesting to note Kuhn's sceptical remarks on the possibility of a neutral language of observation (p. 125), and his statement that the search for 'a pure observation language' can begin only after experience has been determined by a particular theory (p. 128).

not just individual hypotheses but complete theoretical constructions. This view follows from the quite simple fact that it is 'generally' only in association with other hypotheses that an individual hypothesis leads to conclusions which allow it to be tested. In other words, *the test applies*, at bottom, not to a single hypothesis, *but to the whole system of physics as a system of hypotheses*,[95] or at least the system of physics as proposed at any particular time. This provisional system in turn itself determines the observations and the language in which they are reported. This means that empirical checking of hypotheses takes place not within a framework of theoretically neutral observations, but normally as part of a process which Kuhn has described as 'paradigm articulation'.[96] By this Kuhn means the working out of a provisional theory by means of the 'solution of all sorts of complex instrumental, conceptual and mathematical puzzles' which occur when a theory which functions as a paradigm of natural explanation is applied to other areas or, in exceptional cases, used to explain rival theoretical models for 'anomalous' phenomena (52ff). In this way, except for purely instrumental problems, 'every problem that normal science sees as a puzzle can be seen, from another viewpoint, as a counterinstance and thus as a source of crisis' (79), which, when generally recognised, leads to a change in the theory previously accepted as a paradigm. From this point of view Kuhn attacks the 'stereotype of falsification by direct comparison with nature' (77), and says that the decision to reject one theoretical paradigm is always simultaneously a decision in favour of another: accounting for an anomaly always involves 'the comparison of both paradigms with nature *and* with each other' (77). Kuhn admits that the appearance of 'anomalous experiences' is similar to what Popper calls falsification, but denies that it necessarily entails falsification: 'if any and every failure to fit were ground for theory rejection, all theories ought to be rejected at all times' (145). In fact the

---

[95] Carnap, *Logical Syntax of Language*, p. 318, citing Duhem and Poincaré. Carnap's italics. Popper too explicitly accepts this view of Duhem's (*The Poverty of Historicism* (1957), New York 1964, p. 132n., and *Logic*, p. 78, n. 1).

[96] For this idea see Kuhn, p. 35, and on the issue in general the whole of his chapter IV, 'Normal Science as Puzzle-Solving' (pp. 35ff). The page references in the rest of this section are to Kuhn's book.

usual reaction to anomalies is precisely the procedure rejected by Popper as the 'conventional twist' or 'immunisation strategy', in which the defenders of a paradigmatic explanatory model 'devise numerous articulations and *ad hoc* modifications of their theory in order to eliminate any apparent conflict' (78). There is no fundamental difference between this procedure and the articulation and refinement of a paradigmatic theory in the course of its application as long as the 'anomaly' is regarded simply as a 'puzzle' which can in principle be solved within the framework of the existing theory. An anomaly is recognised as a falsification of previously accepted theories not on its first appearance, but only later, after the 'triumph of the new paradigm over the old one' (146).

Kuhn's vivid description of the processes involved in scientific revolutions destroys the illusion that Popper's criterion of falsification can be clearly applied at any time. Whether a particular anomaly falsifies a hypothetical law or turns out to be no more than a puzzle which can be solved by the further application of the hypothesis is recognised not as a question to be settled by the result of a single experiment, but as the subject of an often lengthy process of scientific discussion. This does not mean that the crucial importance of the criterion of falsification is denied, since the process of scientific discussion makes sense only on the assumption that an anomaly could be shown to be a falsification of previous assumptions, instead of a soluble and perhaps speedily solved puzzle. Kuhn's study may in fact be regarded as a contribution to the redefining of the scope and the refinement of the application of Popper's criterion of falsification. Unfortunately, however, Kuhn's discussion obscures the special position of falsification within the general task of comparing different theories to determine 'their ability to explain the evidence at hand (144–5). This formula, which Kuhn puts forward as the residual meaning of verification in Carnap's sense of confirmation after the abandonment of the strict theory (144), is in fact so general as to go far beyond the particular problems of testing proposed laws. It would be equally applicable as a standard for judging hermeneutical models in historical or literary interpretation. The criterion of falsification, on the other hand, stipulates the particular character of the standard which must apply to the testing of proposed laws. Whereas discussion about whether hypotheses are established by their fruitfulness in explaining the existing evidence is not ended by agreement that a hypothesis is securely established so far, discussion about a hypothetical law can be immediately ended as soon as there is agreement that an 'anomaly' which contradicts it must be regarded as a counterexample and therefore as falsifying the hypothesis. Even though discussion of the problem may be reopened later from different points of view, as long as this agreement remains, the falsification of the hypothesis is settled once and for all. In the converse case of the 'establishment' of a paradigmatic theory no such assertion can be made about its logical status, as opposed to its general reputation.

6. Structuralism and History

Logical positivism directed its energies to the discovery of a unitary logic of science, not just of a special methodology for the natural sciences. This idea of 'unified science' also dominates Popper's thinking. He openly admits his belief in 'unity of method', by which he means that 'all theoretical or generalising sciences make use of the same method, whether they are natural sciences or social sciences'.[97] Popper extends this thesis to historical disciplines, in spite of what he admits to be a 'fundamental distinction between theoretical and historical sciences'. This distinction lies not in method, but in interest: 'it is the distinction between the interest in universal laws and the interest in particular facts.' Popper has had to defend himself against the charge that this characterisation of history is old-fashioned, and it is certainly true that recent discussion on the theory of history has largely concentrated on the significance in history of the typical, of what can be expressed in a law.[98]

[97] *The Poverty of Historicism*, p. 130. The quotations which follow come from p. 143.
[98] R. Wittram, for example, says that Popper's position 'no longer totally corresponds to the state of opinion among modern historians, who do not regard as adequate a description of history in terms of its "interest" in actual,

None the less the discussion of the significance of typical or nomothetic structures in history has been influenced to an important extent by Popper's ideas, especially because of an essay by C. G. Hempel.[99] Popper believes that even if the historian is interested in explaining particular events, he must presuppose and make use of general laws, even though in the narrative form of historical description the presupposition is no more than tacit: 'a singular event is the cause of another singular event – which is its effect – only relative to some general laws.'[100] The laws concerned, says Popper, are in the first place sociological, but based on pre-scientific sociological models which are already implicit in the historian's terminology. This makes history an applied generalising science, which, as such, can be included in the concept of unified science.

As a result of the essay of Hempel's mentioned above, these views have provoked an intense and wide-ranging debate in the British and American literature on historical methodology. According to A. C. Danto, 'almost everything since published on the topic has been structured by Hempel's original formulation, whether writers agree with him or not'.[101] The dominant feature of this discussion is an effort to resist the absorption of history into the generalising sciences by emphasising the uniqueness of historical explanation of individual processes. The situation is reversed in the German debate, where the importance of the individual as the object of history and a stress on the 'ideographic' character of history have been almost unchallenged orthodoxy since the rise of historicism.[102] This orthodoxy is now

---

single, specific events' (*Anspruch und Fragwürdigkeit der Geschichte*, Göttingen 1969, p. 108). See also Wittram's book, *Das Interesse an der Geschichte*, 1958, pp. 54ff.

[99] C. G. Hempel, 'The Function of General Laws in History', *Journal of Philosophy* 39 (1942).

[100] *The Poverty of Historicism*, p. 145.

[101] A. C. Danto, *Analytical Philosophy of History*, London and New York 1965, p. 308.

[102] It is well known that the term 'ideographic' comes from W. Windelband, *Geschichte und Naturwissenschaft*, 1894, where it is contrasted with the 'nomothetic' nature of the sciences. Windelband's distinction was systematically developed by H. Rickert in a book which was for long a standard work, *Die Grenzen der naturwissenschaftlichen Begriffsbildung*, 1902.

being challenged by the claim that the comparative approach and
the search for the typical or structural is at least as important in
historical research and history writing.[103] 'Typical' is not used
here in its scientific sense, however, and an emphasis on the
typical may even go with a rejection of the assumption that there
are laws in history. This in itself would make further clarification
of the relation between types and laws of nature essential, and the
British and American discussion of the relation between natural
law explanations and historical explanations provides a valuable
basis for this.

One of the main critics of Hempel and his followers (such as
A. Donagan) has been William Dray,[104] who has developed the
view (previously argued by Michael Oakeshott) that all
historical statements refer to continuous series of individual
events,[105] and take no account of nomothetic regularities. Of the
compromise solutions suggested, one which has attracted
particular interest is M. Scriven's proposal that while laws in
history do not act as premises in a deductive explanation,[106] they
should be regarded as part of the 'justification' of an explanation
of a historical process by giving an account of its origin.[107] This

Rickert connected the concept of individuality with that of cultural values,
which he regarded as the object of the historian's 'value-relating' procedures.

[103] See for example T. Schieder's discussion of the 'object of history' in his
book *Geschichte als Wissenschaft*, 1965, pp. 14ff. Schieder has stressed the
importance of the typical in historical knowledge in a number of books. His
claim that history studies 'the history of the great structures of human
community and the human beings who act within them and shape history' (p.
20) is deliberately designed to break out of the opposition between the
question of regularities in history and the limitation of historical study to the
investigation of individual phenomena.

[104] See his *Laws and Explanations in History*, Oxford 1957, pp. 66ff.

[105] See also the account of Oakeshott's view (based on his book *Experience
and Its Modes*, London 1933) in Dray, *Philosophy of History*, London 1964, 8ff,
esp. 9, where Dray ascribes to Oakeshott 'a "continuous series" model of
explanation': 'the historian may claim to understand one event's following
another, it would seem, if he can "fill in" the intervening events' (Dray, pp.
9–10). The meaning of historical 'continuity' is, however, left unclear by
Oakeshott.

[106] M. Scriven, 'Truisms as Grounds for Historical Explanation', in P.
Gardiner (ed.), *Theories of History*, New York 1959, pp. 464ff.

[107] On 'Explanatory Narrative in History', see the article of that title by W.
Dray, *Philosophical Quarterly* IV/14 (1954), pp. 15–27.

idea has been taken further by A. C. Danto in his *Analytical Philosophy of History* (1965). Danto says that the inclusion of an event under a general law already presupposes a general description of the event, and this description in turn depends on a prior 'historical explanation' of the event as part of a narrative structure.[108] But unlike a narrative sequence, a general law cannot connect the beginning of an event with its end, but only with the general class of events to which it belongs.[109] Now this limitation applies not only to the use of strictly general natural laws in the explanation of historical processes, but also to sociological or specifically historical types or structures of limited generality. While it is impossible to deny the presence of such structures, it is equally impossible to apply them to the conditions which started off the historical process as a basis and explain the end-product of that process. This procedure would give us only the class of events of which the result is a member,[110] and deciding whether something is a member of the class is in turn dependent on the particular sequence of events which can be described only in narrative form. In other words, the classical historicist view that history deals with unrepeatable sequences of unique events – a view argued in Britain by, for example, Oakeshott – turns out to be basically correct,[111] always provided that the appearance in such sequences of regular structures of varying degrees of generality is allowed to be equally the concern of history. The emphasis on the explanatory value of such structures is quite right. It is true that they cannot explain the particular result of every historical process in its individuality, but they do narrow down the possibilities within a sequence of events, giving rise to 'tendencies', which emphasise the relevance of some events as preceding, and to some extent encouraging the occurrence of, others.

[108] Danto, *Analytical Philosophy of History*, pp. 220ff.

[109] Danto, pp. 238ff, esp. 240.

[110] Danto discusses this question on p. 254 with the example of 'laws' specific to history.

[111] The objection that it is impossible for unique events to be the object of linguistic description because language always works with general expressions does not hold, because the reflective form of language makes it quite possible to use general expressions to mean individual and unique states of affairs, although the general form of an expression can of course itself be examined.

It is therefore perfectly possible for historical *interest* to be directed to general factors, but nevertheless the method of deductive explanation described by Popper and Hempel proves inadequate for history because it is unable to explain the individual particularity of historical processes and especially of their results. Historical hypotheses, however, relate to this sort of process even when they concern themselves with their typical structures,[112] and for this reason the falsification criterion cannot apply to them, at least in the form given it by Popper. The assertion of a general rule or law can, at least in principle, be refuted by a single counterexample because the example destroys the strict generality claimed by the law, but the situation is different with assertions about individual facts. These do not have a relation to exemplifiable regularities which permits abstraction from their other characteristic features. With reference to Popper's definition of a basic proposition as a singular there-is statement, Carnap rightly stressed that the task of falsifying such a statement is as impossible to complete as that of full verification of a proposed law. In the second case an infinite number of relevant instances would have to be examined before a strictly general proposition could be regarded as verified, and in the case of a singular there-is statement the whole universe would have to be explored before one could say with complete certainty that the assertion was false.[113] Popper avoided these problems by combining the concept of a basic proposition with that of observability. This automatically presupposes repeatability, particularly when the observability required is observability at any time.[114] There are probably, however, states of affairs which are not observable at all times but the reality of which is not open to question, even though assertions about them are not liable to

[112] The dependence of such structures on time, their restriction to a particular historical period, is important here. On the other hand, the (comparatively) strict universality of scientific laws and their invariability over time (though in the case of very long periods this may be no more than a fiction) often leads scientists to forget that the hypothetical laws of natural science too are concerned with individual sequences of events in irreversible processes.

[113] R. Carnap, *Testability and Meaning,* 1950.

[114] Such a requirement is itself, of course, formally a hypothetical law and as such is open to falsification.

falsification by a single counterexample as in Popper's procedure. This is especially true of past events, which may have been open to repeated observation when they occurred, if they were of sufficient duration (e.g. last year's apple blossom), but are now no longer accessible to any observation. The checking of statements about events of this sort is always historical in character, i.e., by following up currently available leads (evidence) and by making use of all his relevant structural knowledge, the historian must form a judgment about whether the alleged event took place or not. In the case of such historical judgments, as in the case of circumstantial evidence in a court, a single clue is not normally enough to refute an assertion about past events. In this case the asymmetry between falsification and verification cannot be assumed. A decision about this sort of assertion, whether positive or negative, can be based only on the balance of the evidence.

The position is similar in the case of assertions about sequences of events when the sequences are not only linked by general laws which apply to them as indifferent events in a single class, but also connected with each other as individual events in the temporal sequence. This sort of sequence can be called evolutionary when its general tendency, irrespective of individual deviations, is already determined at the start of the process.[115] The description 'contingent sequence of events' applies to the different situation in which the connection in the succession of events comes into being gradually, as each event takes place, with each event related to the preceding members of the series. We may for the moment ignore the question whether evolutionary processes are not ultimately a particular form of contingent sequence, though it is certainly true that historical processes in the narrow sense would normally be expected to follow the pattern of contingent sequences, even if they contain

[115] In the case of sequences of events of this sort historical materialism talks of 'historical laws'. The 'pure type' of such a law is said to be the 'genetic-structural law', in the sense of a structure which determines development (P. Bollhagen, *Soziologie und Geschichte*, Berlin (DDR) 1967, pp. 187, 205ff; cf. the reference in R. Wittram, *Anspruch und Fragwürdigkeit der Geschichte*, 1969, p. 74). A. C. Danto's discussion (*Analytical Philosophy of History*, pp. 253–4) of the formal structure of historical laws leads to a similar view, but Danto leaves open the question of whether such laws in fact exist.

evolutionary phases within them.

A contingent sequence is formed by the temporal succession of events each of which is an individual. The form of the succession itself is also unique and historical. It may be described in narrative form, but the sum of the unique features of its occurrence cannot be described as an instance of the application of a single law. This is still true even if the individual occurrences which are the members of such a sequence of events can be regarded, in abstraction from their unique individuality, as members of classes of events and are from this point of view covered by the relevant laws. Individual observations or pieces of evidence can therefore no more refute assertions about such sequences of events as wholes than they can refute assertions about individual events. The refutation of the former class of assertion requires the introduction of considerations which judge the hypothetical construction of the sequence of events by what is known from the evidence about its members individually.

Both individual events and contingent sequences of events are entities which are unrepeatable in their specific facticity. The only thing that is repeatable, and therefore open to examination, is the logical structure of the historical reconstruction itself. The unrepeatability of historical events is ultimately a result of the uniqueness of individuals which exist in time, and even Popper admits that this uniqueness makes it impossible to explain them by falsifiable laws.[116] The only method which can be used here is the 'situational logic' of a historical interpretation which considers individual events as part of their periods. Popper's remarks on this point contain a clear reminiscence of Dilthey's hermeneutical logic,[117] which also had as its principal aim the consideration of the individual as part of the relevant totality. However, unlike his German champion Albert, who detects in Dilthey the beginnings of 'a technology with a nomological

---

[116] Popper, *The Poverty of Historicism*, pp. 146–7. Popper says explicitly that events can be explained by laws only when they are treated 'as typical, as belonging to kinds or classes of events. For only then is the deductive method of causal explanation applicable' (p. 146). On the other hand, the description of events 'in their particularity or uniqueness' is one of the most important tasks of history.

[117] Popper, pp. 147ff.

basis',[118] Popper's judgement is that at least as regards the unavoidable selectivity of historical interpretation Dilthey is not dealing with hypotheses which are testable or falsifiable in the scientific sense.[119] Interpretations can possibly be judged by their varying degrees of fruitfulness.

Is this only a symptom of the lack of precision of the historical disciplines? Does not the problem of the singular occur even in the natural sciences? Popper believes he can exclude from philosophy of science the 'metaphysical' argument of whether or not unrepeatable events exist,[120] but his own basic propositions must also refer to singular events,[121] to the extent that they are singular there-is statements. It is only the additional requirement of observability which introduces a restriction into those basic propositions where constitutive events are repeatable. This cannot be a feature of the structure of basic propositions, since the distinction between basic propositions and scientific theories would then disappear. The contrast between basic propositions and scientific theories is an expression of the demand that the abstractions of human thought should be tested against the individual entities on whose complexity they are based. Nomothetic structures can be demonstrated only in contingent entities, which always represent, in contrast to the alleged general structure, the particular and relatively unique. This feature is explained by the assumption that the world as a whole is a unique process in time. Given this assumption, all individual events are also, strictly speaking, unique: the concept of repeatability depends in fact on the possibility of neglecting the difference between individual events in favour of their typical structure.[122] Biology and scientific cosmology, as well as

---

[118] H. Albert, *Plädoyer für kritischen Rationalismus*, 1971, p. 129.

[119] It is not quite clear from Popper's account whether this judgement on historical interpretations (Popper, p. 151) is also meant to apply to the previous remarks on 'situational logic'. That it is so meant is implied, however, by the fact that the subject in both cases is the aspect of uniqueness in historical events, which according to Popper is not accessible to explanation in terms of derivation from laws.

[120] *Logic of Scientific Discovery*, p. 46.

[121] 'A singular statement (a basic statement) describes an *occurrence*', *Logic*, p. 23. The second German edition adds 'singular' before 'occurrence' (p. 55).

[122] On these matters see my discussion 'Kontingenz und Naturgesetz' in

historical studies, are also interested in this aspect of the unique, from which the scientific search for laws abstracts. In this sense, historical studies are not further removed from reality than natural science. To deny a scientific character to historical judgments to the extent that they apply to the unique features of particular events is therefore arbitrary.[123] This would, of course, fit in with the Aristotelian notion that knowledge can be only of the general, but the logical consequence would be to make any knowledge of reality problematical. If we are unwilling to exclude the quality of uniqueness from scientific consideration a priori, what are we to say of the unity claimed by philosophy of science for historical and scientific disciplines? Is Popper's idea of the testing and establishing of hypotheses an adequate expression of their basic methodological unity? The foregoing discussion makes clear that it can be so only if it is not restricted to the particular conditions applying to the formulation of scientific laws. These are concerned with the repeatable and typical elements of events in abstraction from their individual particularities, in the same way that the structural approach of the social sciences tries to describe typical forms of behaviour. In fact, however, as T. S. Kuhn has shown, even in the natural sciences the testing of hypothetical laws usually takes the form not of direct attempts to falsify them, but more often of a comparison of 'the ability of different theories to explain the evidence at hand'.[124] It appears from this that the ability to draw together and make sense of the available material is the principal criterion in the testing of scientific as well as of historical hypotheses. Popper admits this criterion for historical interpretations, but denies that it makes them scientific theories because of the impossibility of strict falsification. Within this single method of interpreting

---

Pannenberg and Müller, *Erwägungen zu einer Theologie der Natur*, 1970, pp. 33ff, esp. 47ff and 65ff. Since all nomothetic statements depend on contingent conditions, although these conditions are not made explicit in the laws, it is open to question whether the claim Popper makes for natural science, that it can 'represent only one world: the "real world" or the "world of our experience"' (*Logic of Scientific Discovery*, p. 39), can be said to be true of science exclusively and without restriction.

[123] Nor does Popper do this. He refers explicitly to 'historical sciences', whose objects are singulars.

[124] T. S. Kuhn, *The Structure of Scientific Revolutions*, 1967, p. 192.

phenomena, their inclusion under hypotheses with the constant risk of falsification is the characteristic feature of explanations 'of the evidence at hand' in natural science and all generalising sciences. It would be wrong to extend this characteristic to other sciences which use a different basis for interpreting their material, such as the intimate connection of unique events with their context. This also implies that the concepts of testing and establishment should be be tied, as they are by Popper, to the condition of predictability. This condition can be met, and makes sense, only in connection with the assertion and testing of general rules. Other assertions about the real world can also be tested by their ability to unify and interpret all the relevant aspects of the material with which they are concerned. In this form of testing, however, conclusive falsification and complete verification are often both impossible, i.e. in cases involving neither the assertion of general rules nor the assertion of singular facts. This is the reason why historical hypotheses can rarely be proved or refuted by a single piece of evidence. A provisional judgment is usually a conclusion from the balance of a large number of individual points of view. For this reason also the modification of hypotheses on points where they prove inadequate should be regarded less harshly than it is by Popper. It is the purpose of historical hypotheses to build the total stock of evidence about a historical theme into as comprehensive and complex a hypothesis as possible, but they are not required to formulate general rules which exclude as much as possible. If even in the natural sciences it has to be regarded as doubtful whether the formulation and application of hypotheses are dominated by the ideal of permanent self-sacrifice rather than by the effort to give the simplest and most comprehensive explanation of the available material, it is certain that this effort is predominant in the historical disciplines. All that can be required of historical hypotheses in the interest of testability and possible refutability is the greatest possible clarity in construction, so that a particular historical reconstruction, with its main assumptions and selection of evidence, can be clearly distinguished from alternative hypotheses.

The idea of critical examination can be regarded as a suitable basis for a general theory of science only if it is widened so that it is no longer restricted to hypotheses about general rules, but also includes hypotheses about singular events and contingent sequences of events. Knowledge of reality cannot be limited to a knowledge of general rules.

   If the idea of critical examination is taken in such a general sense, however, it can no longer be used as a criterion for excluding philosophy (or metaphysics) from the class of scientifically meaningful statements. It is true that philosophical assertions do not normally lead to assertions which could be checked by individual observations alone, but the reason for this is that they are not concerned merely with one selected aspect of reality. Philosophical assertions always include reflection on this act of selection as an inherent element, and therefore are concerned with reality in general, the *ti en einai* of things. Consequently philosophical assertions are always about reality as a whole, whether it is all the aspects of a single phenomenon or the whole of reality as the semantic context of every individual phenomenon. If this feature of philosophical statements is kept in mind, it is not surprising that philosophical assertions cannot be falsified in Popper's sense. Reality as a whole does not just consist of abstract structures, but always includes the aspect of the particular and the unique as well, and in the temporal process this always appears as something new. And since reality itself is still in process, still open, our experience of reality is always at any given moment necessarily incomplete, even if we ignore the inevitable limitations of our information. In other words, philosophical statements always have to do with whole phenomena, which show regularities but also have temporal uniqueness as part of their structure and are determined by their relation to all other phenomena. We shall see later that this takes us into the description of the semantic structure of phenomena. In this function philosophical models are bound by the general criterion which applies to the formulation of all scientific theories. Not only must they give a unifying description of the given 'material' in its semantic context, but they must also do this with reference to the problem with which, as philosophical models, they have to deal. A decision on the extent to which a philosophical model can do this can never be final; it is quite possible that the underlying idea may also apply to material which the formulator of the hypothesis did not know about, and it might be capable of clearer and therefore less restricted formulation than it was given by its author. This is the reason why there is always new discussion about philosophical systems of the past, and why this is the only way of finding out the areas in which these systems may still be fruitful. Nevertheless philosophical interpretations of reality as a whole can also be treated as hypotheses.[125] They can be tested for coherence (freedom from contradiction), the efficiency of their interpretative components (the avoidance of unnecessary postulates), and the degree of simplicity and subtlety they achieve in their interpretations of reality. Testing for this last feature is particularly difficult with philosophical assertions because the incompleteness of experience and the nature of reality as a continuing process means not only that new individual cases may turn up – as in the case of induction – but also that they may shift the total structure of events into a new perspective. Conversely, models currently available may in different ways succeed in anticipating the still incomplete totality of reality.

This concern with reality as a whole in all its aspects distinguishes philosophical hypotheses not only from the hypothetical laws of the natural and social sciences, but also from historical hypotheses. We may accept that historical methods are not basically restricted to the area of human action and experience as opposed to non-human nature and that the disciplines of natural history have a genuinely historical character. We may even regard the objects of historical investigation as including the objects of the generalising sciences – which would explain the reciprocal dependence of historical studies on the categories and results of these disciplines. Nevertheless, history [Historie] remains limited to the investigation of past events and processes. It follows from this that historical investigation cannot see all sides of the phenomena it studies: the process of history [Geschichte] has an impetus that takes it beyond the present and will in the future reveal the facts of the past in a new light, disclose new semantic relationships in them. Because of its exclusive concern with the past, history

---

[125] See S. C. Pepper, 'World Hypotheses. A Study in Evidence, 1942, passim.

[*Historie*] leaves the question of the final meaning or essence of the realities it investigates quite open. The question of essence, however, is the *fundamental* question of philosophy. The essence of a thing or (which comes to the same thing) its ultimate truth, its ultimate meaning, can be discovered only with reference to the totality of reality and to the total context of human experience. Because of the incompleteness of human experience and the openness of the world process itself to the still unattained future, the totality of both experience and the world process is accessible only in anticipation. For this reason philosophical theories cannot go beyond the anticipatory stage. But however widely these theories might differ among themselves, their intention is such that all present assertions implicitly presuppose the totality of both reality and human experience. We have seen that this applies also to assertions in the natural sciences, in spite of their deliberate abstractions and limitation to the question of uniform rules in natural processes. Popper in particular has seen that the concept of a hypothesis includes an element of anticipation or conjecture, which also means an anticipatory understanding of truth. This fact in turn forms the basis of the transition from the statements of the empirical sciences to those of philosophy. The transition in the generalising sciences, however, is different from that in history [*Historie*]. The step from the assertions of the generalising sciences to those of philosophy cannot be made by a linear extension of nomological description, but requires a consideration of the language of the generalising sciences and its implications. This follows from the abstract nature of this language. This is not true of the study of history [*Geschichte*] inasmuch as philosophical reflection is carried out at the same level as historical interpretation, namely that of the manifestation of semantic contexts. As a result, historical questions necessarily lead into philosophical ones, since the meaning of a past event can be fully determined only in the total context of history [*Geschichte*] as a whole. This means that the frame of reference in philsophy must include not only past history but also the present and the future, while the historian excludes these from the formal scope of his discipline. [126]

[126] A. C. Danto has an illuminating discussion of the relation between historical and philosophical interpretation, in which he restricts the second to

philosophy of history. According to Danto, both historians and philosophers of history enquire into the meaning or significance of events, which can be determined only by reference to their context. An event has meaning or significance in the historical sense of these terms only 'in the context of a story' (Danto, *Analytical Philosophy of History,* p. 8). It is therefore only hindsight which entitles us 'to say that an episode has a given specific meaning' (p. 8), and this view of the meaning of events must be constantly revised in the light of later experience. Danto says that the philosophers of history make illegitimate use of this method of interpretation (p. 9) by trying to determine finally the meaning of events before the occurrence of the later events which alone will give the first events their (ultimate) meaning. For us the later events are still in the future, but the philosophers of history 'seek . . . to tell the story before the story can properly be told' (p. 11), 'the story of history as a whole' (p. 12). In their 'impatience' the philosophers of history interpret the past on the basis of assumptions about the future. But does not every historian inevitably do this when he attributes any meaning to past events? This always implies an anticipation of the future, of ultimate meaning. The present consciousness of the historian, like that of other people, is always formed by anticipations of the future, even when he is concerned only with the past. The philosopher of history (in the sense of the 'substantive philosophy of history' which Danto rejects) differs in his procedure from the historian only by requiring himself to give a critical account of this state of affairs. His anticipation of the future of history becomes wrong only when he forgets that it is *mere anticipation* under the influence of his historic present and makes definitive judgments about the meaning of past events without qualification. Danto can dismiss the philosophy of history based on anticipation of the ultimate future so completely only because he has failed to see that an anticipation of this sort is already implicitly included in any recognition of a specific meaning in an individual event.

Chapter Two

THE EMANCIPATION OF THE HUMAN SCIENCES
FROM THE NATURAL SCIENCES

THE application of analytical theories of science to the so-called 'human sciences' frequently encounters the objection that methods developed for the natural sciences are not suitable for dealing with the disciplines associated under the term 'human sciences'. The objection implies that the natural sciences and the human sciences are two fundamentally different branches of science, and this assumption has been repeatedly criticised, especially by logical positivists and critical rationalists, who have worked to produce a unitary philosophy of science based primarily on natural science. Conversely, those who most strongly defend the independence of the human sciences also claim a monopoly, or at least superiority, for hermeneutical methods in the field of the human sciences, and declare that these are the only methods appropriate to the particular subject-matter of the human sciences. The concept of the human sciences and the problems of hermeneutic must therefore be regarded as fundamentally connected.

1. The Concept of the 'Human Sciences'

In its German equivalent, *Geisteswissenschaften,* the term 'human sciences' goes back to Wilhelm Dilthey's *Einleitung in die Geisteswissenschaften,* which has become a fundamental work in this area.[127] In this term Dilthey included 'the totality of the sciences which have as their object historical and social reality'

---

[127] Only the first volume appeared, in 1883 (= *Gesammelte Schriften* I).

(4). For Dilthey the human sciences comprised not only the disciplines which deal with the *interpretation of the world* in language, myth, art, religion, philosophy and science', but also those concerned with 'the structures of life in state and society, law, morals, education, the economy and manufacture'.[128] Dilthey justified his grouping of these disciplines under a single heading by their common differences from the natural sciences. Dilthey had previously put forward similar dichotomies in the totality of the sciences, though not always under the same labels, and in particular followed John Stuart Mill's *Logic,* which appeared in 1843. Mill, however, had not distinguished between natural and human sciences, but established a group of disciplines alongside the natural sciences which he named 'moral sciences'. This group of Mill's included empirical psychology, a theoretical characteriology ('ethology'), the science of society and historical science. The composition of this group in itself implies that Mill, like Comte, did not at all regard these sciences as having their own methods and being independent of the natural sciences. This emphasis was in fact the result of the replacement of Mill's term 'moral sciences' by that of 'human sciences', and it is this which has given Dilthey's term its constantly increasing importance. The first appearance of the term is in the German translation of Mill's work, which appeared in 1849; in the original the title of Book 6 is 'The Logic of Moral Sciences', whereas in the translation it reads 'On the Logic of the Geisteswissenschaften or Moral Sciences'.

Before we follow the concept of 'human sciences' to its sources we must clarify the distinction between *physical* and *moral* sciences. Although it occurs in both English and French literature of the seventeenth and eighteenth centuries, it goes back much further, to the Stoic division of sciences into logic, physics and ethics. In this division physics and ethics are the two practical sciences, and ethics includes everything to do with human behaviour and the historical world created by that behaviour. The term *sciences morales* therefore has a very broad meaning, and goes considerably beyond the narrow sense of 'moral'.

The translation of this concept of the 'moral' by that of *Geist*

---

[128] E. Rothacker, *Logik und Systematik der Geisteswissenschaften,* 1947, p. 3.

(mind) took place in Germany under the influence of the philosophy of Hegel. Hegel himself had talked only of a 'philosophy of mind', which he contrasted with natural philosophy and which, with natural philosophy and the introductory 'Logic', formed the three parts of the plan for his 'Encyclopedia of the Philosophical Sciences', which thus followed the Stoic division of the sciences. But since for Hegel philosophy and science were not distinct, but philosophy was indeed science, it is understandable that his pupils could, as early as the 1840s, have used the term 'science of mind' (*Geistwissenschaft*). This, then, is the origin of the description 'human sciences' (*Geisteswissenschaften*), although the term became so generally accepted as a result of the translation of Mill's *Logic* and Dilthey's work that its connection with German idealism was easily forgotten.

Historically, the opposition of philosophy of mind and natural philosophy in Hegel is of course based on the distinction between nature and mind or spirit, which was given its classical modern formulation by Descartes.[129] Descartes' distinction between the *mens sive substantia cogitans*, characterised by the faculty of thought (*cogitatio*) and the *substantia corporea*, characterised by extension (*extensio*) was modified by idealism to make both different manifestations of the one ultimate reality of mind. Descartes' substantial dualism was turned by idealism into a mere dualism of method. Dilthey's distinctions between natural science and the science of mind show the influence of this idealist modification of Cartesian dualism. This enables him to say that by the 'civic freedom of his person' derived from the fact of his personal consciousness man 'is set apart from the whole of nature'. Through his freedom he establishes 'a kingdom of history separate from the kingdom of nature' (6). The 'constitution of the human sciences as autonomous disciplines' is, according to Dilthey, the result of the fact that, alongside the processes externally given through the senses 'the others set themselves apart as a particular range of facts (!), given primarily to internal experience and therefore unaffected by any action of the senses (!) ' (8–9).[130] In other words, for Dilthey the autonomous

---

[129] *Principa philosophiae* (1644) I, p. 51.
[130] The page references are to Dilthey, *Gesammelte Schriften* vol. I. Dilthey

givenness of personal consciousness as the source of 'inner experience' (9) is the source of the autonomy of the human sciences. Dilthey refers to the 'incomparability of material and mental processes', and the 'impossibility of deriving' the latter from the former (11).

Descartes' dualism of corporeal and thinking substance is modified by Dilthey in two respects. Firstly, at least as regards anthropology, the duality of substance becomes a duality of method, which does not prevent Dilthey from stressing man's psycho-physical unity. Secondly, his concept of mind no longer corresponds to Descartes' *substantia cogitans*. In the philosophy influenced by Kant and idealism, thinking substance had become personal consciousness, and the concept of mind also came to include the historical world created by human action as in Hegel's 'objective mind'. In Hegel, however, the 'objective mind' was not just a product and expression of the action of individuals, but revealed the supraindividual (and superhuman) reality of absolute mind as world mind. In Dilthey this absolute mind is replaced by the unity of (intelligent) life which links all individuals, though he regards 'life' as real only in individual human beings.[131]

The human sciences differ from the natural sciences in having their starting-point in the vital 'unity', the 'psycho-physical unity of life', of the individual (15) which is given in 'internal experience', in which not only the unity of personal consciousness (14), but also 'the whole external world . . . is given'

---

could also say, however, following Locke, that 'there is only one sort of experience, but it is used in two ways, and this is the source of the distinction between external and internal experience' (V, p. 434). The idea of the individual as a psycho-physical unity in life (I, p. 15) is related to this. On the importance of empirical anthropology and especially physiology, for Dilthey, see P. Krausser, *Kritik der endlichen Vernunft. Diltheys Revolution der allgemeinen Wissenschafts- und Handlungstheorie*, 1968, pp. 53ff. Krausser regards remarks such as the one just quoted as grounds for interpreting Dilthey's theory of structure in terms of a cybernetic biology of open systems (cf. pp. 93, 109–110, 111–114). On the other hand, Dilthey also insisted that 'full reality' was given only in internal experience (V, p. 431). See H. Diwald, *Wilhelm Dilthey, Erkenntnistheorie und Philosophie der Geschichte*, 1963, pp. 42–3.

[131] On Dilthey's reshaping of Hegel's doctrine of objective mind, see also H. G. Gadamer, *Truth and Method*, London and New York, 1976, pp. 197–204.

(15). This unity of life, 'which fills us with the immediate sense of our undivided existence', is 'broken' by the methodology of the natural sciences (16).

This basic idea is connected in Dilthey with the contrast between 'explanation' and 'understanding' as expressed particularly in the contrast between an explanatory or analytic and an understanding or descriptive psychology.[132] Understanding psychology is concerned with the living wholeness of the individual human being. It interprets the components of human perception as experiential 'events' in so far as they are consciously related to man's vital unity in the direct awareness of his present undivided existence, and understands all activity as an 'expression' of this vital unity. Psychology based on natural science, on the other hand – explanatory or analytic psychology – examines isolated details to discover their causal relations.

In Dilthey's view, at least in his *Einleitung in die Geisteswissenschaften,* the only unity of life in the strict sense was the individual. This is why he could warn against a constructive use of the categories 'unity and multiplicity, whole and part', with reference to society (31).[133] Of course the use of these terms is unavoidable, and Dilthey himself constantly refers to the 'whole' of a society (36; cf. 34), and of history in general.[134] This is, however, a metaphor from the individual unity of life. It has some justification in the fact that the 'interaction of particular individuals, their passions, their vanities and their interests', provides 'the necessary manmade teleological context of human history' (53). Later Dilthey reversed his description, saying that the individual was 'only the point of intersection of the cultural systems and organisations into which his existence is woven', and to this he added the question: 'how can the systems be understood from a consideration of the individual?' (VII, 251). In his last studies, which develop the *Einleitung in die Geisteswissenschaften,*

---

[132] The classical statement of the distinction is in Dilthey's 1896 Academy lecture, 'Ideen über eine beschreibende und zergliedernde Psychologie'.

[133] H. Diwald's *Wilhelm Dilthey. Erkenntnistheorie und Philosophie der Geschichte,* 1963, pp. 81ff, does not take account of this position of Dilthey's in his *Einleitung in die Geisteswissenschaften,* with the result that his account is unduly influenced by the different emphasis of Dilthey's later statements.

[134] *Gesammelte Schriften* I, pp. 35–6, 87, 89, 95.

the idea of a totality of historical and social life in which individuals are only elements or parts becomes more important. Diwald has suggested plausibly that this departure from the individualism which the young Dilthey shared with historicism was an effect of Dilthey's view of the 'selfness of human nature'.[135] In addition to this, the change must be seen in connection with Dilthey's move away from the proposal to base the human sciences on a general psychology, which had been largely influenced by Mill's philosophy of science. Dilthey abandoned this plan as a result of criticism from Husserl.[136] The result of the change was that the task formerly allotted to psychology was now given to hermeneutic. The abstract unity of general psychology was now replaced by the actual unity of mankind in its history, the unity of the historical and social context of which the individual is necessarily a part.

This change of view did not make it necessary for Dilthey to abandon completely his earlier starting-point in the concept of psychic *structure*.[137] He now needed to develop the logic of the mutual relationship between whole and part – a logic which determined the psychic structure – as a *historical* relationship and extend it beyond the individual to his social environment in its historical development. Dilthey did both these things implicitly in his late analyses of semantic structures in the process of historical experience, especially in the third study on the foundations of the human sciences (VII, 70–5). Starting from his fundamental idea of the totality of life, Dilthey had already previously defined structure as the 'interrelations of this whole, determined by real relations to the external world' (VII, 238). The individual elements, which are incorporated into the

[135] *Wilhelm Dilthey. Erkenntnistheorie und Philosophie der Geschichte,* pp. 90ff and 145ff. On the selfhood of human nature, see Dilthey's remarks in VII, pp. 141, 213; V. pp. 270–1, 329–30, 334–5. At V, p. 229 there is a reference to the 'homogeneity of human nature'.

[136] On this see Diwald, p. 75, where he quotes Husserl's argument that psychological description can never determine the objective validity of an experience (Husserl, *Logical Investigations,* London and New York 1971, vol I, pp. 206–7). The move from a psychological to a hermeneutical account of the human sciences is described in Diwald, pp. 121ff.

[137] On the development of this idea in Dilthey see the book by P. Krausser mentioned in note 130 above.

structural context but then themselves become 'structural units' in their own right – the experiences out of which the structure of mental life is built (VII, 21) – are therefore in their turn mediated by relations with the external world and do not form a self-sufficient inner world. The individual human unit is thus necessarily taken up into the wider groupings of society (themselves based on the membership of individuals) in which the individual is a component part constituted by his relationship to the social whole and beyond that to humanity. But, like the wholeness of the individual, these various groupings do not already exist complete[138] but are still in a process of historical formation. For this reason in the process of history the *meaning* of the individual elements of life – 'the characteristic relationship between life's parts' (73) expressing their relation to the whole of life (233) – is constantly changing.

There were, however, two questions implied by the logic of historical experience which Dilthey no longer included in his analysis of the semantic structures of historical experience. The first was how the still uncompleted whole of life – at the various levels of individual life, the life of social groups and the life of society or even mankind as a whole – could be present at each particular moment. The second was how the different modes of the presence of the whole at the various levels of historical life then interrelate so as to make intelligible not only the dependence of individuals on the group and society but also their independence from them. Dilthey may have given no specific answer to the question about the presence of the uncompleted historical totality of life in its individual moments because he regarded it as already answered in a different context, namely in his general conception of life as a totality whose energy is active in all its parts. In the context of such a view, the fact that this life itself is still in process of becoming need not be felt as posing any particular problem. Nevertheless, even assuming such a 'pantheistic' intuition of the stream of life flowing in individuals, Dilthey's opinion that the uncompleted whole of life becomes intelligible to us 'in its parts' (VII, 233) is still unsatisfactory, since according to Dilthey's hermeneutical logic the parts themselves

---

[138] This point marks the limit of Krausser's interpretation of Dilthey's mental 'structure' in terms of a cybernetic system characterised by self-regulation.

are intelligible only if the whole can be presupposed at least implicitly. At this point Dilthey's intuition of the unity of life in individuals clashes with the logic of historical experience produced by his own analyses, and Dilthey fails to resolve the contradiction. On the other hand, in his idea of life as a givenness of experience, though a fundamentally different sort of experience from that with which the natural sciences were concerned, the later Dilthey still remained under the influence of his earlier conception of the human sciences which opposed them to the natural sciences. As a result he could rely only on the subjectivity of one's own experience of historical existence in the hope that out of this experience a supra subjective reality of life could be obtained which would therefore have intersubjective validity. Without this 'metaphysical' assumption on Dilthey's part, the claim of his analysis of hermeneutical experience to 'objectivity', after his abandonment of the attempt to base it on psychology, was left without support. Since Dilthey, under the influence of Comte and Mill, regarded all metaphysics as an expression of a period of human intellectual development which had been left behind, these implications were neither noticed nor, therefore, confronted with his analysis of historical experience. A possible escape from the subjectivism and relativism in which Dilthey's attempts to provide a theoretical account of the human sciences had become entangled seemed to be offered by Rickert's and Husserl's distinction between the meaning-creating structures of the mind and the sphere of mental acts, which was part of their critique of Dilthey's psychology of the human sciences. From this point of view, in order to obtain an intersubjectively valid basis for the human sciences, E. Spranger developed Dilthey's ideas into a distinction between the domain of mind with its logical web of meaning on the one hand and, on the other, the subjectivity of mental experience.[139] Such a distinction, however, has to face the question of the reality of mind. If this question was not to be answered by a return to an idealist metaphysic of mind, the only alternatives were neo-Kantianism's transcendental theories of validity or Husserl's intentionality of consciousness. In both cases, in contrast with Dilthey's view, awareness of meaning

[139] E. Spranger, 'Zur Theorie des Verstehens und zur geisteswissenschaftlichen Psychologie', in *Festschrift Vokelt*, 1918.

was derived from acts of a consciousness which confers meaning.[140] In these views 'meaning' could be taken to be either the object of thought in relation to its noetic content,[141] or alternatively the 'value reference' of the experienced content.[142] As belief in the primacy of epistemology declined, and with it the importance of the problems raised by Husserl of the constitution of the consciousness which creates meaning, it was possible for a general theory of action as the basis of the human sciences to dominate their theoretical problematic. The transition to this situation was provided by Max Weber's attempt to base a humanistic sociology on a theory of action.

2. Sociology as an Understanding Science of Action

The idea of the science of man as sociology goes back to Comte. Mill's more differentiated category of 'moral sciences' had placed sociology on a base of psychology and characteriology. Both Mill and Comte regarded sociology as a generalising science on the model of the natural sciences. In contrast to them, Weber made sociology (as understanding sociology) one of the human sciences,[143] and developed his theory of it within the contemporary discussion about the foundations of the human sciences. Crucial to this was the view which Weber developed from Knies,[144] that the 'specific object' of sociology was human

---

[140]So Edmund Husserl, *Ideas,* London, 1931 pp. 168–9, 246–51, 261–65. The counterpart of Husserl's conferral of meaning in Rickert is the reference to value, since Rickert subsumes the concept of meaning under that of value: *Die Grenzen der naturwissenschaftlichen Begriffsbildung,* 1902, 2nd ed. 1913, pp. 516ff.

[141]Husserl, *Ideas* pp. 361–2, 364–8

[142] Rickert, *Grenzen,* pp. 516ff; see also pp. 333ff.

[143] In 1903 Weber declared that 'the development of human action and human manifestations of any sort is accessible to a meaningful interpretation', and that the 'step beyond the "given" ' taken with every interpretation, 'in spite of Rickert's objections', justified 'treating those sciences that use such interpretations methodically as a separate group (the human sciences) ' (*Gesammelte Aufsätze zur Wissenschaftstheorie* (1922), 3rd ed. 1968, pp. 12–13n.)

[144] *Wissenschaftstheorie,* pp. 46–7. Knies regarded history and 'the related sciences' as sciences of action.

action, and that human action represented 'an intelligible personal relation to "objects", where "intelligible" means characterised by (*subjective*) *meaning,* conscious or not, which someone "had" or "intended" '.[145] This concept of action had already been distinguished by Weber from the more general one of behaviour, and in particular from mere 'external conduct'.[146] The concept of 'subjective meaning' recalls Husserl's intentions of meaning, although in Weber's usage, unlike Husserl's, the main point is not reference to objects *qua* reference,[147] but, as the quoted passage explicitly says, a specific *form* of relation to objects. What are we to understand by the notion of 'meaningful action'? Strangely, in precisely the places where he attempted to give a general account of the basic concepts of understanding sociology, Weber did not see any need to give his concept of meaning a more precise definition.[148] In another context, however, we find the passing remark that 'the meaning we attribute to phenomena' is equivalent to 'their reference to the "values" we live by in practice'.[149] This is not a meaning which phenomena have in themselves, but a meaning we give to them by relating them to 'values' which we apply. The way in which this sort of value reference, which is external to phenomena, relates to the subjectively 'intended' meaning proper to human

[145] *Wissenschaftstheorie,* p. 429 (Uber einige Kategorien der verstehenden Soziologie' (1913); see also pp. 542ff).

[146] *Wissenschaftstheorie,* p. 429; see also pp. 427–8.

[147] See, for example, Husserl, *Ideas,* p. 361–2 and passim.

[148] Jürgen Habermas rightly observes that Weber 'did not sufficiently clarify the category of meaning in its various applications' (*Zur Logik der Sozialwissenschaften* (1967), Frankfurt 1971, p. 87).

[149] Weber, *Wissenschaftslehre,* p. 54. Later in the essay on Knies (p. 93), Weber distinguishes the understanding of meaning from psychological interpretation by citing Simmel's distinction between the subjective interpretation of the motives of a person who is speaking or acting and the objective understanding 'of the meaning of an utterance'. In his discussion with Meyer in 1906 Weber subsequently distinguished his understanding of meaning as a reference to value from the 'interpretation of the linguistic "meaning" of a literary object' (p. 247), and claims that these are fundamentally different processes'. Only the former interpretation of meaning, in terms of value theory, justifies Henrich's claim that Weber 'generally treated the terms sense, meaning and value as identical' (D. Henrich, *Die Einheit der Wissenschaftslehre Max Webers,* 1952, p. 76).

actions becomes clear only on the assumption that human action is already of itself related to value. Human action can be 'understood' only in so far as it is already, of itself, 'referred to meaningful value-judgments', or, where that is not explicitly the case, when it 'at least *can* be referred to them' (126).

In his theory of 'value-based interpretation', Weber constantly relied on Heinrich Rickert, and in particular on his book of 1902, *Die Grenzen der naturwissenschaftlichen Begriffsbildung*. Rickert's view is that the only way of forming the concept of an individual in the context of historical reconstruction is by starting from a view of value which reveals individuals in their unique significance.[150] In other words, the external act of relating things to values is for Rickert the starting-point for the formation of historical concepts. The act of relating things to values has the function of constituting objects transcendentally, and at the same time it takes account of the methodological significance of the conditioning of historical knowledge by the specialised interests which determine in advance the choice of a historical object and its interpretation. But it is surprising how long it takes Rickert to mention that the 'centre' of historical description must be occupied by 'beings' who themselves 'take up an attitude to the values which guide their description'.[151] The values to which these individuals relate are universal values, because the individuals, as social beings, live in communities (505). On the other hand, the values which guide historical reconstruction are also social values (506), 'the common concern of the members of a community' (508) *as 'cultural values'* as opposed to what is given in nature (509). Of 'particular importance', therefore, to historical reconstruction are 'people who adopt an individual

[150] Rickert, *Die Grenzen der naturwissenschaftlichen Begriffsbildung*, pp. 316–17. See also the whole section, pp. 300–33.

[151] *Grenzen*, p. 495. Rickert regarded the view of the historical disciplines as 'human sciences', which he severely criticised, as based ultimately on the fact that historical descriptions are concerned with intelligent beings, and that 'we have an incentive to give a historical account of any events only when these intelligent beings include some who take up a position of their own in relation to the values that govern the account' (pp. 496–7; see also p. 501). 'The main object to which existing historical writing relates everything else is the development of human culture' (p. 505). The following quotations in the text are from Rickert's *Grenzen der naturwissenschaftlichen Begriffsbildung*.

attitude to the universal and normative social values of state, law, economy, art, etc. and so in their individuality are of crucial importance to the development of the culture' (510). 'The "semantic content" of historical interpretations is the "significance" that accrues when things which exist in their own right are subsequently brought into relationship with the interpreter's values' (516).

Weber took over Rickert's value-based technique of interpretation as the key to the historical reality of human behaviour. As he worked out his ideas, however, he came increasingly to regard the subjective value-intentions of individual agents as the proper object of external value-based interpretation. This is part of Weber's general transformation of Rickert's epistemological enquiry into an empirically oriented methodology which in practice, in spite of his heavy dependence on Rickert, represents the 'disintegration' of the neo-Kantian approach.[152] This reversal of approach has left its trace in a shift in the concept of meaning which appears in Weber's later formulations of basic concepts of his sociological theory of action. Here Weber says explicitly that the *subjectively intended* meaning of action is the proper object of understanding. Rickert, on the other hand, had made a sharp distinction between 'the real acts of intending and understanding' and the 'logical meaning' of which they were the 'bearers' and which, in his view, was 'understood jointly by a number of individuals, whereas it is of the essence of the psychic that it really appears only in a single psyche and belongs to no other'.[153] The empirical orientation of Weber's theory of action requires the concept of meaning to be rooted in the 'intended meanings' of individual agents themselves. This trend can be seen quite early in Weber's attraction to

[152] D. Henrich, *Die Einheit der Wissenschaftslehre Max Webers,* 1952, pp. 103–4.

[153] Rickert, *Grenzen,* pp. 516 and 181; see also p. 54. Like Rickert, Weber also distinguished the 'parity of the relation that gives meaning' to the behaviour of individuals from the psychic structure of their behaviour (*Wissenschaftstheorie,* p. 430), but nevertheless did not abandon the level of subjectively *intended* meaning, and this must be regarded as the origin of his theory of ideal types. Weber did not, however, investigate further the changed relationship between objectified meaning and subjective intentions of meaning involved in his position.

Gottl's concept of meaningful action (98ff), and lies behind his central methodological concept of the ideal type.[154] The ideal-type reconstruction, which significantly has no parallel in Rickert, offers a model of the rational structure of subjectively intended meaning and compares it with the actual behaviour of individuals which deviates from the ideal type because of its irrational features.[155] The concept of the ideal type is thus a unique link between an interpretation which attributes value from outside and so transcends the actual behaviour of individuals and the intentions of meaning which motivate the individual's activity. Like Dilthey in his later analyses of the significance of historic processes, Weber used his theory of value to describe the way in which the significance of these processes transcends the processes themselves while nevertheless remaining rooted in them. Weber is also close to Dilthey in his empirical attitude towards the meaning intended in action itself, in spite of his rejection (influenced by Rickert's criticism) of Dilthey's efforts to construe the semantic structure of historic experience in terms of a psychological theory. While Dilthey, however, could perceive implications which went beyond the original events only subsequently, by looking back at changes in significance in the course of historic experience, the emphasis on value in Weber's ideal-type reconstructions enabled him to discern, from the intentional structure of the action itself – in the sense of an intersubjectively valid structure of meaning – the way implication transcended the given material of action, This advantage was gained, however, only at the expense of restricting sematic analysis to actions. Furthermore, individuality was taken into account only as a deviation from the ideal type - a fault from which Ricker's method of historical formation of concepts did not suffer. And finally, as regards subjectively intended meaning, the emphasis on value increasingly bordered on the irrational. increasingly bordered on the irrational.

[154] On this see Henrich, pp. 83ff, and Weber, *Wissenschaftstheorie,* esp. pp. 190ff. The page references in the text are again to this collection.

[155] Compare Weber's description, pp. 561–2. This is also the source of the distinction between 'reconstructions of political economy in terms of ideal types' and the hypothetical laws of the natural sciences (p. 131): the ideal type does not need to have universal application, and because of this also helps to illuminate types of behaviour which deviate from it.

This latter development can be seen in the relation in Weber between value rationality and purposive rationality. The 1906 essay on Knies still refers to the 'rational' construing of human action in terms of the categories of 'purpose' and 'means', that is, the later purposive rationality, as 'a particular form' of value-based interpretation (126ff). But in the *Soziologische Grundbegriffe* of 1921, 'value rationality' appears as a different type of social action *alongside* 'purposive rationality' (565ff). We are still told that 'choice between alternative and conflicting ends and results may well be determined by considerations of absolute value,' but at the same time it may 'take place without a rational orientation to a system of values, merely under the prompting of subjective needs ordered in urgency by the principle of "marginal utility"' (*Theory of Social and Economic Organisation*, p. 117). This development deprives the determination of action by value of its superior function in action theory. Its relegation to the same level as purposive rationality results, however, in its appearing as 'irrational' when considered 'from the point of view of purposive rationality'. The consequences of this for the disputed question of value-judgements cannot be discussed in detail here.[156] Not only in evaluation based on a definite position, but also in value-based interpretation, subjective factors now become central, on the one hand to the description of the role of scientific *interest* in 'the selection of a given subject-matter and the problems of an empirical analysis', and on the other to 'the elaboration of the various possible meaningful attitudes towards a given phenomenon' (*The Methodology of the Social Sciences*, p. 22). The transcendental constitution of historical knowledge in terms of its relation to objective social cultural values, which links the interpreter with the processes he interprets and was heavily emphasised by Rickert, now becomes comparatively unimportant.[157]

[156] It would involve in particular a discussion of Weber's political decisionism. On this see H. Bosse, *Marx-Weber-Troeltsch*, 1970, pp. 27ff.

[157] Typical of this attitude is the fact that the Weber of 1917 no longer allows any intermediate position between 'practical value-judgements' — including the question whether ethical values can claim 'normative dignity', which must be decided by the philosophy of value — on the one hand, and the 'status as truth of a determination of empirical fact' on the other (p. 501; see also p. 50).

In spite of the tendency for Weber's theory of action to become independent of Rickert's value-based interpretation and its epistemological concerns, his interpretive sociology continued to rest on the more general base of the cultural sciences as defined by Rickert, for which Weber also accepted the term 'human sciences' (*Geisteswissenschaften*). Nevertheless, the opposition of value and being led to a situation in which a methodology based on a concept of action could finally condemn the whole concern with values as irrational in comparison with the purposive rationality of action. Inevitably, this created the conditions for a reversal of the relation between action theory and the cultural sciences. This reversal was brought about by T. Parsons' development of a general theory of action as a basis for the cultural sciences.[158]

In opposition to the behaviourist model of behaviour as an externally describable response to stimulus, Parsons insisted on the fundamental importance in the social sciences and the human sciences in general of the category of action as *intentional*, and therefore *meaningful*, behaviour. Parsons' most important reason for regarding the concept of intentionality as essential to a description of action, in view of its role in distinguishing action from externally observable behaviour, is his belief, shared by E. Cassirer and G. H. Mead,[159] that language is essential for directing action.[160] This view has been particularly neatly summarised by Habermas, following W. I. Thomas: 'Only the meaning asserted by the agent himself gives us adequate access to behaviour which is directed towards a situation interpreted by him.'[161] In this process language always pre-exists the individual

[158] The anthology edited by Talcott Parsons and Edward Shils, *Towards a General Theory of Action*, New York, 1951.
became something of a manifesto for this school.
[159] See J. Habermas, *Zur Logik der Sozialwissenschaften* (originally published as *Philosophische Rundschau, Beiheft* 5, (1967), and reprinted with other material, Frankfurt 1970) pp. 78ff, 102–03 (page references are to the 1970 edition).
[160] Parsons, *Societies*, New York and London 1966, p. 5; see also Parsons' book *The Social System* (1951), New York 1964, pp. 3ff, 543–4.
[161] Habermas, *Zur Logik der Sozialwissenschaften*, p. 139. The negative implication of this situation is that 'on the level of intentional action the direct correlation of stimulus and response becomes blurred: the same stimuli can

as part of the social context that transmits meanings which make the subjectively intended meanings of the individual possible and yet also transcend them. Parsons does not, like G. H. Mead,[162] trace such cultural values back to the mutual semantic anticipations of individuals' behavioural expectations in the process of their interaction, but starts from the assumption that the mutuality of behavioural expectations in any given social system already presupposes a system of cultural values. In Parsons' view, the general theory of action therefore divides into three theoretical branches:[163] the theory of personality, the theory of culture and the theory of social systems, which links the other two. The theory of personality forms part of psychology (545–6). A comprehensive 'theory of culture' is, according to Parsons, the aim of anthropology (553). Alongside anthropology are the 'formal' human sciences, the function of which Parsons describes as 'analysis of the content of cultural pattern systems for its own sake without regard to their involvement in systems of action' (554). In these latter Parsons includes logic, mathematics, philosophy of science and 'the analysis of art forms'. The theory of social systems lies in between the theory of personality and the theory of culture. It connects them as part of its function of describing the integration of individuals into the normative structure established by the cultural system.[164] In Parsons' theory the institutionalisation of the processes which provide values for individual behaviour is the particular subject-matter of sociological theory in the narrow sense, together with economics

---

produce different reactions if they are differently interpreted by the subjects' (Habermas, pp. 199–200). This indicates clearly the limits of the usefulness of behaviouristic models of human action.

[162] G. H. Mead, *Mind, Self and Society* (1934), 13th ed., New York 1965, pp. 61ff, 266ff, 281ff. On the incompatibility of this view with Morris's behaviourism, see Habermas Mead's derivation of the identity of linguistic meaning from the mutual anticipation of expectations, i.e. from a process of communication, is important to Habermas's later work: see Habermas and Luhmann, *Theorie der Gesellschaft oder Sozialtechnologie*, 1971, pp. 190ff.

[163] In *The Social System* (1951). In *Societies* Parsons lists 'the behavioral organism' as a further subsystem of action alongside personality (p. 8). Subsequent page references are to *The Social System*, pp. 545ff.

[164] *Societies*, pp. 8ff.

and political science (547ff). Parsons' systematic account of the cultural sciences is based on a theory of action, a reversal of Weber's approach. Weber's theory of action rested on the value theory which Rickert made the basis of all cultural sciences. Cultural values enter Parsons' conception of social systems 'as it were from above',[165] since the cultural system is always presupposed in all the processes by which the behaviour of individuals and groups is institutionalised. At this point it is impossible to avoid asking whether the converse is not also true, namely that cultural values are relative to the social process and are formed and modified in the process of the socialisation of individuals. Although Parsons himself stresses the *interdependence* of society and culture,[166] he prefers to regard this interdependence not as a historical process but as something like a self-regulating cybernetic system within which 'the highest cybernetic level is cultural rather than social and, within the cultural category, religious rather than secular'.[167] Elsewhere he admits that history deals with the social system as a whole, but says that it is better conceived not as a theoretical science of action, but as a 'synthetic empirical science' which 'mobilises' the knowledge of the different systematic disciplines in order to explain social processes and cultural changes in the past.[168] Parsons thus gives history a position subordinate to the theoretical disciplines.

This one-sided emphasis on cultural values at the expense of social processes is central to Jürgen Habermas's criticism of Parsons. Habermas emphasises that the regulative values which Parsons postulates for social systems depend 'on rules of evaluation which themselves have to be worked out in a decision-making procedure which could in principle be described'.[169] This would mean that cultural values to which the

---

[165] Habermas, p. 170. More recently Habermas has described the target of his criticism in even stronger terms as the 'at best . . . circumstantial plausibility' of the combination of action theory and systems theory in Parsons' work. (Habermas–Luhmann, p. 182 n. 1).

[166] *Societies*, p. 30.

[167] *Societies*, pp. 113–14.

[168] *The Social System*, p. 555.

[169] *Zur Logik der Sozialwissenschaften*, p. 177. The subsequent references in this paragraph are also to this book.

regulative values which maintain the balance of the system are, in Parsons' view, related would themselves be 'drawn into the discussion', that is, 'pragmatically examined and purified of their ideological elements'. Habermas had previously asked a similar question about Weber's view, namely, whether 'the methodically determinative value-references could not themselves be included in the sociological analysis as an effective contextual reality at the transcendental level' (19). Habermas argues that value-formation should be referred back to the theory of action as part of the development of the latter into a 'historically significant, functionalistic investigation into social systems' (91), with the aim of distinguishing utopian, purposive-rational and ideological contents in value systems.[170] In this analysis utopian and ideological contents appear as 'instinctual energies' which are 'not integrated' into the purposive rationality of the self-regulating society and 'have no hope of satisfaction in its role systems'. These energies are none the less given interpretations, either 'as utopian anticipations of a group-identity not yet achieved' or as ideological 'justifications of forces which repress drives or of fantasy substitute satisfactions'. The stability of the social system would then depend on the degree to which utopias can be put into practice and ideologies neutralised (92–3).

The key to this argument is the characteristic concept of 'instinctual energies'. This seems to imply that social systems, including the cultural values which shape them, are to be measured by their ability to assimilate or satisfy pre-existing instincts. This takes no account of the fact that the instincts themselves (and not just their 'interpretation') are historically mediated by the socio-cultural environment, and that consequently they provide no independent criterion for judging that environment, but at most can test the capacity of a given social system for self-regulation. It is also unclear, secondly, whether all the instincts which arise in this way can be, or even ought to be, integrated into the as yet unachieved group-identity

[170] op. cit., p. 181. This triad is clearly connected with other, similar, tripartite divisions in Habermas's work, especially the triad of instrumental, communicative and emancipatory cognitive interests (e.g. *Knowledge and Human Interests*, pp. 196ff).

of a future better society, whether destructive instincts must not remain excluded if a 'group-identity' is to be achieved at all. Thirdly, the question arises whether the formal condition of dialogue without domination is alone enough to give the pre-existing 'instinctual energies' a chance of satisfaction without the additional presence of the internal 'value' which guarantees their satisfaction. Connected with this question is the further one of whether in certain aspects of the human condition this internal value should not be looked for among the cultural values. If this is so, the division of cultural values into utopian, ideological and purposive-rational cannot be exhaustive; instead we are required to assume the existence of cultural values which neither are purposive-rational, nor consist in ideological justification of forces which repress drives, nor are just a utopian blueprint for a future order of human relations free from domination, but would be in themselves, as cultural values, a counterweight to all the social processes.[171] Conversely, however, should it not also be asked whether these cultural values do not condition a social system's capacity for integration? With this, our questioning of Habermas brings us back to Parsons. Parsons has shown, from the examples of ancient Israel and Greece, that cultural values are not necessarily dependent on the societies in which they were first expressed.[172] It can be added that these two examples also show that a society can reject its own cultural values, which eventually outlive it. This means that the truth of cultural values is certainly not to be ultimately determined by their contribution to integration in a particular society. The 'instinctual energies' present in a society can perfectly well account for its rejection of the cultural values adopted. Habermas is right to object to Parsons' neglect of the socio-historic mediation of cultural systems, but it does not follow from this that cultural systems are adequately understood as illustrations of pre-existing instinctual energies.

The priority given by Habermas to naturalistic 'instinctual energies' and their corresponding 'needs' over 'cultural values' is part of his general approach, which regards the 'interests' which

[171] On this see Habermas's new definition of the relation between cultural values and interests below.

[172] *Societies*, pp. 94, 108, 110–11.

'stimulate enquiry' as more important than knowledge itself or its truth. Habermas regards these interests as the 'natural basis' of the mind.[173] They are 'the basic orientations rooted in specific fundamental conditions of the possible reproduction and self-constitution of the human species, namely *work* and *interaction*'.[174] This distinguishes them from accidental empirical needs and makes them 'exclusively . . . a function of the objectively constituted problems of the preservation of life that have been solved by the cultural form of existence as such'.[175] While the system of interests which is part of life cannot be 'defined' independently of forms of action and categories of knowledge,[176] it is nevertheless presupposed as a transcendental condition of all knowledge, which in turn is constitutive for the orientation of action: 'it is only the knowledge-constitutive interest that lays down the conditions of the possible objectivity of knowledge'.[177] When interest is made a transcendental concept in this way, knowledge becomes 'experience admitted into structured complexes of action'.[178] The aim of interests is action – instrumental, communicative and emancipatory action[179] – and

[173] *Knowledge and Human Interests*, Boston, Mass. 1971/London 1972, p. 312.

[174] *Knowledge and Human Interests*, p. 196. Habermas develops the distinction between cognitive interest and communication in his 1961 inaugural lecture in Marburg, 'Die klassische Lehre von der Politik in ihrem Verhältnis zur Sozialphilosophie' (reprinted in *Theorie und Praxis*, 1963: see esp. pp. 31, 36–7, 46). The tripartite division occurs also in the 1965 inaugural lecture in Frankfurt, 'Knowledge and Human Interests', included as an appendix to *Knowledge and Human Interests*, pp. 301–17. On Habermas's wavering between identifying and distinguishing communicative and emancipatory interest, cf. M. Theunissen, *Gesellschaft und Geschichte. Zur Kritik der kritischen Theorie*, 1969, pp. 25–6.

[175] Habermas, *Knowledge and Human Interests*, p. 196.

[176] Habermas, *Knowledge and Human Interests*, p. 211.

[177] Habermas, *Knowledge and Human Interests*, p. 178; cf. p. 211–12.

[178] In the course of his discussion with Niklaus Luhmann ('Theorie der Sozialwissenschaft oder Technologie?', in *Theorie der Gesellschaft oder Sozialtechnologie*, pp. 228–9) Habermas modifies his view to take account of an objection made by K. O. Apel. Apel argued that there was a difference 'between the experience of objects admitted into structures of action on the one hand and discourse which is untouched by experience and free from the weight of action, on the other'.

[179] *Knowledge and Human Interests*, pp. 191–4, 211–12, and passim.

in this system of action the function of knowledge is still no more than mediation. To the extent that interests transcendentally 'establish the specific viewpoints from which we can apprehend reality as such',[180] they have taken over the function which Rickert ascribed to cultural values as the transcendental condition of knowledge in history [*Historie*] and the cultural sciences. In this way the process of moving from a view of the cultural sciences as based on a theory of value to one which regards them as based on a theory of action, which began with Weber, is completed in Habermas – or, more accurately, in this phase of his thought. Characteristic of the move is the claim that 'epistemology can be elaborated only as social theory'. [181]

The transfer of the concept of the transcendental from the self-reflection of consciousness to the investigation of the conditions which make phenomena (in the Kantian sense) such as 'the human species' [182] possible, not only brings a totally new range of problems into 'transcendental' philosophy, but also implies 'a naturalistic reduction of transcendental-logical properties to empirical ones', which is just what Habermas wishes to avoid.[183] The fact that 'on the human level the reproduction of life is determined culturally by work and interaction' does not take us outside 'the biological frame of reference of reproduction and the preservation of the species',[184] but simply indicates the modification undergone by this frame of reference in human biology. Habermas criticises Nietzsche for 'necessarily' misunderstanding knowledge-constitutive interest 'in naturalistic terms' because of his (Nietzsche's) view that 'interest and instinct are immediately identical',[185] but it is hard to see what difference it makes when Habermas declares

---

[180] *Knowledge and Human Interests*, p. 311. The idea of viewpoint, which was also used by Rickert, is important here. Cf. also p. 293, where interests are said to be the only thing that can give 'meaning' to scientific knowledge.

[181] *Knowledge and Human Interests*, Chapter 12, n. 20.

[182] Particularly clear in the lecture 'Knowledge and Human Interests', pp. 311–12.

[183] *Knowledge and Human Interests*, p. 196. Cf. Theunissen's discussion (*Gesellschaft und Geschichte. Zur Kritik der kritischen Theorie*, pp. 23ff).

[184] *Knowledge and Human Interests*, p. 196.

[185] *Knowledge and Human Interests*, p. 298.

knowledge-constitutive interest to be transcendental.[186] How can self-reflection lead beyond a transcendental frame of reference given to it in advance and rooted in the 'natural basis' of the mind if this course is laid down for it already by an emancipatory interest which derives from this very basis? It is impossible to see how, by starting from interest, Habermas intends to avoid Nietzsche's conclusion that 'the subjective conditions of the objectivity of possible knowledge affect the meaning of the distinction between illusion and knowledge'.[187] Habermas's use here of Kant's idea of the 'pure interest' of reason in itself, which is identical with knowledge,[188] is illegitimate because it is characteristic of the purity of the self-interest of reason in Kant that it is independent of the natural basis of material or empirical interests, from which Habermas derives all interests. In these circumstances there is no way of excluding the possibility that all reflection might, as a result of this basis in interests, be part of a 'systematically distorted form of communication'.[189] There can be no way out of this impasse through 'the idea of truth as a function of true consensus, a consensus which has come into being without constraint or distortion'.[190] Niklaus Luhmann has rightly wondered 'whether the phenomenon of consensus-formation through lengthy, free group discussion has to do not with truth — but rather with a reduction of complexity through the assimilation and consistent use of symbolic schemas'.[191] When Habermas replies to Luhmann that 'truth can certainly be reached

---

[186] The main point of his criticism of Nietszche is that 'he could not acknowledge to himself that his critique of the objective self-understanding of science was a critique of knowledge' (*Knowledge and Human Interests*, p. 298).

[187] ibid., loc. cit.

[188] *Knowledge and Human Interests*, pp. 200–05; *Technik und Wissenschaft als 'Ideologie'*, 1968, p. 164.

[189] This problem is the subject of the essay 'Der Universalitätsanspruch der Hermeneutik', in *Hermeneutik und Dialektik I, Festschrift für H.-G. Gadamer*, 1970, pp. 73–104, reprinted in the collection *Hermeneutik und Ideologiekritik*, 1971, pp. 120–59.

[190] *Hermeneutik und Ideologiekritik*, pp. 155, 153. See also the earlier (1965) essay 'Knowledge and Human Interests', p. 314. Habermas has developed his consensus theory of truth further in his discussion with Luhmann (*Theorie der Gesellschaft oder Sozialtechnologie*, p. 223; cf. 123ff. See also note 402 below.

[191] N. Luhmann in *Theorie der Gesellschaft oder Sozialtechnologie*, p. 343n.

by a "liberation" of communication, and only in this way,' [192] this is nothing more as yet than a mere assertion. The criterion of the absence of constraint alone cannot exclude the possibility that consensus may rest on pure convention.

In his discussion with Luhmann, Habermas has drastically altered the conception of 'knowledge and interest' by explicitly giving up the idea of the human species as a subject which constitutes itself through its history.[193] This change inevitably affects the concept of knowledge-constitutive interests, since by definition these 'basic orientations' can acquire the transcendental function of knowledge-constitutive interests only 'within the conception of a *history of the species* comprehended as a *self-formative process* . . . in which the species subject first constitutes itself'.[194] Instead of replacing the collective subject by the at first sight obvious alternative of the concept of system,[195] Habermas now joins Luhmann in pronouncing the transcendental concept of subject a monological abstraction from 'the process of the intersubjective constitution of a world of meaningful objects' (173–4) and has become a firm supporter of a 'theory of ordinary-language communication' (180). In this theory 'interests' have no more than subsidiary importance as needs isolated from the communicative consensus and 'wishes that have once more become monological' (252). Human action is not oriented to competing interests until 'the consensus about the norms in force (and the varying chances of satisfying needs conditionally and legitimately, breaks down, in other words, when the legitimations of the norms in force are undermined and the balance of the systems of interaction controlled by these norms is destroyed' (253). In contrast, in the 'normal case' (253) of a 'group united by a common cultural tradition' the needs underlying the interests have found intersubjectively valid interpretation and recognition within the framework of – cultural values! 'Communicative action is oriented to cultural values; strategic (monological) action is interest-oriented' (252).

[192] *Theorie der Gesellschaft oder Sozialtechnologie*, p. 242.

[193] *Theorie der Gesellschaft oder Sozialtechnologie*, pp. 173ff, esp. 179.

[194] *Knowledge and Human Interests*, p. 197.

[195] *Theorie der Gesellschaft oder Sozialtechnologie*, p. 271. The page references in this and the following paragraphs are to this book.

It might be expected that this return to a view which gives 'cultural values' priority over 'the need-imperative of the isolated agent' (252)[196] would show up the basis of the theory of action itself as a 'monological' abstraction from intersubjective semantic systems. This would be a logical consequence of the abandonment of a theory of action which claimed a transcendental function, but so far Habermas has been unwilling to draw it. He has, however, in some 'preliminary observations to a theory of communicative competence' (ibid. 101ff), made a distinction between 'language-games derived from experience and reinforced by norms' in the context of communicative action, and 'discourse' − a form of communication unobstructed by action (114ff) − which alone serves the interests of mutual understanding (115) and 'can substantiate the disputed claims of opinions and norms to authority' (117). As the discussion between Habermas and Luhmann shows, however, Habermas still defines the function of discourse in relation to theory of action; he postulates discourse as a way out of the difficulties of action theory rather than as an autonomous and more fundamental feature of human life, within which the concept of action itself should be included. For him, it is 'only when the natural approach to living becomes inadequate, when its unspoken claim to authority is questioned, that 'we enter discourse' (198). According to Habermas, communicative action itself is dependent on discourse (202), and properly speaking that should lead him to offer an 'explication of semantic structures', with which discourse is 'exclusively' concerned (200), as a more fundamental topic than the entire theory of action. Instead he broaches the subject of discourse (and therefore of awareness of meaning) only as something already 'embedded' in the structure of interaction (213). It is impossible to see, however, especially if we 'establish objects of possible experience only in the

---

[196] Nevertheless the departure of special interests from a collapsing communicative consensus and especially the social system's assertion of itself against them by repression or attempts to divert them into projections remains for Habermas a criterion of inauthentic, distorted, communication such as is exposed by critiques of domination and ideology (pp. 353ff). The ambivalence and historical relativity of the needs which underly the interests (cf. p. 89 above) remains even now unrecognised, however.

reference-system of action', if, in other words, a transcendental function as a condition of possibility for any kind of experience is ascribed to the action system, how the framework of interaction can lose its effectiveness, become 'virtualised' (ibid.) or 'suspended', where discourse is concerned. The 'anticipation of the ideal linguistic situation' (136, 140f) alleged by Habermas cannot solve the problem, even if it takes place in an interaction context which is not already constituted by such anticipation. The reason is that the transcendental function of the 'reference-system of action' casts doubt on the possibility of such an anticipation. If, however, the anticipation of meaning is *always* in one way or another constitutive of action, we should have to explain the awareness of meaning in itself, independently of a theory of action, so that phenomena like action which are constituted by awareness of meaning become adequately accessible.

The concept of meaning and its relation to the theory of action are at the centre of the discussion between Habermas and Luhmann. In Luhmann's view the theory of action on its own does not provide an adequate basis for sociology. He regards it as illegitimate to 'restrict meaning a priori to the meaning of actions', because 'even the meaning of actions always implies the world as a whole. Snow, property, justice, plates, capitalism etc. can become relevant in a system of action without being action themselves' (76). Luhmann therefore claims a 'primacy of experience' in the perception of meaning (306, cf. 75ff), [197] and a corresponding superiority in sociology for an approach based on a theory of systems as against one based on a theory of action (319).

Habermas's objections to this are similar to objections he has already made to the treatment of cultural values by Parsons (and before him by Weber) as a mere *assumption* of sociological investigation. For Habermas, the intersubjectivity of reliance on meanings requires 'in the first place a reconstruction of the emergence of the "community" (Dilthey) in which the identity of meaning has its basis' (188). In Dilthey, however, the problem of such a formative process was obscured by the assumption of the unity of 'life' in individuals. Habermas would like to locate

[197] Instead of 'perception of meaning' Luhmann uses the term 'constitution of meaning'. The problems involved in this term will be discussed again below.

the origin of this community, following G. H. Mead (190ff), in the communication process and in the 'mutual anticipation' which develops in that process 'of expectations about subjects who regard each other as subjects'. This, for him, would be the source of 'the intersubjectivity of validity, that is, the semantic identity of symbols' (192). Crucial to this view is the assumption that the expectations are mutual and that the mutual expectations have identical content. This means that Habermas must make it a requirement that 'the identity of meaning must be reduced to the intersubjective recognition of *rules*' (189, italics added). By so doing, however, he lays himself open to Luhmann's objection that 'rules themselves must be meaningful in order to provide a basis for anything', and that therefore 'the problem of meaning is more fundamental than the problem of rules' (303).

In fact the ability to go beyond the self to the 'universal' is implicit in the ability of an individual agent to recognise another person as 'another I' (Luhmann, 51–2) and to take part in a process of communication. Inherent in Luhmann's view of meaning as 'an extension of the potentialities of actual experience by an apprehension and representation of what has not been experienced' (40), that is, of latent 'possibilities of further experience and action' (32, cf. 37) is the basic, vague awareness of the universal by negation of the particular,[198] and this shows the connection with insights into the constitution of ego-consciousness which go back to Hegel. Since this is not the universal conceived of as such (in the abstract), Luhmann rightly uses instead the term 'experience of meaning'. The ability implied in this to apprehend the universal as 'the immanent transcendence of experience' (31) over what is given here and now cannot be derived – as Habermas and Mead try to derive it – from a process of communication, since it is rather a precondition of all human communication and all inter-

[198] Habermas comments on this that he 'finds it hard to imagine what negation can mean prior to language, in other words, apart from saying no' (pp. 187–8). The ability to detach oneself from impressions must, however, be accepted as a precondition of the development of language, and this already includes the logical factor of negation. The positive correlate of negation, which in fact can be apprehended only in language, may still remain indefinite. There is therefore no need to deny that 'identical meanings' are first made possible by language (p. 188).

subjectivity. When Habermas claims that 'meaning is inconceivable without intersubjective validity' (195, cf. 188), he overlooks the prior conditioning of intersubjectivity itself by the 'immanent transcendence' of experience by virtue of the element of universality it contains. Nevertheless Habermas must be admitted to be right when he says that there can be no assertion or articulation of this experience of meaning without intersubjectivity in ordinary-language communication. This does not mean, however, that the basic phenomenon of awareness of meaning is only the result of the process of this communication: it is not a linguistic *product* but rather a prior condition of the indeterminate universality of linguistic symbols. On the other hand, this does not exclude, but is rather the basis of, the fact that a *determinate* view of semantic structures (and therefore also the formation of something like 'value-systems') takes place through the process of communication in ordinary language. But the semantic structures which are implicitly contained in present experience underlie the interpretation which gives them explicit definition in the process of ordinary-language communication, *and only because of this can there be argument about different semantic constructions.* It is also only because of this, however, that a consensus in understanding – whether in the form of a tacit 'agreement',[199] or by an explicit attachment to traditional meanings or meanings developed in dialogue with tradition – can be more than mere convention and can for that reason remain open to further processes of critical reflection.

Habermas's suspicion of Luhmann's concept of experience of meaning and of the claim that this experience is prior to action is partly understandable in view of Luhmann's assertion that meaning is 'constituted' by experience (53–4, 60, 67). Habermas rightly sees this view as based on Husserl's constitution theory of knowledge (180), and because of the constitution by the absolute consciousness of the experiencing ego Luhmann's concept of meaning is in fact still 'monological'. As Habermas says, 'the

[199] Weber himself analysed this phenomenon (*Gesammelte Aufsätze zur Wissenschaftslehre,* pp. 452ff), but without realising that it shows the limitations of his concept of meaning as based on value-intentions, since the indefiniteness of a directly experienced agreement is not exhausted by a connection with this or that specific value.

isolated subject remains the starting-point of his analysis' (188), [200] a position which contradicts Luhmann's own criticism of the rejection of the view of meaning as subjective intention (26–7). Luhmann's intention is to define the concept of meaning 'without reference to the concept of subject because the concept of subject as a meaningfully constituted identity already presupposes the concept of meaning' (28). It is for this reason that Luhmann prefers the systems theory to the theory of action (28–9). His objections to the use of theories of action as a foundation for the social sciences (318–9, 75ff) can be summarised in the statement that the concept of action itself presupposes a monological model of transcendental subjectivity [201], and his rejection of the view of meaning as subjective intention (26–7). want to develop the concept of meaning on the level of intersubjectivity independently of a prior connection with the intentionality of a 'monological' subject, [202] and each sees the other's attempt as unsuccessful. In fact both have still not completely overcome the limitations of a view of 'meaning' as intentional (whether pure object intention or value intention) derived from the prior concept of subject. This view is particularly influential wherever meaning is construed as a value-reference, since values by definition exist only for a valuing

[200] This can also be seen from the way meaning and interpretation merge in Luhmann's writing. For example, he can give the following definition of meaning: 'Meaning is a particular strategy (sic) of selective behaviour (sic) under the condition of high complexity' (p. 12; cf. p. 302). This blatantly defines meaning as a form of activity, or at least as 'behaviour' or a behavioural strategy, which clearly contradicts Luhmann's description of semantic perception as the awareness of the implicit presence of a range of 'possibilities' in actual experience. The *reduction* of this multiplicity by 'meaningful identifications' to 'create unity out of the abundance of the possible' (p. 12) can perhaps be understood as *interpretation,* which 'reduces' the indeterminate complexity of original perception of meaning.

[201] See Luhmann's discussion, pp. 51–2, esp. n. 25, quoted approvingly by Habermas, pp. 173ff.

[202] This is not true of Habermas's earlier statements, however. In these the basic concept is treated as fully 'intentional', but clearly intentionality is thought of not in Husserl's sense of 'consciousness of something' (Husserl, *Ideas* pp. 119–126), but as something closer to value rationality. It is in this sense that Habermas talks in this discussion with Luhmann (p. 181), with reference to Parsons, of the 'concept of intentional value-orientated action . . . which is attributed to a subject construing his situation).

subject. To escape from these dilemmas it would be necessary to return to the reappraisal of Dilthey, which, as will be seen later, Habermas broke off prematurely. In Dilthey *perception* of meaning is similarly relative to the subject which experiences, but the concept of meaning has already been defined by the categories of whole and part. The problems of the subjectivity and relativity of the perception of meaning arise from the fact that, in the uncompleted process of history, the horizon of the 'whole' within which the 'parts' have their significance is constantly shifting (see below, however, note 257).

Luhmann comes very close to Dilthey's contextual concept of meaning when he talks about the presence in actual experience of what an individual has not yet experienced (40). The horizon of latent semantic references within which actual experience takes place is admittedly not only 'the abundance of the possible' (12), although it does *open up* a multiplicity of possibilities for explicitly confirming the implicit components of actual experience. It represents, rather, in spite of its mobility and flexibility, the 'totality' of the context which defines the significance of each individual experience. This is true not only of the presence of the future and the past within the present moment (54ff), but also of the relation of form and content as 'guide-lines for the progressive apprehension of meaning which are visible in meaning itself' (69), in so far as form is a 'perceivable and constructive anticipation of the totality of possible contents' (68). The anticipation of wholeness guides the subject's progressive penetration into the semantic structures present us the meaning apprehended in actual experience, because semantic references have or acquire precision only in their total context. Hence even the meaning of actions 'always implies the world as a whole' (70). The wider contextual complex which fixes the significance of individual experiences and actions and thus constitutes their meaning[203] is omitted from the picture if

[203] Thus it is not experience which constitutes meaning (as maintained by Luhmann, pp. 53–4) but the reverse: the totality of the (historically open) context and so the structure of meaning constitute the significance, the value, of the individual experience. This is the only way of carrying out Luhmann's intention 'not to define meaning by subject but instead subject by meaning' (p. 12).

meaning is reduced to intentions of action. The meaning supposedly produced by processes of communicative action is then in fact determined by unnoticed anticipations of meaning. This is ideology, concealing real semantic links in the interests of unexamined semantic constructs. On the other hand, 'world views', even when they 'legitimate' existing or future social systems (which have always so far been systems of domination) are by no means 'always ideological', as Habermas believes (259). That could be maintained only if they allowed no 'unconstrained discourse', since in such discourse, 'if it were permitted, existing institutions would be convicted of making a false claim' (ibid.). One cannot, however, deny a priori that particular social systems – again this has always meant particular structures of domination – are appropriate to the objective conditions and possibilities of their time and, relative to these conditions, offer a maximum of freedom. A world-view which allows this sort of evaluation of a particular social system, without encouraging false claims about its permanent validity, would not necessarily be ideological or fear 'unconstrained discourse'. On the contrary, every social order, even the most liberal, needs such 'legitimation' by 'world-views', which enable the members to *measure* how far social norms can be regarded as adequate in relation to the continuity of experience and meaning of the 'world as a whole' already given in experience. 'Unconstrained discourse' is therefore needed in order that claims to this sort of correspondence may be constantly reviewed. This review has two aspects. It considers firstly how far the 'world as a whole' already given in experience is adequately anticipated in the form of a particular world-view, and secondly, how far the system of social norms requires correction when judged by the standard of this anticipation. If world-views in history have in this way encouraged criticism of social norms as well as helping to establish them, it is the social system's very need for justification which has created the possibility of criticism. Only to the extent that a social order represents the 'meaning' of experienced reality as a whole, *including the semantic deficiencies experienced in it,* need its norms not be felt by individuals as repressive, that is as the ultimately arbitrary imposition of norms by other individuals.

Anticipation of the semantic totality of a cultural world, which exposes the limitations of an analysis solely in terms of systems of action and the intended meanings they contain, is therefore also constitutive *as a criterion of the difference between repression and emancipation.* This anticipation, which has been discussed here under the concept of world-view, has appeared in the cultural systems of the past mainly in the form of religion. It is constitutive because 'cultural values' themselves are the product of the totality of a culture's awareness of meaning. The concept of a cultural value itself reduces the range of meaning latent in experience to mere preparation for action, and this has made cultural values, taken as isolated norms, into arbitrary axioms of systems of action. Unless we resort to conventionalist solutions – to which even an approach restricted to processes of communicative action must lead – Habermas's persistent search for the formative process which produces these cultural values can be successful only if it includes consideration of the fact that cultural norms of action are mediated by a culture's whole semantic awareness – which is interwoven with its web of experience and action – or rather by the meaning that that awareness discloses, the 'spirit' of a culture or cultural epoch.[204] Our subsequent discussion of Ernst Troeltsch's study of the perception of religious meanings within the limitations of the concept of value will also lead to this conclusion.

This investigation has shown that sociological theories of action are always dependent on semantic constructions, which in

[204] H. Rickert, *Die Grenzen der naturwissenschaftlichen Begriffsbildung,* 2nd ed. 1913, pp. 354ff, took the opposite view and maintained that any conception of a 'whole' in history is conditioned by its reference to a value distinct from that whole. The 'general structure into which history has to fit particular individuals' is in other words, according to Rickert, 'also an individual', so that its unity can derive only from relation to a value (p. 358). Each whole is thus part of a larger whole. According to Rickert, however, the ultimate *historical* whole can be not the universe but merely human history, since otherwise the constitution of a whole (and that means of any historical object) by individualising extraction from a wider context on the basis of a value-reference to the most extensive whole would be impossible (p. 359). In fact, the unity of both individuals and historical totalities does not depend on subjective values, as maintained by Rickert's theory of the historical individual with its derivation of individual unity from uniqueness (pp. 308ff), but is apprehended as a unity of *form,* in which the form, here as elsewhere, anticipates the complex totality of the semantic content.

turn are related to the totality of meaning which constitutes the horizon of any given human grouping's experience. It makes no difference to this dependence that such semantic constructions remain disputed historically as attempts to articulate a totality of meaning is a fundamental sociological concept, the study of of this dependence, theories of action cannot, however, at least not on their own, provide a theoretical basis for the cultural or human sciences. However, although – and indeed because – meaning is a fundamental sociological concept, the thematic of meaning could not be carried to completion within the restricted limits of a discussion of the basis of sociology. One of the main obstacles here is the rigid division between sociology, as a structural science, and history. If the formative process which leads to the production of 'cultural values' can be traced only in the changes in semantic awareness in the history of a socio-cultural grouping, all investigations of 'typical' structural interrelations are already dependent on the semantic assumptions resulting from that process. A theoretical foundation for the human sciences as a whole can therefore be expected only from a theoretical consideration of the conditions governing historical knowledge and the historical formation of concepts. But this in turn can take place only when the theoretical investigation includes all the dimensions of human reality studied by the various disciplines within the human sciences (including sociology). Here again it is impossible to escape from the mutuality of expectations; these may be conditioned by a prior totality of meaning, but of its nature that totality can never be finally and unequivocally captured in a particular form.

3. Ernst Troeltsch: Theology as a Human Science

Although Troeltsch's writings are often classified as a theological variety of historicism, his theory of theology might be more accurately described as based on the human sciences. This takes account of the close connection of his ideas with the approaches of Dilthey and Rickert,[205] and of his affinity with the view of sociology as a human science developed by Max Weber. Seen from this point of view, Troeltsch, like these other writers, is not so much himself a historicist as an heir to historicism.

Like Dilthey's early efforts to construct a theory of the human sciences, Troeltsch's concern with 'Autonomy of Religion' (1895) assumes a basis in psychology, though a philosophical rather than an empirical variety.[206] The particular form of this psychology in Troeltsch was influenced especially by Wundt.[207] Nevertheless, Troeltsch's discussions of psychology concentrated entirely on the psychology of religion, and are particularly concerned to refute views which assume 'a gradual process of the filling of empty psyches from the external world of sense', and which correspondingly try to interpret morality, aesthetics and religion 'in terms of purely sensory experience' (387). Alongside the 'sensory sphere' Troeltsch asserted the existence of an autonomous ideal sphere of common fundamental psychic functions concerned with 'ideal perceptions of intellectual realities and ideal feelings of value with the corresponding desires' (390). Unlike the contents of sensory perception, the ideal contents were, in Troeltsch's view, inseparable from

---

[205] Writing in 1913, Troeltsch referred to a 'shift' in his philosophical position after the publication of his first major study, *The Christian World-view and its Counter-Currents* (1894), a shift 'from Dilthey and Lotze to Windelband and Rickert' (*Gesammelte Schriften* II, 1922, p. 227). Interesting in the context is the remark made by Troeltsch in his lengthy review of Rickert's book *Die Grenzen der naturwissenschaftlichen Begriffsbildung* (originally in the *Theologische Rundschau* in 1904, reprinted in *Ges. Schriften* II, pp. 673–728) that Dilthey had opposed only a 'psychological metaphysic of history' to the mechanistic and atomistic metaphysics (pp. 680–1). Nevertheless in this review Troeltsch still adheres to a psychology which, contrary to Rickert's recommendations, is not part of a nomothetic natural science and is described as 'the basis of transcendentalism'. Only a year later, in 1905, in his essay 'Psychology and Epistemology in the Study of Religion', Troeltsch accepted the primacy of epistemology over psychology. On Troeltsch's relationship with his teacher, (II, p. 754) Dilthey, see also E. Spiess, *Die Religionstheorie Ernst Troeltschs,* 1927, pp. 77–104, and with Rickert, cf. E. Lessing, *Die Geschichtsphilosophie Ernst Troeltschs,* 1965, pp. 60–1.

[206] E. Lessing rightly describes psychology as the 'basis of Troeltsch's system' (*Die Geschichtsphilosophie Ernst Troeltschs,* p. 56).

[207] *ZThK* 5 (1895), pp. 380ff. The page references in this paragraph are to this article, which was continued in *ZThK* 6 (1896).

emotional and volitional components (391). Indeed, for Troeltsch, the 'evidence' for this whole sphere of experience of the beautiful, the good and the divine rests on the power of these 'ideas' to 'raise and direct the mind', and, in contrast to the contents of sensory perception, which press themselves on us of their own accord, the power of the ideas 'has to be accepted submissively, if we do not want their seeds to wither' (392). This description already contains a statement of the fundamental importance of religion for the whole of the psychic life, since religious experience is precisely about the 'relation to an infinite ... power' (396) on which the existence of this whole sphere of ideal experience depends. Religion is 'the belief in a power which contains these ideals within itself, establishes them in the world and by so doing ensures the salvation of men' (398).

The link between psychology and history was expressed for Troeltsch in Schleiermacher's idea that the general becomes real only in individual forms. Ideal perception, and in particular religious perception, is historically real only in the form of individual conceptions of the ideal, in which the divine power makes itself known 'to human minds'.[208] Because of the permanent association of perception in the ideal sphere with feelings of value and aspirations of the will, Troeltsch can also later speak of *values,* which the aspirations of the will make into *purposes.* This terminology does not yet appear in the early essay on *The Autonomy of Religion;* Troeltsch says only that in the relation to this infinite power 'the practical character of religion as a striving for the highest good is always an ineradicable element'.[209] Later, in *The Absoluteness of Christianity,* ideals themselves are described as values,[210] though Troeltsch is not

[208] *ZThK* 6 (1896), pp. 76ff and pp. 79–80. In this respect Troeltsch, even at this period, recognises a difference between his psychology and Dilthey's; in the latter, as for Kant, 'consciousness appears as the producer both of the sensible and of the ideal world' (*ZThK* 5 (1895), p. 416). In other respects, however, Troeltsch wants to analyse the historical phenomena of religion 'in something like the sense' which Dilthey 'seems to be trying to outline' in his *Einleitung in die Geisteswissenschaften* (p. 415).

[209] *ZThK* 5 (1895), p. 396.

[210] In 1895 Troeltsch is not yet prepared to describe this whole 'sphere' as one of value-judgments (*ZThK* 5 (1895), p. 391) because the 'practical sensations of value must always be related to a prior idea'. In his discussion

aware of the problems introduced by this implicit restriction of his approach to one based on a theory of action.

The main part of Troeltsch's argument bears a close parallel to Dilthey's. Individual differences in personal ideals and conceptions of value must be assessed, says Troeltsch, within the framework of the 'homogeneity' of human intellectual and moral life.[211] These presuppositions makes sense of 'the idea that every man is a microcosm, capable of acquiring an understanding of the nature and function of apparently alien situations' by means of 'definite points of correspondence between them and himself. This means, therefore, that the different value orientations of mankind have something in common. It is this common factor that impels us to compare and contrast the values they embody and further, to establish criteria and form judgements about human history – just as we do about individual personalities – on the basis of the conclusions arrived at in the course of such comparative assessment'.[212] In Troeltsch's view, this rivalry and conflict between 'competing values' (92) moves the different

with J. Kaftan ('Geschichte und Metaphysik', *ZThK* 8 (1898), pp. 1–69) about whether ideals 'can be derived from an analysis of historical facts' (ibid., p. 30) there is already a reference to a 'belief in the "ideal" based on value-judgments' (p. 3; cf. p. 46), but generally the subject is treated in terms of the relation between history and the ideal. Again, in *The Absoluteness of Christianity and the History of Religions* (1902), Troeltsch can still write: 'We have to do, rather, with substantive components and principles of life (*Lebensideale*) that take shape in the depths of the human soul and then rise to a place alongside the natural structures that condition and serve human need. Such components and principles are not mere products of antecedents or environment, but are creative regulators of historical life. Their claims to validity are based not on the causal necessity of their origin but on their truth' (Richmond, Va. 1971, London 1972, p. 88). These 'principles', are also, however, described as 'values' (pp. 89, 90, 92, 94). That the same situation is envisaged is made clear by the occasional association of terms such as 'goal and ideal' (p. 106; cf. p. 98); the connection with the concept of value derives from the teleological element in the concept of an ideal.

[211] *ZThK* 8 (1898), pp. 37–8. The key term 'homogeneity' occurs on p. 38. Note also the fundamental importance of this idea for Troeltsch's conception of historical method, and in particular for his view of the principle of analogy as an instrument of historical criticism (*Ges. Schriften* II, pp. 745–6, III, p. 62).

[212] *The Absoluteness of Christianity and the History of Religions*, Richmond, Va., 1971/London 1972, p. 89. The page references in this paragraph are also to this book.

lines of historical development towards a common goal which corresponds to the homogeneity of human nature as expressed in the common fundamental direction underlying individual conceptions of value. The idea of this 'common goal' (95) enables the 'free interaction of ideas' to produce a standard by which they may be judged. This idea of 'a common, orienting goal that may from time to time manifest itself in history in clear and distinct preparatory forms but always remains a goal "out in front" ' (99), which Troeltsch elsewhere describes as the highest good,[213] grows out of the interaction of the individual and common human elements in the particular purposes and aspirations of human beings, which, in Troeltsch's view, always involve the perception of the ideal. This is why Troeltsch could, from the very beginning, stress the emergence of ideals and values from the interactions of history itself.[214] The 'final goal' of human development, 'considered as something perfect and complete', remains 'beyond history' (94). Nevertheless, 'though transcending history . . . this goal can be manifested within history at different points along the ascent toward the higher orientations of life in ways adapted to each historical situation and its presuppositions. These different manifestations can be measured and compared with one another' (95). The criteria for this comparison must be 'constantly rediscovered' in the 'free interaction' of the ideas themselves (95).

The picture of the history of religion which takes shape in Troeltsch's work is very similar to Dilthey's conception of the 'interrelation of purposes in the history of mankind' formed from individual purposes and their 'interaction', but 'reaches through' individual 'wills' and their intentions.[215] In Dilthey, however,

[213] Already in *ZThK* 5 (1895), p. 396, and later esp. in 'Grundprobleme der Ethik', *ZThK* 12 (1902), p. 153. The whole argument on pp. 125–78 of the latter essay is also relevant.

[214] *ZThK* 5 (1895), p. 370. The discussion between Troeltsch and J. Kaftan in *ZThK* 1896–8 was rooted in this very question, whether values or ideals were external additions to the historical and factual by means of a confessional assessment or whether they were the product of the historical process itself and could be read off in a simple description. Cf. esp. Troeltsch, 'Geschichte und Metaphysik' (*ZThK* 8 (1898), pp. 1–69), esp. pp. 17 and 30ff.

[215] Dilthey, *Ges. Schriften* I, p. 53. The metaphor of 'reaching through' recalls the old image of the decree of providence prevailing behind the backs

unlike Troeltsch, the idea of an interrelation of the purposes of
mankind does not lead to the concept of a 'final purpose' which
lies in front of all individual purposes but is never finally realised
in history at any point. Dilthey goes no further than the idea of a
plurality of social purposive systems (I.63) which reflects the
common nature of individuals and their tasks and purposes
(I.65ff). This must be seen as a consequence of Dilthey's
attachment to a 'contemplative concept of truth', which has been
well described and criticised by Habermas. Dilthey's emphasis on
the need to recreate experience, his 'intuitive model of
understanding',[216] is not the only reflection of his contemplative
attitude to history. This also appears in his exclusive interest in
past history and its 'immeasurable variety of individual values'
which creates 'the meaning of historical reality' as an
'extraordinary composite'.[217] If Dilthey had included in his
consideration the future-orientated tendencies introduced into
historical processes as a result of the concern with purposes and
values present in individual behaviour, his postulate of the unity
of psychic life in all individuals would have led him, like
Troeltsch, to the problematic concept of a common final goal
which is historically accessible only in the competing purposes of
individuals and social groups. In this respect Troeltsch's
philosophy of history shows itself superior to Dilthey's. By
taking account of the future it was already preparing the ground
for the utopian philosophy of history of our own day – in spite of
Troeltsch's offhand dismissal of Ernst Bloch's *Geist der Utopie* as

of individual agents, while Troeltsch – though not ruling out this aspect –
imagines individual aims competing in the perspective of an ultimately
common final goal. See also Troeltsch's comments on Dilthey's rejection of
the question of the 'Purpose and Meaning of History as a Whole' (Troeltsch,
Ges. Schriften III, p. 525). In spite of all their differences both Troeltsch and
Dilthey could speak of a unification of individuals pursuing their separate aims
in a transcendent continuity of purpose.

[216] J. Habermas, *Knowledge and Human Interests*, p. 182. For my part I cannot
see that Dilthey's retention of the principle of 'objectivity' even in the
knowledge acquired by the human sciences owes anything to this
contemplative tendency in Dilthey. An impression that it did could have
arisen only in the context of an attitude which looked for the measure of
knowledge not in itself – i.e. in its claim to truth – but in an interest
pre-ordered to it.

[217] Dilthey I, pp. 97–8.

one of the 'ephemera of the world war'[218] — and for a theology aware of eschatology. J. Weiss's realisation of the influence of a futuristic eschatology on the message of Jesus and in particular on his idea of the kingdom of God had been revolutionary, and Troeltsch was perhaps the only systematic theologian who could incorporate it into his theology without losing sight of the real futurity of the rule of God. Opposing supernaturalist assertions of an absolute within history, he was able to base his argument on the fact that Jesus himself had consigned 'absolute religion' to 'the world to come'. 'Only this future would bring complete deliverance, perfect knowledge, and permanent victory,'[219] and Jesus could therefore be the model of a 'living piety that speaks out of its relation with God' and 'has left the matter of absolute truth to the future, to the end of history'.[220] Jesus' message of the rule of God, interpreted eschatologically, seemed to match Troeltsch's philosophy of history, which, like it, pointed to a final common goal for all mankind beyond all historical realisation: 'Such a philosophy of history admittedly leads, in the last analysis, to the question of the ultimate end and to that of the participation of the individual in that end. It leads, that is to say, to questions which cannot be answered without the concept of something that lies beyond earthly history.'[221] But since this ultimate end, as goal and 'highest good', provided the criteria for all values and purposes within history, Troeltsch was able to set it up in opposition to W. Herrmann's argument from intentional ethics in their dispute on 'Fundamental problems of ethics'.[222] Troeltsch appealed to the power 'of the eschatological idea the influence of which is now universally admitted to extend throughout the Gospel' and which he called 'the magnificent expression of the unique value of the religious purpose'. 'The proximity of the kingdom of God resulted in the subordination of all other ideas to the immediate domination of the final purpose, and this is the key to the Gospel's attitude to other

---

[218] Troeltsch, *Ges. Schriften* III, p. 74n.

[219] *The Absoluteness of Christianity*, p. 123 (emended).

[220] Ibid., loc. cit.

[221] Ibid., p. 99.

[222] *ZThK* 12 (1902), pp. 44–94, 125–78. The quotations are from pp. 151 and 154.

objective goods, including this-worldly morality.' According to Troeltsch, to enable this-worldly values to recover their status 'all that is required is that the religious purpose should lose the all-powerful force of its imminent realisation. This may be the only way in which it can be recognised as the highest value and the one which should dominate all others; it may be that it could have come to birth only out of eschatology. But it can still endure even if this immediate realisation moves away into the future, and it can renew itself only by sinking back into the image of the classical primeval age, when it stood alone before the human heart.

Troeltsch's philosophy of history succeeds impressively in giving a place both to the futuristic eschatology of the primitive Christian expectation of the end and to the significance of the delay of the parousia. His interpretation remains problematic, however, especially on a point which reveals both the merits and limitations of his general idea of history. The category of purpose which is so central for Troeltsch does not fit the eschatology of the kingdom of God, because in Jesus' message the coming kingdom is not an extension of human purposes, but comes without any human intervention. Because Troeltsch draws excessively on the theory of action, his analysis of historical experience suffers from an exclusive concern with the orientation of human conduct to purpose and value, and the result, which has the theological disadvantage just mentioned, is that he fails to see the wider context of the historical experience of meaning. Moreover, the influence of the category of final purpose makes Troeltsch give a one-sided emphasis to the kingdom of God as something in the future, at the expense of the presence of this future in the history of Jesus, an aspect to which he allows only passing significance. Connected with this must also be Troeltsch's inability completely to escape from the difficulties of relativism. Precisely because his idea of the absolute was a final goal in the sense of something totally beyond the present experience of history, present experience in his account necessarily lacks the absolute: its truth lies outside itself. The reason for this is that the category of purpose, however much it connects present and future, at the same time keeps them apart.

The concept of purpose does not owe its central position in

Troeltsch's work to Rickert's use of a theory of value, but rather the reverse: it is more likely that the roots of the concept in Troeltsch's early, psychologically-based theory of history encouraged his interest in Rickert. The only connection between Troeltsch's early psychological views, which were based on Wundt and Lotze, and the experience of history was the individuality of the experience of ideal contents, which become purposes for those who turn to them. This gave 'purpose' a much more important function in Troeltsch's conception of history than it had had in Dilthey's, even though in Troeltsch's work, unlike Dilthey's structuralism, psychology is not derived from an analysis of historical experience, and not even worked out with history in mind. Troeltsch's general philosophical remarks are directed much more to providing a context for the psychology of religion, from which the young Troeltsch still hoped for an answer to the question of the truth of religious experience in general.[223] Later Troeltsch was convinced by Rickert that psychology could not do this, and therefore adopted an epistemological basis for the philosophy of religion, built on the idea of the 'religious a priori'.[224] In his later years his epistemological framework widened, in opposition to neo-Kantian apriorism, to include metaphysics. This brought Troeltsch in his late work, *Der Historismus und seine Probleme* (1922),[225] back to a position close to Dilthey's. He now regarded neo-Kantianism, with its 'theory of the creation of the object by thought' as 'totally unacceptable in history' (660). The 'fixed position of the closed substantial individual consciousness' could lead 'only to a priori or empirical structural forms of a merely given reality seen from outside' (673–4). On the other hand he still regarded it as impossible to describe 'the structural relations' of history in terms of psychology, as Dilthey had done: by holding on to this, Dilthey 'comes into permanent conflict with

[223] *ZThK* 5 (1895), p. 370.

[224] Especially in his 1905 essay, 'Psychology and Epistemology in the Study of Religion'. As late as 1904 Troeltsch had criticised Rickert's view of psychology 'as nothing but a nomothetic natural science' and described it as an 'autonomous philosophical discipline . . . which in many respects forms the presupposition (!) of transcendentalism' (II, p. 720n.).

[225] Published in 1922 as vol. III of the *Gesammelte Schriften*. The page references in this and the following paragraphs refer to this work.

every psychic science which gives rise to any form of psychology,[226] or he simply turns psychology into history[227] and in losing psychology loses any methodological foundation' (659). But above all Troeltsch regards it as 'the limitation of all psychology as compared with history that, no matter whether naturalistically or with the methods of the human sciences . . . it yearns for fixed and unchanging quantities, which history simply complicates and conditions, whereas in reality in the confluence of motives history can signify something genuinely new' (60). Troeltsch might well have used similar arguments against attempts to base an understanding of history on a theory of action or sociology. A psychology which intends to include a study of the tension-laden relation between individual and totality in history (44) and of 'the fact, confirmed by history a thousand-fold, that our actions, feelings, instincts, longings and decisions are the result of many more influences than we know and may have a much greater or totally other importance for the total course of events than we may have realised', a psychology which wishes to take account of this 'overflow of content beyond what is at any moment consciously perceived and of the origin in unknown depths of what is consciously perceived, must study in the school of history, not the other way round' (47).

[226] In his description of Dilthey's position in *Ges. Schriften* III, pp. 509–30 Troeltsch emphasised its closeness to positivism and in particular to Mill. According to Troeltsch, Mill's psychologism had been 'the real foundation of his (Dilthey's) doctrine' (p. 513). On the difficulties of what Troeltsch regarded as Dilthey's failure to be consistent in replacing a psychology based on causal explanations by one based on 'understanding', see ibid. pp. 516ff. Troeltsch also declared himself sceptical of the concept of human science as based on psychology, which was that of both Dilthey and Mill. He argued that both logic and epistemology on the one hand and ethics and history on the other should be regarded as 'completely autonomous major disciplines' and not derived from psychology (III, p. 80n.).

[227] With his reference to turning psychology into history Troeltsch has accurately summed up in advance the direction of Dilthey's last drafts, which were unknown to him when he wrote. Nor can the judgment which follows be described as wholly inappropriate, since the abandonment of psychology in fact left Dilthey with only the subjectivity of experience, and his assertion, which he never withdrew, of the intersubjective ('objective') validity of historical knowledge could therefore rest only on the 'metaphysic' he constantly rejected, i.e. his assumption of the unity of intelligent life.

Remarks such as these show Troeltsch moving in a similar direction to that taken by Dilthey in his late work on the analysis of historical experience (the manuscripts of which were still unpublished when Troeltsch wrote), away from a philosophy of history based on psychology and towards a hermeneutic of historical experience. In turning to a theory of historical experience, Troeltsch leaves behind him not only the concept of a psychological theory of history, but also the limitations of a theory of history based only on a theory of action, and reaches a broader analysis of historical structures in terms of meaning. In his new position Troeltsch, unlike Dilthey, regards the 'continuity of significance' (42) or 'continuity of meaning' of historical experience, in which what is permanent 'makes itself known only through the meaning and significance of its function within the whole' (43), not as a hermeneutical process, but as the subject-matter of an epistemology (673) of history requiring a metaphysical basis. He thought he had found the key to this epistemology in Leibniz's doctrine of monads, which he regarded as expressing the vital continuity of the infinite mind 'while preserving the finitude and individuality of the former' (675). Troeltsch had referred to the need for a metaphysical basis for historical knowledge even before his interest in epistemology,[228] but at that time he had used the term to cover no more than a philosophical anthropology or psychology and its extrapolation to the idea of a final goal. Now, in contrast, he was interested in the relation of the finite to the infinite, of the individual to the whole, as the only factor capable of determining the structure of meaning and significance of historical events. These are essentially the problems which dominate Dilthey's late work, and their ultimate metaphysical implications are spelt out in Troeltsch's work on historicism.

[228] Notably in 'Geschichte und Metaphysik', *ZThK* 8 (1898), pp. 1–69. What he envisaged was a 'metaphysic of the human mind' (p. 40) or 'of history and the human mind' (p. 41) – in other words what was also called philosophical psychology and later was distinguished from psychology as 'epistemology' (pp. 45–6). Troeltsch maintained that the 'close connection of this metaphysics of mind with the other areas of metaphysics' should not be 'ignored', but he still thought he could limit himself to the metaphysics of mind and leave natural philosophy and the metaphysics of the absolute to others (p. 45).

Nevertheless the way in which Troeltsch discusses them does not include an analysis of the temporal nature of historical experience as a hermeneutical process, as Dilthey's late drafts had begun to do. Troeltsch treats the semantic continuity of whole and part in a merely abstract way as something fundamentally 'proper' to history (665). Unlike Dilthey, he does not trace the origin of its temporal concretion from the process of historical experience. Hence he never realised the incompleteness of this totality of meaning in this process or the dependence of that totality on the future. This latter point remained obscured by Dilthey's contemplative attitude until its importance was pointed out by Heidegger, though even then only for isolated existences. The discovery would have brought the reference to the future of Troeltsch's category of purpose into a new and wider perspective, and both it and the category of development would inevitably have lost their dominant position, since the narrowness of their exclusive theory-of-action perspective would have been seen for what it was in the wider context of the experience of meaning in history. But since Troeltsch fails to see the future-based temporality of this totality of meaning, he regards it as sufficient to formulate the metaphysical implications of the basic historical relationship between whole and part in terms of Leibniz's doctrine of monads and so fails to do justice to his own awareness of the openness of the process of historical experience. His metaphysical categories form a complement to this experience instead of deriving from an analysis of it, and this means that they remain extraneous to their proper problematic. Nevertheless Troeltsch's struggle with the problems of historicism remains important as a complement to Dilthey's hermeneutic. Because the subjectivity of hermeneutical experience can provide no basis for its intersubjective validity, the conditions which enable it to go beyond the experience of individuals must be explicitly analysed. It is possible to look for these conditions in the social mechanisms of communication processes and define their investigation as part of sociology. But this does not answer the question about the conditions which make communication itself possible, which are also the conditions which enable the individual's experience to attain intersubjective validity. The mutuality of the expectations of those involved in the process of communication cuts across all differences and presupposes some prior unity in awareness of meanings, however problematic. From the point of view of the positions which enter communication this unity of awareness is explicable in terms of whole and part even when the 'parts', as different anticipations of the whole, at first contradict each other and acquire lasting significance as *parts* of the whole only as *moments* of this whole in the process in which their contradictions develop. Willingness to communicate is already an anticipation of possible agreement, to which a totality of meaning corresponds and the contours of which may still be undefined and may indeed need to be fixed by explicit interpretation only to the degree required by the differences in understanding that have to be overcome in communication. But in every case the totality of meaning present in this sort of agreement has 'metaphysical' dimensions. At least potentially, it integrates the semantic structures of the experiences and possibilities of action of the individuals involved in the communication and so constitutes the unity of the social environment. Troeltsch was therefore right to let the question of the 'objectivity' of historical knowledge lead him to the question of the relation of the individual to the whole in reality in general. By so doing he left behind the formal universality of basic concepts derived from psychology and sociology and reached the higher universality of a formation of concepts which is 'transcendental' in the pre-Kantian sense and in which the general and the particular coincide to the extent that every particular requires the same general characteristics for its analysis. Troeltsch was aware that the level of such a 'metalogic' (678), the problems of which he had always previously avoided,[229] also transcended the two oppositions of nature and mind and human and natural science and contained 'a basis for the unity of the areas of social science, logic and natural science, which are now divided' (107). By insisting on an account of historical knowledge in terms of a 'metaphysically' based epistemology, Troeltsch in his own way went beyond both the dualism of method separating the natural from the human

[229] See the previous note, and further *ZThK* 3 (1893), pp. 510–11; *ZThK* 5 (1895), pp. 432 and 377ff; *ZThk* 6 (1896), pp. 95–6 and esp. 81; *ZThK* 12 (1902), p. 136.

sciences and the limits of his own attempt to give a theoretical account of theology in terms of the human sciences alone.

4. Critique of the Division between Natural and Human Sciences

Originally the classification of the sciences according to the Cartesian dualism of nature and mind was based on the assumption of a fundamental difference in kind between the objects described by these terms, and upholders of it reasoned from this assumption to the necessity of a corresponding difference in the methods used in their scientific study. Many objections have been made to this approach. For example, it is possible to doubt whether the actual difference in scientific procedure can be connected to a difference between the objects studied, and, even if the connection *is* accepted, whether the distinction between mind and nature is an accurate general division and definition of these sorts of objects. Again, the internal unity of each of these two groups of sciences has been questioned. It has been pointed out that the differences in scientific procedure do not coincide with the classification of objects of study: not only are traditional human sciences increasingly using methods regarded as belonging to the natural sciences, but conversely there are also natural sciences which pursue 'historical' investigations. In this situation, and especially in view of the increasing use of the methods of natural science in the human sciences, the assumption of mind's basic independence of nature has lost much of its plausibility.

The inclusion of all the disciplines to be distinguished from the natural sciences under the description 'human sciences' was criticised very early. If there is no prior ontological distinction between mind and nature, the 'systematic human sciences' – logic and mathematics – seem definitely to have a closer connection with the 'exact' procedures of the natural sciences than with the historical or philological disciplines. Many different writers observed that, in spite of Dilthey's efforts to develop a humanistic psychology, psychology had been overwhelmingly included among the natural sciences. Among Dilthey's critics, Rickert in particular argued forcefully and effectively that the psychology put forward by Mill and Dilthey as a basis for the 'moral' or 'human' sciences was, in method and subject-matter, not a human science at all.[230] For the remaining disciplines, but particularly with sociology and historical and philological disciplines in mind, Rickert introduced the term 'cultural sciences' to replace *Geisteswissenschaften,* which for him smacked of Hegelianism.[231]

The basis of Rickert's theoretical approach was not a classification of sciences by subject-matter, but a distinction between scientific procedures. Earlier, in 1894, Wilhelm Windelband, in his rectoral address 'History and Natural Science', had supported a division of sciences not by subject-matter, but by method. Windelband had distinguished between the 'nomothetical' procedures of the natural sciences and the 'ideographic' method of history and philology, and Rickert developed this approach, notably in his book *Die Grenzen der naturwissenschaftlichen Begriffsbildung,* of 1902. He contrasted the generalising procedures used mainly by the natural sciences with the individualising approach characteristic of historical disciplines. Rickert did not, however, intend the association of the generalising procedures with the natural sciences and the individualising with the human sciences to be a rigid distinction. He was well aware that generalising procedures 'typical' of the natural sciences can be used in historical research and that conversely natural sciences can concern themselves with individual situations.[232] The distinction of methods or of

---

[230] Rickert, *Die Grenzen der naturwissenschaftlichen Begriffsbildung* (1902), 2nd. ed. 1913, pp. 122ff, 151ff, 173ff, 179.

[231] Rickert, *Science and History,* Princeton, New York, London 1962, pp. 10–14. See also *Die Grenzen der naturwissenschaftlichen Begriffsbildung,* pp. 175ff, 501ff, 27–8.

[232] *Grenzen,* pp. 235ff. Rickert insists that '*all* reality is historical in the broadest, purely logical sense of the word, i.e. is individual' (*Grenzen,* p. 226). But the single empirical reality can be considered from two points of view: 'It becomes nature when we consider it with regard to the general and history when we consider it with regard to the particular and individual' (p. 224). Rickert therefore does not deny that 'the fortunes of civilised humanity *could* be the object of a description in terms of natural science, i.e. a generalising one' (p. 226). But the result would no longer be 'history'.

'concept-formation' is not to be confused with differences in subject-matter. The association of the one with the other means only that in history cognitive interest is directed more at individuals whereas in the areas of non-human nature it is directed to generalising explanation and description, which is the way in which 'finite mind is able to overcome vast complexity and so take the physical world into its knowledge'. [233]

In the discussion on Rickert's view of philosophy of science, questions have been raised not only about the association of the distinction between the formation of generalising and individualising concepts with the division of sciences into natural and cultural sciences, but also about the general value of the distinction in philosophy of science. Where this criticism went so far as to deny the generalising character of the knowledge embodied in the laws of natural science, as in the work of Cassirer,[234] Rickert's view may be regarded as having been vindicated.[235] But even if the distinction between generalising and individualising procedures is accepted in itself, it is still open to question whether it is a suitable principle of classification for the sciences, particularly since Rickert himself has admitted that the boundaries of the distinction are not quite the same as those of the two groups of cultural and natural sciences. E. Becher, in a particularly comprehensive study of Rickert's view,[236] which

[233] *Grenzen*, p. 1.

[234] Ernst Cassirer, *Substance and Function*, London 1910, pp. 221ff. Cassirer claims that the theoretical concepts of the mathematical natural sciences involve a 'series principle' by which 'the diversity' of similar impressions 'should appear' (p. 148), and that therefore 'no insuperable gap can arise' in this area 'between the "universal" and the "particular"' (p. 224). Series construction, however, is possible only within a continuum which is homogeneous in Rickert's sense (*Grenzen*, p. 36) and which – in contrast with the 'heterogeneous continuum' of prescientific experience – is itself based on generalising abstraction.

[235] See Rickert, *Grenzen*, pp. 62ff and esp 65n., where he takes issue with the critics of his thesis that all natural science generalises. Every concept of natural science, he says, is characterised by the fact 'that the events to which it is meant to apply can be covered by it only as examples conceived in isolation' (p. 64).

[236] E. Becher, *Geisteswissenschaften und Naturwissenschaften. Untersuchungen zur Theorie und Einteilung der Realwissenschaften*, 1921, pp. 125–64. The page references in the rest of this paragraph are to Becher's book.

summarised all the previous objections, came to the conclusion that the overlapping was so extensive, particularly where generalising and individualising approaches were combined within a single discipline (157ff), that the theory provided no basis for a classification of the sciences. According to Becher, only a 'one-sided emphasis on history' (149) at the expense of other cultural sciences such as sociology and linguistics had enabled Rickert to ignore the importance of generalising methods in a number of human sciences. More recent developments, particularly those influenced by structuralism, tend to reinforce these observations of Becher's. The same may also be said of historical studies, whose use of collective 'concepts of totality', rules and typifying approaches had already been mentioned by Becher himself.[237] On his findings, Becher could allow the contrast between generalisation and individualisation only minor importance in the classification of the physical sciences (156ff). He contrasted these as a group with the ideal sciences such as logic and mathematics (24ff), and within the group retained the distinction between natural and human sciences in spite of all the criticism to which he and others had subjected it. Becher departed from Windelband and Rickert in reintroducing psychology as one of the human sciences, with the result that in his system the cultural sciences still form no more than one group among the human sciences.[238]

In more recent discussion, the increasingly wide use of methods from the natural sciences in the so-called human sciences has led commentators to disagree with Becher and question the autonomy of this latter group as distinct sciences. J. von Kempski believes that the increasing use of structuralist methods, and especially of mathematical description, in the 'human sciences' has made this term, with its implied contrast with the natural sciences, a mere honorific.[239] According to him the theoretical

[237] See also the defence of the assumption of historical 'laws' in Becher, pp. 167–76, esp. 174, though Becher remarks that such 'laws' would be 'more accurately described as rules' (p. 176).

[238] Becher, pp. 97ff, 105ff. Decisive, in Becher's view, for the inclusion of psychology in the human sciences is the distinction between sense-perception and self-perception as the 'basic methods' underlying the two groups of sciences. (pp. 116ff).

[239] J. von Kempski, *Brechungen. Kritische Versuche zur Philosophie der*

social sciences are already using mathematics 'in very important areas of investigation in just the . . . same way as theoretical physics' (225). Kempski goes further, and assumes that the normative social sciences (law and ethics) can be treated in a similar way (225). Just as in the natural sciences, so also in the theoretical social sciences empirical reality is apprehended 'with the help of abstract structures' (228). Not only in economics, but also in social science and psychology, and today particularly in modern structural linguistics, valuable results are being obtained from structuralist approaches which at least 'flirt with' mathematics (228). Kempski claims that there is no need to build a 'bridge' between these disciplines, 'from theoretical physics to linguistics'; the bridge already exists 'in principle' in mathematics, (229) which is a 'general science of structures'. Of the so-called human and cultural sciences, this leaves only history and 'the philologies', more precisely literary studies. But according to Kempski not even for history can there be a claim for autonomy of method as against the structural sciences. History must be regarded rather, he says, as 'the least autonomous of the sciences', as Huizinga put it, since in order to explain historical events it must use as a basis theories from economics and the social sciences, psychology and law (87ff). Since these sciences are structural sciences — Kempski himself has produced a structuralist theory of law[240] — history cannot be opposed to them. Even the specific elements of history take second place to structure. In Kempski's view it would be quite wrong to 'place mind, ideas and ideals at the centre of history' (91). History, he says, must be regarded rather as a 'network of actions' (89), and this means structures which historical research must investigate. Kempski admits that an exact science of action is today only in its beginnings (98),[241] but he clearly expects crucial advances in this area from further developments in cybernetics, and in particular

---

Gegenwart, 1964, p. 225 The essay 'Misguided Bridgebuilding', from which this quotation comes, first appeared in 1962. The page references in this and the following paragraph are to Kempski's book.

[240] J. von Kempski, Recht und Politik. Studien zur Einheit der Sozialwissenschaft, 1965.

[241] On this see Kempski, 'Der Aufbau der Erfahrung und das Handeln', in Brechungen, pp. 295–309.

from games theory. This will give a description of a 'field of possible action' which will allow the historian for the first time to make exact statements about *real* action (98). In this way the autonomy of the human sciences completely disappears in Kempski's work. They are included in principle in an approach dominated by the search for general structures with mathematics as its basic discipline. The only disciplines left in hermeneutic by Kempski are literary studies (98ff), and even here he thinks it possible to develop a 'logic of philology' (99) which would replace previous hermeneutical methods.

The price to be paid for such a reduction of the traditional cultural sciences to theories of general structures and to approaches capable in principle of mathematical formulation is indicated by Kempski's remark that science thus defined merely describes a 'field of possible action', from which real action is excluded (98). The latter falls outside the models Platonism of models which characterises normative structuralism. [242] Kempski himself admits that because of the distinction between real and possible action a 'fundamental' (sic) distinction continues to exist between history and the natural sciences (99). But if this is so, it means that the reduction of human sciences to normative structuralist theories is only an illusion because real action (and experience), with its semantic implications which are irremovably fixed in the historical process, are beyond the reach of abstract-universal structuralist theories.

Where Kempski finds no use for the term 'human sciences' as a contrasting term to 'natural sciences' because of the universal applicability of mathematical techniques, Ernst Topitsch attacks the distinction with arguments from ideological criticism. [243] Topitsch derives all views which do not correspond to the positivist model of science (which he takes for granted) from

[242] The concept of 'Platonism of models' derives from Hans Albert. It is applied by Habermas (*Zur Logik der Sozialwissenschaften*, p. 132) to Kempski's normativistic theory of action: 'The basic premises relate to idealised action on pure principles and cannot be the basis of hypothetical laws with any empirical content' (Habermas, ibid., loc. cit.).

[243] E. Topitsch, *Das Verhältnis zwischen Sozial- und Naturwissenschaften. Eine methodologisch-ideologiekritische Untersuchung*, 1963, reprinted in E. Topitsch (ed.), *Logik der Sozialwissenschaften*, 1965. The page references in this and the following paragraphs are to this book.

mythical or magical origins. He traces back dialectic, for example, to the gnostic drama of redemption. Dialectical patterns of thought are only a formalised expression of the dramatic fall of the soul and the world from their divine home and their return through redemption (62ff). Ultimately, both dialectic and 'the crude dualism of "mind" and "nature" originate . . . in magic and ecstatic ideas which were rationalised by philosophy into the doctrine that man's deepest core ("reason" or "mind") is essentially beyond the reach of the pressure of reality or can be placed beyond its reach by means of a saving knowledge'. [244] Such 'archaic roots' (64) are also the source of the distinction between 'nomothetical' natural sciences and 'ideographic' human sciences (64).

Topitsch has yet to produce proofs of these assertions. The fact that in antiquity there existed in Eastern Persia and other parts of Central Asia a belief in the soul connected with shamanistic techniques for producing trances by means of marijuana is not in itself a proof that all human ideas about the independence of the soul or mind from the physical world, such as those of Greek philosophy, derive historically from these beliefs. Topitsch the critic of ideology is here engaging in speculations of a sort which the metaphysical philosophies of history he rejects as unscientific rarely allowed themselves.

Apart from this, however, even if Topitsch's historico-genetic derivation of the ideas of mind, reason and dialectic could be taken seriously, the historical origin of an idea or concept does not in itself tell us whether this origin has a permanent real influence on the present form of the idea. [245] Topitsch himself

---

[244] Topitsch, p. 62, referring to the essay 'Seelenglauben und Selbstinterpretation' in E. Topitsch, *Sozialphilosophie zwischen Ideologie und Wissenschaft*, 1961, pp. 155ff.

[245] The classical form of this problem is secularisation. The origin of secularised ideas in Christian sources says nothing about their continued dependence on those sources. Similarly, however, just as the Christian origin of historical thought, of the concept of person and of the independence of man from the world is not in itself a proof that the ideas of person and history *now* depend on theological premises, so an alleged mythological background to Hegel's ideas, within the framework of which the modes of the dialectic were developed, is no proof that the dialectic is ultimately a mythical pattern of thought: that would have to be proved independently.

makes use of this distinction. He rightly points out that when images from society are transferred to other areas, as in Darwin's application of the idea of the competitive struggle to the biological doctrine of evolution, what determines the meaning is not the image but the new content it is given in the association with the new material to which it has been heuristically transferred (60).

Topitsch advances only one relevant argument against the distinction between ideographic and nomothetical sciences. This is the fact, which was stressed by Rickert himself and was prominent in the discussion he stimulated, that not only are structuralist techniques of enquiry used in the social and cultural sciences, but conversely ideographic approaches are used in the natural sciences. In support of this claim Topitsch quotes E. J. Walter:[246]

Large areas of the natural sciences deal with individual phenomena which can be approached only by means of a causal, genetic analysis, such as the problems of malformations in embryology, genetics, the study of heredity, the individual formation of specific mineral groups, the development of natural landscapes, etc. Even in meteorology it is found necessary to use individualising techniques of observation and description, for example in the study of typhoons and low-pressure areas.[247] On the other hand, it would be rash to claim a priori that universal rules or laws were inconceivable in the so-called human sciences: psychology, political theory, economics, sociology.'

This remark leads back to the hard core of the critique of the dualism of human and natural sciences. Windelband and Rickert

[246] E. J. Walter, 'Von der Sozialphilosophie zur empirischen Sozialforschung', *Schweizerische Zeitschrift für Volkswirtschaft und Statistik* 95 (1959, p. 320, quoted by Topitsch, p. 65.)

[247] The list could be made even longer. The most obvious addition would be physical cosmology, which, according to C. F. von Weizsäcker, forms the third main branch of physics alongside the physics of elementary particles and quantum physics (see Weizsäcker, *Die Einheit der Natur,* pp. 220–1).

long ago suggested that the distinction of the two spheres of nature and mind should be transformed into a distinction between two complementary methods, both of which could in principle be used either in the investigation of nature or in the cultural and social sciences. Today it must be stressed, even more firmly than it was by Rickert, that the distinction between individualising and generalising approaches has nothing to do with the distinction between human and natural sciences. The basis of the distinction between the two procedures is based on the complementarity of the two aspects of contingency and regularity in all events. Laws or regularities can be found only in the contingent, uniqueness only in contrast to the normal or typical. The association of nomothetical and ideographic methods with the areas of 'nature' and 'mind' or 'culture' respectively contains an element of truth in so far as ideographic methods have many more applications to the study of man because of the greater complexity and individualisation of human beings. But this is not a reason for maintaining a dualism of nature and mind. Today this dualism is unsatisfactory both in itself and as a principle of classification in the sciences. It is unsatisfactory in itself because the evolutionary approach has superseded the Cartesian dualism of extended and thinking substance. In philosophy of science the opposition is open to objection because it encourages a reification of methodological discrepancies which in fact represent no more than a transitory phase in the development of scientific procedures. The individual sciences, at least the physical ones, are distinguished by their area and depth of study, but this can never give rise to a categorial dichotomy. This does not, however, exclude the grouping of related disciplines under a common description, although these groupings are of no more than secondary importance and remain liable to revision as a result of changes of interest within particular sciences.

But is this perhaps still not a sufficiently sharp definition of the specific principle of the human or cultural sciences? Ernst Cassirer has attempted to locate this principle at a level deeper than the distinction between nomothetical and ideographic method, in a 'perception of expression' which differs from the perception of meaning and apprehends structures of meaning.[248]

With its concentration on the 'totality' of a semantic plexus which makes itself known in phenomena of expression, Cassirer's view of the unique features of the cultural sciences is a return to Dilthey's idea, although Cassirer does not mention his name. Dilthey had already made the understanding of meaning in terms of whole and part the object of his understanding psychology and later of hermeneutic. In the line of Dilthey's analysis, the understanding of meaning is regarded even in the modern discussion between hermeneutic and positivism as the study which accounts for the special position of the human sciences in relation to the natural sciences.[249]

Under these circumstances it was logical that Hans Albert's criticism of the division between natural and human sciences should have been directed in particular at the view that 'meaningful action is beyond the scope of nomological interpretation', and accessible only to hermeneutical methods.[250] Albert criticises this view for 'removing man and his activities from the causal system of nature and transplanting them to an area in which there are no universal structural limitations' (ibid.). He therefore calls for nomological interpretation to be applied 'also to behaviour which can be understood as meaningful action, without necessarily denying the possibility or usefulness of the distinction' (152).

Albert's assumption, however, is mistaken. It is not true that the supporters of the view he attacks claim that man and the human world are completely outside the field of description by natural laws. In asserting the competence of hermeneutic to describe man and his historical world, neither H. G. Gadamer nor J. Habermas intends to 'remove man from the causal system of nature', as Albert suggests. Their argument is merely that description by means of natural laws cannot deal with a particular but essential aspect of the human world, that of the perception of meaning.

[248] Cassirer, *The Logic of the Humanities,* New York, 1961, pp. 93ff, 97–8, 164ff, 170–1. Cassirer's earlier criticisms of Windelband and Rickert reappear here in modified form (pp. 88–90).

[249] Representative of this position is H. G. Gadamer, *Truth and Method,* pp. 6ff, 59–60, 259ff.

[250] H. Albert, *Traktat über kritische Vernunft,* 1968, p. 153. The page references in this and the following paragraphs are to this book.

Albert attacks hermeneutic for its explicit 'rejection of the concept of method used by modern science', and calls it 'a continuation of theology by other means' (132). This judgment applies to hermeneutic the interpretation first put forward by Popper of the two main forms of modern epistemology as secularisations of a model of cognition based on revelation. Evidence for this is provided by the fact that, in Albert's view, a study which uses hermeneutical methods attempts to do no more than expound a given text, not to subject it to critical examination. In accusing hermeneutic in particular of attempting to 'carry on theology by other means',[251] Albert nevertheless fails to mention that the same reproach in Popper's sense must be made against both the modern empirical tradition and the aprioristic idealism of transcendental philosophy.

Albert's essay 'Hermeneutik und Realwissenschaft' further develops his criticism of hermeneutic.[252] He now sees the 'theological ancestry' of the hermeneutical approach as expressed 'primarily' in its 'anti-naturalism', its 'rejection of natural science's method in the analysis of socio-historical reality'. Albert locates the continuing theological motif in secular hermeneutic 'in the effort to preserve the absolutely special position of man which was based on theological tradition', after the realm of nature had been lost to theology through modern natural science, which has made the existence of God a redundant hypothesis for the explanation of nature.

It must be admitted that this argument of Albert's contains some truth.[253] It is true that ever since proofs of the existence of God from nature have proved untenable, modern theology has connected the question of God with a theory of man. Theology has now settled down in the new situation, even though by limiting its frame of reference to man it has risked allowing the

[251] The eccentric use of the term 'theology' in such arguments, as 'a reproach against academic opponents to discredit their intellectual efforts', is examined by T. Rendtorff, 'Was heisst "interdiziplinäre Arbeit" für die Theologie?' in J. B. Metz and T. Rendtorff, Die Theologie in der interdiziplinären Forschung, 1971, p. 50.
[252] The essay is reprinted in Hans Albert, Plädoyer für kritischen Rationalismus, 1971. The quotations are from p. 107.
[253] Albert appeals here to K. Löwith, Gott, Mensch und Welt in der Metaphysik von Descartes bis zu Nietzsche, 1967.

Christian belief in creation to atrophy. There have been efforts even in quite recent times to develop a theology of nature or a theology of evolution (as by Teilhard de Chardin), but on the whole theology in recent times has tried to find a basis more or less exclusively in the idea of man's subjectivity and self-understanding. This has inevitably meant a theological interest in seeing the anthropological and historical sciences autonomous and independent of a natural science which seemed no longer to offer theology a purchase of any kind. Albert's arguments show the difficulties theology faces when it makes this sort of alliance with the human sciences. If theology builds to such an extent on the autonomy of the human sciences and ignores the natural sciences, it may, together with the philosophical tendencies on which it relies, incur suspicion of making a self-interested attempt (117) to shield the world of man and history from the methods of discovery of natural science.

But even if this charge is accepted, it must be described as an amazing exaggeration of the influence of theology on the intellectual and scientific history of the recent past when Albert describes Christian theology's interest in continued existence as the decisive or even the only inspiration for the dualism of human and natural sciences in modern times. Many of the thinkers connected with transcendental philosophy and with the claim of a special position for the human sciences and hermeneutic have had no particularly marked interest in Christian theology. Primary responsibility for the dualism of mind and nature in modern thought should be attributed to the Greek, and especially Platonic, dualism of reason and matter. The responsibility of Christian theology is secondary, although that theology did enter at a very early stage into a complicated symbiosis with the Platonic tradition, and this may have been a reason why it was able to adapt so easily to the Cartesian dualism of mind and nature. Eventually, however, after some initial encouragement for its dualistic tendencies, the new questions of the modern period forced the Platonic analogy between soul and cosmos as firmly into the background as it did the Christian belief in creation. None the less the dualism of nature and mind points back primarily to a Platonic prehistory, even if this was for long periods transmitted by Christianity. In a search for the intellectual sources of the opposition of mind and nature, not to mention its Platonic roots while concentrating on the theological interest behind the dualism of the human and natural sciences is a complete misrepresentation.

But here, as generally, the tracing of intellectual ancestry is of very limited relevance. What has been crucial to the influence of the dualism of mind and nature is that there were a number of fundamental situations and phenomena which seemed to require some such view. An argument such as Albert's, which so vigorously and justifiably attacks the view which reduces the scientific approach to alleged or actual 'interests' which condition knowledge while neglecting the question of whether they are justified or not (ibid. 113) should also not pass over the real reasons which led to the hardening of the opposition of nature and mind in modern philosophy of science.

For Descartes these reasons included the fact that a natural science which was still conceived in purely mechanistic terms was in fact incapable of explaining the existence of a living and thinking creature. For Kant it was the deterministic character of classical physics, which seemed irreconcilable with the experience of human freedom and in that way encouraged the dualism of mind and nature. The discovery that all objective knowledge and even perception itself was subjectively conditioned pushed in the same direction. In historicism a dualism of nature and mind was encouraged by the nomological bias in the scientific ideal of knowledge, its concentration on universal laws, which contrasted with the individualising approach necessarily used by historians. Lastly, Dilthey had the experience of finding that the psychology inspired by the natural science of his day offered no basis for the total view of man which seemed to him required by the nature of the subject. There is thus reason to suppose that sometimes a particular problematic has accepted an ontological nature-mind dualism only as a secondary component.

Some of these factors today no longer exist. Natural science is no longer mechanistic, nor is it any longer, as classical physics was, deterministic. Arguments for the special position of man or the mind based on these two circumstances are therefore no longer valid. This is not true of the subjective conditioning of all knowledge of objects. This problem is still specifically present in the critique of Popper's 'basic propositions'. The enduring attraction of Kant's transcendental approach must be largely the result of this situation, in view of the attempt to reconcile subjectivity and universal validity, a problem which has still not received a convincing solution that avoids the difficulties of transcendentalism.

In the self-understanding of the human sciences, however, the crucial argument for a status distinct from that of the natural sciences has, since Dilthey, been the role of meaning in human experience, the fact of meaningful behaviour and the experience of meaning. Since the experience of meaning both objectively and subjectively requires the evaluation of individual phenomena in the network of the relevant whole, there is a need for a total consideration which cannot be replaced by a causal analysis. This is the premise of both hermeneutical and dialectical method.

But the search for the 'meaning' of parts in the network of a 'whole' is by no means restricted to the study of human experience or even of organic life. As long ago as 1939, Andreas Angyal related the concept of 'whole' to that of 'system'.[254] Whereas in the case of an aggregate the relations of the parts are determined by their individual characteristics, the constituents of a system are made such 'by means of their distribution or arrangement within the system' (28). The constituents of a system are therefore linked 'by the mediation of the system itself' (30), even when they have no direct relation to each other (32). The concept of system enables us to maintain the truth of the old saying that a whole is more than the sum of its parts without the need to follow vitalist biologists and similarly inclined gestalt psychologists in taking refuge in a mysterious 'formal quality' which has to be added to the sum of the parts. The 'more' of the whole is merely the ordering of the parts into a system as opposed to their merely additive relations in an aggregate.

Ernest Nagel, in his essay 'The Whole is More than the Sum of its Parts',[255] has used similar arguments to criticise the claim of a

---

[254] A. Angyal, 'The Structure of Wholes', *Philosophy of Science* VI (1939), pp. 25–37. The page references in the text are to Angyal's article.

[255] First published in 1955, and reprinted as chap. 11 of E. Nagel, *The Structure of Science*, New York/London 1961, esp. pp: 380ff (the references in

special scientific status for totalist views. Although Nagel, unlike Angyal, argues against a theoretical distinction between 'individual wholes' and mere 'aggregates' (225), the actual content of his discussion largely agrees with the view put forward by Angyal. Of particular interest is Nagel's discussion of a favourite example of the gestalt psychologists, and one which Angyal also mentions in passing: melody. In the statement that a melody is not identical with the mere sum of the tones which are its constituents, 'sum' is often implicitly used to mean 'the unordered class of individual tones' (388). The term 'whole', on the other hand, refers here 'to a pattern or configuration formed by elements standing to each other in certain relations'. In this sense, says Nagel, the statement that the whole is more than the sum of its parts is 'perfectly true though trivial' (388). But exactly the same is true of Angyal's interpretation (with which Nagel disagrees) of the phrase in question, according to which the element, the part, is *determined* by the character of the whole (cf. 388–9). This is true to the extent that the individual element is a *constituent of a 'pattern'* which gives the 'whole' its character. Angyal also rightly pointed out that it is not only in organic but also in dynamic systems that 'the parts function differently when they form part of one or another whole'.[256] Part of the constitutive meaning of 'pattern' – or 'structure' in Dilthey's sense – for each whole and its parts is, as Nagel emphasises, the implication that 'the distinction between wholes that are the sum of their parts and those that are not is *relative to some assumed theory T* in terms of which the analysis of a system is undertaken' (390). Dilthey's view of experience and the understanding of meaning makes the perceived meaning relative not only to the individual system of the 'vital unit' which perceives meaning, but also to the transcendent system of a totality of meaning in which the individual who *perceives* meaning experiences his own existence as meaningful.[257]

---

the text are to the book). Cf. M. Schlick, 'Ueber den Begriff der Ganzheit', in *Gesammelte Aufsätze,* 1938, an article that forms part of the debate with H. Driesch.

[256] Angyal, 'The Structure of Wholes', p. 36.

[257] Dilthey made a particular point of 'insisting . . . that meaning is connected with the totality of the conceiving subject' (VII, p. 230), that is,

This means that the introduction of the concept of system and related cybernetic considerations can correct the exclusive association of questions of meaning with the human sciences and clarify the meaning of such fundamental hermeneutical concepts as whole and part by relating them to the problems of general systems-theory. The unique characteristics of human experience as the perception of meaning are to be sought not in the fact that semantic networks first appear on the level of human reality, but in the fact that human beings not only create structures of meaning as individual systems but are also capable of experiencing semantic networks, and ones at that which go infinitely beyond the reality of their own existence.

There seems therefore to be hope, after all, of overcoming the exclusion of the subject of meaning from the methods of natural science. In this context Albert's reference to the 'exaggeration' of the importance of questions of meaning in the human sciences is not very helpful.[258] It is impossible to exaggerate these questions in human studies because the understanding of meaning is an

---

involves a whole of the sort which is present to itself. He seems to have had in mind something fundamentally and qualitatively different from other sorts of relations between whole and part, since he goes on: 'If the term ["meaning"] is generalised to cover any relation of a subject between whole and part, and therefore includes the object of the process of thought or rather the relation of the parts in objective thought or the formation of a purpose, and thus also the general idea which forms the individual images, then the term meaning means nothing more than membership of a whole. In this whole the riddle of life, how a whole can have organic or psychic reality, is eliminated' (ibid.). This 'riddle of life' coincides with a dualism of subject and object which is no more than an assumption and which forgets that the subject in its reflection must treat even itself as an object. If this sort of 'vitalist philosophy' dualism is not allowed to become a formal position, the self-givenness of the totality of the individual person who *experiences* himself as a totality has to be recognised as a *modification* of the general systematic structure of the relation between parts and wholes. This would entail an investigation of the origin of this peculiarity in the self-transcendence of man. There would then be no longer any need to deny that we discover meaning and significance not only by intuition in the phenomena of life, but also in every other relation of wholes and parts.

[258] Albert, *Traktat über kritische Vernunft*, 1968, p. 148. Albert talks about a 'dramatisation' of questions of meaning in *Plädoyer für kritischen Rationalismus*, p. 109.

inherent element in the use of language, which is fundamental for human behaviour. Perhaps Albert is in fact attacking only an exaggeration of the importance of questions of meaning as a justification for a fundamental distinction between natural and human sciences. His own efforts are directed towards breaking down the distinction by means of a 'nomological' description of the perception of meaning. This approach to a connection between the perception of meaning and the cognitional forms of natural science seems, however, to offer less prospect of success than that via systems-theory. The reason for this is that the 'nomological' approach must abstract from individuality, which is the characteristic feature of the semantic phenomena investigated by the cultural sciences. Albert claims that even Dilthey, the father both of the theory of the human sciences and of modern hermeneutic, aimed at an analysis of understanding which might be described as 'a technology on a nomological basis' (129). Albert bases this claim primarily on Dilthey's concept of the 'structure of psychic life' (132), but in doing so he overlooks the fact that for Dilthey the concept of structure is a fundamental concept of *understanding* psychology as opposed to the analytical psychology based on natural science.[259] As Dilthey uses it, the concept of 'structure' in no way suggests a 'nomological X-ray' of understanding (135); it describes not a general consistency in the perception of meaning or in meaningful behaviour, but an individual vital unity. Nevertheless Albert is quite right when he emphasises that for Dilthey 'universal judgements ... contribute to every act of understanding as items of practical experience'.[260] In fact, of course, 'there is no reason ... to start from the idea that there are no rules in this field' (136). The question is only whether the specifically hermeneutical rules display the sort of consistency that Albert claims. The general rule that the individual thing is to be understood in relation to the whole of which it forms a part cannot be applied nomothetically to the 'instances' it governs. This would involve the assumption that these individual cases

[259] Albert mentions this opposition only in a different context, that of the theory of 'internal perception' (*Plädoyer*, p. 133, n. 60). He ignores the close connection of this concept with Dilthey's concept of structure.

[260] Dilthey, V, pp. 334ff, quoted Albert, *Plädoyer*, p. 132.

were in themselves unimportant and interchangeable. If the rule is understood in this sense, it no longer has the character of *guidelines* for deducing the individual semantic structure of a particular phenomenon from the relation of a whole to its parts. The relation to its field of application of a universal rule understood as a hermeneutical guideline is different from that of laws, which must always be supplemented by rules for their application.

Dilthey's concept of 'psychic structure' as a particular network of meanings[261] must not be confused with the further development of the concept of structure by Bertrand Russell and Rudolf Carnap.[262] The positivist concept of structure as a 'relation number' in the sense defined by Russell treats structure as a general abstract formation. In 1928, it is true, Carnap could claim that the concept of structure used in the theory of relations provided 'a suitable basis' for the 'logic of individuality' called for by Dilthey, Windelband and Rickert,[263] but his remark can be understood only in connection with his reference to a statement of Cassirer's. Cassirer had argued against Rickert that the formation of concepts in the natural sciences, which is based on the formation of series, lies beyond the opposition between individual and universal and demonstrates, as it has gradually developed, its 'ability to *distinguish* the particular'.[264] But if we

---

[261] Dilthey, VII, p. 238; cf. V, pp. 204ff.

[262] Russell, *Introduction to Mathematical Philosophy* (1919); Carnap, *The Logical Structure of the World* (1928, English 1967). On both see F. Kambartel, *Erfahrung und Struktur. Bausteine zu einer Kritik des Empirismus und Formalismus,* 1968, pp. 149ff, esp. 170ff.

[263] Carnap, *The Logical Structure of the World,* pp. 23–4. Kambartel (*Erfahrung und Struktur,* p. 246) quotes this statement as evidence that 'for both Russell and Carnap the difference between the intentions of Hilbert's early work and the true meaning of the Dilthey school's concept of structure' seemed to be very small (Kambartel, p. 245). Kambartel believes that there is also 'in fact' a parallel, in that 'both in the investigation of formal systems of axioms and in the analysis which examined the theoretical expressions of individual life in terms of typology or ideal types no claim for (substantial) truth or validity was made for the premises or model' (p. 246). No evidence for the truth of this statement in Dilthey's case is offered, however, and would presumably be hard to find.

[264] Carnap (*Logical Structure,* pp. 23–4) refers to Cassirer, *Substance and Function,* pp. 224–5, where the argument reproduced above may be found.

accept Rickert's judgment that the concepts of relation contained in the laws of natural science, including the homogeneous continuum to which they refer, are as abstractly universal as the generic categories of Greek philosophy,[265] we cannot locate individuals on this approach. For this reason the concept of structure used by formalism can be clearly distinguished from Dilthey's concept of the psychic structure as the structure of the sum of an individual life which must be analysed through the categories of part and whole. The concept of meaning can, of course, be used wherever interrelations of whole and part occur, including abstract systems or Cassirer's forms,[266] and it is also quite proper on the terms of Dilthey's concept of structure to talk about formal structures. However, the particular problem of meaning for the sciences that deal with man derives from the fact that man is meaninful as in *individual* system, that forms himself by descriptively apprehending, as the basis of his personal identity, semantic networks which transcend his existence. This role of meaning in human existence, which expresses itself in acts of freedom, also gives a new point to the description of the sciences which deal with it as 'human' sciences, without involving a relapse into the mind-nature dualism. The systematic models of the natural sciences, however, also operate in the same sphere of 'human' structures of meaning which is the specific field of the human sciences.

If it is the aim of the method of the human sciences to describe the meaning of the individual in the continuity of the relevant whole as that continuity takes shape in the individual understanding of meaning, the discussion of the uniqueness of the hermeneutical or dialectical method of the human sciences leads back to the central significance of the individual and individualising techniques in these disciplines. However, this also means that the study of meaning cannot in itself be the private reserve of the human sciences and cannot justify a theoretical opposition between human and natural sciences. The uniqueness of the human sciences can be described only in terms of their special form of perception of this common object. This special

[265] See above, note 135.

[266] E. Cassirer, *Logic,* pp. 157ff. Note also the introduction of the concept of structure, pp. 88–90.

form is a concentration on the historical character of the formation of meaning, which is intimately connected with its mediation by individual perception of meaning.

5. Understanding and Explanation

The dichotomy of explanation and understanding was connected with the 'total view' of the so-called 'human sciences' in Dilthey's original formulation. 'Explanation' in this context is generally taken to mean the inclusion of individual phenomena under a general rule, in contrast to understanding, which considers the individual in the context of the whole to which it belongs.[267]

In E. Rothacker's view,[268] the understanding of an individual experience differs from both the grasping of a content and the explanation of a phenomenon because of its dependence on external conditions. Rothacker makes no distinction between contingent-historical dependence and the sorts of dependence which must be described by the inclusion of phenomena as instances under a general rule. He too shares the view that explanation is characteristic of the naturalistic approach to a phenomenon.

Critics of the dualism of human and natural sciences have mostly rejected this opposition of explanation and understanding. This is logical, because the opposition is no more than the methodal expression of the view that there exists a fundamental distinction between mind and nature, and of the theoretical distinction, deduced from this, between the natural and the human sciences as two groups of sciences: the method of explanation by the application of universal laws is contrasted with the methods of understanding, the hermeneutical methods, of the human sciences. On the other hand, a group of writers which includes Topitsch and Albert (see above) argue that the

[267] The distinction between understanding and explanation has occasionally been developed in theology into a contrast between understanding and knowledge in general (e.g. G. Ebeling, *Wort and Glaube I*, pp. 399–400)

[268] E. Rothacker, *Logik und Systematik der Geisteswissenschaften*, 1947, p. 127.

intention of such claims is to remove the sphere of human life from the scope of explanatory science.[269] In his essay '*Hermeneutik und Realwissenschaft*', Albert goes still further, and claims that 'intersubjective communication itself' can be made 'the object of a science of an explanatory character' (119). Albert finds a 'point of departure' (128) for this agument in no less a person than Dilthey, who, he says, attempted 'to grasp understanding as a universal human activity . . . in terms of its structure' (128). In this way, ays Albert, Dilthey helps us 'to explain understanding' (130, cf. 137).

In the sense in which the term is used by Albert, 'explanation' requires 'a nomological basis'.[270] In other words, Albert seems to presuppose the deductive-nomological (DN) model of understanding. This model goes back through John Stuart Mill to David Hume and presents scientific explanation as the inclusion of individual phenomena under natural laws.[271] The best known modern spokesman for this theory of explanation is Karl Popper, and Popper's version has been taken further by C. G. Hempel and P. Oppenheim.[272] The most detailed explanation and discussion of the theory in German is by W. Stegmüller.[273]

Is it true that 'understanding' in Dilthey's sense can be reduced to deductive-nomological explanation, with the result that the claim for autonomy on behalf of the human sciences loses its basis as 'understanding' loses its independence of 'explanation'? Albert says that Dilthey's hermeneutical theory aspired to a 'technology on a nomological basis',[274] and that in Dilthey's own view understanding itself rested on a knowledge of laws. This, says Albert, would mean that the difference between understanding and explanation disappears because understanding too now has to

---

[269] See H. Albert, *Traktat über kritische Vernunft*, pp. 135ff.

[270] Albert, *Traktat*, p. 85; cf. pp. 152ff.

[271] W. Stegmüller, *Wissenschaftliche Erklärung und Begründung* (= *Probleme und Resultate der Wissenschaftstheorie und Analytischen Philosophie* I), 1968, p. 78.

[272] C. G. Hempel and P. Oppenheim, 'Studies in the Logic of Explanation', *Philosophy of Science* 15 (1948), pp. 135–75. See also C. G. Hempel, *Aspects of Scientific Explanation*, New York 1965; K. Popper, *The Logic of Scientific Discovery* (1934, English 1959, 2nd ed. 1968).

[273] Stegmüller, *Wissenschaftliche Erklärung und Begründung*, esp. pp. 72–207.

[274] *Plädoyer für kritischen Rationalismus*, 1971, p. 129. The following page references are to this book.

be included under knowledge of laws. However, even if we accept that Dilthey's concept of structure requires understanding to have a universal nomothetical structure (128, cf. 137), and so indeed serves to 'explain understanding', this is no more than an explanatory statement *about* the process of understanding. It by no means follows from it that the process explained in this way itself has an explanatory character. Albert is confusing the process of understanding with statements about it which describe its 'structure'. It is not true, however, that the process of understanding consists in bringing an individual feature under its general structure; understanding relates the individual to a whole as a constituent of it or a factor in it, and it is this which creates the 'structure' of life as Dilthey sees it. Understanding takes place by establishing a system, and that system is an individual, 'open' and autonomous one, but not a universal under which the particular is to be subsumed.

The reduction of understanding to the pattern of deductive-nomological explanation thus turns out to be impossible even though understanding itself can perfectly well be the object of this type of explanation. A better way of thinking about the relation of explanation and understanding is to say that the former always presupposes the latter. This can mean that scientific explanation in terms of laws is only a special form of understanding, or even a 'derivative mode' of understanding, to use Heidegger's term.[275] But to say that understanding precedes explanation can also be taken to mean that understanding is only a preliminary form of explanation, an incomplete explanation. This view was taken by H. Gomperz, who described understanding as 'a stage preliminary to explanation', which 'in some circumstances' could even be a substitute for it, namely 'in fields where explanation is undeveloped'.[276] Gomperz argued against Dilthey that there is 'no question of "understanding", as opposed to "explanation", being the higher form of knowledge in relation to all outside psychic life' (216). 'I say it is lower, but still something if we cannot have the other' (217). Gomperz's

---

[275] M. Heidegger, *Being and Time*, trans. John Macquarrie and Edward Robinson, London 1962, pp. 194–5; cf. pp. 195ff.

[276] H. Gomperz, *Ueber Sinn und Sinngebilde. Verstehen und Erklären*, 1929, pp. 210, 212. The page references in the rest of this paragraph are to this book.

interpretation of understanding as a 'stage preliminary to explanation' rests on the assumption that understanding adds an element of 'readiness', this in turn a habit, and that the habit presupposes 'a corresponding regularity' (161, cf. 163). 'What ... usually occurs seems familiar to us, and we are ready to expect it again.' [277]

The view of understanding as a 'stage preliminary to explanation' is close to the interpretation of it as a *heuristic* procedure which has been put forward by Stegmüller, following T. Abel. Stegmüller describes 'the "explanation-understanding" alternative' as 'a totally distorted description'. [278] For the purpose of historical explanation, the 'method of intuitive understanding' is in his view neither adequate nor necessary (364). It is 'at most a heuristic device, used to reach hypotheses which may prove accurate' (368). Albert has taken this view further and described understanding itself as the use of a 'nomological basis' such as is involved in explanation, [279] which is not very far from Gomperz's view.

But there is a difficulty which faces all views which regard understanding as a preliminary version of explanation, and this is the fact that explanation itself has understanding as its goal. J. Passmore has made this clear by showing that the need for an explanation arises in everyday life whenever something surprising and unexpected occurs which cannot be immediately fitted into the framework of the existing understanding of reality. [280] In this situation, Passmore says, the function of the explanation is not, as has been thought, [281] to make the unknown intelligible by reference to the already known. Something that

---

[277] Gomperz, Uber *Sinn und Sinngebilde*, p. 163. Cf. the role of the 'homogeneity' of intellectual life in Dilthey's hermeneutic, although unlike Gomperz Dilthey treats it as an a priori condition of understanding.

[278] *Wissenschaftliche Erklärung und Begründung*, p. 362. Cf. T. Abel, 'The Operation called Verstehen', in H. Feigl and M. Brodbeck, *Readings in the Philosophy of Science*, New York 1953, pp. 677–88.

[279] *Plädoyer für kritischen Rationalismus*, p. 130.

[280] J. Passmore, 'Explanation in Everyday Life, in Science and in History', *History and Theory* 2 (1962), pp. 105–123, esp. 107. See also W. Dray, *Laws and Explanations in History*, Oxford 1957, pp. 72ff. and 61.

[281] Gomperz, for example, calls explanation 'pointing to a familiar feature in something unfamiliar' (*Uber Sinn und Sinngebilde*, p. 87).

surprises us seems to us to require explanation precisely because it bursts through the framework of the familiar, current understanding of the world, because it is not intelligible within the framework of the already known. The explanation puts forward a new frame of reference within which the previously unintelligible event now becomes intelligible. A frame of reference of this sort can be set up by a hypothetical law, but also by other things. Stephen Toulmin has described the main effect of explanation as 'making sense' of previously unintelligible observations.[282] In Toulmin's view this takes place not only through the construction of hypotheses but also quite generally in the construction of 'ideals of the natural order' (54–99) which are used by human beings as 'explanatory paradigms ... to make nature intelligible to them' (70, 98). This remark implies, even though Toulmin does not stress it explicitly, a starting-point in systems-theory rather than in a merely nomological notion of explanation. The nomological model now becomes no more than

<hr/>

[282] Toulmin, *Foresight and Understanding*, London and New York 1961, p. 33. Toulmin particularly criticises associating the concept of explanation with prediction, in the manner, for example, of Popper, *Logic of Scientific Discovery*, pp. 59ff. He points out that the theoretical speculations of the Ionian natural philosophers gave rise to no predictions but still had explanatory value, whereas 'the Babylonians acquired great *forecasting power*' in astronomy, but 'conspicuously lacked *understanding*' (p. 30). The forecasting power of a theory is so far from constituting the criterion of that theory's explanatory strength that 'prediction itself can meet the case only if we import into it the idea of "explaining" and "making sense of" natural connections' (p. 34). Stegmüller (*Wissenschaftliche Erklärung und Begründung*, 1969, pp. 153–267) also rejects the 'thesis that explanation and prediction have the same structure', although he regards a number of objections to it, including Toulmin's 'description argument', as unsatisfactory (pp. 178ff). But in his brief discussion Stegmüller does not look in detail at Toulmin's idea of explanation as 'making sense'. He therefore interprets Toulmin's description argument too narrowly and fails to see its connection with Darwin's theory or to notice that it calls in question, at least implicitly, the deductive-nomological concept of explanation on which Stegmüller's own argument is based. Stegmüller's own solution, which involves a distinction between real and rational grounds, related to the distinction between explanation and prediction in such a way that prediction is not required to offer real grounds (p. 198), has been criticised for remaining 'in the fog of an unexamined metaphysic' (E. Ströker, 'Erklärung und Begründung in den Erfahrungswissenschaften', *Philosophische Rundschau* 18 (1971), p. 14).

a special case of the former, in the sense that nomothetical hypotheses construct a theoretical framework of the 'natural order', or at least contribute to the formation of a theoretical framework, into which previously unintelligible phenomena can be fitted. In the terms of the concept of explanation used in systems-theory, the hermeneutical method can now be seen as similarly being a form of explanation, in the sense that interpretation sets a semantic horizon – constructs a semantic whole, to use Dilthey's terminology – in relation to which the statements of the text to be interpreted become intelligible. Together with deductive-nomological explanation, the hermeneutical method now appears as another form of explanation, concerned not with subsuming cases unimportant in themselves into the universal schema of an unordered class, but with arranging individual phenomena into a whole which has the character of an ordered class and in which the individual member is regarded as important because of its particular characteristics.

The inadequacy of the concept of deductive-nomological explanation is shown by W. Stegmüller's careful discussion, paradoxically, because Stegmüller tries to develop the deductive-nomological concept as consistently as possible. His discussion shows that the concept of deductive-nomological explanation itself requires a broader concept of explanation even to be intelligible as an individual form of explanation, and that it alone is inadequate to show how deductive-nomological arguments function as an explanation.

Stegmüller limits the concept of explanation in advance to answers to why-questions as opposed to simple description, which is an answer to what-questions or how-questions.[283] The class of why-questions itself, however, is again divided (on a principle suggested by C. G. Hempel)[284] into questions about the evidence supporting a *statement,* that is, questions of an 'epistemic' character, and questions which ask for the causes of *real events.*

---

[283] W. Stegmüller, *Wissenschaftliche Erklärung,* pp. 76ff; cf. p. 760. The page references in the rest of this paragraph are to this book.

[284] C. G. Hempel, *Aspects of Scientific Explanation,* 1965, pp. 334–5, quoted Stegmüller, p. 75 (cf. p. 701).

Stegmüller applies the term 'explanation' only to answers to questions of the second type. However, towards the end of his investigation into the logical-systematic concept of explanation characteristic of the deductive-nomological type of explanation, Stegmüller comes to the conclusion that deductive-nomological 'explanation' seems to be much closer to the more general type of proof. This can be seen from the fact that the negational inversion of a deductive-nomological explanation, which retains the same logical structure, does not produce an explanation (761). Stegmüller therefore considers it 'more useful' to follow a suggestion by M. Käsbauer and use the term 'proof' in all references to deductive-nomological explanation (760–1, cf. 783, n. 26). This means that deductive-nomological arguments can lead only to a logical subsumption; they cannot *in themselves* supply the real cause of any particular event which requires explanation.[285] There is only one situation in which a deductive-nomological proof becomes an explanation, and that is when a reference to a law or laws, under which the event which requires explanation can be included, leads to the cause of the event. This means that additional practical conditions are required for the concept of proof to be narrowed down to that of explanation, namely a connection with a situation which requires explanation (702). Even to distinguish a proof from pseudo-proof. This can be seen from the fact that the negative pragmatic framework (768ff). E. Ströker has called this an 'indirect admission that a logical-systematic analysis of science which hopes to attain purity by simply ignoring all the practical

---

[285] Before Stegmüller, J. Passmore ('Explanation in Everyday Life, in Science and in History', *History and Theory* 2 (1962), p. 109) has also pointed out that 'there can be no purely formal definition of an explanation'. As an example he gives the syllogism: 'All American drugstores sell cigars, this is an American drugstore, therefore this drugstore sells cigars.' This utterance *may* have an explantory function for a stranger who is puzzled about why drugstores sell cigars. Alternatively it may function as an invitation or as a prediction. For an American, who for certain special reasons is puzzled by the fact that he obtains cigars in a particular drugstore, this general statement provides no explanation whatever. 'Explaining, in short, is a particular way of using a form of argument; it has no logical form particular to it' (Passmore, ibid.). Note, however, with reference to the last remark, that the use of arguments itself has a structure and therefore a logical form.

circumstances of scientific investigation is a fiction',[286] though, given this conclusion, Stegmüller's book might equally well be called a total destruction of the positivistic concept of explanation made all the more effective by its conservative technique.

It must certainly follow from Stegmüller's conclusion that it is totally impossible any longer to regard the concept of explanation as being the bringing of data under laws. It must be worked out instead from 'practical' situations, in which a datum (or its absence) is felt as unintelligible and therefore as requiring explanation.

Attempts to develop a theory of explanation along these lines have been made by J. Passmore and earlier by W. Dray. Both writers have drawn attention to the variety of sorts of explanation which may be required in ordinary life. They range from explanations of the terms used in explanations of how something works and what purposes it serves to explanations of the origin of a thing and ultimately of the causes of a state of affairs.[287] If, as proved to be the case, deductive-nomological arguments which bring events under hypothetical laws are in themselves not explanations at all, it follows that they are also not superior forms of explanation to others used in everyday life.[288]

---

[286] E. Ströker, 'Erklärung und Begründung in den Erfahrungswissenschaften', p. 35.

[287] Passmore, pp. 106–7.

[288] As maintained, curiously, by Passmore, in spite of his realisation that it is not the abstract logical structure of an argument, but only its use, which determines its explanatory character. Passmore says that explanations accepted as adequate in everyday life can be regarded by the scientist as no more than 'tentative hypotheses' which must be made more precise by a search for conditions which are necessary and sufficient (p. 117). The historian's explanations, which are modelled on those of everyday life, are also and for the same reason, in Passmore's estimation, superficial from a scientific point of view (p. 121; cf. the remark, p. 106, that he wants to show 'to how slight a degree history is scientific'). But by arguing in this way Passmore ignores his own distinction between the logical structure of a deduction and its explanatory function. As regards the inclusion of a datum under hypothetical laws the requirements of natural science for intelligibility and sufficiency are certainly much more rigorous than those of the historian, but this affects only the structure of the proof, not the explanatory function. The historian's argument, which is less 'exact' in the structure of its proof and from a formal-logical point of view less strict, may very well explain more to

There is now no longer any reason to restrict the concept of explanation to answers to why-questions. A much better approach is to look for what is common to the different sorts of explanation. Passmore's answer to this question of common denominator is; 'The only common factor, so far as I can see, is that in each instance I am puzzled; the explanation sets out to resolve my puzzlement.' [289] Corresponding to the common factor of puzzlement, of inability to understand, in the situation which gives rise to the need for an explanation, is the positive fact that the explanation makes what was previously not understood intelligible in the relevant respect. This confirms the interpretation of the concept of explanation given by Toulmin, who says that an explanation 'gives a meaning' to previously unintelligible observations (see above, n. 282). This interpretation in terms of systems-theory can be applied to all the types of explanation listed by Passmore, since they all act as explanations by placing the fact to be explained in a context in which it can be understood as meaningful.

In its connection with the particular practical situation in which an explanation is required, the concept of explanation used by systems-theory coincides with the method of hermeneutic. In addition, as well as allowing for the possibility that knowledge of natural laws may acquire an explanatory function within an appropriate pragmatic context, it also leaves room for the model of historical explanation constructed by W. Dray. In the course of his argument against Popper, Hempel and the development of their 'covering law' theory by P. Gardiner,[290] Dray shows that bringing events under a general law or a theory of natural law fails to grasp them in their historical uniqueness and is therefore inadequate as an explanation of them as historical events. To explain historical events, he argues, requires more than bringing them under general laws in this way.[291] Historical explanation requires the demonstration of a

---

someone whose interest in a fact is historical than would bringing it under a natural law.

[289] Passmore, p. 107. Cf. above, note 280, the analogous conclusions of W. Dray.

[290] P. Gardiner, *The Nature of Historical Explanation*, London 1952.

[291] W. Dray, *Laws and Explanation in History*, London 1957, pp. 28ff, 58ff.

continuous series of events leading up to the event which is to be explained (66ff). In the case of history, such an explanation does not have to give adequate answers to why-questions, but simply to describe 'how' the event which is felt to require explanation came about (156ff). The historian has to reconstruct the 'ladder' (162–3) of conditions which made the event in question possible (164ff).

Stegmüller has tried to show that what he calls Dray's 'historico-genetic' form of explanation can quite easily be reduced to the deductive-nomological type. In the first place, he argues, the 'concept of explanation of how something is possible' belongs to 'the category of *pragmatic* concepts, since it must be concerned expressly with *convincing* somebody' (op. cit. 377). But because this pragmatic aspect is involved, says Stegmüller, it is 'misleading of Dray to play off *how* something is possible against *why* something is possible'. The why of an event is a purely formal concept which abstracts from pragmatic aspects.

This criticism of Dray is not very convincing since at the end of his book Stegmüller has already admitted that the *explanatory force* of formal arguments depends totally on their connection with a pragmatic situation of understanding. In any case, the subjective conditions of understanding are not the only aspect involved. The construction of the 'ladder' of conditions is an application of the 'continuous series' model of explanation, to which Dray (81) says historical explanations conform. Dray's assumption that this model takes more account of the uniqueness of historical events than the deductive-nomological one (44ff) seems quite reasonable. Dray says that his model of historico-genetic explanation does without hypothetical laws completely. Stegmüller, on the other hand (365ff), has tried to interpret historico-genetic explanation, following Hempel, in such a way that each individual step is covered by a general law, with the difference that as the argument develops 'great masses of

---

Unless otherwise indicated, the page references in the next two paragraphs are to this book. See also the discussion in W. Dray, *Philosophy of History*, 1964, pp. 5ff., where in particular the close connection between Dray's concept of explanation by the construction of a 'continuous series' and the ideas of Oakeshott (*Experience and Its Modes*, 1933), with their stress on the uniqueness of historical events, is made clearer (esp. pp. 8ff).

purely descriptive detail are introduced' which in this context are not 'explained by means of other facts with reference to laws' (358).

Neither individual events nor the individual steps in a historico-genetic explanation can, however, according to Dray, be explained by reducing them to general laws. This is not just because of the need for a connection with a practical situation in which the law can be understood as an explanation; it also has something to do with the situation to be explained. A law, which is universal, cannot take account of the particularity of a unique event, but to the extent that it is made more specific it loses its universality and in extreme cases becomes simply a description of a unique situation.[292] To this Stegmüller replies that 'a law which in fact has only a single instance nevertheless *could* have other instances, and therefore could in principle *be used in other explanations and predictions*' (102). However, this reply is not convincing, since Stegmüller himself has said that explanations, as answers to why-questions, have to do with matters of fact and therefore cannot operate with mere possibilities. A general structural statement is not a law until it has more than one instance. In other circumstances it is a description, though it *could* be a law if it ever had more than one instance.

A. C. Danto has expressed a view on this point similar to Dray's.[293] Danto emphasises that a law deals only with a general *class* of events, though in fact the events themselves are not homogeneous, and this means that bringing an individual event under a law does not explain its particularity.

It has, of course, frequently been denied that historical explanations can have individual events, in their unrepeatable uniqueness, as their objects. Stegmüller, for instance, says that an individual event can 'never be explained in its full totality',[294] not

[292] Dray, *Laws and Explanations,* pp. 32ff, esp. p. 39.
[293] A. C. Danto, *Analytical Theory of History,* 2nd ed., pp. 225ff. Danto's premise is that every explanation presupposes a description of what is to be explained (p. 220), and that for one and the same event descriptions of varying degrees of generality can be given (p. 221).
[294] Stegmüller, *Wissenschaftliche Erklärung und Begründung,* p. 337; cf. C. G. Hempel, 'Deductive-Nomological vs Statistical Explanation', in Feigl and Maxwell (edd.), *Scientific Explanation, Space and Time* (Minnesota Studies in Philosophy of Science 3), Minneapolis 1962, pp. 98–169.

even by the historian. Indeed, even the historian uses general expressions, or 'species concepts', to describe the objects he is dealing with. This means, says Stegmüller, that *neither a complete description nor a complete explanation of an individual event is possible*' (337–8). So far the argument holds. However, using species concepts to describe a general class of objects is not the same as using them in combination to describe the complex uniqueness of an individual event. Because he ignores this distinction, Stegmüller's conclusion, that 'in *this* respect, a distinction between explanations in natural science and in the human sciences is, on logical grounds, impossible', (337–8) is premature.

Historico-genetic explanations of events make use of 'continuous series' or 'ladders' of events leading up to the one to be explained. They assume a multiplicity of laws working together in the individual events and the series they form and thereby explaining them. But this does not mean that this type of explanation can be reduced to the deductive-nomological pattern.[295] This is because the combination of these laws presupposes a description of the situation in which they interact and a description of the situation which preceded their operation – which is what Dray calls a historical explanation. The invocation of laws or general rules can be relevant here only as a proof or justification of an explanation already given, not as an explanation in itself.[296] In other words, in historical explanations the difference between explanation and proof appears as a difference in content. This explains why historical explanations seldom refer explicitly to general laws – a fact which has led supporters of the deductive-nomological model to assume that historical explanations are no more than 'working hypotheses'.[297]

---

[295] Cf. M Scriven, 'Truisms as Grounds for Historical Explanation', in P. be no restriction to just one "covering law" but adds that his own model and his previous work' must be understood as permitting reference to *any number* of laws in the explanation of a given phenomenon'.

[296] CF. M. Scriven, 'Truisms as Grounds for Historical Explanation', in P. Gardiner (ed.), *Theories of History*, Glencoe 1960, pp. 443–75. Scriven abandons the requirement of strict universality and prefers to speak of rules which apply under normal circumstances.

[297] C.G. Hempel, art. cit., p. 106. cf. Stegmüller, pp. 110–11, 346ff.

Dray has argued against Scriven that the general rules entailed by historical explanations are in many cases, and especially in explanations of human behaviour, 'evaluative norms of behaviour', but not empirical generalisations in the positivist sense.[298] This sort of explanation comes close to what Dray himself has described as a 'rational explanation' of human behaviour by reference to purpose.[299] In turn this view is related to Max Weber's concept of explanation by ideal types, but does not go so far as Weber's, in that Weber's ideal types also explain irrational behaviour which deviates from them, whereas Dray and Collingwood postulate a rational structure as at least underlying every instance of behaviour. C. G. Hempel has rightly observed that the rational structure view ignores the importance of the unconscious and irrational motives discovered by modern psychology.[300]

K. O. Apel has used Dray's concept of 'rational explanation' to support his argument that history, unlike the natural sciences, whose function is *explanation,* is concerned with *understanding* human actions.[301] Following Habermas, Apel traces the inaccessibility of human actions to explanation by natural science more specifically to their intentional structure (27), which, as Habermas has shown,[302] cannot be reduced entirely to observable behaviour and responses to stimuli. Again like Habermas, Apel takes it for granted that the semantic intentions by which human action is influenced are controlled by fundamental cognitive interests (31). Of these, the technical mastery of the natural conditions of existence is the function of the knowledge of the natural sciences, but the intersubjective communication necessary for the transmission of tradition (31) is an equally fundamental human interest. In Apel's view it is the connection of the *hermeneutical* disciplines with this process of the transmission of

[298] W. Dray, *Philosophy of History,* p. 16.
[299] Dray, 10ff; cf. Dray, *Laws and Explanation in History,* pp. 118ff., esp. 125 and 131ff. Dray himself draws attention to the connection of this form of explanation with R. G. Collingwood.
[300] Hempel, art. cit., 108.
[301] K. O. Apel, 'Scientistik, Hermeneutik, Ideologiekritik', *Wiener Jahrbuch für Philosophie* I (1968), pp. 15–45, esp. 24. The page references in this paragraph are to this article.
[302] See above, note 161.

tradition which accounts for their independence of the natural sciences and for the difference in method between understanding in the human sciences and explanation in natural science.

Albert has rightly described this argument as a new attempt to justify a dualism of natural and human sciences.[303] Apel has given a one-sided twist to Dray's and especially Danto's accounts of the particularities of historical explanation in order to use them to support a hermeneutical theory of the 'human sciences', when the real basis of these accounts is on a different level. The real point of Dray's and Danto's remarks is the singularity of historical events, or the historian's interest in the singular aspect of an event which for other purposes may certainly be investigated by the methods of natural science. In Dray's argument it is because of the singular character of historical events that they are still only partially explained when they are taken as instances of alleged general laws; what this leaves out is, precisely, their historical relevance. This is also why the interrelations between historical events depend on the connections between their complex individualities and not just on their conformity with laws. It is for this reason that the connected series of events itself is needed to explain historical events if the explanation is to understand what is to be explained in its various interrelations. Dray's argument on this point implies, though he does not develop the idea, an alternative to the deductive-nomological concept of 'explanation' in the shape of a general concept of explanation involving the fitting of what has to be explained into its appropriate 'context'.[304] From this point of view, which is not that of Dray himself, historical explanation no longer appears as a simple opposite to explanation in terms of natural laws, but both types appear as special cases of a more general concept of

[303] H. Albert, 'Hermeneutik und Realwissenschaft', *Plädoyer für kritischen Rationalismus*, pp. 114ff.

[304] Dray occasionally touches on this wider question, as when he agrees with P. Gardiner's idea that the use of the concept of cause in history needs 'contextual reference' (*Laws and Explanation in History*, pp. 16–17, 20) and must be related to the context of a specific situation (p. 104, cf. p. 196). Dray clearly regards the use of 'contextual reference' as a peculiarity of historical interpretation, without noticing that the theoretical framework of the laws of natural science provides an analogous systematic context, which alone gives the inclusion of phenomena under laws an explanatory function.

systematic explanation, understood as the fitting of what is to be explained into its appropriate systematic framework. In historical explanation this system is provided by the series of events, and in scientific explanation by the theoretical framework of a 'natural order' in Toulmin's sense (see above, n. 282). In its most general form the 'context' of the explanation also includes the practical situation in which the need for an explanation arises. In contrast, the concept of a 'purely' systematic explanation is a result of narrowing the perspective down to systems of objects.

The way in which historical explanation makes individual events intelligible *in their context* by fitting them into a series of events has been described in more detailed by A. C. Danto in his discussion of the function of narrative in historical explanation.[305] Danto's discussion refines Dray's model of the 'continuous series' so as to bring out its connection with the task of hermeneutic, which was contained in Dray's theory under the title 'rational explanation' but remained unconnected with his concept of the 'continuous series'.

Danto starts from the assumption that in the historical sequence the event to be explained always represents a *change* in relation to previous events (233). It is not just that the earlier event explains the later (235), but rather that both are parts of a 'temporal whole' which is the object of the explanation and within which the 'parts', in particular the beginning and the end of the change, are explained (ibid.). According to Danto, what produces the explanation is the discovery of the transition from the beginning to the end which unites both to form the whole that is the object of the narrative system (236).[306] However, Danto does not square this emphasis on the function of the transitional member, which he uses as the starting-point for remarks on the role of laws in history (236ff), with his remark that the narrative as a whole, and therefore also its beginning, is determined by its end (248): narrative propositions are, he says, always a 'retroactive re-alignment of the past' (168). It is true that a statement such as: 'In 1618 the Thirty Years' War started' could not have been

[305] A. C. Danto, *Analytical Philosophy of History*, pp. 143ff, 233ff. The page references in the rest of this paragraph are to this book.

[306] Each narrative system in turn forms part of a wider historical system (p. 241).

written by a chronicler of the year 1618, but could have been made only after 1648. But a statement of this sort can be regarded as an explanation of the events of 1618 *now*. Therefore not only the transition from the beginning to the end, but also the end itself, has an explanatory function, and it would seem odd to deny that the beginning also has one. Danto's analysis would have to be enlarged in the light of these considerations so as to include the beginning and end of the historical process – as well as the transition from one to the other – *as mutually explanatory factors in the context of the historical whole* (determined by its end) which is the subject of the narrative. This view makes Dray's continuous series model a special case of the concept of explanation used in systems-theory. It can now be shown that the narrative unity of series of events in history is rooted in the historical nature of human perception of meaning. In Dilthey's terms, this perception has a similarly temporal structure as a result of which the semantic horizon which determines significance can be anticipated, albeit one-sidedly, in the historical present although it depends on the end of a process of historical experience. This description makes it unnecessary for the role of the meanings perceived by historical agents in explanations of the course of history to be added as an external element, like Dray's 'rational explanation', to the model of the series of events to make up the specifically historical form of explanation. On this view perception of meaning can be regarded as inherent in the explanation. This account maintains that human perceptions of meaning are unique and cannot be fully grasped by explanations in terms of natural laws, however much these may be able to clarify them. The reason for this, however, is not the intentionality of these perceptions, but their historical character, by virtue of which they partake as an *individual open system* in the uniqueness of historical events and processes.[307] For this reason there is no need to postulate a fundamental distinction between historical and hermeneutical explanation and explanation in the

---

[307] I have discussed the derivation of hermeneutic from the historical nature of the perception of meaning and the resulting connection with the problematic of history as a whole in my discussion with H. G. Gadamer, 'Hermeneutic and Universal History', W. Pannenberg, *Basic Concepts in Theology,* London 1970, vol. 1, pp. 96–136.

natural sciences such as Apel makes under the influence of his dualism of 'explanation' and 'understanding'. Instead, our reminder of the practical context in which all explanation functions has already suggested a concept of explanation as the fitting of particulars into a whole which could provide a common basis for a theory of explanatory procedures in both hermeneutic and the natural sciences. A strong argument in favour of this is the fact that both inclusion under laws and the historical forms of explanation mentioned above have an explantory function only in relation to a practical need for explanation.

The way in which the fitting of explananda into a context of meaning also forms part of explanation in the natural sciences has recently been more closely investigated by E. Scheibe, who starts from the practical situation which creates the need for an explanation.[308] According to Scheibe, we ask for a cause or an explanation when something surprising or unexpected occurs, something which 'is not among the implications of the assumptions from which I started and which should not occur in a world constructed according to these assumptions' (263). Following J. König, Scheibe stresses, against Hume's interpretation of causality as an expression of habit, that surprise is the impulse of a search for causes.[309] Similarly in physics, the need for an explanation does not arise until a proposition or a theoretical system which has previously been adequate begins to reveal limitations. When this happens, however, not only the unexpected event, but also the weakness in the theory which has until this point been regarded as universally valid, require explanation. These two requirements can be met only by the construction of a new theory on a higher level of generality which explains not only 'how the respective phenomena fall under a comprehensive theory, but also how the previous theory fits into the new one and what is responsible for the fact that one theory accounts for the phenomenon in question but the other

---

[308] E. Scheibe, 'Ursache und Erklärung', in L. Krüger (ed.), *Erkenntnisprobleme der Naturwissenschaften*, 1970, pp. 253–75. The page references in the following paragraphs are to this article.

[309] Scheibe, 'Ursache und Erklärung', p. 257. See also Popper's criticisms of Hume, *Conjectures and Refutations*, pp. 42ff.

does not' (273). This view in principle confirms Toulmin's interpretation of scientific explanation as giving meaning by providing explanatory paradigms, but it adds a refinement which makes it even clearer that explanations of this sort also function by fitting parts into a semantic whole in the way attributed above to systems-theory. The additional postulate requires the explanation to take account not only of the previously unintelligible observations but also of the earlier theoretical views with which these conflict. The contradiction must be resolved in a new theoretical framework which shows the previously contradictory elements as reconcilable in the semantic web of a new systematic. On the other hand, as Scheibe emphasises, logical deductions are 'not the *decisive* element in the explanation' (271), however much explanations in natural science may take the form of deductions.

Even in Scheibe's approach, deduction, in the sense of inclusion under hypothetical laws, is altogether more important in scientific than in historical explanations. In historical explanations the deductive aspects are at the most implicit, presuppositional, while the basic method, as we have just seen, is determined by other aspects. However, Scheibe's general description of the situation in which a need for explanation arises can also be applied to philosophical and theological discussion as well as to historical disciplines. In these uses it holds not only for the special case of causal explanation, with which Scheibe is primarily concerned, but quite generally. A need for explanation arises wherever states of affairs are discovered which cannot be fitted into the existing theory in the field in question, but conflict with it. The explanation required in such a situation in historical, philosophical and theological investigations has to make sense not only of these states of affairs, but also of the limitations of the previously accepted theory and the extent to which it retains validity (its 'elements of truth'). In historical and philosophical disciplines a single postulate may not be able to do both, but even in these disciplines the explanations of the two aspects of the problem must harmonise.

Scheibe's extension of the concept of explanation provides a common basis from which the specific features of explanation in the various fields of natural science, history, and philosophy and theology, can be understood. This basis is best described in the language of systems-theory as the function of fitting parts into a total pattern of meaning. Not only does this view explain the relation of scientific method in the natural sciences to scientific method in historical and philosophical disciplines, but it also implies that the concept of explanation can no longer be rejected as inapplicable in historical and philosophical disciplines in favour of a concept of understanding allegedly specific to the human sciences. The relationship between understanding and explanation must itself now be redefined.

A starting-point for the work of redefinition is provided by a comment of Scheibe's on the history of physics. In the framework of the explanation provided by Newton's theory of gravitation, he says, 'we *understand* (!) ... both why in a particular case, such as that of our solar system, there is a lot to be said for Kepler's laws, and why deviations from them must occur' (272). In other words, *understanding* operates within a frame of reference which in this case is provided by the *explanation* offered by Newton's theory. An explanation can therefore provide a framework for understanding, which is concerned with the relation of individual phenomena – in this case Kepler's laws and deviations from them – within this framework.[310]

Understanding, however, does not always presuppose an explanation. 'It is truer to say that understanding is more fundamental and that explanation always begins where understanding reaches its limits.'[311] Where we understand, no explanations are needed. It is only where we do not understand that explanations are required. When people find this or that

---

[310] Max Weber describes the relation of explanation and understanding differently. He says that it is the task of sociology 'to understand social action by interpreting it and thereby to give a causal explanation of it in its effects' (*Wissenschaftslehre*, p. 542). Explanation is described here as the *result* of understanding. Against this view it must be maintained that explanation is no longer needed where there is understanding, while conversely an explanation may be very necessary to enable something previously unintelligible to be understood.

[311] O. F. Bollnow, *Die Methode der Geisteswissenschaften*, 1950, p. 15. Bollnow defines understanding as the 'transparency of a familiar context' (ibid.). The page references in the rest of this paragraph are to this book.

unintelligible, in need of explanation, it is always in a context of general understanding of and familiarity with their world. Unlike the understanding produced by explanation, this prior understanding is not related to any *explicit* frame of reference. The semantic horizon of this basic understanding fades into indefinite distance, however much it may be coloured by tradition and custom and however little it blurs the sharpness of the outlines in the immediate sphere of life. The indeterminacy of this semantic horizon is matched by that of the basic confidence which keeps reasserting itself in human life, in spite of all disappointments, as long as life goes on. It is only to the extent that particular segments of this semantic horizon are made uncertain by surprising experiences that an *explanation* is required. The explanation explicitates the existing frame of reference used by the person who seeks understanding, and at the same time partly replaces it with an intellectual construction of the totality of meaning under question. It is not just the sciences which do this; the process also occurs in religion and art. Nevertheless in the history of our culture the sciences have acquired more and more importance in this role, though it is filled equally by the so-called human sciences, including philosophy and theology. F. Bollnow has rightly emphasised that 'understanding is not restricted to the human sciences, or explanation to the natural sciences' (14). Both produce explanations where 'the original understanding has broken down' (18). It might be added that breakdowns are quite often caused by the natural sciences themselves, which cultivate doubt as part of their method. Doubt in the natural sciences is not an aim in itself, however, but is directed to the acquisition of more reliable foundations for human dealings with reality based on understanding. The sciences produce these foundations in the form of explanatory hypotheses, and by so doing 'reconstruct the lost meaningfulness of the world' (18). This applies as much to the human sciences, including philosophy and theology, as it does to the natural sciences. Where there are differences between them, they relate not to the explanatory process itself, but to the methods used in the different disciplines to produce explanations. In this view explanation in terms of a system of natural-law theory can be seen as a particular case of the construction of networks of meaning and significance which takes place in another mode in historical and hermeneutical explanation and the general form of which is the construction of philosophical theories.

Chapter Three

HERMENEUTIC: A METHODOLOGY FOR UNDERSTANDING MEANING

HERMENEUTIC has already come into the argument of Chapter 2. In that chapter three points emerged.

1. The aim of hermeneutic is the understanding of meaning, and meaning is to be understood in this context as the relation of parts to whole within a structure of life or experience.

2. It proved possible to connect the idea of whole with E. Nagel's idea of pattern, and in this sense with that of system, which in turn made possible a connection between theory construction in hermeneutic and theory construction in natural science. The claim that the experience of meaning is the specific field of the human sciences was found to be justified only to the extent that the *totality of life* which is a basic element of experience and which is the object of interpretations in hermeneutic is not an abstract systematic scaffolding. That is to say, it is not like the abstract model of natural events offered by classical mechanics which, precisely for that reason, consists of timeless, universal rules. What Dilthey called the 'unity of life', which is accessible in experience, is a temporally determined, individually existing 'open system', with the specific characteristic that the system is present to itself, inheres in itself, in experience. However, it proved impossible to justify a restriction of the concept of meaning to individual systems of this sort, since a geometrical figure or a physical theory has just as good a claim to be called meaningful in itself. Every system, whether temporal and individual or timeless and universal, includes relations between parts and whole, and to that extent at least every system is meaningful in itself, even if it is not present to itself as meaningful.

3. We also saw that the distinction frequently said to exist between 'understanding', in the sense of the understanding of meaning, and 'explanation' by means of hypothetical laws cannot be maintained in a sense which implies the existence of fundamentally distinct intellectual functions. Rather, every guide to understanding, and so every hermeneutical aid to understanding, must itself be treated as an explanation. Explanation of this sort may take the form of inclusion under hypothetical laws, but it is not limited to this form. In particular, where the objects to be explained are unique structures, as in a historical event, laws have only limited explanatory force compared with interpretation, which can reveal the individual structure of the complex of events. On the other hand, such an interpretation is itself an explanation when it meets a need for understanding, and in the light of such an explanation – if it is informative – what was previously unintelligible can be understood.

The results of this discussion have given us the framework for an explicit consideration of hermeneutic. This chapter cannot give a full systematic account of its foundations, but sets out merely to introduce the problems raised by the rival views of hermeneutic put forward in the current discussion.

1. General Hermeneutic

The art of hermeneutic is first mentioned in the pseudo-Platonic dialogue *Epinomis*,[312] where it means construing religious tradition, as opposed to divination, the 'mantic' art. Neither hermeneutic nor divination, however, can of itself decide on the truth of what is transmitted. This decision is the responsibility of science and dialectic.

In a manner which is not fully clear, the word 'hermeneutic' is connected with the name of the god Hermes, the messenger of the gods who announces their decisions. By analogy with this function of Hermes, and in a phrase which says much about Greek religion in general, Plato in his *Ion* calls poets 'interpreters

---

[312] *Epinomis*, 975 c 6: hermeneutike techne.

of the gods' (*hermēnēs tōn theōn*, 534e), in contrast with the bards, who merely recited Homer and were only 'an interpreter's interpreters' (535a).[313]

Unlike the terms 'hermeneutic' and *hermēneus* ('interpreter'), the word *hermēneia* had a secular use in Greek. Aristotle's *Peri hermeneias* (known in Latin as *De Interpretatione*) deals simply with the theory of the statement, though the title might also imply an essay 'on (linguistic) expression'.

From classical rhetoric and Stoic philosophy, which had developed an allegorical method of construing the mythical tradition, reflection on the rules of hermeneutic was taken over into Christian exegesis of scripture. Typological reconstruction, a product of the Christian use of the scriptures, was now added to the literal and allegorical forms. The name hermeneutic was used for the study of the rules of exegesis, and a distinction was made between *hermeneutica sacra* and secular hermeneutic. Hermeneutic was developed into an independent discipline in 1567 by Flacius, who hoped, by formulating universally valid rules of interpretation, to establish the possibility of a universally valid scriptural exegesis in opposition to post-Tridentine Catholic theology.[314]

The modern history of hermeneutic begins with Schleiermacher.[315] Although the traditional division between

[313] See the definition of the relationship of Moses and Aaron (Ex 4: 13–16), according to which Aaron is to be Moses' 'mouth' and Moses (like the prophets generally, see Jr 15:19) is to be the mouth of God. It is not surprising that Philo of Alexandria should have interpreted this situation in terms of the corresponding Platonic idea and presented Aaron as the interpreter of Moses and Moses and prophets in general as interpreters of God (references in J. Behm, TDNT vol. II, 664–5). The mediating function of the interpreter (*hermeneutēs*) is no doubt also the explanation for the emergence of Hermes as a redeemer figure in the Hellenistic period.

[314] The term *hermeneutica sacra* was used as a book title by J. C. Dannhauer in 1654. On the connection of the development of hermeneutic with the history of biblical exegesis, see G. Ebeling, 'Hermeneutik', RGG, 3rd ed. 1959, pp. 242–62, and Dilthey's outline, which is still instructive, 'Die Entstehung der Hermeneutik' (1900), vol. V, pp. 317–31.

[315] Schleiermacher's writings on hermeneutic were published in a new edition with an introduction by H. Kimmerle in 1959: F. D. E. Schleiermacher, *Hermeneutik* (Abhandlungen der Heidelberger Akademie der Wissenschaften, Phil.-hist. Klasse, 1959).

exegesis and criticism is retained in his work, Schleiermacher does not restrict hermeneutic to a collection of rules for textual interpretation. For him hermeneutic is the theory of understanding in general in all forms of communication between people. This is the source of Schleiermacher's historic significance in the development of hermeneutic.

According to Schleiermacher, that people can understand one another results from the fact that individuals in their dealings with each other begin by assuming the unity of the human species. Individuals are linked by species consciousness in so far as each one of them is interested in what is human in general and in what is of significance for man. This shared species consciousness makes understanding between individuals possible by enabling one to understand not only the words and gestures, but also the tone variations and mimicry, of another as an individual variation of human nature in general.[316]

Schleiermacher however did not develop general considerations of this sort into the central theme of hermeneutic as such, but treated them merely as an introduction, from which he immediately passed to the problems of textual interpretation. This meant that he did not pay much attention to the differences between the understanding of face-to-face speech, in which both the speaker and hearer are physically present at the moment of utterance and to that extent participate in the same situation, and the interpretation of a text, where this is not so. His analysis of the relation between the situation of understanding and that of the utterance to be understood is also poorly developed because Schleiermacher treats knowledge of historical structures not as an element in understanding itself but only as a precondition of it.[317]

[316] See R. R. Niebuhr, 'Schleiermacher on Language and Feeling', *Theology Today*, 17 (1960). See also Dilthey, *Leben Schleiermachers*, vol. II, ed. M. Redeker, 1966, pp. 691ff, esp. 693–4, 696ff, 706–7, 720ff.
[317] Kimmerle rightly points this out in the introduction to his edition of Schleiermacher's *Hermeneutik*, pp. 15–16. Dilthey (*Leben Schleiermachers*, vol. II, p. 778) had objected that Schleiermacher's view of psychological interpretation, which was derived from ethics, allowed 'no room for the progress of historical development'. H. G. Gadamer also (*Truth and Method*, pp. 168ff) saw that Schleiermacher's hermeneutic was concerned less with the problem of overcoming historical distance in time than with individual variations in the universally human, and he suggested that the reason for this

This is another symptom of the fact that after his general introductory remarks Schleiermacher turned immediately to the interpretation of texts. Significant here is the distinction between grammatical and 'technical' or psychological interpretation. The second became steadily more important in Schleiermacher's work. Whereas technical interpretation was concerned originally with the individual features of an author's usage, the addresses to the Academy of 1829 gave psychological interpretation the task of reconstructing the origin of the text in the author's thought, with the implication that the interpreter could transpose himself into that thought.[318]

Dilthey based himself on Schleiermacher's work, but again extended the scope of hermeneutic. He developed Schleiermacher's approach by treating understanding as a 'psychological reproduction', which reconstructed the 'creative process' of the origin of a text. This view was in harmony with the status he accorded psychology as the discipline underlying all the human sciences. When the *Einleitung in die Geisteswissenschaften* was completed in 1883, Dilthey was still attracted by the idea of a general psychology which would provide a basis for hermeneutic.[319] The development of

---

may have been that Schleiermacher's hermeneutic was 'really' designed 'for texts whose authority was established' (p. 173). Schleiermacher's concern, according to Gadamer, 'was not a historian's but a theologian's'.

[318] H. Kimmerle (Schleiermacher, *Hermeneutik*, p. 23) has rightly criticised the way in which Schleiermacher's psychological interpretation describes only 'the process of the emergence from the interiority of thought into language'; 'understanding is no longer of *something*, but only of *how* something can be the empirical modification of an ideal datum'. The only doubt attaches to Kimmerle's assumption that this point represents a deviation on Schleiermacher's part from an original view of hermeneutic which was concerned also with the content of language. Already in the early distinction between general word-meaning and individual nuances in language use ('Aphorismen von 1805 und 1809', p. 34 of Kimmerle's ed.) we find a statement of the problem of the movement from general word-meaning to individual nuance, i.e., the problem which was later solved by psychological construction.

[319] Dilthey, *Gesammelte Schriften*, vol. I, pp. 29ff, 32. The difference between him and Schleiermacher was that in Schleiermacher's work − as Dilthey himself stressed in his *Life* (see above, n. 316) − ethics and not psychology formed the general anthropological basis for hermeneutic. At this point

Schleiermacher's approach in his work is connected particularly with his category of expression. For Dilthey, the expression of individuality meant not just texts and possible discourse, but any occurrence whatever, in so far it was connected with human actions and in particular in so far as it was a product of those actions.[320] This enabled Dilthey to develop hermeneutic still further into a general theory of historical consciousness, although this was overshadowed in the last phase of his thought by his ambition to provide a basis for the human sciences in a 'descriptive psychology'. Droysen's idea that 'History is the *gnōthi seauton* of mankind, its consciousness, "its conscience"'[321] now became established in Dilthey's thought with its full impact. Its main result was an insight into the historical nature of the semantic structures of experience which emerges in Dilthey's last drafts as the continuation of his *Einleitung in die Geisteswissenschaften.* Here Dilthey came close to abandoning his concept of structure as an already existing unity of life when he saw that life and its semantic structures were necessarily incomplete because historical. 'We should have to wait for the end of life and should only at the moment of death

Dilthey took a different path under the influence of Mill's view of psychology as the fundamental discipline of the human sciences.

[320] Though it took a long time for the crucial importance of the external expression of objectivations of life in its external manifestations to become a central concern of Dilthey's. The 'Ideen über eine beschreibende und zergliedernde Psychologie' (1894, vol. V, pp. 139ff) still attempts to derive the 'descriptive psychology' on which the human sciences are based from 'inner perception' (vol. V, p. 170, and passim). The emphasis on the importance for the human sciences of the 'objective products of psychic life' is no more than marginal (pp. 199–200; see also p. 265). In the essay, 'Die Entstehung der Hermeneutik' (1900), however, 'awareness of one's own states' is said to be the object of understanding only in a loose sense. It is described now as a process 'in which we become aware of a psychic entity through sensible signs which are its manifestations' (p. 318). In the later drafts which developed the 'Einleitung in die Geisteswissenschaften', this view, and with it the concept of expression (VII, p. 131; see also pp. 124, 205, 208ff, 279, 319–20), becomes increasingly important. The parallel use of the term 'objectivations of life' (vol. VII, pp. 146ff, 118, etc.) and that of 'objective mind' (pp. 148ff) indicates that in this field Dilthey had been stimulated by Hegel.

[321] J. G. Droysen, *Historik. Vorlesungen über Enzyklopädie und Methodologie der Geschichte,* ed. R. Hübner, 3rd ed. 1958, p. 267.

be able to see the *whole* in terms of which the relation of its parts
could be determined. We should have to wait for the end of
history to possess all the evidence needed to determine history's
meaning.'[322] The consequence of this for the concept of structure
should have been an awareness of the dependence of the
structural unity of life, in the sense of that of the totality of
meaning of the individual life, on its eschatological future, but
Dilthey evaded it by claiming that the whole also became
'intelligible in its parts' (233). Such a claim is still problematic,
however, without the assumption of a prior knowledge of the
whole. We saw above that knowledge of this sort does play a
part in Dilthey's work in the shape of his conviction of the unity
of psychic 'life' in all individuals. As a result of this he could still
look for an understanding of the whole in terms of its parts, that
is to say, to start from the structural 'unity of life' as something
given. It is this direction that M. Heidegger has taken in
reincorporating Dilthey's analysis of meaning into a structural
concept of existence, in which existential structure takes the place
of the descriptive psychology which Dilthey sought as the basis
of hermeneutic. As a 'being', which, as being in the world, is an
issue for itself,[323] existence, according to Heidegger, outlines itself
on its possibilities (its 'for-the-sake-of-which'), and thereby
places itself in advance in a position of possible understanding. In
the process, the 'involvement' of its world is laid bare through an
anticipation which discloses the world as a totality of
significance.[324] The primacy of this anticipation for
understanding is a result of man's search for a
for-the-sake-of-which for his existence and corresponds to
Heidegger's idea of the primacy of the future for the temporality
of human existence (378). In its 'authentic' form, the anticipation
of understanding reaches out to the uttermost possibility of
existence, death; according to Heidegger, only the prospect of
death discloses the possibility of existing as a
'potentiality-for-Being-a-whole' (264). What thus comes to
understanding has meaning: 'Meaning is that wherein the

[322] Dilthey, *Gesammelte Schriften*, vol. VII, p. 233; see also p. 237.
[323] Martin Heidegger, *Being and Time*, London 1962, p. 182. See also the
whole section 'Being-there as Understanding', pp. 181ff.
[324] *Being and Time*, pp. 190–2 ('Understanding and Interpretation').

intelligibility of something maintains itself' (193). For Heidegger, who thus disagrees with the value philosophy of Rickert, meaning is 'not a property of beings' in general; only the existence of man can 'be meaningful or meaningless' (193). All other 'beings', according to Heidegger, are 'unmeaning', devoid of any meaning at all (194). This leaves the question of the transsubjective truth of human experience of meaning as open as it was for Dilthey. The same is true of the relevance of the historical conditioning of understanding for the structure of experience and its possibilities. H. G. Gadamer has taken both these questions beyond the context in which they were discussed by Heidegger.[325]

Gadamer regards even Dilthey's attempt to base the human sciences on hermeneutic and to assert their independence of the natural sciences as yet another misleading attempt to make the human sciences conform to the methodological ideal of the natural sciences. Dilthey believed that scientific knowledge involved 'breaking the connection with life, getting away from one's own history' (5). This objectification, analogous to the approach of natural science, derives from the psychological interpretation which is the culmination of hermeneutic in Schleiermacher and was taken over and developed by Dilthey.

In psychological objectification, says Gadamer, the interpreter must attribute to the author he is trying to understand the interiority of his own experience.[326] Thus it proves, like all methodological objectification, to be monological, and its monological structure completely prevents it from reaching the other as a not-I.

Gadamer wants to eliminate this contradiction and so eliminate 'objectifying' procedures from hermeneutic. He takes his model for this attempt from Hegel's idea that 'the essence of the historical attitude is not the restoration of the past, but

---

[325] H.G. Gadamer, *Truth and Method*, London and New York, 1976, p. 36–37. The English edition is a translation of the 2nd, revised German edition of *Wahrheit und Methode*, Tübingen, 1965. Subsesquent page references in the text are to this book.

[326] H. G. Gadamer, 'Hermeneutik und Historismus', *Philosophische Rundschau* 9 (1962), esp. p. 243; English translation included in the English edition of *Wahrheit und Methode*, pp. 460–91.

thoughtful mediation with contemporary life' (161). This task is to be performed in Gadamer's work by the device of 'fusing horizons' (269–74). The first stage of this is the recognition of the distinctness of the text or the alien utterance from the present of the interpreter. The second is to look for a common horizon to link the interpreter with the text and its context and with tradition in general.

Abandoning the 'monological' nature of the objectifying method in the sciences, Gadamer starts from the premise that the tradition which the so-called human sciences seek to interpret is given in advance: 'We stand always within traditions, and this is no objectifying process, i.e. we do not conceive of what the tradition says as something other, something alien. On the contrary, it is always part of us, a model and an exemplar, a self-recognition, which our later historical judgement would hardly see as a kind of knowledge, but as the simplest preservation of the tradition' (p. 250). In the first stage of the fusion of horizons – establishing the distance between the utterance to be interpreted and the interpreter's horizon – the main task is to recognise the priority of tradition over our understanding, its 'claim' (p. 324), and 'openness' to this claim is the distinguishing feature of 'an awareness conditioned by history'. Nevertheless, 'in an overall view . . . the power of history does not depend on its being recognised. This epitomises the power of history over finite[327] human consciousness, that it predominates even where men deny their own historical nature as a result of belief in method'.[328]

This emphasis on the predominance of tradition distinguishes Gadamer from Dilthey, who stressed much more the transformation of the past in the light of present experience and the emancipation from the dogmatic claims of tradition which

---

[327] Gadamer's point is the finitude of man in historical experience.

[328] Following this line of thought, Gadamer arrives at the 'ontological development of hermeneutic' as a linguistic realisation of the tradition in which the individual man is necessarily involved as a finite being. Connected with this is Gadamer's criticism of an objectifying understanding of language itself as 'statement' (pp. 426ff.), which does not reveal the 'unexpressed horizon of meaning' of the linguistic event. In similar terms, Heidegger argued in *Being and Time* that assertions no longer reach out into a 'totality of involvements'.

resulted from historical consciousness. In Dilthey's view, 'historical consciousness of the finitude of every historical phenomenon, of every human or social condition, of the relativity of every kind of belief is the last step before the liberation of man.' [329] Gadamer, on the other hand, is less interested in the finitude of historical phenomena than in the 'finitude of our historical experience' itself (p. 415), in other words in the finitude of man in relation to tradition (244, 320–22). Intimately connected with this is his critical attack on an objectivity allegedly to be attained through scientific method (p. 321). The link with the process of tradition also leads to a characteristic reshaping of the primacy of the future in the temporality of human existence which Heidegger demonstrated, a reshaping in which the anticipation of understanding is itself made once more relative to tradition. According to Gadamer, 'the anticipation of meaning that guides our understanding of a text is not an act of subjectivity, but proceeds from the communality that binds us to tradition' (261). This approach of Gadamer's is a further refinement of Heidegger's idea of the circular structure of knowledge which is peculiar to knowledge because knowledge is always shaped by a pre-understanding of the thing which is to be understood and by the anticipation which guides the interpretation. [330] For Gadamer belonging to tradition is fulfilled in the 'fact that we share fundamental prejudices with it' (262). But Heidegger had also concluded from the connection of understanding with preunderstanding and prejudice that the hermeneutical process was unscientific: 'In a scientific proof, we may not presuppose what it is our task to prove.' Consequently, 'the business of historiological interpretation is excluded a priori from the domain of rigorous knowledge.' [331]

'The loss of objectivity which is the result of Gadamer's doctrine' is the target of the criticism of Gadamer by E. Betti. [332] Betti regards Gadamer's argument as in large part following the

[329] Dilthey, vol. VII, p. 290.

[330] Heidegger, *Being and Time,* pp. 190–5.

[331] Heidegger, ibid., p. 194.

[332] E. Betti, *'Die Hermeneutik als allgemeine Methodik der Geisteswissenschaften,* 1962, p. 41. Subsequent page references in the text are to this book.

line taken by Rudolf Bultmann in 1958 in his *History and Eschatology*. Against both, Betti insists that 'for every position or point of view, within the limitations of available perspectives, objective truth can be seen' (27). Betti believes, however, that the only way to ensure the objectivity of interpretation – and here he differs not only from Bultmann and Gadamer, but also in practice from Dilthey[333] – is by separating the meaning of a phenomenon from its significance for the interpreter. He also insists, against Gadamer, on a separation of historical interpretation and application (57–8), and makes a fundamental distinction between cognitive hermeneutic and normative hermeneutic, in which latter he includes the 'eschatological attribution of meaning' in which he regards Bultmann as engaged, and which, he says, must not be confused with 'historical interpretation' (31ff). With such distinctions between a *quaestio facti* and a *quaestio iuris*, between a value-related and a purely cognitively oriented interpretation (25ff), Betti goes back to a stage not only before Dilthey, who recognised values as products of the historical process itself,[334] but also before Rickert, who did separate value and being but still treated *all* historical knowledge as 'value-relative'.[335] In particular, in order to keep the eschatological attribution of meaning distinct from cognitive interpretation, Betti has to restrict Dilthey's insight that the meaning of a historical phenomenon is influenced by the continuation of historical experience so that it applies only to the 'historical repercussions and consequences' of that experience (23). For Dilthey, on the other hand, the result of both the consequences of an occurrence and the changing context of experience generally is a change in the meaning of past events and experience, so that it would only be at the end of a life or at

[333] In Dilthey's work the term 'significance' (*Bedeutsamkeit*) refers to the 'definiteness of the meaning of a part for a whole' (vol. VII, pp. 238–9; see also p. 168). In other words significance no less than meaning refers to a state of affairs which exists in manifestations of life, not a subjective value given to them by the interpreter.

[334] Dilthey, vol. VII, pp. 153ff.

[335] Reluctance to accept the notion of 'value-related' interpretation is perhaps due to the influence on Betti of Max Weber, even though Weber's distinction between value rationality and purposive rationality obscures the fact that in Weber's use the latter is also 'value-related' in Rickert's sense.

the end of history that the meaning of events taking place in the course of them could be finally decided. Betti explicitly rejects Bultmann's assertion, which is influenced by the late formulations of Dilthey, that a historical phenomenon 'will show itself in its very essence only when history has reached its end',[336] even though he himself shares the underlying analysis of the way in which the structures of meaning of historical phenomenon are determined by context. This analysis derives from Dilthey and leads ultimately to questions about universal history and an eschatological future which determines all individual meaning. Betti is wrong in thinking that this makes the determining of an interpretation by the interpreter's anticipations of the future an inseparable part of the process of historical interpretation, and not a subsequent addition of 'value-relative' interpretation. Because of this mistake he also completely misses the point of Gadamer's statement in a letter to him that he 'regards it as the only scientific method *to recognise what is,* instead of starting from what ought to be or could be'. In his replies to Betti's criticism, therefore, Gadamer has needed to do no more than reiterate this position.[337]

For all the inadequacy of his arguments, Betti's insistence on the requirement of 'objectivity' in historical interpretation is nevertheless justified. 'Objectivity' in this context obviously cannot mean a complete independence of the interpretation from the interpreter's position, but only that for every such position the thing to be interpreted must be distinguishable from the subjectivity of the interpreter, and that its distinctness must be given full weight.[338] This distinction is not simply a theoretical

---

[336] Betti, *Hermeneutik,* p. 30, criticising R. Bultmann, *History and Eschatology,* p. 120.
For a contrary view, see Dilthey, vol. VII, pp. 233, 237.
[337] Gadamer, 'Hermeneutics and Historicism', *Truth and Method,* pp. 460–91. Betti had quoted the passage from Gadamer's letter on p. 51 of his book.
[338] Betti rightly regards the possibility of distinguishing the 'meaningful forms' which have to be interpreted, in their specific features, and therefore in their historical distance, as endangered by Gadamer's inclusion of 'application' in historical hermeneutic (Betti, pp. 47–8, on *Truth and Method,* pp. 303–04). In reply to Gadamer's appeal to legal hermeneutic, which treats the meaning of a law as becoming 'completely specific' only in its applications (p. 308), Betti cites the difference between the 'position of the legal historian and the lawyer

requirement, but is made a possibility by virtue of the detachment inherent in human experience, a detachment which operates automatically in the representational function of language and its corresponding linguistic mode, the statement. In the statement, the speaker distinguishes the stated content from his own subjectivity as a content which has an identity in itself and which can therefore be communicated to others and understood by them as having that identity. Characteristically, Gadamer does not allow for the constitutive importance of the statement as the expression of the representational function of language for the specifically human relation to the world,[339] although he does stress the importance of the fundamental anthropological phenomenon of the factual nature of experience of the world (402–03). Gadamer's critical view of the statement is directed, and rightly, against attempts to detach or isolate what is said from its unexpressed associations, but in taking this position he nevertheless seems not to allow the element of *objectification* in the statement its full theoretical legitimacy, not to recognise it as a fundamental structural element of language itself. Although his own theory of interpretation as a fusion of horizons recognises in the reconstruction of what is to the interpreter the alien horizon of the text he is interpreting, in its historical distance, an ineradicable element of the event of interpretation, Gadamer does not notice that this process involves objectification. This must be a result of the influence of Heidegger's thesis of the hermeneutical circle and Gadamer's own extension of it in the idea that all understanding rests on a structure of prejudice

whose task it is to apply the law' (p. 44), which he says Gadamer ignores.

[339] See the negative assessment of the statement in Gadamer, *Truth and Method,* p. 426. This devaluing of the statement was the central point of my critical discussion of Gadamer's work ('Hermeneutic and Universal History' (1963), in W. Pannenberg, *Basic Questions in Theology,* vol. 1, pp. 96–136, esp. 125ff). I argued that it was connected with the separation of the linguistic event in the process of tradition from the actual content of what is historical and its dependence on universal history. In his reply, ('Rhetorik, Hermeneutik und Ideologiekritik. Metakritische Erörterungen zu "Wahrheit und Methode"', *Kleine Schriften,* vol. I, 1967, pp. 113ff, reprinted in *Hermeneutik und Ideologiekritik,* 1971, pp. 57ff, esp. 76–7), Gadamer is sympathetic to my remarks on universal history, but not to my criticism of his devaluing of the statement.

conditioned by tradition. However, it is only the exclusion of the constitutive significance of the objectifying function of the statement for the objectivity of language which enables Gadamer to contrast the hermeneutical events of tradition and the 'methodical' procedures of natural science, which operate with statements. Again it is this exclusion which gives rise to the equally problematic affinity of Gadamer's hermeneutic with a theological 'hermeneutic of the language-event' which attempts to relieve the interpretation and current appropriation of the biblical texts of the awkward problems associated with the historical facticity of the events transmitted by tradition and to reduce them to their existential relevance for present-day man.

2. Hermeneutical Theology

Gadamer's hermeneutic might be expected to show the influence of Rudolf Bultmann at a number of points. This influence seems to be perceptible particularly in the statement that the tradition confronts the interpreter with a 'claim'.[340] Another point of contact with Bultmann is Gadamer's description of the situation of understanding as based on the question which human existence necessarily poses.[341]

[340] See Gadamer, *Truth and Method*, pp. 321–25, esp. 324, where the claim of tradition is explicitly mentioned. Compare Bultmann's reference to a 'claim which confronts us in work' ('Das Problem der Hermeneutik' (1950), *Glauben und Verstehen*, vol. II, 1952, pp. 211–35, esp. p. 226). Bultmann refers in a similar way to the 'claim of the New Testament' (*Glauben und Verstehen*, vol. III, 1960, p. 32) but more frequently speaks of man's being 'addressed' by tradition, kerygma or Word of God, where 'address' describes the making of the claim (see Bultmann, *Faith and Understanding*, trans. L. P. Smith, London and New York, 1969, pp. 188-93, 204–09, 212, 218, 241, 287–88, 297–302; *Existence and Faith*, trans. S. M. Ogden, New York, 1959, London 1961, pp. 100–3.) Betti (*Hermeneutik*, p. 41; see also p. 31) associates Gadamer's idea of the claim of tradition with N. Hartmann's term 'demand' (N. Hartmann, *Das Problem des geistigen Seins*, 1933, pp. 140–1), though Gadamer himself speaks explicitly of the theological origin of the term in connection with hermeneutical questions (*Truth and Method*, p. 112).

[341] Though Gadamer interprets the uncertainty of existence in terms of the Platonic dialectic (*Truth and Method*, pp. 325–33).

According to Bultmann the person who attempts to understand approaches his text as a questioner because the structure of human existence itself is questionable. Bultmann believes that man exists essentially as a question about himself, and cannot – and here he differs from Heidegger – himself answer the question he is in his existence without failing to do justice to his existence.[342] Man is therefore driven by the structure of his existence to meet the claim which confronts him in the traditions by which he lives.

This is what is meant by saying that interpretation requires a 'relation of life . . . to the matter' which is given expression in the traditional text. The particular 'matter' about which information is sought from the text depends on the interest behind the interpretation. Bultmann calls this interest, which guides the interpretation but does not in any sense anticipate its findings, 'pre-understanding',[343] and this term has become notorious as a result of the widespread misunderstanding that it means a prejudgement on the content of the text. The interest which approaches the transmitted text may be psychological, aesthetic or historical. The most general or most fundamental interest which can govern an interpretation, however, is the interest 'in history as the sphere of life in which human existence moves and in which it acquires and develops its possibilities' (128). The evidence of history hands down to us, in Heidegger's words, 'the "monumental" possibilities of human existence'. Human existence is open to these 'by repetition' because of its orientation to the future. Our relationship to history is the 'repetition of the heritage of possibilities'.[344]

In interpreting New Testament texts, therefore, Bultmann examines 'the understanding of human existence expressed in the scripture' (232). The reason why 'existentialist interpretation' takes this approach becomes clear only when it is realised that,

[342] *Glauben und Verstehen*, vol. I, p. 304. Heidegger on the other hand says that Dasein itself answers the question of its potentiality-for-Being-a-whole 'as resolute' (*Being and Time*, p. 357).
[343] Bultmann, 'Das Problem der Hermeneutik', *Glauben und Verstehen*, vol. II, pp. 219–20. The immediately following page references in the text are also to this essay.
[344] Heidegger, *Being and Time*, pp. 448 and 442.

according to Bultmann, we know about God only through asking about ourselves. Bultmann's essay, 'What Does It Mean to Speak of God?' (1925), is fundamental both to this thesis and to the programme of giving an existentialist interpretation of Christian discourse about God. In this essay Bultmann tries to show that talk about God 'is only possible as talk of ourselves'. [345] For faith the converse is also true, namely that our existence 'is non-existent outside God', with the result that understanding our existence is also understanding God. For the unbelieving man, however, the possibility of understanding his existence through God's claim is a possibility which is excluded in advance by the exercise of his freedom; he seizes his freedom by giving his own answer to the question of his existence. [346]

Bultmann's interpretation of understanding in terms of the question inherent in human existence takes up Dilthey's insight that it is only by an understanding perception of history as an expression of the possibilities of human existence that we come to a knowledge of our own possibilities. [347] Bultmann, however, abandons Dilthey's psychological interpretation by restricting the pre-understanding to the openness of the enquiry which is answered by the claim of the traditional text. This idea of Bultmann's has been taken over by Gadamer in his development of Dilthey's idea of a history of influences, but Gadamer, unlike Bultmann, does not narrow down the claim of the transmitted text to the question of the authenticity or inauthenticity of existence. Gadamer, faithful to Dilthey's approach, never loses sight of the unlimited plurality of tradition. He therefore regards it as impossible to exhaust tradition simply by reflection. On the other hand, when Bultmann says that the New Testament writings are relevant only as a possibility of understanding human existence, what he is ultimately interested in is simply the opposition authenticity – inauthenticity. In 'obedience' to the kerygma the believer receives the authenticity of his existence which the unbeliever tries to obtain by the exercise of his freedom. Seen from the standpoint of faith, the freedom to

[345] R. Bultmann, *Faith and Understanding*, p. 61. The next quotation is from p. 63.

[346] *Glauben und Verstehen*, vol. I, p. 304. See above, n. 342.

[347] *Glauben und Verstehen*, vol. II, pp. 225–6.

dispose of one's own life appears as nothing less than the loss of the authentic possibility of existence, in other words, as sin. Sin is self will,[348] whereas faith is the surrender of the arbitrariness of existence. Gadamer has called this 'a privative experience of human self-determination'.[349] The phrase sums up very well the peculiar formalism of Bultmann's existentialist interpretation, which reduces the rich content of tradition to the thinness of this single fundamental act of existence.

Bultmann's idea of the claim of the traditional text, which has a theological counterpart in the view that man is addressed by the kerygma, has been used by E. Fuchs and G. Ebeling in their work on hermeneutic.[350] Fuchs has interpreted the way a text addresses man on the model of Heidegger's analysis of the call of conscience in *Being and Time*.[351] According to Fuchs, man's I is 'always intrinsically a called I' (133). As an I, it is called to itself. The particular forms in which the call goes out to man depend on history and tradition. Fuchs describes this situation in terms which point forwards to the hypostasisation of the language of tradition in Gadamer: 'History is essentially "saga", and therefore a history of language'. This means on the one hand that

---

[348] *Kerygma und Mythos*, vol. I, 1948, p. 41.

[349] Gadamer, *Truth and Method*, p. 477. I have myself tried to use Bultmann's view of the 'claim' of a text transmitted by tradition as a question to the self-understanding of the interpreter as the basis for a demonstration of the need to go beyond the limits of Bultmann's 'existentialist abridgement' of hermeneutic. Only by doing this can we connect the full content of the past situation out of which the text, with its understanding of self and the world, grew with the present of the interpreter while at the same time respecting its separate identity. The basis of the connection is the realisation that both have a place of their own in one and the same history ('Hermeneutic and Universal History', *Basic Concepts in Theology*, vol. 1, pp. 112–3).

[350] G. Ebeling, 'The Word of God and Hermeneutics' (1959), in Ebeling, *Word and Faith*, London and Philadelphia, 1963, pp. 305–32. E. Fuchs, *Hermeneutik*, 1954, 2nd ed. 1958, esp. pp. 137ff.

[351] Fuchs, *Hermeneutik*, p. 64. The quotations in the text are from pp. 133 and 137. J. M. Robinson, in his introduction to the collection of essays he edited with J. B. Cobb (*The New Hermeneutic*, New York and London, 1964) correctly points out that Fuchs has 'a somewhat different understanding of language from that of Heidegger himself' (p. 50). The main difference is that for Fuchs language and the call of conscience are connected with the claim of tradition.

history offers our self-understanding a 'linguistic challenge', on the other that this process involves 'that essential language in which we always answer 'with ourselves' (137).

Fuchs's work shows the effect of Bultmann's restricted view of hermeneutic, which limits the task of interpretation to the problem of self-understanding. As used by Fuchs, the formal alternative of authenticity – inauthenticity is even more clearly recognisable as an analogue and form of expression for the theological opposition of law and Gospel, guilt and forgiveness. In his arbitrariness man denies his guilt. Forgiveness frees man from this arbitrariness and so also from his guilt. In the process the message of forgiveness presupposes that man experiences himself as a moral being. Fuchs says that the New Testament makes a 'hermeneutical presupposition': it presupposes 'that man "relates" to himself and can therefore understand when he is addressed on the subject of himself. The New Testament makes this presupposition particularly when it assumes that we all know what *guilt* is'.[352] Perceptible behind this description is the pietistic derivation of theology from the experience of guilt, which, by showing the need for man to be forgiven, is also held to legitimate the Christian belief in forgiveness and justification. These arguments, which were characteristic of revival theology and persisted in W. Herrmann, appear in Fuchs's work in the guise of theological hermeneutic.[353]

A different starting-point nevertheless leads to a similar conclusion in a fundamental essay of Ebeling's written some years ago. Just as hermeneutic in general is the theory of understanding

---

[352] Fuchs, p. 117; cf. p. 56. See also R. Bultmann, 'Kirche und Lehre im Neuen Testament' (1929), *Glauben und Verstehen*, vol. I, p. 160.

[353] For details of the theological background to the development of hermeneutical theology, see my article, 'Die Krise des Ethischen und die Theologie', *Theologische Literaturzeitung* 87 (1962), pp. 7–16, which challenges particularly Ebeling's assertion of the 'self-evidence of ethics'. Ebeling's reply (*Wort und Glaube*, vol. II, 1969, pp. 42–55) did not dispute my description of the theological background. On the term 'hermeneutical theology', see also Ebeling's lecture 'Hermeneutische Theologie?' (1965), in *Wort und Glaube*, II, pp. 99–120. In this account the restrictive ethicising description of hermeneutic largely gives way to a more general definition of the task of theology as 'doing hermeneutical service to a previous word-event by keeping open its inherent hermeneutical potential' (p. 107).

and therefore of the word which discloses understanding in the act of discourse or as a verbal event,[354] so theological hermeneutic is defined as the theory of the word of God (323). But what is the word of God? According to Ebeling, it is 'not . . . any special supernatural Word', but simply 'true, proper, finally valid Word' (324). But this means that theological hermeneutic has the same subject as hermeneutic in general, that is 'word as word and understanding as understanding' (324). At this point, therefore, says Ebeling, theological hermeneutic must 'enter into conflict' with non-theological hermeneutic about what constitutes 'truth'.

Theology, says Ebeling, understands word historically, as the word-event which unlocks understanding. In this it corresponds to the understanding of word in ancient Israel, where 'the questions as to the content and power of words' were 'identical' (326).[355] Therefore – argues Ebeling – the basic structure of word is 'not statement – that is, an abstract variety of word-event – but message', and message in the sense not of *information* but of *communication*. As communication in this sense, word is not just a 'means of communication': 'where word happens rightly, existence is illumined' (327). These remarks follow the interpretation of message in Heidegger as the 'disclosing of existence', in contrast to the objectifying statement, which is dismissed as a 'derivative mode' of understanding and language.[356]

According to Ebeling, the true nature of word and language as the communication of existence and the word which opens up

---

[354] *Word and Faith*, pp. 323ff.

[355] In this idea both Ebeling and Fuchs show the influence of Heidegger's 'new hermeneutic', in which utterances are no longer, as they were for Dilthey, the objectifications of human life. According to the 'new hermeneutic', language itself 'prior to or without connection with any subjective intention seeks to emerge in meaningful utterance' (H. Franz, 'Das Wesen des Textes', *ZThK* 59 (1962), p. 204; cf. J. M. Robinson, *The New Hermeneutic*, pp. 45ff). The basis for such a theory of the subjectivity of language is, however, already present in Bultmann's idea of the Word of God as kerygma or 'address' (see esp. *Faith and Understanding*, pp. 287–8).

[356] *Being and Time*, p. 205, discussing the relation between (derivative) 'assertion' or statement and 'communication', which, as the 'disclosing of existence', makes language 'the Articulation of Being with one another understandingly'. See also the whole of section 34. Fuchs also treats the category of 'communication' as fundamental to the understanding of language (*Hermeneutik*, 1954, pp. 98ff).

existence is to be *promise*: 'As communication the word is promise' (327). This nature of the word is given its purest fulfilment where the speaker promises himself in his word and thereby opens a future to the other by awakening faith through his word. It now becomes clear that Ebeling sees the true nature of word and language in general fulfilled in the Gospel as the *promissio Dei*. It is now possible to make sense of the at first sight peculiar claim that the word of God, as *promissio Dei*, is nothing other than word as such, true and definitive word.

The Gospel as the word which unlocks existence and opens up the future comes into conflict, Ebeling explains, with the word of law, which closes off the future. So Ebeling ends with a conclusion similar to Fuchs's, which limits the work of the hermeneutical 'aid to understanding' to the function of 'communication' in the word, interpreted in the existentialist sense as the opening up of existence, to which there corresponds the alternative possibility of closing off existence. This conclusion, like Fuchs's, relates the meaning of language exclusively to ethical questions,[357] and turns out, not altogether surprisingly, to be identical with the Reformers' basic distinction between law and Gospel.

The foundations of this theological doctrine of understanding as an aid to man's self-understanding had already been laid by Bultmann. Bultmann had also held the view that existentialist interpretation was the fundamental form of interpretation in general. In his work too, existentialist interpretation is already directed towards the alternative of authentic — inauthentic self-understanding, and he had already linked this alternative with the Reformation teaching on law and Gospel. Fuchs and Ebeling took this approach further by linking the call of the kerygma with the question of the nature of language. Once the

---

[357] Ebeling, *Word and Faith*, pp. 331–2. In his subsequent writings Ebeling has been increasingly cautious. In particular, his *Einführung in die theologische Sprachlehre* (Tübingen 1971) discusses the complexity of the phenomenon of language, including those aspects stressed by linguistic analysis (pp. 183ff), in much more detail and more sympathetically than his previous works. The distinction between law and Gospel retains 'decisive importance' (p. 248), but now seems to be generalised to cover more than ethics alone. This second change is less clear in Ebeling's 'Erwägungen zu einer evangelischen Fundamentaltheologie', *ZThK* 67 (1970), pp. 516–7.

true meaning of language was defined as the 'communication' which unlocks existence, makes authentic existence possible, identifying the Gospel of the forgiveness of sins or of God's promise of himself with the true nature of language in general was an obvious step.

The difficulty of the claim that the true nature of language consists in the experience of guilt and forgiveness is that it takes no account of the complexity of the actual structures and contents of language. The abstract nature of this approach can be seen in the way its efforts to understand language exclude the whole area of the statement and therefore all the various factual contents of language,[357a] in favour of an exclusive concentration on the function of communicating existence. This recalls the similar reluctance of Heidegger and Gadamer to allow the statement form fundamental importance in human language. This devaluation of the statement must clearly be regarded as a characteristic of existentialist hermeneutic in both its philosophical and its theological forms, though the minimising of the function of the statement in analyses of language use does not necessarily mean the reduction of language and understanding to the formal either – or of authenticity and inauthenticity. In particular, the philosophy of existentialist hermeneutic does not connect this formal alternative with a particular historical tradition which it interprets as the opening up of authentic existence. This is much more the specific feature of existentialist hermeneutical theology, which identifies the formal (existentialist) concept of the revealing of authenticity with the actual historical content of the Christian Gospel. In contrast, Gadamer's hermeneutical philosophy never loses sight of the complexity of historical tradition, even though its understanding appropriation is dominated by man's questions about himself and takes the form of an application of the text to be interpreted to

[357a] Ebeling's more recent discussions of the question no longer exclude the statement element in language. In his *Einführung in die theologische Sprachlehre*, pp. 207ff, the interrelation and connection of the linguistic process and the content of utterances is distinguished and convincingly described in a way which clearly (though implicitly) corrects the earlier analysis. See also *Einführung*, pp. 112ff ('Sprache und Sache'). Ebeling's more recent works have broken out of the limitations of the existentialist hermeneutical approach to theology discussed in the previous section.

the immediate situation of the interpreter. However, for Gadamer, the identity of the interpreter in his present can itself be acquired only in the complexity of historical tradition. Man's self has no prior basis in an ethical reflection which is independent of history.

3. Interpretation of Language: Existentialist Hermeneutic and Linguistic Analysis

One starting-point for a critique of hermeneutical theology is its claim to be an accurate interpretation of the meaning of the biblical writings. Is it an adequate account of the primitive Christian kerygma to treat the message of the cross of Jesus as the word of judgment on man's arrogance, and the Christian message of Easter as the expression of the significance of the cross, as a way of saying that this judgment means liberation? Is the historical figure of Jesus fully represented when his message of the coming kingdom is neglected and he is treated merely as a preacher of forgiving and helping love? Critical questions of this sort have occupied most of the discussion about the programme of demythologisation. However, a critique of the attempt to base theology on hermeneutic can be directed equally at its general philosophical foundations. An example of this is the concentration of criticism on the narrowing of the understanding of language which has resulted from the devaluation of the linguistic function of the statement in hermeneutical theology and in the work of Heidegger and his successors. What is the cause of this narrowing? What justification is given for dismissing the statement as a 'derivative mode' of articulation of descriptive being-in-the-world?

Heidegger says that the content of a statement is 'cut off' from the 'reference-relations . . . of significance' which are the environment of the 'concernful understanding' to which the things of its own world are 'ready to hand' as equipment in a 'totality of involvements'.[358] Gadamer has taken over this

---

[358] *Being and Time*, pp. 200–1. These remarks on the 'derivative nature' of the statement amount to a judgment on it in advance of the discussion of its phenomenal structure in subsequent paragraphs.

position in his assertion that the unexpressed semantic horizon of the original proposition remains obscured in the statement because the statement isolates and so objectifies the meaning content it displays.

Underlying the description of the 'objectifying' statement as an isolation of contents, an isolation which by its action makes the contents capable of being identically reproduced and conveyed, is the assumption that man is essentially a native of a world that is ready to hand. Against this view it has been argued,[359] rightly, that what distinguishes man from the animals is precisely the fact that he, unlike them, is not part of an environment in which he is at home in such a way that the things of his world, in their original state, are to hand. It is truer to say that man is open to the world, and therefore by nature foreign to it. He is adapted to the world not by behavioural mechanisms in the normal sense, but by his intelligence, which requires him to establish a relation between himself and the world, just as he has to construct his own environment by producing a culture. It is only in the cultural world created by his mastery of the natural conditions of his existence that man can feel at home, feel that things are to hand. But the cultural world is fragile. The primal threat to man can always reappear when his cultural world is shaken. This means that man's original relation to things, prior to the creation of any culture, is characterised not by dealings with things ready formed, as Heidegger describes it, but more by a detachment largely freed from instinctual pressures which allows things to be seen as themselves, in all their many aspects, and thus as self-subsistent, existing as the unity of their qualities. This situation supports the assumption that imagining things as objective is in fact a characteristic feature of the specifically human relation to the world. If this is so, the specific detachment of man's characteristic relation to the world would be expected to show itself in the representational function of language, which is most highly developed in the statement. It is therefore questionable whether the representational function of language should be regarded as a secondary factor in man's understanding of himself in his relation to the world. Even conversation, which

[359] For example, by M. Landmann, *Philosophische Anthropologie*, 1955, pp. 215–6.

Gadamer takes as the paradigm of the hermeneutical event, always operates in statements and sets of statements, and indeed without this there could be no communication about the same thing between the parties to a conversation. If one party is to understand what the other wishes to communicate to him as precisely what the other intends to communicate, this presupposes the separability of the content of the communication from the subjective characteristics of both speaker and hearer, in other words, a degree of objectification sufficient to allow the content to be communicated unchanged. It is the social nature of language which encourages the element of objectification in speaking and stimulates the effort for objectivity. At the same time, the need to communicate oneself helps to bring about a situation in which man reaches an understanding of himself only in others, and not only in other people, but also in understanding the things and situations with which he is in contact.

However, the existentialist devaluation of the statement is based on an important, though possibly overweighted, fact. This is expressed in Heidegger's remark that every proposition is part of the referential frame of a 'totality of involvements' and that its meaning is rooted in this totality. Gadamer has developed this idea into the thesis that every proposition includes within itself an 'unexpressed horizon of meaning'. This is a convincing view, with far-reaching consequences, but not necessarily in conflict with the factor of objectification. Rather, one of the peculiarities of language is that in the process of speaking the expressed and the unexpressed, the defined and the undefined, are all held together. There is therefore no need for the 'unexpressed horizon of meaning' in what is said to be determined in advance in the totality of involvements of an essentially available world. It is more plausible to suppose that the referential framework of every proposition and every experience of meaning fades into the indeterminacy of a totality of meaning which acquires precise boundaries only within the narrower confines of actual experience and speech.[360]

[360] There is no room to go into this here. The starting-point for a demonstration would be the indefiniteness of words, which acquire their definiteness (which is in any case always limited) only from the proposition and the wider context of speech. The fact that even in the context of a

In contrast to the interpretation of language offered by existentialist hermeneutic, analytical philosophies of language take the statement, and therefore the referential function of language, as their starting-point. This is true above all of logical positivism, but Wittgenstein too, in his *Tractatus,* took the statement, that is, the assertive proposition, as the basic form of language in general. According to Wittgenstein, the proposition is an image of the state of affairs among objects. That is its meaning.[361] The individual words in a proposition are names (3.202). They name the objects which are connected in the state of affairs. Since images cannot be made of isolated objects, but only of states of affairs, the words which are names *mean* their objects only in the context of the proposition, which corresponds in the arrangement of its words to the arrangement of objects in the state of affairs (3.21).

As K. O. Apel has stressed, Wittgenstein's early view of the meaning of propositions as images of states of affairs is an attack on the claim of traditional (for example, metaphysical) texts to have meaning.[362] In the hermeneutical tradition, on the other hand, the meaningfulness of the material to be interpreted was never called in question, with the result that 'from Luther to Dilthey it was the claim of the works to be interpreted to possess meaning and truth that remained the standard of all understanding in hermeneutic' (51). This remark makes it clear that the emphasis on the statement-structure of language is connected, in contrast to hermeneutic, with a strongly critical attitude to tradition.

Apel has shown that Wittgenstein's early work removed the hermeneutical problem of communication between individuals through his programme of creating a single language which

---

proposition words only partly lose their indefiniteness shows that while the uttered proposition or propositional context may point beyond itself to unexpressed semantic networks, it does so only in a vague way. Only in the narrower range of meaning of a proposition does this reference acquire a more precise structure.

[361] Wittgenstein, *Tractatus Logico-philosophicus,* 2.221. Subsequent references in the text are to the numbered paragraphs of the *Tractatus.*

[362] K. O. Apel, 'Wittgenstein und das Problem des hermeneutischen Verstehens', *ZThK,* 63 (1966), pp. 49–87, quoted from p. 57. The two subsequent quotations are from p. 51.

would reflect the world; if this could replace natural languages it would automatically put individuals in communication. But both in the history of logical positivism and in Wittgenstein's personal development, it has turned out that the hermeneutical problem of establishing communication could not be so easily bypassed. Logical positivism's attempts to construct a single language capable of unambiguous analysis have failed because every formalised language ultimately presupposes ordinary language; it is only in ordinary language that the meaning of its rules and axioms can be explained.[362a] In his late work, the posthumously published *Philosophical Investigations* (1953), Wittgenstein gave up the idea of a single world-reflecting language and made ordinary language itself the object of his philosophical study. He did not, however, treat ordinary language as a single entity, a unitary model of the world, but as a plurality of language-games. The concept of the language-game originated in Wittgenstein's mathematical work and is related to the concept of calculation.[363] As used by Wittgenstein, it emphasises that 'the *speaking* of a language is part of an activity or a form of life'. As examples of such language games, in addition to 'naming' and 'explaining', Wittgenstein gives the following rough list: 'Giving orders, and obeying them; describing the appearance of an object, or giving its measurements; constructing an object from a description (a drawing); reporting an event . . . play-acting . . . guessing riddles . . . translating . . . asking, thanking, cursing, greeting, praying.'[364] These are all activities which belong to a particular social situation in ordinary life. Wittgenstein uses the concept of the game because every game has its own rules. This crucial feature connects the language-game with calculation, formalised language.[365] The activities named as examples of language-games are also carried out according to certain rules, rules which are not arbitrary, but connected with the character of the particular activity in its area of life. The rules are also reflected in the way we speak. It is in this sense that we must understand Wittgenstein's

[362a] Apel, 'Wittgenstein'.

[363] See K. Wuchterl, *Struktur und Sprachspiel bei Wittgenstein*, 1969, pp. 110ff.

[364] Wittgenstein, *Philosophical Investigations*, Oxford 1963, para. 23. References to the *Philosophical Investigations* are to its numbered paragraphs.

[365] K. Wuchterl, pp. 132ff. Cf. Wittgenstein, *Philosophical Investigations*, 81.

statement that 'the meaning of a word is its use in the language' (43). Meaning is no longer defined in cognitive terms as the representation of pre-existing objects, but pragmatically, in connection with a particular for of activity, in the context of which people speak in a particular way. Wittgenstein's thesis is that language is rooted in such forms of everyday life and has a determinable meaning only in relation to them. Consequently he retains his critical attitude to metaphysics in spite of the change in his view of language since the *Tractatus*: 'What *we* do is to bring words back from their metaphysical to their everyday use' (116)

Criticising the breaking down of language into a plurality of language-games, Apel argues that this too – though in a different way from the unitary language of the *Tractatus* – ignores the problem of how linguistic communication can take the form of the elimination of incomprehension. Even in Wittgenstein's later work, says Apel, the hermeneutical problem is left out of account. We understand only when we are already taking part in the appropriate language game, participating in the form of life in which language is used in this way. But how does one obtain this understanding if one is not already familiar with the way of life? In practice, Wittgenstein always assumes familiarity, in his early work familiarity with the unitary world-reflecting language, and later familiarity with the various forms of life or language-games. The process of communication which can lead to this familiarity, or restore common understanding when it has broken down, is, however, never discussed by Wittgenstein.[366] As a result, he also ignores the historical nature of language, ways of life and language-games (Apel, 86). In this way, because of the lacuna here, linguistic analysis itself shows the need for hermeneutical processes in communication, and also for a hermeneutical approach to the investigation of language. On the other hand, linguistic analysis has revealed particular aspects of language which had certainly been neglected in existentialist hermeneutic from Heidegger to Gadamer. This is true both of the object-reference of language in the world-reflecting language of the *Tractatus*,[367] and of the connection of language and social

---

[366] K. O. Apel, 'Wittgenstein', pp. 82, 84–85. Subsequent page references in the text are to this article.

life-forms in Wittgenstein's later philosophy. The hermeneutical
approach must also incorporate these aspects of language. This is
what Apel sets out to do in his hermeneutical critique and
reworking of Wittgenstein's investigations. According to Apel,
understanding and communication have to do with the
perception of objects and the reciprocal adjustment of behaviour
in the context of social situations. Language and communication
are not normally concerned directly with self-understanding and
the authenticity of existence. The disclosure of existence
generally takes place only indirectly, by means of
communication about the world of objects and about coexistence
in social situations. The attention paid by Dilthey, in his
pioneering work in hermeneutic, to the objectification of life in
linguistic and other expressions of life makes his work more
suited to this general hermeneutical task than existentialist
hermeneutic with its concentration on a view of language as a
communication which discloses existence and its rejection of the
statement.

If the approach of linguistic analysis can be regarded as in
many respects a corrective to the interpretation of language put
forward by existentialist hermeneutic, there can also be seen in
the later work of Wittgenstein a remarkable convergence with
the analysis of understanding offered by Heidegger in *Being and
Time*. Heidegger's interpretation of understanding as the
openness of an available world comes close to the pragmatic
approach of Wittgenstein's language-games. The question asked
of Heidegger, how such an available world came into being, is
raised in a similar way by the life-forms and associated
language-games of Wittgenstein's analysis. Language is required
for the initial creation of such a cultural world and its life forms.
It can therefore also provide the power to transform them and is
not limited to being a means of communication in a familiar
sphere of life.

Although Heidegger's later statements on language move
away from it again, this convergence explains why both
Wittgenstein's later linguistic philosophy and Gadamer's

---

[367] Even in his later period, Wittgenstein regarded the language of the
Tractatus as valid as one language-game among others: see *Philosophical
Investigations*, 353, on 'verification'.

hermeneutic have been criticised for being expressions of an uncritical acceptance of linguistic tradition. It is true that in Wittgenstein's later work everyday language plays an authoritative role similar to that of tradition in Gadamer's hermeneutic. In both, factual knowledge, which is rooted in the representational function of language and is given linguistic form in the objectifying statement, is an indispensable corrective. Objectifying knowledge articulated in statements is essential to a critical analysis of and a critical attitude to traditional language and the institutions of our social environment. In addition, however, even everyday communication is possible, as was emphasised previously, only by means of objectification in the message; it must be communication about situations described in statements. The content intended by the speaker must be capable of being separated with sufficient precision from this subject and of being perceived by another as the same content. This separability of the content of a thought from its link with a particular subject necessarily implies its objectification. However, this affects only one part of the complex of meaning in which the idea first appears, and only a subsidiary aspect of the state of affairs referred to, and therefore the 'unexpressed horizon of meaning' in which all linguistic utterances, including statements, are always rooted is indeed crucial to a correct understanding. This unexpressed horizon can often be grasped automatically when the hearer shares the situation of the speaker or can insert himself into it. He then 'understands' what is said. Even in this case, however, understanding normally starts from what is actually said, the content communicated and inevitably objectified in the act of communication.

In cases in which understanding presents difficulties, hermeneutical clarification of the complex of meaning, and therefore a further objectification of the horizon of meaning left unexpressed in the original utterance, is necessary. The interpretation explicitates the nuances and associations at work in the utterance, often unknown to the speaker or author. The interpretation assists understanding by putting this horizon into an explicit statement. 'The interpreted text is precisely the text which has been *objectified* with respect to the previously unanticipated proportions of its horizon of meaning.' [368]

4. Hermeneutic and Dialectic

K. O. Apel has attempted to demonstrate the necessity of a hermeneutical approach in his criticism of the interpretation of language offered by linguistic analysis as an alternative to that of existentialist hermeneutic. In the process, hermeneutic as Apel understands it becomes something different from what it was for Heidegger and Gadamer. As early as 1963 Apel was maintaining the possibility even in the human sciences of having theoretical knowledge which was not dogmatic and not dominated by unexaminable prejudices.[369] Later, in 1968 in a criticism of Gadamer, he remarked that the idea of 'overthrowing tradition' by historical understanding did contain an element of truth, not in the sense of 'overthrowing history totally as a medium of tradition', but in that of 'the overthrowing of specific "traditions", i.e., their contents, deriving from a pre-industrial or pre-scientific age'.[370] Apel has called for the task of understanding to be re-established as a theoretical one, involving a 'possibly only provisional objectification and distancing of the meaning to be understood', distinct from the determination of its present validity, and for it to be spearated from the task of application, which, he says, belongs not to the human sciences but to philosophy – 'in particular to the philosophy of history' (38). The 'implicit assumption that the application of their understanding was obligatory', whether in the Marxist or in the existentialist sense, produced 'exactly the same ideological corruption in the human sciences as that which resulted from the positivist refusal to acknowledge historical involvement as one condition of the possibility of their understanding meaning' (38). Apel thus gives the activity of hermeneutic a different context from Heidegger and Gadamer, namely an emphatically theoretical reflection on the part of the human sciences.

J. Habermas has done the same thing in a different way. Like

---

[368] W. Pannenberg, 'Hermeneutic and Universal History', in *Basic Concepts in Systematic Theology,* vol. 1, p. 184.

[369] See Apel's review of Gadamer's hermeneutic in *Hegel-Studien* 2 (1962), pp. 314ff, esp. p. 321.

[370] K. O. Apel, 'Scientistik, Hermeneutik, Ideologiekritik', *Wiener Jahrbuch für Philosophie* I (1968), p. 37. The subsequent quotations are from p. 38.

Apel, Habermas has tried to demonstrate the need for a hermeneutical approach by means of a critical comparison with non-hermeneutical positions. In his case these were not the philosophy of linguistic analysis, but the whole spectrum of attempts, from different points of view, to provide a theoretical basis for the social sciences.[371] Against the behaviourists, Habermas insists, with Weber and Talcott Parsons, that social behaviour 'belongs to the class of intentional actions which we understand by reconstructing their meaning' (13). But Habermas rejects a Parsons-type functionalist reduction of the intentionality of action to a given social system, since, in Habermas's view, this approach ignores the 'reactive constraints' in the life of society (94) and the element in individual meaning-intentions which looks beyond the incomplete present (92–3). With reference to linguistics and analytical philosophy, Habermas stresses the importance of 'the tendency inherent in linguistic practice to transcend itself' in the direction of a 'unity of reason in the plurality of languages' (151). The fact that the historical *movement* of linguistic communication became the subject-matter of hermeneutic in Gadamer's work is the basis of Habermas's interest in this form of hermeneutic (152–3). He takes over the description of the process of communication as a fusion of horizons (261ff), but criticises Gadamer's 'rehabilitation of prejudice in its own right' (283), and the connected thesis of the predominance of tradition. The 'substance of the historically pre-given' does not remain 'unaffected by being taken up into reflection' (284). 'Gadamer,' he says, 'ignores the power of reflection shown in understanding' (283). For Habermas, one of the proofs of this power is that reflection can 'also reject the claims of traditions' (284). The right of reflection ('the inalienable legacy bequeathed to us from the spirit of the eighteenth century by German idealism', 285) 'demands a frame of reference which transcends the continuity of tradition; only then can the process of tradition be criticised' (285).[372]

---

[371] J. Habermas, *Zur Logik der Sozialwissenschaften*, Frankfurt 1971 (originally published in 1967 as Beiheft 5 of the *Philosophische Rundschau*). The subsequent page references in the text are to this work.

[372] In his reply, 'Rhetorik, Hermeneutik and Ideologiekritik' (see note 339 above), Gadamer called for the 'exposure' of 'the opposition between a

Habermas's 'frame of reference' which allows us to defend ourselves against the superior power of tradition is supplied by universal history (290), which Habermas regards as the basis of all historical understanding. According to Habermas: 'For all practical purposes, historians anticipate *final states* which enable them to organise the multiplicity of events into separate histories which give some guidance for action.'[373] In the process, expectations constantly build up 'the fragments of existing traditions hypothetically into the totality of a pre-understood universal history, in the light of which each relevant event can in principle be as fully described as is possible for the practically effective self-understanding of a social life-world' (273). The anticipatory expectations have first to create the 'whole' in the context of which the 'parts' of the historically given have their significance: 'only because we sketch out the provisional end of a referential system from within the perspective of practical life can

---

tradition which is still alive and naturally growing and its reflective appropriation' as 'dogmatic', as the expression of a dogmatic 'objectivism which also distorts the concept of reflection' (p. 68). It must certainly be recognised (as Habermas does, 'Der Universalitätsanspruch der Hermeneutik' (1970), quoted as in *Hermeneutik und Ideologiekritik, 1971*, p. 158) that reflection itself is always determined by its historical situation and therefore by the process of tradition. As a result of this, even criticism which is a product of reflection cannot escape from the process of tradition in its totality – even when it thematises it as a totality. Nevertheless, even if reflection cannot escape from or overthrow history, it can 'bring about the overthrow of particular traditions', in the sense of their contents, deriving from a pre-industrial or pre-scientific age (K. O. Apel, 'Scientistik, Hermeneutik, Ideologiekritik', quoted as in *Hermeneutik und Ideologiekritik*, p. 34). Gadamer's protest against the charge of 'turning cultural tradition into an absolute' (loc. cit., p. 71; see also pp. 296ff) would be convincing only if the 'productive factor in understanding' (*Truth and Method*, p. 111) were understood not just in terms of a 'history of influences', as concerned with the still unappropriated meaning of traditional texts, but also in terms of the open future of history, which gives the interpreter his freedom. It has to be thought of as a productive function of an understanding 'which necessarily includes critique and forgetting', as H. R. Jauss puts it in his essay on the aesthetics of reception (*Literaturgeschichte als Provokation*, 1970, p. 189). It is this freedom of the interpreter that makes critical reflection on tradition in relation to a future which is still open possible, and it is by appropriating tradition in its otherness that the interpreter achieves awareness of his own situation.

[373] Habermas, *Zur Logik der Sozialwissenschaften*, p. 273; see also p. 271.

interpretations of events organised into a history in virtue of a projected end, and interpretations of parts decipherable only as fragments of an anticipated totality, have any informational content at all for that practical life' (275).

In an attempt to solve the problems left by Gadamer's book, Habermas is here transferring to the understanding of history G. H. Mead's idea of the anticipation of meaning as the basis of communication between human beings. The primary function of the anticipation of the totality of history in terms of its 'provisional' end is, for Habermas, the exposure and elimination of existing distortions in communication. This is a subject to which Habermas constantly returns. Anticipations of a 'final state' (273), as 'the final state of a formative process' (303), open up a critical understanding of the present. Habermas's constant model for such a critical social philosophy is psychoanalysis (see *Sozialwissenschaften*, 297–305). He wants to do for the problems of society what Freud did for the problems of individual life. Like psychoanalysis, critical social philosophy must be 'liberating reflection'.[374]

In his essay on 'The Claim of Hermeneutic to Universality', Habermas criticises Gadamer's 'hypostasisation of the continuity of tradition' and the 'ontologisation of language' which goes with it. He has a deep suspicion that consensus in the context of traditional language may be 'a forced product of pseudo-communication' (153). What guarantee is there that there could not be a 'systematic distortion' of communication as a result of which men could no longer understand their own true intentions? Hermeneutic as developed by Gadamer is no help here. Instead, we need to anticipate 'the concept of a truth measured by idealised agreement sought in unrestricted and unconstrained communication' and 'the structure of coexistence in unconstrained communication'. Only against the background of such an 'anticipation of right living' (154) will the distortions of the present state become visible.

---

[374] On this, see especially the last chapter of Habermas's *Knowledge and Human Interests*, and Habermas's contribution to the Gadamer *Festschrift* ('Der Universalitäsanspruch der Hermeneutik', *Hermeneutik und Dialektik*, I, 1970, reprinted in *Hermeneutik und Ideologiekritik*, 1971, pp. 120–59. The immediately following page references in the text are to the reprint in the latter volume).

In place of a hermeneutic which merely 'understands meaning subjectively', Habermas wants to put a theory of society combining the approach of hermeneutic with the insights of Marx and Freud.[375] Such a theory, 'understanding meaning objectively', would see society as a formative process moving towards a final state of 'right living' in unconstrained communication. In his book *Knowledge and Human Interests,* originally published in 1968, Habermas distinguishes this approach from the 'critiques' produced by positivism, pragmatism and historical hermeneutic. Nevertheless, the method of the critical social theory which is his aim is fundamentally and avowedly hermeneutical.[376] Habermas refers to 'hermeneutical understanding expanded into criticism',[377] and confines his attack to a hermeneutic which understands meaning subjectively.[378] The expansion of hermeneutic into criticism is brought about through the previously mentioned anticipation of the goal of history as that of the process of the formation of mankind. This means that Habermas can describe his method of criticising present society in the light of an anticipated totality of human history as a dialectical one.

Dialectic and hermeneutic share the fundamental feature of being concerned with the analysis of the interrelation of wholes and parts.[379] However, whereas hermeneutic sees the whole only as a horizon which establishes the meaning of all the details and whose transformations initiate the continuing process of interpretation, and can therefore remain uncertain about the final form of this whole, dialectic considers the totality as such, without which the individual element could have no definitive meaning. Because dialectic analyses the categories which

---

[375] Habermas, 'Analytische Wissenschaftstheorie und Dialektik' (1963), in *Der Positivismusstreit in der deutschen Soziologie,* 1969, p. 164.

[376] *Positivismusstreit,* p. 164.

[377] *Hermeneutik und Ideologiekritik,* p. 158.

[378] *Positivismusstreit,* p. 164.

[379] This idea, in a formulation of Adorno's, is Habermas's starting-point in the article 'Analytische Wissenschaftstheorie und Dialektik' (*Positivismusstreit,* p. 155). On the same subject see K. Kosik, *Die Dialektik des Konkreten,* 1967. Stalin, in his essay, *On Dialectical and Historical Materialism,* also discusses the relation of part and whole in first place among the 'basic features of the dialectical method'.

hermeneutic applies in its practical work, it has to make explicit the totality which hermeneutic assumes only implicitly and for that reason can leave uncertain. This has always led to the accusation that dialectic claims a totality which goes beyond the limitations of human experience and human knowledge and therefore can only be ideological. This criticism has been made of Habermas both by positivists, more accurately by critical rationalists, and by Gadamer.

Hans Albert has described the dialectical theory of the social sciences outlined by Habermas in 1963 in his essay attacking Popper, 'Analytical Philosophy of Science and Dialectic', as 'a myth of total reason'.[380] The description refers to Habermas's use of the category of totality when he defines the concept of a dialectical theory of society as one which asserts 'the dependence of individual phenomena on the totality'.[381] In this essay, however, Habermas had formulated his position in a way which made it vulnerable to criticism by Albert on a number of points. In the first place it was left unclear how dialectic obtains the idea of the totality of society 'in the dimension of a process of development unique as a whole and irreversible in its stages' (163). In this essay Habermas did not yet consistently use the concept of anticipation,[382] but relied mainly on alleged 'tendencies' in historical development: 'If history itself is to be theoretically explicable in hermeneutic's objective understanding of meaning, the study of history must . . . become open to the future. In the tendencies of its historical development, society reveals itself . . . first in terms of what it is not' (165; cf. 164). These tendencies were also claimed to be 'laws' of the historical movement of society, though naturally laws of a different kind from those allowed by the 'restrictive concept of law' used in the analytical sciences (163). Popper had already attacked reference to laws in terms so characteristic of traditional marxism,[383] and

[380] H. Albert, 'Der Mythos der totalen Vernunft' (1964), included among the essays in Der Positivismusstreit in der deutschen Soziologie, pp. 193–234.

[381] Habermas, 'Analytische Wissenschaftstheorie und Dialektik', Positivismusstreit, p. 163. Page-references in the text to Albert's and Habermas's articles are to this volume.

[382] The hermeneutical 'anticipation of totality' is mentioned only once (p. 161), in passing.

[383] K. Popper, The Poverty of Historicism, London 1957.

now Albert asked, reasonably enough, 'What does the logical structure of these laws look like ... and how can they be examined? In what sense can a law relating to a specific historical totality, to a unique and irreversible process, be anything but a singular statement?' [384]

The idea of 'laws' as a description of the 'tendencies' in the unique historical process of human history involves real difficulties, and by demolishing it Albert imagines himself to have also eliminated the idea of totality, which he regards as unclear both in itself and in its applications. Habermas also made this criticism all the easier by a number of formulations in his essay. First, he claimed that the dialectical concept of whole 'transcends ... the limits of formal logic' (155). The second assertion was that there existed a distinction between system and totality which, however, could not be 'directly defined' (156) because it was necessarily 'broken down ... in the language of formal logic and transcended in the language of dialectic'. Thirdly, he called for the social sciences to make sure in advance that their categories were 'appropriate to their object' (157).

1. The announcement that 'the dialectical concept of the whole transcends the limits of formal logic' (198) is, in Albert's view, indicative of an 'immunisation strategy' by means of which 'Habermas tries to deny the possibility of giving a logical analysis of his concept of totality' (199). In his reply to Albert's criticism Habermas says on this point merely that reasoning in dialectic 'gets into tangles', 'not because it ignores the rules of formal logic, but by following them particularly stubbornly'. [385] However, he neither withdraws his claim that the dialectical concept of the whole transcends the limits of formal logic nor shows how this concept arises out of reason's stubborn attachment to the laws of formal logic. To this extent Albert can claim with some justice that the 'question of what dialectic really consists of ... and what methods it uses has received no answer in his reply'. [386] It is hard to see why Habermas did not describe the

[384] H. Albert, 'Der Mythos der totalen Vernunft', pp. 210–11. The following references are to this essay.

[385] Habermas, *Gegen einen positivistisch halbierten Rationalismus* (1964).

[386] Albert, 'Im Rücken des Positivismus?', *Positivismusstreit*, p. 304. On the other hand, the remark omitted from the quotation above, namely that

relation of part and whole as a logical one which can be shown
to exist in all experience of meaning and so to belong to the
foundations of hermeneutical logic as laid by Dilthey. Whatever
the reason, Habermas's statement that the dialectical concept of
the whole transcends the limits of formal logic has only caused
confusion.

Albert also regards the contrast between totality and system as
another example of diplomatic immunity from the laws of logic
on behalf of the basic concepts of dialectic.

2. Whereas E. Nagel defines the concept of whole in terms of
that of a system or of a theory which describes a system, Habermas claims a difference between dialectical totality and system. It
becomes clear that this claim is an expression of the view that the
concept of system remains 'as external to the area of experience
analysed' as the theoretical propositions which articulate it,
whereas the social sciences must first examine the appropriateness
of their categories to their objects (157) because the subject itself
belongs to the area of objects to be analysed (158). This means,
Habermas believes, that there is 'this revenge of the object . . . in
the social sciences in that the subject, in the middle of its attempt
to understand, remains trapped by the pressures of the very
sphere it is trying to analyse'.[387]

The view of the concept of system as a category which remains
external to the area of experience it describes also explains the
suspicion with which Habermas greeted the use of the concept of
system by Niklaus Luhmann. The truth is that theoretical systems
composed of abstract and universal nomothetical statements are
always external to reality, which is always actual and individual.
But this 'externality' means only that theoretical systems of this
sort are limited to abstract and universal statements which are
unable to grasp the unique process of history and the
individuality of its components. The concept of system itself is

---

Habermas has not indicated 'what advantages [dialectic] has over other views'
(p. 304), is not justified. It should be sufficiently clear that Habermas claims
that only dialectic makes it possible to understand individual items in the
context of the actual totality of history.

[387] Habermas, 'Analytische Wissenschaftstheorie', p. 158. Note the real
similarity with the problems of liberating reflection, which have a parallel in
psychoanalysis.

not limited to this sphere of abstract universals. Systems of this sort, built out of abstract theories, are not to be confused with the cybernetic, self-regulating systems which exist as specific totalities. Among these there is a special class of 'open systems' which can change themselves by including their environment. To the extent that living beings can be described as 'open systems' of this sort, the concept of system can no longer be presented as external to the area of experience analysed. On the contrary, in this use the concept of system describes no more than the actual totality which Habermas is attempting to grasp with the resources of dialectic. It is true that Habermas is interested not just in the totality of the individual but also in that of society, but it is quite conceivable that societies and historical processes as phases of social life should be describable as open systems, even though neither society nor a historical period is present to itself in the same way as a conscious human individual.

In this sense, therefore, even the totality of the process of human history as a whole can be logically described as a system and so is amenable to Nagel's analysis of the category of whole.

3. The positive counterpart of Habermas's rejection of the concept of system as 'external' is his statement that the subjectivity of the investigator in the social sciences is part of the field to be investigated, which means that these sciences must 'begin by examining the appropriateness of their categories to their object' (157). Their procedures disclose 'an object of whose structure I must in fact have *previously* understood something, if the categories selected are not to be external to it' (158). This is what forms the 'circle' which can 'be analysed dialectically only by working from the natural hermeneutic of the social world'. Consequently in this field the 'hermeneutical articulation of meaning' replaces the 'hypothetico-deductive system of propositions' characteristic of the analytical sciences. Habermas's use of the term 'pre-understanding' (189; cf. 181) is clearly to be understood in terms of this pre-understanding of the object, which here refers not only, as with Bultmann, to an existential relation to the matter in the sense of an open interest in the subject, but also to the 'directional understanding of meaning' (189) which 'programmatically' guides the individual analyses. Habermas detects such a pre-understanding at work even in

Popper's basic propositions, which, according to him, derive their 'empirical validity from a *previous* integration of individual perceptions into the mass of unproblematic and by and large established convictions' (182). This is meant not as a criticism but as a description of an ineradicable element in knowledge, and one which requires particular attention in the social sciences because in these the subject and object of theory construction coincide. 'Previous experience of society steers the drafting of the theory' of that society (160). Albert sees in this the danger that 'inherited errors ... may also to some extent influence the "steering"' (207). With such claims, Habermas, he feels, is coming close to the 'linguistic tendency' of Wittgensteinian linguistic analysis, whose methods, in Albert's view, 'are likely to turn the knowledge embodied in everyday language into dogma' (204).

Habermas, however, in his controversy with Gadamer, has himself taken on the role of spokesman for the critics of linguistic tradition, and even in the statements which Albert criticises there is a repeated emphasis on the corrective influence of theory on the previous familiarity with the object out of which the theory itself grew. Nevertheless Habermas's arguments are open to misunderstanding in so far as they fail to distinguish the 'hermeneutical anticipation of totality' (161) from the previous familiarity with the object and the 'directional' pre-understanding arising out of this. This distinction is necessary, however, if only because in comparison with the indeterminacy of pre-understanding the dialectical *preconcept* of totality is marked by theoretical precision. It is the preconcept, which takes as its subject the total system of the life and meaning of a society, which first makes a (hypothetical) definition of the totality which is presupposed in the prior human familiarity with the social context of life in a more implicit but still indeterminate form. If this distinction between preunderstanding and preconcept (or preliminary model) is kept in mind, the circular appearance of hermeneutical arguments disappears: however much an *existential relation* with the matter with which the interpretation is concerned is presupposed in establishing the interpretation, the explicit preconcept always remains distinguishable from the matter as a hypothetical description of its structure. Although therefore the subjectivity of the social scientist – or historian or anthropologist – is always part of his professional field of investigation, this in no way presupposes what can be discovered only by his investigation. The fact that the social scientist's subjectivity itself falls within the field for which he develops theories does not prejudice the testing of explanatory models he puts forward, but is merely a reason for the requirement that, once they deal with society as a whole or have general sociological implications, they must pass the additional test of application to themselves. In other words, the fact that the social scientist himself is one of the objects about which he constructs theories is not identical with the phenomenon of pre-understanding in the sense of a previous familiarity with these objects. The previous familiarity with his subject-matter should be regarded less as a required qualification for the social scientist than as an existentially unavoidable factor which makes no difference, for better or worse, to the validity of a theoretical model. On the one hand it is the psychological basis for the formulation of hypothetical constructions, and on the other it is the object of analysis when it is the process by which these constructions are produced which is being studied. In neither case is there any obvious reason why it should prevent the appropriateness of sociological categories to their objects from being tested as a second-order operation within the relevant theory in the same way as other hypothetical statements are tested against the appropriate material.

To sum up the results of our discussion of these three points, we see that the dialectical concept of whole as a social totality can perfectly well be represented theoretically with a hypothetical description. It is also describable as an individual system and is wholly susceptible of logical analysis; that is to say, it does not need to be removed, as it was by Habermas, from the competence of logic. But what leads Habermas to isolate and mystify dialectic in this way? What makes him reluctant to point to the presence of the concept of totality in the structure of the perception of meaning itself, which always includes an implicit assumption of totality as a prerequisite of perceiving anything at all as meaningful? An analysis of the perception of meaning would have shown that the introduction of the idea of totality is

neither a dispensable luxury nor an arrogant claim to total
knowledge, not a myth of total reason, but merely a matter of
explicitly recognising a process which takes place implicitly in all
perception of meaning and therefore in all experience whatever.
That is to say, it involves making the semantic whole of the
human perception of meaning, which is always implicit in
experience, explicit in such a way that hypotheses could be
formulated about it which could then be judged by their ability
to integrate individual perceived meanings into their contexts of
meaning. Why did Habermas not set about justifying his concept
of dialectical totality in this way?

An answer to this question can be given only if we remember
Habermas's peculiarly ambivalent attitude to hermeneutic. The
approach to a justification of the concept of dialectical totality
outlined above consists in showing that it is an *implication* of the
perception of meaning. Habermas, on the other hand, introduces
dialectical totality as a *complement* to the hermeneutical thematic
and can then no longer derive it from the inherent logic of
hermeneutic. Habermas's procedure is explained by his aim of
producing a foundation for a social theory of action. This aim is
clearly associated with his tendency to classify the understanding
or perception of meaning as simply one aspect of the concept of
action.[388] It is at this point that Gadamer's counter-criticisms and
questions to Habermas begin. Gadamer attacks the classification
of the understanding of meaning as merely an aspect of social
reality. 'It is a reduction of the universality of the hermeneutical
dimension to set one area of intelligible meaning ("cultural
tradition") apart from other determinants of social reality which
are recognisable merely as active factors.'[389] According to
Gadamer, Habermas has not seen that hermeneutic is by no
means concerned only with subjectively intended meaning. 'The
only reason', says Gadamer, 'why the hermeneutical problem is
so universal and fundamental to all inter-human experience,
whether of history or of the present, is that meaning can be
perceived even where it was not intended' (ibid.). What
Habermas calls 'depth hermeneutic', that is, the idea that 'the

[388] See above, pp. 75ff.
[389] *Hermeneutik und Ideologiekritik*, p. 70. The immediately following
page-references are also to this volume.

understanding of meaning cannot be limited either to the *mens auctoris* or to the *mens actoris*', is, in Gadamer's opinion, 'the most characteristic point' (313) of his own hermeneutic. And it is true that Habermas can bring forward this position in opposition to 'hermeneutic's claim to universality' only because at this point he gives hermeneutic a more restricted sense,[390] restricted, that is, to subjectively intended meaning. One result of this is that he believes he can no longer come to grips with 'systematically distorted' communication as a conscious participant, but only as the doctor, analyst or therapist of society as a whole (Gadamer, 81). But what can substantiate the claim implied here that one can leave the dialogue of contrary positions, the struggle to be convinced by the better view, to agree in submission to 'the idea of reason itself' (309), and describe this area of disagreement as one of systematically distorted communication, as a complex of delusion, within which there can no longer be meaningful argument but which can be exposed only as a whole? As Gadamer says, 'To speak of delusion in this context seems to imply sole possession of the correct view' (307). This is perhaps Gadamer's strongest argument against the attempt to replace a hermeneutic which emphasises communication by a sociological 'depth hermeneutic' modelled on psychoanalysis. In Gadamer's view 'depth hermeneutic' entails 'willy nilly the role of the social engineer who creates but does not liberate' (315). This is the ultimate conclusion of the subordination of the understanding of meaning to action. Conversely Gadamer can also accept the need for a 'depth hermeneutic' which transcends both *mens auctoris* and *mens actoris,* but this time as the task of understanding itself, which, 'beyond the limited perspectives of individuals, has to draw out the lines of meaning everywhere and so make historical tradition eloquent' (313). When Habermas agrees that critical analysis of an element of tradition goes deeper than that element's subjectively intended meaning–content, this penetration may still be an appropriation of the tradition's 'true' or 'deeper' meaning. It is only when criticism can incorporate the 'truth' of tradition that it can get past the 'temporally conditioned' form of its subjectively intended meaning, instead

[390] See Habermas's essay, 'Der Universalitätsanspruch der Hermeneutik', also in *Hermeneutik und Ideologiekritik*, pp. 57ff.

of facing a permanent challenge from the possible truth of tradition. But this is more than just drawing out the tradition's lines of meaning in the direction in which they are already laid down in the tradition. Rather, the hermeneutical process as a process of productive appropriation is possible only because the elements of the tradition, both in their content and in the process of their transmission, stand in relation to a truth which lies ahead of them and which in its own shape is still open, and which because of this can be made to refute its own 'temporally conditioned' shape by the freedom of the interpreter. Whether this critical analysis really captures the meaning of tradition can admittedly be proved only by reference to the lines of meaning which the tradition puts out. On the other hand, because these lines of meaning, the unexpressed semantic background of the statements of tradition, include an element of indeterminacy and become explicit only in interpretation, the freedom of analysis is expressed in the provisional clarity of its rendering of the significance ascribed to tradition. In this situation the meaning of a tradition could be exhausted only if the future of its truth could be captured once and for all, but no interpretation and no criticism can claim this power for itself. Just as the statement to be interpreted, with the truth-claim of its expressed content, reaches forward towards the totality of an unexpressed semantic horizon whose precise outlines are as yet undefined, interpretation and criticism also reach forward towards the final truth of the tradition. This need not imply any prejudice in favour of the unity of the tradition with its truth, such as is contained in Gadamer's 'anticipation of completeness': the truth of the tradition can be established critically despite the form in which it has been transmitted. But in either case both interpretation and criticism must be judged by the extent to which the truth they attribute to a tradition can count as identical with the truth which the tradition itself anticipates.

We have argued that the ability of the critical appropriation of a tradition to go beyond the tradition's subjective meaning in the light of an anticipated totality can be justified by the movement of the understanding of meaning itself and does not require us to go beyond this whole level of reflection to another one. Why then, in these circumstances, has Habermas still thought it necessary to leave the hermeneutical concern with an understanding of meaning for a theory of action? Discussion of this question, which is so important for Habermas's thought, must take account of the critique of Dilthey which Habermas presented in his book *Knowledge and Human Interests.*

In this book Habermas refers to a 'circular process of concept formation' in the hermeneutical sciences.[391] 'Hermeneutical procedures' are said to move 'in an inevitable circle' (170), since apprehension of the whole automatically presupposes knowledge of the parts, and conversely the parts cannot be apprehended without the whole. It is the same 'hermeneutical circle' (171) which made Heidegger deny to the hermeneutical disciplines, and in particular 'historiological interpretation', the character of strict knowledge and consequently scientific status.[392] This circle is also mentioned by Dilthey, but since he did not give it such theoretical importance for the formal procedures of hermeneutic he also did not draw Heidegger's pessimistic conclusion about the possibility of objective historical knowledge.[393] If we accept the thesis of the circular character of all hermeneutical arguments, as Habermas does, it certainly makes no sense to continue to claim scientific status for hermeneutical procedures or to use the term 'hermeneutical sciences'. Habermas nevertheless attempts to present the so-called hermeneutical circle as no more than an apparent circle (171). His solution of the 'dilemma' is that the meaning of ordinary language in a particular situation is determined, and can be interpreted, not merely by 'intralinguistic reconstruction', but also 'non-verbally', by the 'non-verbal life-expressions' associated with utterances in practical life (168).[394] It is only this 'intermingling of language and praxis' which explains why hermeneutical procedures 'cannot be called circular in the logical sense'. We can now see why Habermas did not defend the dialectical concept of the whole solely in terms of

---

[391] Habermas, *Knowledge and Human Interests,* Boston, Mass. and London 1972, p. 171, and the whole section, pp. 171–86. Subsequent references in the text are to this book.

[392] *Being and Time,* p. 194.

[393] Dilthey, *Gesammelte Schriften,* vol. VII, p. 262.

[394] Habermas describes this as the 'reflexivity of ordinary language' (*Knowledge and Human Interests,* pp. 168 and 172).

linguistically articulated perception of meaning and its 'language-internal' relations. In his view, it is only by associating linguistic analysis with 'experience', in other words by combining it with 'the empirical content of indirectly communicated life-experience' (172), that the appearance of a logically objectionable circularity in the process of interpretation can be removed. The hermeneutical approach thereby becomes an element, which cannot in itself be scientific, in a theory of practical life which must look for its basis in the concept of action. But by abandoning an argument based on the internal logic of the perception of meaning, Habermas has surrendered the ability to defend the concept of dialectical totality in his controversy with Albert. This concept can be proved to be indispensable only in the context of the dialectic of the perception of meaning with its interrelations of whole and parts, not in terms of a concept of action, which cannot go beyond the plurality of subjects of action. The interaction of the subjects can be seen as a unity only in terms of a semantic unity already underlying their actions. Originally, however, before his later distinction between communicative action and discourse, Habermas restricted the theme of totality of meaning by making it part of the concept of action in such a way that the totality of meaning was merely a description of the whole of social interaction as a historical process moving towards unconstrained communication,[395] in which discourse was then 'embedded'. This excludes from reflection the metaphysical and philosophy of religion aspects of the totality of meaning which are implicit in every experience of meaning. However, this concept of the total meaning, which is restricted to society by the concept of action, can no longer be proved to be an indispensable theme of hermeneutical reflection. The immanent analysis of the perception of meaning, on the other hand, can easily show that

[395] *Hermeneutik und Ideologiekritik*, p. 154. However, this description of the goal implies a totality of meaning which transcends the concept of action and moves towards that of an understanding of meaning on which action itself is based. Gadamer also describes as 'very familiar in metaphysics' this 'criterion of truth which derives the idea of the true from the idea of the good and being from the concept of "pure" intelligence' (*Hermeneutik und Ideologiekritik*, p. 304), though he also points out the vacuousness of such a general 'idea of right living' (p. 316).

all perception of individual meanings has as an implicit component the assumption of a totality of meaning, by reference to which the individual perception first receives its determinate meaning.

But is it really true that the perception of meaning is 'circular' in its intra-linguistic logic and therefore incapable of being scientific? Let us remember what was said before. We saw that while all perception of the meaning of particulars always simultaneously presupposes an understanding of the whole, the implicit pre-understanding of this whole is not identical with an explicit and therefore more clearly defined preconcept of it, which has much more the status of a hypothesis about the whole implicitly presupposed by the particulars. Conversely, such a hypothesis presumes the particulars only in the way that any hypothesis relates to the material it has to interpret. Although in the social sciences, as in hermeneutic and philosophy, 'the process of investigation initiated by subjects itself belongs to the objective complex which is to be known through the act of cognition',[396] it does not follow from this that the structure of the argument itself must be circular in form.

The more important difficulty of all reflection on the totality of meaning involved in experience is of a different kind. It arises out of the unfinished nature of the process of experience, the later stages of which influence the meaning of earlier experiences with the result that only by anticipation of them can any meaning at all be attributed to past and present. If the contextual dependence of the individual perception makes it necessary for analysis to make explicit the totality of meaning which belongs to the context, although in the process of perception it remains open, this unfinished nature also means that every statement about the whole is provisional and has the limitations of a mere anticipation. These anticipations are themselves determined by their place in the process of historical experience, though they consider it as a totality, and this is the source of the mutual relationships of part and whole which characterises the limitations of human understanding. Nevertheless the two-way movement between part and whole in the psychological process

---

[396] Habermas, 'Analytische Wissenschaftstheorie', *Positivismusstreit*, p. 156.

of understanding does not entail circularity in the logical process of the argument.

This means that, if we bear in mind the difference between pre-understanding and preconcept, we can disprove the assumption that understanding is circular merely by reference to the inner logic of hermeneutical analysis, which makes explicit the implicit components of understanding. The move outside the inner logic of the understanding of meaning is not necessary. This is not of course to deny that non-linguistic features of expression also belong to the context of linguistic expression. Schleiermacher saw this, and Dilthey made generous allowance for it in his late work when he extended hermeneutic to cover all features of expression, whatever their nature. Non-linguistic features of expression have a different theoretical status for interpretation from traditional texts only in that they give no explicit guidance for their interpretation. Both forms alike can be material for interpretative hypotheses, and these hypotheses can be tested by reference to both sorts of expression phenomena. There is no obvious reason for Habermas to deny 'hypothetical status' to interpretation in the form of 'linguistic analysis' of texts when he allows this status when dealing with the 'empirical content of individualised situations'.[397]

Habermas attempts to subsume understanding under the allegedly broader concept of 'life activity' because he assumes that the 'linguistic' preoccupations of understanding have to be transcended in order to avoid the hermeneutical circle, but this is refuted by his own awareness that action is itself constituted by the understanding of meaning. It is quite impossible to carry on 'life activity' except through the medium of the understanding of meaning. Conversely, a concept of understanding which was not rooted in the multidimensionality of 'life activity' could be described as 'diluted by idealism'.[398] On the other hand, the coextensiveness of 'life-activity' and the descriptive perception of meaning can be appreciated in its full significance only when it realised that 'meaning can be perceived even where it was not

[397] *Knowledge and Human Interests,* p. 173.

[398] This is Gadamer's criticism of the 'reduction of hermeneutic to cultural tradition and the ideal of semantic transparency, which is supposed to exist in this area' (*Hermeneutik und Ideologiekritik,* p. 283).

intended'.[399] The fundamental significance of the understanding of meaning for 'life activity' becomes fully clear only when the concept of meaning is not narrowed down to intentions of action or 'embedded' as discourse in the system of action. What conflicts with the intentions of agents is also experienced as meaningful, even when the substance of its meaning is unclear and problematic. 'Life activity' takes shape in a flow of experiences of meaning which mutually influence each other, and of these the intended meanings which guide one's own action are only one component among others. But the basis of the primacy of hermeneutic in the investigation of life activity is the fact that praxis is disclosed to itself only in the movement of understanding and only in this way becomes an object of investigation. This does not mean at all that the understanding of meaning is purely contemplative. Its restriction to contemplation by Dilthey is rightly criticised by Habermas.[400] Dilthey's contemplative attitude was connected with his overemphasis on the connection of understanding with memory and thus with interest in the past. In this Dilthey was a prisoner of historicism. His analyses must be extended to allow for the way in which the totality of meaning, the all-embracing semantic horizon, to whose outlines as they change in the course of experience all understanding is at least implicitly related, is accessible only in the anticipation of a still open future. Heidegger has developed this in the limits of his analysis of existence, and Habermas has recovered this awareness in relation to the social context of life. But the totality of meaning as the universe of meaning experienced and implicit in experience also transcends society. Society is not the embodiment of all reality and meaning, but needs itself in its particular current form to be rooted in and corrected by an absolute confidence in meaning which can transcend both conflicts between individual and society and the tension between man and nature. This absolute confidence in meaning has historically been embodied in religions as the basis of particular social orders and also as the potential for their renewal. Even religious confidence in meaning need not thereby be purely contemplative. It can combine with the historical

[399] Gadamer, *Hermeneutik und Ideologiekritik*, p. 70.
[400] Habermas, *Knowledge and Human Interests*, p. 179.

nature of the perception of meaning and build it into a totality of meaning in the perspective of an eschatological future understood as the ultimate horizon of a history of changing meanings. It is hard to see how anything other than such a religious or quasi-religious anticipation of a definitive future can provide the direction for action in search of which Habermas left the confines of a merely contemplative hermeneutic. [401] However, it is neither necessary nor useful to abandon the analysis of interpretive life activity in favour of a theory of action which – contrary to Habermas's intentions – reveals that activity only from outside, from the point of view of the analyst who unmasks it to find the interests allegedly lying behind it. [402]

[401] See above, n. 395, for Gadamer's remark on the metaphysical origin of the 'idea of right living' contained in the concept of unconstrained consensus. In the case of the Platonic idea of the good, the religious and philosophical implications of such a conception are also clear.

[402] Habermas combines the inclusion of a perception of meaning reduced to intentions of action in the concept of action with the assertion of the primacy of interest over knowledge (see above, pp. 90ff.). He justifies this by citing Dilthey's statement that the elementary forms of understanding grow 'in the interests of life activity' (Dilthey, vol. VII, p. 207, quoted in *Knowledge and Human Interests,* p. 173). Dilthey, however, unlike Habermas, did not give these interests a 'knowledge-constitutive' function. Because of his insight into the historical nature of the perception of meaning, which caused him to turn from psychology to hermeneutic, Dilthey outgrew the need to find a transcendental foundation for knowledge, but this need reappears in Habermas as a result of his removal of knowledge from the context of the perception of meaning. However, by identifying the transcendental conditions of knowledge with 'knowledge-constitutive interests', Habermas also goes outside the area of transcendental reflection, as he previously went outside that of meaning-perception, and reduces knowledge to its natural conditions. In adopting this position he is clearly influenced by Peirce's pragmatistic interpretation of the natural sciences. Consequently, the interest in 'agreement that dictates conduct' is in Habermas's view 'analogous' to interest in 'technical control over objectified processes of nature' (*Knowledge and Human Interests,* pp. 175, 191).

The instrumentalistic interpretation of the natural sciences presupposed here as a model has been convincingly attacked by Hans Albert ('Der Mythos der totalen Vernunft', *Positivismusstreit,* pp. 201ff, see also 282ff). Albert argues that 'the fact that informative theories of a nomological character have in many fields shown themselves capable of technical exploitation is in no sense an adequate characterisation of the cognitive interests which underly them' (pp. 201–2). He points out that the instrumentalistic interpretation is refuted by the

Insistence on the primacy of the understanding of meaning as a disclosure of 'life activity' even in its religious and universal-historical dimensions does not mean a restriction to a merely subjective hermeneutic because the totality of meaning present in experience always transcends the meanings apprehended in intention. For the same reason, however, the objective understanding of meaning of history, which in its movement 'breaks open . . . subjectively attributed meaning',[403] does not appear as something alien to subjectivity. On the contrary, subjective experience of meaning is drawn by its own action, if it does not close itself to reflection, into the movement of a history which analyses its contents and its truth.

practice in fundamental research in natural science itself rejects considerations of technical applicability. The natural sciences are concerned primarily with discovering 'the structure of reality and therewith of what actually happens' (p. 202). Habermas now rejects the theory of truth presupposed here – correspondence with a given reality (the correspondence theory – *Positivismusstreit*, pp. 256ff; see also *Theorie der Gesellschaft oder Sozialtechnologie*, 1971, pp. 123–4), and wants to base the concept of truth solely on the mutual empirical statements (Habermas, *Theorie der Gesellschaft*, pp. 124ff), 221ff; see also *Hermeneutik und Ideologiekritik*, pp. 154–5 and *Positivismusstreit*, p. 254). However, A. Beckermann has shown that Habermas himself does not keep to a consensus theory of truth, but that, particularly in his concept of competence and in his appeal to 'non-conventionalist ways' of checking empirical statements (Habermas, *Theorie der Gesellschaft*, pp. 124ff) 'unacknowledged realistic presuppositions are used' which imply the correspondence theory of truth which Habermas rejects ('Die realistischen Voraussetzungen der Konsensustheorie von J. Habermas', *Zeitschrift für allgemeine Wissenschaftstheorie* 3 (1972), pp. 63–80, quoted from p. 65; cf. p. 75). While knowledge cannot be thought of exclusively as the forming of pictures of things in the mind, since the entity to which the idea is supposed to correspond can itself be apprehended only as an idea, the intention of knowledge does seek factual truth. A connection with fact is the only principle by which the criterion of truth as the agreement of those who are seeking knowledge can be distinguished from a merely conventional conformity of opinion, the effect of which is just to obscure truth.

In contrast to the theory of knowledge-constitutive interests, which tends to exclude a relation to an object from the concept of truth, the perception of meaning has no difficulty in finding room for both aspects of the concept of truth, factual correspondence and the consensus of subjects. Intersubjective agreement about truth is always reached in relation to objects encountered in experience.

[403] Habermas, 'Analytische Wissenschaftstheorie und Dialektik', *Positivismusstreit*, p. 164.

206 THEOLOGY AND THE PHILOSOPHY OF SCIENCE

5. The Perception of Meaning and Science

The subject-matter of the human sciences is not limited to the inner mental world accessible to introspection, but also includes the objectifications of man's perception of meaning, though these can be recognised as expressing a perception of meaning only by a personal consciousness. That this is so seems to be widely agreed. Nevertheless this agreement involves problems, because the underlying concept of 'meaning' is used in very different ways. The problem of these different uses is very often not realised, or only partly realised, which makes the confusion even worse.

Writing in 1923, C. K. Ogden and I. A. Richards counted sixteen 'meanings of meaning', each with its subdivisions,[404] but the views of meaning which have emerged from more recent discussion can be divided into three main types, referential, intentional and contextual.[405]

The referential view of meaning, which predominates in linguistics, was developed in recent philosophy mainly by the logical positivists. It goes back to Frege's distinction of two forms of meaning, 'sense' and 'reference'.[406] In Frege's view, the 'reference' of a word, or more precisely of a name which designates an object, consists in this function of denoting, its character as a sign, whereas its 'sense' is based on the context in which the word or expression occurs. In other words, 'sense' attaches to the context, and in the first place to the sentence, in which the individual word appears, not to the individual word

[404] *The Meaning of Meaning* (1923), 10th ed., London 1972, esp. pp. 185ff.

[405] Traditional linguistic semantics usually divides theories of meaning into two groups, analytical (referential) and operational (contextual): thus S. Ullmann, *Semantics. An Introduction to the Science of Meanings*, Oxford 1962, pp. 54ff. See also K. Heger, *Monem, Wort und Satz*, Tübingen 1971, pp. 22ff, and S. J. Schmidt, *Bedeutung und Begriff*, 1969. This division takes no account of intention. Linguistic semantics limits itself to the investigation of the elements of meaning contained in language as opposed to those involved in the speech act.

[406] Especially in his essay 'On Sense and Reference' in *The Philosophical Writings of Gottlob Frege*, Oxford 1952, pp. 56–78. On Frege's theory of meaning, see also C. Thiel, *Sinn und Bedeutung in der Logik Gottlob Freges*, 1962, pp. 85ff, and A. Nygren, *Meaning and Method*, London 1972, pp. 229ff, where its relationship to the views of Russell and Wittgenstein is discussed.

on its own. But sentences too have 'reference' as well as 'sense' in so far as they are concerned with states of affairs. Word-reference is only part of the relation to an object asserted by the sentence. In similar terms, Wittgenstein in 1921 wrote in the *Tractatus* that the 'meaning' of a name was its object (3.203), but that 'only in the nexus of a proposition does a name have meaning' (3.3), and it is as this nexus that the proposition itself has 'sense'.

Since words or names have their meanings only in the context of sentences, and since sentences in turn also have meaning in the sense of a relation to an object, Frege's distinction between 'sense' and 'reference' was easily blurred. Russell, for example, [407] treated the two terms of Frege's distinction as interchangeable ways of describing relation to an object, [408] and even Wittgenstein's early *Tractatus*, which departs from the logical atomism of Russell, Wittgenstein's teacher, in its emphasis on the contextual dependence of word-meanings, occasionally uses the term 'sense'

[407] Bertrand Russell, 'On Denoting', originally published in *Mind* in 1905, reprinted in Russell, *Logic and Knowledge*, London 1956. For discussion, see C. Thiel, *Sinn und Bedeutung in der Logik Gottlob Freges*, pp. 108ff, and P. F. Strawson, 'On Referring', *Mind* 59 (1950), reprinted in A. Flew (ed.), *Essays in Conceptual Analysis*, London 1956, and in G. H. R. Parkinson (ed.), *The Theory of Meaning*, London and New York 1968, pp. 61–85.

[408] Both terms are also frequently used in linguistic semantics to describe the relations of words to objects. According to Ullmann, the lexical symbol does not refer to the thing directly, but through its 'sense', and this relationship between word and 'sense' is what Ullmann calls 'meaning': 'If one hears the word one will think of the thing, and if one thinks of the thing one will say the word. It is this reciprocal and reversible relationship between sound and sense which I propose to call the "meaning" of the word' (*Semantics*, p. 57; see also *The Principles of Semantics*, Glasgow and Oxford 1957, pp. 69–70.) In this view, in contrast to Frege's, the meaning is not identical with the object referred to, though the term 'sense', too, which is analogous to Frege's concept of 'reference', lies in between the lexical symbol and the object, which makes it similar to Husserl's meaning-intentions.

H. Weinrich is closer to Frege's position. He also attributes 'reference' to the individual word and 'sense' to the text. His position differs from Frege's, however, in that his 'sense' does not coincide with the object referred to, but is described as the 'totality of the features of an object defined as relevant by a linguistic community' (*Linguistik der Lüge*, 4th ed., 1970, p. 17). The 'wide reference' of a word is turned by the context into public opinion (Weinrich, p. 24).

to describe the object-relation, representation or reflection (2.221). According to the *Tractatus*, the 'sense' of a proposition lies in its showing 'how things stand *if* it is true' (4.022; cf. 4.2). This enabled logical positivism to formulate its now famous criterion of meaning, which says that the meaning of a proposition depends on the possibility of giving its truth-conditions: sentences for which no verifiable conditions can be given under which they would or would not be true must be regarded as meaningless. In this view, which treats language as a reflection of the world, the concept of meaning was completely taken over by the object-relation for which Frege used the term 'reference'. In the process, Frege's insight that 'sense' had to do with the combination of words in a proposition and in the wider context of a discourse, was lost.

The interpretation of meaning as the intentional object of experience, which was put forward by Edmund Husserl,[409] also makes no terminological distinction between 'sense' and 'reference' (304–5; cf. 325). Husserl understands attributed meaning (*vermeinter Sinn*) as the intentional object of consciousness (316ff), which 'can be expressed by "meanings" (*Bedeutungen*) (305). In this formulation Husserl combines Brentano's concept of intentionality (which denoted the relationship of consciousness to objects) with Frege's concept of 'reference'. In particular, he shares Frege's anxiety to give a purely logical account of meaning-contents, without any reference to mental acts,[410] though he treats meanings which have become separated from existent objects as intentions of a subject, in contrast with the lexicographical analysis of meaning used by later semantics. In the terminology of sociological action theory since the time of Max Weber, Husserl's intentionality has been translated back from the sphere of transcendental reflection into an empirical context. For writers from Weber to Habermas, subjectively attributed (or intended) meaning is a characteristic of the teleological structure of action. These writers see action as acquiring its meaning from the values or interests by which it is

---

[409] E. Husserl, *Ideas*, London 1931, pp. 261–2 and passim. The immediately following references in the text are to this book.

[410] See C. H. van Peursen, *Phänomenologie und analytische Philosophie*, 1969, pp. 22ff.

governed.[411]

The reduction of 'meaning' to the relation of propositions to objects in the sense of their verifiability a priori excludes the specific semantic thematic of the human sciences in favour of a language which reflects the world. On the other hand, the connection of the concept of meaning with intentionality, and in particular with the purposive nature of action, gives the human sciences a field of their own – the reference-intentions of agents – but fails to make any connection between that and the field and thought-forms of the natural sciences. The result is that the attempt to give the human sciences an independent base in an understanding of meaning interpreted in terms of intentionality falls back into the old dualism of human and natural sciences. As mentioned earlier, Hans Albert has brought this charge against K.O. Apel's attempt to show that the inaccessibility of human actions to explanation by the natural sciences is the result of their intentional structure, i.e., of the fact that they express subjective meanings.[412] Of course it was no part of Apel's intention, or of Habermas's, to 'remove human action from the causal system of nature'. In fact Apel, in an earlier essay,[413] had expressly tried to investigate human action and its objectifications by combining Hempel's nomological explanation with a hermeneutical approach. According to this essay, objectifying methods must be applied even in the human sciences in cases where hermeneutical communication is no longer (or not yet) possible. His examples are psychoanalysis and the critique of ideology. But even in normal conversation it may happen that 'the immediate context of communication which is the basis of

[411] See above, n. 149, on Max Weber, and pp. 96ff. on the discussion of the concept of meaning between Luhmann and Habermas; on Habermas esp. notes 202 and 180. W. Kamlah and P. Lorenzen similarly feel obliged 'to follow the tendency . . . to use the word "meaning" *mainly in connection with actions'*, with particular reference to the connection of action with purpose (*Logische Propädeutik*, 1967, pp. 130–1). No reasons are given by these authors for their stress on this aspect of meaning in preference to the various alternatives.

[412] See above, pp. 147–9.

[413] K. O. Apel, 'Die Entfaltung der "sprachanalytischen" Philosophie und das Problem der "Geisteswissenschaften"', *Philosophisches Jahrbuch* 72 (1964/65), pp. 239–89, esp. pp. 260ff. The page-references which follow in the text are to this article.

intersubjective conversation is suddenly broken and the other person is placed at a distance as an object' (260). When the other person's interpretation of himself is no longer intelligible to me, I see him as an object whose behaviour I have to interpret. But in this process even the 'objectification of the factors in human behaviour which are not (yet) capable of articulation in the language of self-understanding is in the service of this self-understanding' (289) and directed towards a resumption of communication. This strand in Apel's thought is paralleled by his references to the need for intersubjective understanding in the natural sciences, and specifically for the interpretation of basic propositions (258). This approach has been taken further by G. Radnitsky, who talks about a complementarity in the methods of natural science and hermeneutic, such that each is mediated by the other (65).[414] In fact, however, the concept of complementarity itself shows that neither Radnitsky nor Apel regards these two areas of science as mediating each other's content, but only as externally related. If the understanding of meaning which is the aim of the human sciences is conceived as concerned only with intentional acts, there is no basis for a continuity of content with the aims and methods of the natural sciences, and the most that can be shown is an external mediation of the methods of the one by those of the other.

The understanding of meaning as the intentional object of subjective acts has provoked a variety of criticism. Schlick, Carnap and Ryle have attacked Husserl's view of meanings as essences. Instead, the logical empiricists have treated 'meanings' as mere functions, ways of using expressions.[415] It has also been denied that the purposive character of action can be derived from explanations of a nomological type.[416] More important, however, is Ogden and Richards' remark that the intention of a speaker, i.e., 'subjectively intended meaning', by no means

[414] *Contemporary Schools of Metascience* (1968), 2nd ed., Lund 1970, vol II, pp. 59ff. The next reference is also to this book.

[415] On this, see C. H. van Peursen, *Phänomenologie und analytische Philosophie*, pp. 52–3.

[416] This question is at the centre of much of the criticism directed by the logical positivists at Dray's 'rational explanation'; see W. Stegmüller, *Wissenschaftliche Erklärung und Begründung*, 1969.

necessarily coincides with what he in fact says: 'we very often mean what we do not mean; i.e., we refer to what we do not intend . . .'[417] If intentionality is not isolated from language, which is the only medium in which intended meanings take on articulated form, it immediately becomes clear that meaning cannot be reduced to subjective meaning-intentions. The reason for this is that the speaker's intentions are not the sole, exclusive context within which his utterances are to be understood. The utterance enters a different context with each hearer, and the speaker himself also remembers his utterance later within an altered framework of experience and understanding. Because the domain into which the uttered word enters is intersubjective, and because of the historical nature of the participants, the meaning which the utterance in fact has in the intersubjective situation goes beyond the intentional horizon of both the speaker and any person originally spoken to or listening. It is these ways in which semantic references transcend the *mens auctoris* which give the practice of hermeneutic its special fascination.

With the referential view of meaning the problems are reversed. The definition of meaning in terms of subjective intention could not escape the objection that the spoken word has contents additional to and different from those intended in the utterance; but the ambiguity of the objective reference of a linguistic utterance is a result of the fact that the reference is influenced by the different intentions of the speaker, the person addressed and the interpreter. Is the meaning of an expression that to which the speaker is *in fact* referring, or that to which he *thinks* his utterance refers, or that to which the *interpreter* thinks the speaker is referring, or that to which his utterance would naturally refer in normal usage?[418] That such questions can be asked shows that the relation of a linguistic utterance to its object cannot be determined without a consideration of its social and historical context.

This insight emerged in the philosophy of linguistic analysis in

[417] *The Meaning of Meaning*, pp. 194–5.
[418] Ogden and Richards, *The Meaning of Meaning*, pp. 205–8. Although Ogden and Richards themselves tend towards a referential theory of meaning, considerations of this sort in fact introduce the crucial role of context dependence in word meaning.

the later work of Wittgenstein. His concept of the 'language-game' has been plausibly interpreted by A. Nygren as the equivalent of a 'context of meaning',[419] and Stephen Ullmann regards him as the most important advocate of a contextual view of meaning.[420] Wittgenstein himself, however, did not explain his term 'language-game' explicitly as 'context of meaning', but he does frequently say that a thing 'has not even *got* a name, except in the language-game', and again that 'this was what Frege meant too, when he said that a word had meaning only as part of a sentence'.[421] But the sentence too is part of a wider context (§ 595), just as any 'proceeding' possesses 'significance' only in its 'context' or 'surroundings' (§ 584): 'What is happening now has significance – in these surroundings. The surroundings give it its importance' (§ 583). This enabled Wittgenstein to say that instead of asking for the meaning of a word we should ask about the sort of context in which it occurs (II, ix, p. 188). It is not until this point that his view that the meaning of a word is equivalent to its use in language can be properly understood.[422] And yet the concept of the use of a word is itself still ambiguous: it may mean either an *individual* use in one of many unique speech situations, or a *typical* use in specific, typically recurring situations. The second of these senses predominates in Wittgenstein's later philosophy through the connection of language use and language-game. The concept of the language-game refers to a typical context of language use which abstracts from all the individual contexts of an utterance. It is only of such typical contexts that it makes sense to ask what are the rules which govern the use of language in a particular context as in a calculus (§ 81). It is this concern with the typical that brings the idea of context in Wittgenstein's language-game into contact with that of linguistic semantics, which distinguishes

---

[419] A. Nygren, *Meaning and Method*, pp. 252–3.

[420] S. Ullmann, *Semantics*, pp. 64ff.

[421] L. Wittgenstein, *Philosophical Investigations*, par. 49. The immediately following references in the text are also to this book.

[422] In this connection it is interesting that the firm equation of the 'use' of a word and its 'meaning' made in the Blue Book (*The Blue and Brown Books*, Oxford, 2nd ed., 1964) is softened in the *Philosophical Investigations* by the observation that this equation holds 'for a *large* class of cases – though not for all' (par. 43; cf. 561).

between linguistic contexts and contexts of utterance.[423] This means that the language-game theory must be concerned with constant social structures, 'life-forms', and not with the abstractions of a language conceived lexically. The latter is, however, the concern of the word-field theory of J. Trier and L. Weisgerber, in which language, in the sense of a collection of lexical items, is regarded as the expression of a linguistic 'picture of the world'.[424] When one considers, however, that meanings listed in a dictionary are abstracted from a set of representative examples of actual word use in real utterances, it would seem that word-meaning must be based on this rather than on a language system allegedly prior to linguistic use. Ullmann claims that consideration of the real context of utterance gives rise to a 'direct threat to the relative independence of the word' and the 'semantic identity' of lexical symbols,[425] though he rightly points also to the relative stability of word-meanings, particularly in the case of 'object words'. Ullmann calls the 'context theory . . . the most influential single factor in the growth of twentieth-century semantics', and says that because of its position 'there is no risk of underestimating its significance by asserting that it is perfectly compatible with a certain measure of word-autonomy' (65). However, since every utterance depends on its context, the relative constancy of word-meanings becomes less obvious and in its turn requires explanation. There can be no doubt that an important contribution to such an explanation has been made by

[423] Ullmann, *The Principles of Semantics*, p. 61. In his later work, *Semantics* (1962), Ullmann associates the operational or context theory totally with speech, as opposed to language, where he claims that the referential view of meaning applies. K. Heger (*Monem, Wort und Satz*, p. 23) distinguishes between two forms of the 'operational' theory of meaning: in relation to the 'individual act of communication', he says, it is 'only of marginal interest' to linguistics and belongs to the level of *parole* as opposed to that of *langue*, whereas it is important in so far as it concerns 'the conditions of the possibility of acts of communication', as in the language-game model or the word-field theory. See also W. Schmidt, *Lexikalische und aktuelle Bedeutung*, 1963, p. 24.

[424] On the arguments for and against the word-field theory, see H. Geckeler, *Strukturelle Semantik und Wortfeldtheorie*, 1971, pp. 84–176: on the lexematic character of the word-field theory, esp. pp. 86–7: cf. pp. 169, 89 (how it differs from the more comprehensive 'field of meaning').

[425] Ullmann, *The Principles of Semantics*, p. 61. The immediately following page-references in the text are also to this book.

the language-game theory through the attention it has drawn to the dependence of language on the 'life-forms' of a society.[426] These life-forms are characterised by a constancy which also influences individual behaviour. Nevertheless, it is important to realise that the language-game theory itself represents a narrowing as compared with the search for the meaning of a word in its various individual contexts. This is particularly clear in the work of Peter Winch, who, developing Wittgenstein, wants 'to give the concept of "rule" a central position in the analysis of meaningful behaviour', and claims that 'all behaviour which is meaningful (therefore all specifically human behaviour) is *ipso facto* rule-governed'.[427] Does that mean that individual behaviour which deviated from every existing rule would not be meaningful? Or would it be meaningful only by virtue of its negative relation to the rule? Is it not meaningful even before any relation to a rule simply because, as individual behaviour, it has a relation to its individual context and acquires a particular value in it? If this were so, the fact that there are also *typical* contexts or 'life-forms', and therefore also rules which determine behaviour in such contexts, would then be a special case of a more fundamental and more general situation. This would also take account of the objection made by Luhmann to Habermas's adoption of Winch's proposal to define the concept of meaning in terms of that of rule. Luhmann argues that 'rules must first be meaningful themselves before they can account for anything', that is, before they can give meaning to actions.[428] A rule acquires its meaning from the fact that the totality of rules expresses the typical features of the relevant life-form. The fact that obeying a rule already presupposes understanding is a further indication that in the individual case, which may deviate from the rule, understanding precedes observance of the rule.[429]

[426] H. Weinrich (*Linguistik der Lüge*) stresses, in addition to the dependence of words on context, the social conditioning of their meaning by the 'linguistic community'. However, he does not regard word-meaning itself as dependent on actual contexts of utterance; only its limitation by 'public opinion' is so dependent.

[427] P. Winch, *The Idea of a Social Science,* London and New York 1958, p. 52.

[428] See above, pp. 96–8.

[429] See K. O. Apel, 'Die Entfaltung der "sprachanalytischen" Philosophie', *Philosophisches Jahrbuch* 72 (1965), pp. 271ff, esp. 279.

However, the relation of whole and part within which understanding operates does not have the character of a rule as opposed to the individual and deviant, but determines the structure of *every* perception of meaning precisely in its particular individuality.

We saw that the contextual concept of meaning was developed mainly by Dilthey from Schleiermacher's work and introduced by him into the self-understanding of hermeneutic. This approach differs from Frege's and from that which prevails in linguistics by relating the concepts of both sense and reference to the context of the appropriate semantic whole.[430] The concept of meaning includes not only the relation of the sign to what it stands for, but also the relation between the parts of a semantic whole and their relation to this whole (see above, pp. 77–8). The meaning of a word does not consist simply in the fact that as a name it refers to 'something', in other words designates an object in a particular way;[431] the word always means 'something for

[430] In linguistics, even contextual theories of meaning often begin with lexical word-meaning. H. Geckeler says of the contextual definition of meaning: 'Here the meaning of a word is identified with the sum of the different contexts in which it appears' (*Strukturelle Semantik und Wortfeldtheorie*, 1971, p. 49). Earlier, J. R. Firth wrote, similarly: 'Meaning, then, we use for the whole complex of functions which a linguistic form may have' ('The Technique of Semantics', 1935, in *Papers in Linguistics*, London 1957, p. 33). Word-field theory adopts the same approach (Geckeler, pp. 78ff), but even Weinrich presupposes a lexically based theory of significance in his description of the determination of significance by the context to conform to current opinion (see above, n. 426).

[431] Whereas Frege treated the object referred to by the lexical symbol as itself the significance of the sign (see his essay 'On Sense and Reference', p. 57; see also 60), present-day semantics distinguishes meaning and object, and frequently stresses the difference between significance and reference (see Geckeler, pp. 78ff). E. Coseriu says: 'Significance is conceptual, but reference involves objects' (quoted Geckeler, p. 83). This distinction assumes that 'significance' is envisaged in general lexical terms, while reference naturally relates to a specific object. However, when the concept of significance is defined in terms of real contexts of utterance, its objective reference is always necessarily specific, and to that extent significance coincides with reference. This does not affect the 'transsignificatory' character of a word's significance, since as sign a word also hints simultaneously at the associations in the semantic context. See B. Liebrucks, *Sprache und Bewusstsein*, II, 1965, pp. 121ff, 132ff, and E. Heintel, *Einführung in die Sprachphilosophie*, 1972, pp. 40ff.

something', that is to say for the context of the sentences and for the composite meaning it expresses. Only now can we see the point of Frege's remark that the meaning of a word depends on the context of the proposition. The explanation of this dependence is that meaning is intrinsically related to this context. In other words, lexical meaning is a complex relation. It includes both object-relation (reference) and the value the individual word acquires in the proposition and in the semantic context of the discourse (significance).[432] This makes the attempt to distinguish between 'sense' and 'reference' even more difficult. Both clearly overlap in the area of relations between parts and wholes, although the object-relation is presumably characteristic of 'reference', while the closed unity of a semantic network can be expressed only by 'sense'.

In so far as there exists, for any semantic whole, a context which transcends it, the whole itself possesses its meaning only in relation to that context, as its 'reference' within it. It follows from this that no unity of meaning and no perception of meaning is autonomous in itself. Every specialised meaning depends on a final, all-embracing totality of meaning in which all individual meanings are linked to form a semantic whole. Because every individual meaning depends on this whole, the latter is implicitly invoked in every experience of particular meaning. This is not to say that this semantic whole is somehow present in fully defined form in every perception of particular meaning. The proposition, in particular the affirmative proposition, possesses a relative autonomy of definition, as does a complete section of discourse, but they too are admitted into their 'unexpressed semantic horizon'. Within this they are surrounded by a greater or lesser

---

[432] This point is often ignored, in linguistic semantics as much as in philosophical linguistic analysis. Even A. Nygren (*Meaning and Method*, 1972, pp. 229ff) does not discuss the fact that 'meaning' itself always includes a relation to the context (significance) as well as a relation to an object (reference). 'Significance' is an appropriate term for the first of these, provided it is taken in Dilthey's sense as the objective positional value of the part in the relevant whole, rather than in Betti's definition, as the relevance for the evaluating subject (Dilthey, *Gesammelte Schriften*, vol. VII, pp. 238–9). Dilthey's definitions of the concept of meaning also remained incomplete, since they did not draw attention to the object-relation and did not discuss its relation to the contextual relation within the concept of meaning.

area of definition, but beyond this the boundaries of meaning shade off into indefiniteness.[433] This combination of definition and indefiniteness also exists in language; indeed it is only because the words of a language are incompletely defined that propositions can be formulated with precise definition.[434] The proposition's comparative autonomy of meaning exists as the semantic anticipation of an indefinite semantic whole which transcends it and which is revealed in the proposition and acquires explicit, though only partial, definition in it.

While every individual perception of meaning implies a totality of meaning, not in fully defined form but at most as a guide to hermeneutical reflection in its continued attempt to penetrate its complexes of meaning, the fact of individual perceptions of particular meaning by no means implies that reality as a

[433] H. G. Gadamer's 'unexpressed horizon of meaning' of an utterance is related to the area which M. Polanyi calls the 'tacit coefficient of speech' (*Personal Knowledge. Toward a Post-Critical Philosophy* (1958), New York 1964, pp. 86ff). Particularly illuminating in this connection is the example of reading given by Augustine in his *De Magistro*. When we read a letter, Augustine says, we are conscious only of what is at the centre of our attention, and the letters and words we read are only latent in our consciousness. Polanyi, however, does not distinguish between the inexpressibility of rational structures of meaning and emotional components such as attention, passions and commitments; see esp. pp. 134, 173.

[434] J. Stenzel, *Philosophie der Sprache*, 1934, pp. 16–17, 48ff. B. Liebrucks description is even closer: according to him, 'the specific meaning of the *whole* emerges only retrospectively' when the last sound of the sentence has been uttered (*Sprache und Bewusstsein*, vol. II, 1965, p. 134). Liebrucks also speaks of the 'undefined range of possibility' which surrounds the individual word on utterance (242–3) and provides the 'scope' for progress of thought. Because of their remoteness from the process of speech, remarks of this kind are rare in linguistic semantics, but see H. Weinrich, above, n. 426.

[435] W. Weischedel (*Der Gott der Philosophen*, vol. II, 1972, p. 172) claims that 'if anything at all is claimed to have valid meaning, this implicitly presupposes absolute meaning' (see also my remarks on Dilthey's treatment of meaning, *Basic Questions in Theology*, vol. 1, pp. 162ff). However, Weischedel immediately abandons this implication because of the possibility of the experience of meaninglessness – as if such an implication could be refuted if it were really contained in each individual perception of meaning! Weischedel also claims that even the nihilist 'performs individual acts, even though they seem to imply meaning' (p. 177). The possibility of the nihilist's surmounting this 'in an attitude of self-mockery' seems less likely than Weischedel

whole must have a positive underlying meaning. [435] On the contrary, the totality of meaning implied in the perception of particular meaning is implied, by virtue of its indefiniteness, only as a problem, and so makes particular experiences of meaning also problematic. This situation shows how the impression of meaninglessness can arise. The experience of meaninglessness itself has the character of an experience of particular meaning in the formal sense of the word used here, and itself implies a definite totality of meaning. This totality is, as generally in experiences of particular meaning, implicit in such a way that it can become a guide for its continued exploration by means of hermeneutic. In this case, as generally, it may happen that the hermeneutical exploration of the unexpressed horizon of meaning reveals the immediate self-understanding connected with the experience of particular meaning – in this case the impression 'it is all meaningless' – as inappropriate to the actual contents of the experienced meaning, i.e., it may expose the immediate self-understanding as 'false consciousness'. This possibility is connected with the way in which the hermeneutical method understands meaning objectively, by going back behind the *mens*

---

imagines, if what is involved are undeniable implications of one's own authentic actions; in such a case self-mockery might be expected to lead instead to repression. However, since Weischedel makes even philosophy a matter of a 'basic resolve' (pp. 180ff), and so moves on to a level of unquestionable justifications of theology through irrational religious commitments, he is bound to accept such an attitude on the part of the nihilist. Acceptance of the logical possibility of the experience of meaninglessness, on the other hand, means looking for its basis in the structure of the perception of meaning itself, as was attempted above. Unfortunately Weischedel's discussion of the concept of meaning is always rather obscure. From the definition of meaning as 'intelligibility' (p. 166), it is not clear that understanding itself has to do with meaning and therefore presupposes what is meant by the term. According to Weischedel, 'meaning' is 'pointing to something' (p. 167), but not in the sense of designating (neither linguistic semantics nor Frege and analytical philosophy have any place in Weischedel's reflections); instead the pointing is said to be 'at something . . . from which meaning and sense derive' (p. 167). The metaphysician Weischedel envisages the 'establishment of meaning' which this explanation describes on the model of Platonic participation: 'What is meaningful *has* the meaning; the other thing to which it points *is* the meaning' (p. 168). The problem of context is not raised by the analysis of meaning, but appears only in the claim that what confers meaning is 'in every case the all-embracing' (pp. 170–1).

auctoris, which is only incompletely aware of the implications of its expression of its own experience. The possibility that the interpretation may be able to criticise the self-understanding of the author it is interpreting in turn raises the question of the relation between the understanding of meaning and truth.

As well as intellectual components of meaning, every contextual totality of meaning includes the relation to the world of the subject which perceives particular meaning. Indeed, we must say that this relation to the world is inherent in the components of particular meaning because of the complexity of the concept of particular meaning. Particular meaning includes not only the contribution of the individual experience of meaning to its semantic network, but also its relation to the world of objects. Dilthey long ago emphasised that 'life activity' does not possess its relation to the world as something outside itself, but includes it. The complexity of the concept of particular meaning enables us to describe this situation more precisely.

The fact that the experienced particular meaning has objects as its contents naturally does not mean that the meaning asserted is correct. The element of assertion in the structure of a proposition's meaning, even in the case of a pure statement, offers no guarantee of its truth.

Nevertheless the question of truth is not a problem introduced from outside into the discussion of sense and reference. This might be suspected in advance, since the two aspects combined in the concept of particular meaning – object-relation and context-relation – correspond strikingly to the two aspects of the concept of truth which have traditionally formed the basis for opposite interpretations, correspondence with the object and coherence or consensus.[436] While a pure consensus theory of truth is as incomplete as the classical correspondence theory, we may agree with W. Kamlah and P. Lorenzen that the correspondence of statement with the facts cannot be determined without reference to the judgment of others who 'speak the same language as us'.[437] These must, however, be 'competent judges'

[436] The aspect of coherence and the aspect of consensus can be taken together because systematic continuity and intersubjective agreement are both subsidiary aspects of the contextual totality of meaning.

[437] W. Kamlah and P. Lorenzen, *Logische Propädeutik,* p. 120.

or 'experts' (119), so in this way the factual aspect is reasserted as a critical principle preventing pure conventionalism. Nevertheless, since it is possible only for *subjects* to learn about facts, interpersonal agreement retains a predominance in decisions about the truth of statements. Since interpersonal consensus is only one aspect of the general harmony of all the factors of experience, that is, of the coherence of experience, so that a conventionally accepted view may be rejected if it is irreconcilable with the content of an individual's experience, it may be maintained that the internal coherence of the semantic totality which embraces all experience coincides with truth, since there could be no further experience outside it to cast doubt on the truth of its meaning. In the all-encompassing totality of meaning, therefore, meaning and truth coincide. To this extent it is an intrinsic part of the hermeneutical consideration of the composite meanings of linguistic utterances to investigate their truth. This is so even when the limitations of the semantic horizon of the utterances are shown to be the source of their untruth, in that every assertion claims to possess the truth about its object and by doing so within a limited horizon of meaning sets itself in opposition to the totality of truth.[438] On the other hand, every assertion, and to a correspondingly greater degree every outline of systematic networks of meaning which integrates perceived meaning and makes interpersonal agreement possible, anticipates truth. This element of anticipation is expressed in the very *form* of an assertion, in that as an assertion the proposition claims to be true while at the same time laying itself open to refutation.

Explicit outlines of comprehensive networks of meaning, describing the indefinite totality of meaning experienced in any given area of human experience, were produced in the form of myths, which were combined into mythologies. Philosophy and science also produce general outlines of meaning which give explicit form to the totality of meaning which is the basis of the

---

[438] Untruth, or rather partial truth (appearance), is consequently regarded as asthenic because it conflicts with the rest of experience, while the stability and permanence which both the Greeks and the Hebrews associated with truth are attributed to the semantic whole which embraces experience. Cf. my remarks on the concept of truth in *Basic Questions in Theology*, Vol. II, 1971, pp. 1–27.

particular meaning of individual phenomena. Philosophy and
science differ from myth in producing systematic interpretations
in the form of models of meaning which are intended to be free
from internal contradiction and contain no more than what can
be shown to be logically necessary for the explanation of
networks of phenomena. In both, the explicit presentation of
systematic networks of meaning has an explanatory function to
the extent that explanation is the basis of an understanding
concerned with fitting individual features into a whole (see
above, pp. 151ff). Both also show themselves to be related in that
the weight of the explanation in the sciences as well as in
philosophy is carried by the systematic theories of the various
fields of study, into which the hypotheses are fitted and to
support which they are designed. Theories of this sort should not
be thought of as final summaries of individual discoveries; on the
contrary, discovery begins with paradigmatic models of
systematic explanation for whole areas of phenomena, and the
details are worked out subsequently in the process of 'refining the
paradigm' (see above, pp. 55ff).

   The sciences in the narrow sense differ from philosophy by
restricting their statements to a formalised language and/or to
those which can be tested against empirical data of a specified
sort. These data then define the field of investigation of the
science in question. Mathematics and logic are examples of the
first type, the empirical sciences of the second. The difference
between the empirical sciences and philosophy, however, does
not derive from the hypothetical method of concept-formation in
the former or from the possibility of empirical testing as such.
Philosophical statements can also satisfy such conditions, which
simply make explicit what holds for any assertion in its character
as a mere anticipation of the truth. Philosophical statements
cannot, however, submit to the restrictions mentioned without
losing their characteristic feature of unrestricted reflection. The
definition of the task of philosophy in recent times as linguistic
analysis or the analysis of meaning is not so novel as it may seem.
Since the beginnings of philosophy, philosophical statements
have always justified themselves by an analysis of other
statements in which experience was articulated or even reflected
on already. But the process of unrestricted reflection, which

challenges immediate assumptions about meaning, can stop only when it has revealed the totality of meaning which encompasses all experience. Moreover, every formulation of a result of philosophical analysis can again become the object of a similar analysis, so that philosophy never reaches definite partial results or makes simple linear advances in knowledge. Its advances are always made by means of total revisions, though these derive their rigour and justification from a consideration of the difficulties of previous positions, and so themselves receive something like empirical confirmation.

This endless process of examining the unexpressed semantic context of experience which is articulated in language is cut short in the individual sciences by the restriction to a formalised language and by the demand for verifiability by data of a specified sort. The definition of an expression restricts its content to those features explicitly mentioned. This gives it precision by ignoring the unexpressed semantic horizon which accompanies its various individual applications. By doing this it both guarantees the intersubjective identity of the expression's meaning-content and restricts consideration of its implications to such elements of meaning as satisfy the same criteria. In this way the empirical sciences, unlike philosophy, can concern themselves with a limited area of subject-matter without having to become involved in all the implications of meaning which philosophical reflection must investigate. Finally, the empirical sciences, since they can presuppose a defined operational language, though one which always implies a general description of its object, can devote themselves entirely to their material and to the development and testing of theories and hypotheses about it. Scientific revolutions to modify such a language are still possible, but they can take place only within limits definable in advance by the language's own resources.

We saw that the difference between the human sciences and the historical disciplines was the result of this sort of restriction of scientific description and explanation to a single aspect of a whole phenomenon. The restriction to the nomothetic aspect is already present in the geometrical description of natural processes, which excludes their individuality (see above, nn. 234, 235). This restriction to the nomothetic aspect of events also implies the falsification principle, which can be applied only to hypothetical laws, not to hypotheses about unique sequences of events, of the sort with which the historical disciplines are concerned (see above, pp. 58, 61ff.). Hypotheses of this second sort can be tested only for their ability to integrate the relevant evidence, though this is also true in the natural sciences in view of the difficulty of deciding whether a single case amounts to falsification (pp. 66–7).

Sciences based on the exclusion of aspects of the general networks of meaning to which phenomena belong retain a relation to these networks of meaning by virtue of this act of exclusion. Formal languages, for example, depend for their interpretation on everyday language. The same situation can be seen in the generalising sciences, where statements of laws themselves have to be related to contingent initial and marginal conditions. These are introduced by 'basic propositions', the interpretation of which in turn is a subject of discussion in the interpretive community of those engaged in this investigation. The 'ideographic' approach of the historical disciplines is not detached from the nomothetic aspect in the same way, but uses the available knowledge of laws as a tool of historical criticism and investigation. It in turn, however, also relies on this wider meaning as something presupposed by historical investigation, though not explicitly discussed. Similar problems to those created for the generalising sciences by the contingent and individual aspect of events arise in the historical disciplines with regard to the future. The networks of meaning which the historian describes in past phenomena depend on a present understanding of reality (which the historian shares with his contemporaries) and on a future which is still open. At this point, consideration of the semantic networks constructed by the historian leads into philosophical consideration of the totality of meaning.

Philosophical analysis of meaning, in its treatment of the phenomena it has to analyse and in the results of its analyses, proceeds by hypothesis just as much as the particular sciences. This realisation is certainly inescapable once the assumption that there exist self-evident premises for philosophical reflection is exposed as an assumption, and indeed as a false dogmatism.

Philosophical analysis of meaning can operate only by systematically describing the totality of meaning which guides its reflection, although a systematic account of this sort is itself no more than an anticipation of the implicit and only partly defined totality of meaning of all experience, to which it is related and in which it possesses its truth. It can demonstrate its truth only by its ability to integrate, and so illuminate, actual experiences of meaning.

It may be assumed in advance that the situation of theology will prove to be similar. Theology also deals with the totality of meaning of experience and must be aware of this if it is to know what it is saying when it talks about God.

PART TWO

Theology as a Science

THEOLOGY AS A SCIENCE

THE discussion of the philosophy of science in Part 1 has laid the foundations for a clarification of the question whether, and in what sense, theology can count as a science. Before we deal with this question systematically, however, we shall look at the most important forms which theology's understanding of itself as a science has taken in the course of its history. Consideration of these and their own problems will provide a background for the modern discussion.

Chapter Four

THEOLOGY AS A SCIENCE IN THE HISTORY OF THEOLOGY

1. Theology as a Derived Science

We saw in the Introduction how ancient theology – in the west particularly under the influence of Augustine – thought of itself as wisdom in contrast to related sciences' knowledge of the world (7ff). But this began to change in the twelfth century, and by the thirteenth, with the foundation of the first universities, the change was capable of definition. From then on theological wisdom was also thought of as a science in the Aristotelian sense, and indeed as the highest science.

In the twelfth century a movement in the schools had already grown up, based on the principles of *auctoritas* and *ratio*, which gave the art of argument a high status.[439] From mid-century onwards the school of Chartres debated the Aristotelian system of knowledge which they had received through Boethius. This system set (philosophical) theology among the theoretical, as opposed to the practical, disciplines, and unlike logic and ethics grouped it with the speculative sciences which included physics and mathematics as well as metaphysics or theology.[440] Axioms as in mathematics were now also sought in *sacra doctrina*. By the end of the century Alan of Lille had compiled a set of *regulae theologicae* to be the basis for all theological propositions.

[439] See A. Lang, *Die theologische Prinzipienlehre der mittelalterlichen Scholastik*, 1964, pp. 21ff: 'Die Hochschätzung der "ars" '.

[440] On the scientific system of Gilbert de la Porrée and his school, see Lang, *Prinzipienlehre*, pp. 41–57, and M. A. Schmidt, *Gottheit und Trinität nach dem Kommentar des Gilbert Porreta zu Boethius' De Trinitate*, 1956, pp. 24ff, 59, 179–209.

Nicholas of Amiens in his *Ars catholicae fidei* had also tried to construct a set of axioms for theology on the model of Euclid.[441] But the scientific status of theology still remained unclear because such axioms or rules were derived from the faith of the Church.

In the first half of the thirteenth century, knowledge of what the Aristotelian concept of science entailed became more exact. Some denied that theology could be such a science and others affirmed it only with strong reservations. Alexander of Hales, for example, held that theology offered no *certitudo evidentiae* but only *certitudo adherentiae*.[442] A good century before, Anselm of Canterbury had taught that theology could give *rationes necessariae* for believing the teachings of the faith; now the lack of evidence for these beliefs was emphasised. This arose from a concern with the merit in believing,[443] for according to Gregory the Great, '*fides non habet meritum cui humana ratio praebet experimentum*'.[444] But this had to be brought into line with the demand in 1 P 3:15 to give an account (*rationem reddere*) 'of the hope which is in you' and also, according to Augustine, of the faith.

In spite of this scepticism about the scientific status of theology in the Aristotelian sense, the thirteenth century saw the continuation of the pursuit of theological principles or axioms. Now the articles of faith were seen as principles or presuppositions from which other theological propositions could be derived. Theology proceeded deductively from principles, in an analogous manner to a science in the Aristotelian sense; the principles of the rational sciences depended on the *lumen rationis*, the articles of faith were given by the *lumen fidei*. With this reservation theology could count as a science in the broad sense of the word.[445]

Thomas Aquinas tried to give a more exact account of the scientific status of theology by calling it a derived science and

[441] Lang, pp. 75–93.

[442] Lang, p. 160.

[443] J. Finkenzeller, *Offenbarung und Theologie nach der Lehre des Johannes Duns Scotus*, 1960, p. 172, and esp. A. Lang, *Die Entfaltung des apologetischen Problems in der Scholastik des Mittelalters*, 1962, pp. 38ff. See also M. Grabmann, *Die Geschichte der scholastichen Methode*, vol. II (1911), 2nd ed. 1956, pp. 545ff.

[444] Lang, *Entfaltung*, p. 39; see Grabmann, vol. II, p. 189.

[445] Lang, *Prinzipienlehre*, pp. 157ff.

thus claiming for it the right to be called a science in the full sense of the word. In his *Posterior Analytics*, Aristotle had used the term derived or subordinate science with reference to the relation of optics to geometry and harmonics to arithmetic (*Post. Anal.*, 1, 7, 75 b). The principles of such a science came not from itself but from the prior science from which it was derived. (*Post. Anal.*, 1, 7, 75 b). Thus harmonics rested on principles derived not from itself but from arithmetic. Thomas Aquinas transferred this model to theology. He saw the knowledge possessed by God and the saints as the prior or superior science. For them the articles of faith were objects of knowledge, whereas our theology must accept them on authority.[446]

Thomas Aquinas used this concept of a derived or subordinate science to overcome the difficulty that the articles of faith are not so obvious to our understanding as principles or axioms must be in an Aristotelian science. Furthermore these articles of faith are used as a starting point from which we proceed to demonstrate conclusions in a scientific manner. However by the beginning of the fourteenth century, even in his own Dominican order, doubt was already evinced over Thomas's solution. The Dominican theologians William Petri de Godino, John Picardi von Lichtenberg and in particular Hervaeus Natalis again restricted theology's claim to be a science in the strict Aristotelian sense, because its principles were not self-evident to reason.[447]

Duns Scotus went further with this criticism by distinguishing between what can be proved by one particular science and what is evident to the mind as the subject of all sciences. If we speak of a relationship between a prior and a subordinate science, we must not overlook the relationship of both these sciences to our own intellect. When we pursue a subordinate science, its principles must be present and evident to our intellect even though these principles may derive from another science. Because the superior

---

[446] *Summa theologiae*, I, 1, ad 2: 'Et hoc modo sacra doctrina est scientia, quia procedit ex principiis notis lumine superioris scientiae, quae scilicet est scientia Dei et beatorum. Unde sicut musica credit principia tradita sibi ab arithmetico, ita doctrina sacra credit principia revelata sibi a Deo.' On the idea of a *scientia subordinata* in Aquinas, see M. D. Chenu, *La théologie comme science au XIIIe siècle*, 3rd ed., Paris 1957, pp. 67–72, and Lang, *Prinzipienlehre*, pp. 163ff.

[447] Finkenzeller, *Offenbarung und Theologie*, pp. 201ff.

or prior science is at a higher level of universality, its principles must be known to the intellect before those of the subordinate science[448] and be the cause of the discoveries we make in it.[449] Duns Scotus did not think such proof was attainable in the case of *theologia viatorum*. Neither can we justify the separation of God's knowledge of himself and human theology into two sciences, the one subordinate to the other, by a difference of either subject or point of view.

These objections made by Duns Scotus and other theologians to the theory of a subordinate science were accepted almost universally, and the theory 'was no longer very important in the fourteenth century'[450]. It was revived by a later Thomism, and as part of neo-scholasticism and with the authority of St Thomas as *doctor communis* it has continued to influence Catholic theology to this day.[451] However, the objections to it made at the turn of the thirteenth century did not lose their force in the meantime.

2. Theology as a practical science

Early thirteenth century theologians like William of Auxerre, Alexander of Hales and Bonaventure were not convinced that theology was a science in the strict Aristotelian sense. They were inclined to emphasise the practical side of theology aimed at the awakening of fear and love of God as the highest good.

[448] Finkenzeller (p. 213) gives the reference to this argument as *Ordinatio*, prol. pars 4, qu. 2 (ed. Vat., vol. I, p. 148–9, n. 216), though it is there shown to be an interpolation from *Ordinatio*, III, Suppl., d. 24, qu. un., n. 4. The argument does however appear in the sentence from n. 214 (pp. 146–7) criticising the subordination of theology to metaphysics: 'Nec etiam ipsa sibi aliquam aliam subalternat, quia nulla alia accipit principia ab ipsa, *nam quaelibet alia in genere cognitionis naturalis habet resolutionem suam ultimo ad aliqua principia immediata naturaliter nota.*' On Duns Scotus's other arguments, see Finkenzeller, pp. 212ff.

[449] *Ordinatio*, prol. pars 4, qu. 2, n. 216 (vol. I, p. 148).

[450] Lang, *Prinzipienlehre*, p. 187. On the attitude of the late scholastic theologians to the theory of subalternation, see the detailed treatment by B. Meller, *Studien zur Erkenntnislehre des Petrus von Ailly*, 1954, pp. 254ff.

[451] Examples include the following: M. J. Scheeben, *Handbuch der Katholischen Dogmatik*, vol. I (1873), 2nd ed. 1948, pp. 403–4 (n. 914); F.

Theology used to be called *sapientia*, and they thought this term united the theoretical and practical sides of theology in a striving towards the good.[452] Thomas Aquinas tried to show that theology was a speculative, theoretical science in the Aristotelian sense because theoretical knowledge is an end in itself and therefore of higher value than practical knowledge which is directed towards other ends. Richard of Mediavilla in opposition to this view defended theology as a *scientia practica* because it was more concerned with God as our goal and most lovable highest good than with pure knowledge. Duns Scotus followed him and tried to show that theology was a practical science by means of Aristotelian philosophy.

Aristotle had distinguished the theoretical from the practical and the productive (poetic) sciences, but did not go very deeply into the latter two in his reflections on the theory of science. In his school these three branches were soon reduced to two, theoretical and practical philosophy.[453] The medieval Christian theologian who defended theology as a practical science, because *sacra doctrina* should be directed towards doing good, could quote the sentence in the second book of the *Metaphysics* that the goal of a theoretical science is truth and the goal of a practical science is action.[454] As against this St Thomas used the judgment of the Philosopher in the first book of the *Metaphysics* that sciences pursued for knowledge's sake are a higher wisdom than sciences

Diekamp, *Katholische Dogmatik nach den Grundsätzen des hl Thomas*, vol. I (1917), 6th ed., 1930, p. 5; L. Ott, *Fundamentals of Catholic Dogma* (1952), E. T. Cork 1957, 6th ed. 1963, pp. 2–3; M. Schmaus, *Katholische Dogmatik*, vol. I (1937), 3rd ed. 1948, pp. 32ff. Schmaus gives 'the modern' concept of science equal status with the Aristotelian – Thomistic one (pp. 37–8), and interprets its use of 'science' to mean 'any attempt to obtain knowledge of a particular single object by a single method adapted to that object, with the aim of obtaining coherent knowledge which can be passed on to others' (p. 37).

[452] Finkenzeller, pp. 242ff, who also has material on the following section.

[453] See E. Zeller, *Die Philosophie der Griechen in ihrer geschichtlichen Entwicklung*, II/2, 5th ed. 1963, pp. 176ff. According to Zeller, the division into two parts can be found as far back as Alexander of Aphrodisias. Aristotle's distinction between theoretical, practical and poetic philosophy is set out notably in the *Topics* (145 a 15–16) and the *Metaphysics* (1025 b 25ff).

[454] Met. 993 b 20–1, quoted by Aquinas, *S. T.* I, 1, 4 as the first of the two introductory arguments.

pursued for their practical usefulness.[455] Duns Scotus contended
that this latter group meant purely practical disciplines and was
not relevant to the question of theology. When it was a question
of knowledge of a goal, *cognitio practica* was superior to mere
speculative knowledge.[456] In this argument Duns Scotus
presupposed that theology was concerned with God as the
highest good and thus the final goal of man.

According to Aristotle, practical knowledge started from a
knowledge of the goal desired and then chose the most suitable
means to reach it.[457] Does practical knowledge confine itself to
action, that is either to the selection of means or, if it also
considers the goal itself, only from the point of view of action?
This was the view of Henry of Ghent. He described theology
which was concerned with God in himself and not merely as the
goal of man as speculative knowledge, of the sort presupposed by
all practical activity.[458] We must have some objective knowledge
of the goal, as an object and not just as a goal, before we can
make it our goal or take any practical steps towards it. This is
why Duns Scotus regarded objective knowledge of the goal as
part of practical knowledge. He referred to Aristotle's
description of ethical reflection (*Nic. Eth.*, 1139 a 30f) and called
it 'inappropriate' to exclude the knowledge which governed the
training of the will from the concept of the practical.[459] This
knowledge which governs action is concerned with the goal not
as a *goal* but in its own reality,[460] that objective reality with
which the goal desired by the will must conform.[461] Thus
practical knowledge presupposes not that something is in fact
already a goal set by the will, but only that it is suited to be so. A
goal can be a goal for the will only if it has this suitability

[455] Met. 982 a 14ff, quoted by Aquinas, *I Sent.*, prol. 1, 3, contra.
[456] *Ordinatio*, prol. pars 5, qq. 1–2 (ed. Vat. vol. I, p. 229, n. 353).
[457] *Nic. Eth.*, 1112 b 15ff.
[458] Henry of Ghent, *Summa Aurea*, 8, 3, ad 3 (vol. I, 65 y–66 z), quoted by
Duns Scotus, *Ordinatio*, I, n. 270 (pp. 183–4).
[459] *Ordinatio*, vol. I, n. 297 (p. 196).
[460] *Ordinatio*, vol, I, n. 260 (p. 176); cf. the remarks on exegesis of Aristotle,
n. 226 (p. 154).
[461] In so far as it follows *recta ratio* (*Ordinatio*, vol. I, n. 234 (p. 159); see n. 265
(p. 179).

(*aptitudo*).[462] Questions about the nature of this object come before its adoption by the will as a goal, and therefore, according to Duns Scotus, must be part of practical knowledge. Determining the nature of the goal helps in the selection of the practical measures necessary to attain it.

In this sense God is the final goal of man. Theology as a practical science is directed towards God in so far as he in his own reality can and should be the goal of the human will. Thus the question of God in his own reality remains central to theology even when theology is seen as a practical science.

What is the difference, therefore, between theology conceived as a practical science and theology conceived as a purely theoretical knowledge of God? The difference is mainly that for the first time making theological discourse relative to man who is asking about God is included in the concept of theology itself. In fact, of course, humanity had been at the centre of theology for a long time before this. This approach is characteristic of the Augustinian tradition, and the *Summa* of St Thomas is also concerned largely with questions about man and his salvation, which follow properly from the Christian belief in the incarnation. Duns Scotus's concept of theology as a practical science in this wider sense now made it possible to develop this human aspect systematically, beginning with the doctrine of God itself. However, Duns Scotus did not complete this task because his doctrine of God, like that of the other scholastics, was founded on cosmologically oriented proofs of God's existence. The full fruits of the idea of theology as a practical science did not ripen until much later, in modern times. It was not only external criticism of the cosmological 'proofs of the existence of God' that led to taking our human self-knowledge as a starting point for talking about God. The idea of theology as a practical science had already prepared the way long ago.

The development of this idea of theology as a practical science freed it from the narrow schema of the Aristotelian concept of a theoretical science based on first principles. But in the process, the Aristotelian concept of practical science was radically altered to include not only ethics but also the doctrine of God and an

---

[462] On Duns Scotus's arguments, *Ordinatio*, vol. I, n. 237, (pp. 161–2) and n. 252 (pp. 169–70), see Finkenzeller, *Offenbarung und Theologie*, pp. 251, 255.

understanding of the world based on it. [463] The fact that 'practised' could also include the particular and the accidental which are part of the salvation-history material of theology, whereas a theoretical science in the Aristotelian sense was bound to exclude them, must have been a powerful argument on the 'practical' side for late medieval theologians so deeply troubled by the problem of contingency.

The tradition of theology's self-understanding begun with Duns Scotus and carried on in the school of Ockham also gave rise to a Protestant theology in the sixteenth and seventeenth centuries. Luther took it as self-evident that theology is a practical and not a theoretical science: '*vera theologia est practica . . . speculativa igitur theologia* belongs with the devil in hell.' [464] Luther saw the proper study of theology not as God (in accordance with the literal meaning of the word theology), [465] but the relationship between man and God: '*theologiae proprium subjectum est homo* (!) *peccati reus et perditus, et Deus justificans ac salvator hominis peccatoris*'. [466] Thus with its acceptance by Luther as a practical science, theology became more existential and pastoral.

Luther took over the concept of theology but changed its content with his *theologia crucis*. Melanchthon, on the other hand, tried to avoid the term theology altogether preferring *doctrina christiana*, [467] even though he sometimes had to use the term theology, even in titles to his own works, because it was the common name of a subject of study. However, Lutheran theologians of the late sixteenth century, for example M. Flacius (1567), J. Wigand (1568), J. Heerbrand (1573) and M. Chemnitz (1590), used the term freely, as did other reformed theologians of the time. [468]

---

[463] See also Finkenzeller, pp. 264–5.

[464] Luther, *Werhe*, Weimarer Ausgabe, TR 1, No. 153.

[465] This is why, according to Aquinas, theology deals with all other objects only *sub ratione Dei*, 'vel quia sunt ipse Deus, vel quia habent ordinem ad Deum, ut ad principium et finem' (*S.T.*, I, 1, 7).

[466] Luther, WA, 40, 2, 328, 17 (Enn. Ps. 51); see also WA, TR 5, No. 5757; on this and in general on Luther's concept of theology, see J. Wallmann, *Der Theologiebegriff bei Johann Gerhard und Georg Calixt*, 1961, pp. 17ff.

[467] Wallmann, pp. 19ff.

[468] Wallmann's view (*Der Theologiebegriff*, pp. 23–4) that even apart from

A fresh understanding of the implications of the concept of theology around 1600 led theologians back to the scholastic definitions and reawakened interest in the question of whether theology was a practical or a theoretical science. Theology as a practical science then became permanently linked, at least in Lutheran orthodoxy, with the so-called 'analytical' methods. These analysed and discussed the object under review with reference to its purpose, under the headings of end, subject and means to the end. However, this link between practical theology and such methods was not without its difficulties.

In his *Clavis scripturae sacrae* (1567) Flacius distinguished three scientific processes which could also be applied to theology. The first was the *synthetic* process which built up the object under review from its elements, principles or causes, and in theology starts with God as the simplest element, principle and mover. The next was the *analytical* process that started with the relationship between the object and its *usus* (and so in theology started from its final end, eternal life) and then worked back to its ultimate roots and elements. Thirdly there was the *heuristic* process which started with definitions and proceeded by making distinctions. According to Flacius this last is the shortest process and leads most quickly to the goal, but it is an art rather than a science. Flacius also sees the analytical process as limited to the practical interpretation of scripture.[469]

The analytical method was first applied to the theology of the schools by the Heidelberg reformed theologian B. Keckermann in his *Systema sacrosanctae theologiae* (1602). In using it he strongly emphasised its practical nature.[470] It is this practical nature which distinguishes theological *prudentia religiosa ad salutem perveniendi* from theosophy, the highest form of theoretical knowledge. But theosophy must also derive what it says about God from scripture

---

Melanchthon sixteenth-century Luterhan theology had been cautious in its attitude to the term 'theology', so that a new 'acceptance of the concept of theology' had to occur with J. Gerhard (who followed Chemnitz), will not stand up to examination.

[469] *Clavis*, pars II, pp. 54–9, quoted by C. H. Ratschow, *Lutherische Dogmatik zwischen Reformation und Aufklärung*, vol. I, 1964, pp. 38–9.

[470] E. Weber, *Der Einfluss der protestantischen Schulphilosophie auf die orthodox-lutherische Dogmatik*, 1908, pp. 20ff, is a survey of the history of the analytical method in theology, with particular emphasis on Keckermann.

and so, like theology, rests on revelation.[471] This distinction between theology and theosophy shows that here the concept of practical knowledge, possibly under the influence of G. Zabarella,[472] has a more strictly Aristotelian sense than in Duns Scotus, that is to say that practical knowledge is limited to that which is of practical use to human desires and actions. This may partly explain why reformed theologians gave the theory that theology has a practical character and the analytical method a mixed reception.[473] For example J. G. Alsted, who otherwise inclined towards the practical view, did not accept the term for his *Theologia scholastica* of 1618, evidently because for him the term practical was confined to the narrower sense of ethics and casuistry.[474] In Lutheran orthodoxy, the acceptance of theology

[471] On Keckermann's theory of science, see P. Althaus, *Die Prinzipienlehre der deutschen reformierten Dogmatik im Zeitalter der aristotelischen Scholastik* (1914), 2nd ed. 1967, pp. 20ff; on theology and theosophy, pp. 26ff. Note also the distinction between *scientia* in the narrow sense and *prudentia* (p. 21).

[472] Zabarella's views on the philosophy of science have been described by B. Hägglund, *Die Heilige Schrift und ihre Deutung in der Theologie Johann Gerhards,* 1951, pp. 45ff. Cf. Id., *History of Theology,* 3rd. Swedish ed. 1966, E. T. Saint Louis London 1968, 300–1. On his influence on Keckermann, see Althaus, pp. 22–3.

[473] Here too, any accurate study must distinguish between the two topics. Althaus, for example, stresses that the description of theology as a practical science, which had been advocated by Keckermann, 'found general acceptance in dogmatics' (p. 33), while the analytical method did not 'take root' there (pp. 55ff). Similarly E. Weber previously described Keckermann's attempt to introduce the analytical method into Reformed theology as meeting 'little response' (p. 41), but, unlike Althaus, he combined this judgment with the assumption that neither was the practical character of theology clearly recognised in Reformed dogmatics. According to Weber, the awareness was 'fairly widespread' in Reformed dogmatics, but mainly in the form of a 'belief in the hybrid theoretical-practical character of the theological *habitus'* (p. 39). See Althaus, pp. 55–6. The differences in the judgments of Weber and Althaus can be largely explained by the fact that both fail to take account of the distinctions in the concept of the practical which existed at the end of the fifteenth century. Weber in particular even claimed to find in the early Lutheran texts a modern view of the practical character of religious knowledge which derives from Ritschl's theology. Althaus rightly objected to this (p. 62).

[474] See Althaus, pp. 37–8. See also J. G. Alsted, *Methodus sacrosanctae theologiae,* pp. 47ff, for objections to the exclusive classification of theology with either the theoretical or the practical disciplines.

as a practical science did not necessarily entail the use of the analytical methods developed by Keckermann. Hasenreffer had already spoken in favour of the practical nature of theology in 1600,[475] and so had J. Gerhard in the introduction to the first volume of his *Loci theologici* in 1610. However, Gerhard used the term practical theology in the Scotist sense and unlike Keckermann included the doctrine of God in the determination of the goal of theology. The reformed theologian A. Polanus of Basle did likewise, but he differed from J. Gerhard in distinguishing a double goal of theology, the glorification of God and mankind's attainment of eternal salvation.[477] Gerhard did not build his theology on analytical methods, which is understandable considering that both Keckermann and Zabarella tied them to a much narrower concept of the practical. The Lutheran understanding of theology as a practical science does not confine the term practical to human behaviour in the sense of ethico-religious practice.[478] It also includes the exploration of the ontological structure of the human creature whose final end is God. Even in G. Calixt we find that the analytical methods, in the form in which they were introduced into theology by Keckermann, are not immediately applicable to the metaphysical conception of man in his relationship to God. In his *Epitome theologiae* (1619) Calixt, following B. Mentzer (1610), was one of the first Lutheran theologians to use the analytical methods and

---

[475] For Hasenreffer, see M. Keller-Hüschemenger, *Das Problem der Fundamentalartikel bei J. Hülsemann in seinem theologiegeschichtlichen Zusammenhang*, 1939, p. 115; for Mentzer and Calixt, see E. Weber, pp. 21 and 26–7.

[476] Althaus, pp. 53–54. Althaus later (p. 60) stresses that Polanus cited Duns Scotus in support of his thesis of the practical character of theology.

[477] *Loci theologici*, vol. I, Proem., n. 26. Johann Gerhard's concept of theology has been described in detail in J. Wallmann's dissertation (1961, see above n. 464). For the practical character of theology see Wallmann, pp. 50ff. The significance of Gerhard's return to the Scotist concept of the practical, which was wider than that of Aristotle, in his description of theology as a *scientia practica* is missed both by Wallmann and in the literature generally, since there is clearly no understanding of the relationship of Scotus to Aristotle on this point. Althaus singles out as a striking lack Keckermann's 'inability to subordinate the doctrine of God to the *finis*, as Lutheran theology generally did later' (p. 42), but is himself unable to recognise the connection with a more precise definition of the term *scienta practica*.

made the threefold division which was continued after him: the goal, the subject who strives towards this goal, and the ways and means of reaching it. However the doctrine of God was treated not under the first aspect, the goal itself, but under the second aspect of man striving for this blessedness as God's creature. Thus the doctrine of God was merely a preliminary to the actual subject matter of this second part.[479] Not until J. Hülsemann do we find the analytical method linked with the idea of theology as a practical science and God treated under the first aspect of the final goal itself. In the *Extensio* to his *Breviarium theologicum*, the latter published in 1640, the former in 1648, 'the victory of the analytical method was finally achieved'.[480] Using the distinction already made by J. Gerhard, Hülsemann described God as the primary goal of theology. In the first volume of his *Systema locorum theologicorum*, published in 1655, A. Calov explains that theology treats of God not in a theoretical but in a practical way as the final end of man[481] and attacks Musäus' designation of God as the 'object' instead of the final cause (finis) of theology.[482] J. F. König and J. A. Quenstedt also call God the objective final cause of theology as distinct from human blessedness which is its subjective end.[483]

The development of the idea of theology as a practical science in early Protestantism shows that this description does not confine the term practical to the devotional and ethical, but has an ontological or anthropological – salvation-history background. Seeing human existence as directed towards God made it easier to treat the entire salvation-history thematic of theology as a single theoretical whole. But the emphasis on the

---

[478] Althaus (pp. 56–57) has rightly objected to E. Weber's view that the concept of theology as a practical science in Lutheran orthodoxy was primarily contained in its view of faith as 'a function of life concerned with practical religion' (see Weber, p. 50).

[479] E. Weber, pp.29–30.

[480] M. Keller-Hüschemenger, *Das Problem der Fundamentalartikel*, p. 118; see also ibid. the quotation from the *Ext. Breviarii*, 17, for the inclusion of the concept of God in the category of goal.

[481] A. Calov, *Systema locorum theologicorum*, vol. I, 1655, p. 33, quoted by Althaus, pp. 59–60.

[482] E. Weber, pp. 60–1; for Musäus, see pp. 52ff.

[483] E. Weber, pp. 35–6 (on König).

practical in the sense of the ethico-religious, as for example in the work of E. Weber, was also important. This can already be clearly seen in J. Gerhard's defence of the practical nature of theology. The adoption of the Scotist concept of theology as a practical science can also be seen as the theoretical expression of this practical religious interest, just as it was in the medieval Franciscan school. This interest, however, was already apparent in Melanchthon's *loci* method, which was superseded in the seventeenth century by the analytical method.

The ethico-practical perspective of Melanchthon's theology becomes especially clear when we consider the humanistic background of his *loci* method.[484] We saw earlier how the school of Chartres in the twelfth century was already trying to produce a theological *Topics* on the basis of the Aristotelian *Topics* (see p. 228 above). The concept of *loci communes* in Melanchthon, on the other hand, is more closely connected with rhetoric. As in humanism, it indicates the basic concepts of ethics. The *loci communes* are the points on which, as Melanchthon writes in 1521, the *rerum summa* depend.[485] The speaker must refer to them in order to convince his audience or, in humanistic terms, to have a good influence on their emotions. In his *Rhetoric* of 1519 Melancthon enumerates many such *loci communes*: vices, virtues, fate, life, death, riches, knowledge. He goes on to say that the number of such *loci* is as great as the multiplicity of life itself; he is concerned with the anthropological points of contact to be found with humanistic moral teaching.

Because the Reformed theologians held that human emotions are disordered by sin and can no longer react in the right way, Melanchthon had to postulate particular *loci theologici*. Instead of speaking of the good example which arouses our desire to do good, the preacher must speak of the incapacity of human powers for doing good, of sin and the law of God, as well as of the Gospel which frees us from the law's condemnation, justifies us and makes us capable of loving God and our neighbour.

In the last edition of his *Loci theologici* (1559), Melanchthon

---

[484] On this see E. Mühlenberg, 'Humanistisches Bildungsprogramm und reformatorische Lehre beim jungen Melanchthon', *ZThK* 65 (1968), pp. 431–44.
[485] *Corpus Reformatorum* 21, 84.

limited himself less strictly to the anthropologico – ethical and turned more towards the divine history of salvation. The first edition of 1521 had claimed to be an expostion of Paul's epistle to the Romans, which was itself regarded as a compendium of Christian doctrine. But in order to do justice to scripture, the study of human ethical problems had to be broadened in the new edition to cover salvation history too. The 1559 edition consequently begins with God, and there then follows the *historica series* of the biblical accounts from the creation up to the birth, crucifixion and resurrection of Christ and Paul's *disputationes.*[486]

In spite of this wider coverage, the later edition of Melanchthon's *Loci theologici* still concentrates on the ethico-religious. This continued to be the orthodoxy of the early seventeenth century as we may see from the prologue to Gerhard's *Loci*. But a more strictly scientific form was sought for this ethical and religious interest. Was this an intellectualising aberration? Melanchthon had already realised that this practical interest can achieve its true end only in subordination to the knowledge of God given through the authority of scripture. Early Protestant dogmatic theology was also concerned with the directing of human life towards God and his will. This is why it strove for scientific strength and clarity in its exposition of the knowledge we have of God. For if man striving for salvation must seek to conform to God's will and God's nature, then the knowledge of God is the first thing necessary for regulating ethico-religious praxis and must precede all reflection on human behaviour and its practical demands. The question therefore arises: how can man in his earthly state be certain that God exists? This was no problem, however, for early Protestant dogmatics: the divine authority of scripture constituted a self-evident certainty. But in modern theology this has given rise to the question of certainty in theology and of the Christian tradition on which theology is based. As we shall see later, later Protestant theology has specifically developed the concept of certainty in theology and the understanding of theology as a practical science.

[486] *CR* 21, 605; see Althaus, p. 45.

3. Theology as a Positive Science

There is still much that we do not know about the history of the concept of positive theology. One thing, however, is clear: positive theology did not originally mean Christian theology as a whole as distinct from natural theology: rather it was a single discipline within theology, side by side with other theological disciplines.

a) In his encyclopedic *Apparatus theologicus* of 1628, G. Calixt distinguished between school theology (*theologica scholastica*), sometimes now called 'academic' to avoid the term 'scholastic', and ecclesiastical theology, whose object was not to study all theological issues in learned detail (*plene et exacte*) but to concentrate on the main points of the Christian religion (*capita religionis christianae*) without systematic proofs and without polemic. This ecclesiastical theology could also be called didactic or 'positive' theology.[487] Other theological disciplines named by Calixt are exegesis, church history, apologetics and practical theology. The purpose of positive theology was 'to equip the future clergy' who, as Calixt pointed out, often spent no more than two years at university, 'with adequate means to fulfil the duties of their office in a proper manner.'[488]

This notion of positive theology was frequent in the seventeenth and early eighteenth centuries. The compendia of J. C. Dannhauer (1649), J. F. König (1664), A. Calov (1682) and J. W. Baier (1686) all used the word in their titles. In J. F. Buddeus's encyclopedic *Introduction to Theology* (1727) we have the phrase *theologia thetica seu positiva*, meaning the same as dogmatic theology. Buddeus also maintained the distinction

---

[487] G. Calixt, *Apparatus theologici sive introductionis in studium et disciplinam sanctae theologiae editio altera*, Helmstedt 1661, p. 174: 'Dici quoque potest *didactica* vel *positiva*, quod quae necessaria et certa sunt, doceat et ponat, nec ad quaestiones opinionesque minus aut necessarias aut certas dilabatur. Nos, ut distinguatur ab Academica, Ecclesiasticam appellabimus.' See also p. 167, n. 5, and Wallmann, *Theologiebegriff*, pp. 154–5. Wallmann there quotes the division made by Calixt in 1629 in his introduction to Augustine's *De doctrina christiana*, which is similar to the later one but limited to ecclesiastical (positive), exegetical, historical and academic theology (see Wallmann, p. 155, n. 3).

[488] Wallmann, pp. 154–5.

between positive and scholastic which had become customary in Catholic theology.[489] He clearly did not realise, however, that the Catholics were using the term positive theology in a somewhat different sense from the early Protestant theologians.

b) Petrus Annatus, whom Buddeus quoted as an authority together with L. E. Du Pin and Honorius de S. Maria, distinguished between positive and scholastic theology (1700) by the fact that the former was founded on *principia positiva* which were not proved but presupposed and believed on the authority of scripture and tradition, while scholastic theology, although it covered the same ground, had to approach its subject matter with greater subtlety and precision by means of rational argument.[490] This distinction was already regarded as normal by Du Pin, and we can find its like at least a hundred years earlier in Luigi Carbonia and Gregory of Valencia.[491] It goes right back to Melchior Cano's *De locis theologicis,* which first appeared in 1563.

Unlike Melanchthon and others, including Catholic writers of the sixteenth century, Cano did not regard the main points of Christian doctrine as *loci theologici*. For him the *loci theologici* were the sources from which the theologian drew his arguments and sought his proofs.[492] This sort of work was useful to

[489] J. F. Buddei *Isagoge historico-theologica ad theologiam universam singulasque eius partes,* Leipzig 1727, p. 302. The identification of positive theology with dogmatics may go back to a misunderstanding by Buddeus of a remark by the Jansenist L. E. Du Pin. Buddeus cites Du Pin, who in his *Méthode pour étudier la théologie* (1687), Paris 1768, refers to a 'part of positive theology which treats the mysteries and points of our religion dogmatically'.

[490] P. Annatus, *Apparatus ad positivam theologiam methodicus* (Paris 1700), Erfurt 1726, p. 3: 'Positiva dicitur, dum suas discurrendo conclusiones probat per *principia positiva,* hoc est per principia quae non probantur, sed supponuntur et creduntur, qualia sunt ea, quae desumuntur ex verbo Dei scripto vel tradito, nobisque per Ecclesiam proposito.'

[491] L. Carbonia, *Introductio in sacram theologiam,* Venice 1589, Bk I, chap. 8; Gregory of Valencia, *Commentaria theologica,* vol. I, qu. 1, 1, quoted by A. Lang, *Die Loci theologici des Melchior Cano und die Methode des dogmatischen Beweises. Ein Beitrag zur theologischen Methodologie und ihrer Geschichte,* 1925, p. 209, n. 1.

[492] M. Cano, *De locis theologicis libri duodecim,* Salamanca 1563, Bk I, chap. 3. Cano explains that he does not want to write 'de capitibus rerum illustrium, quae nunc etiam communes appellantur loci, ut de justificatione, de gratia, de peccato, de fide, deque aliis huius generis . . . sed quemadmodum Aristoteles

post-Tridentine theology because, unlike the Protestants, it did
not regard scripture as the one and only source from which proof
might be sought. Early Protestant theology began producing a
similar phenomenon to Cano's methodically interpreted *Loci*;
towards the end of the sixteenth century introductory loci *De
sacra scriptura* became common. According to Cano, the *principles*
of theology must first be derived from ten probative sources –
from scripture and tradition to the authority of human history.
The object was not to prove the *content* of these principles but
only to establish that they had these authoritative sources. Cano
described this work as *positio principiorum,*[493] as opposed to
probatio, and later the theological discipline engaged in it was
called 'positive theology', although Cano himself did not use this
expression. The purpose of the exercise was to refer principles
derived from other sources back to scripture itself. Thus Gregory
of Valencia wrote in 1591 that 'positive' theology was so called
because it sought to find in scripture the principles for all
theological conclusions.[494]

This distinction between 'positive' and 'scholastic' or
(according to new usage) 'speculative' theology is still current in
Catholic theology today. Thus according to M. Schmaus,
positive theology tries 'by means of historical and philological
research to answer the question: what is the truth revealed by
God?', whereas the task of speculative theology is to make a deep
and comprehensive study of the content of this revelation.[495]

in Topicis proposuit communes locos, quasi argumentorum sedes et notas, ex
quibus omnis argumentatio ad omnem disputationem inveniretur: sic nos
peculiares quosdam Theologiae locos proponimus, tamquam domicilia
omnium argumentorum Theologicorum.' See Lang, *Die Loci theologici des
Melchior Cano,* pp. 65ff, where in particular Cano's dependence on the
interpretation of Aristotle's *Topics* of R. Agricola is mentioned (p. 67).
Agricola, in his *Inventio dialectica,* looked for the *topoi* not in particular
propositions, as was Aristotle's intention, but in the general aspects and
features of things contained in the propositions.
[493] Loci, XIII, 2 (348b); see Lang, *Melchior Cano,* p. 90.
[494] *Commentaria theologica,* I, 1, 1: 'quasi principia firma aliarum
conclusionum Theologicarum ponit et ideo positiva videtur dicta, quia scilicet
ponit atque statuit ex Scriptura principia Theologiae firma' (quoted by Lang,
p. 209, n. 1, the same page which bears Lang's statement that Cano did not use
the expression 'positive theology').
[495] M. Schmaus, *Katholische Dogmatik,* vol. I, p. 39.

Schmaus equates positive theology with biblical studies and church history.[496] Others distinguish between exegetical and historical theology on the one hand and positive theology on the other, on the ground that the task of positive theology is to assess the dogmatic status of the findings of those disciplines.[497]

c) Early Protestant theology took over Cano's distinction but also adapted it. In 1623 J. H. Alsted mentioned the distinction 'customary in the schools' between positive and scholastic theology and took scripture itself, the *positiones sacrae scripturae* on which scholastic theology was based, as equivalent to positive theology.[498] This corresponded to the reformation view that scripture itself was the principle and foundation of Christian doctrine. However, it was Calixt's view of the distinction mentioned earlier (see note 487), rather than this view of Alsted's, which became generally accepted. Even *his* interpretation, however, was still based on Cano's distinction in so far as positive theology drew out the doctrinal content of scripture without elaborating, proving or defending it. But neither Calixt nor Alsted required positive theology as a separate discipline at the basis of theology to establish the truths of revelation; both of them held these truths to be clearly given by scripture alone. However, whereas Alsted therefore identified positive theology with scripture, Calixt maintained it was a separate discipline whose particular purpose was the education of the clergy because it gave a 'positive' exposition of 'basic doctrine' without any learned additions. The limitation of

[496] Schmaus, I, 41.

[497] Thus A. Lang, *Melchior Cabo*, p. 210 and n. 3, with a reference to M. Jacquin, in *Revue de sciences philosophiques et théologiques* (1907), pp. 345ff.

[498] J. H. Alsted, *Methodus ss. theologiae*, p. 121: 'Usitata est in Scholis distinctio Theologiae in positivam, scholasticam, in practicam et in controversam.

'Positivam Theologiam appellunt ipsam sacram Scripturam, seu divinam historiam, quam vulgo vocamus Biblia, item Testamentum . . . Dicitur autem *Theologia positiva*, quia legibus ratiocinationum, definitionum ac divisionum non coarctatur, nec in eam tradendam cadit omnino disceptandi ratio, quam Scholasticae penitior adhibetur . . . Haec Theologia positiva est universae Theologiae, quatenus in subjecto est, basis et fundamentum . . .'

P. 122: 'Theologia *scholastica* est quae positiones sacrae Scripturae, seu Theologiae positivae, in methodum redigit, et conclusiones rationibus petitis imprimis e sacris litteris probat.'

positive theology to what was necessary and completely certain led to a favourite conclusion of Calixt, viz. that if we concentrated on fundamentals all other dogmatic controversies became relative in importance.

d) The concept of positive theology moved on again during the Enlightenment. In the past it had been opposed to scholastic theology; now it was opposed to natural theology. Behind this was the opposition between natural and positive religion as formulated, for example, by G. E. Lessing in his fragment (written before 1760) 'The origin of revealed religion'. Here he argued that when people came to make religion a community affair for everybody, it became necessary 'to construct a positive religion from natural religion because all men were not capable of practising this natural religion in the same way, just as a positive law was constructed from natural law'. [499] Thus the young Lessing, like other thinkers of the Enlightenment, held that positive religion was merely a politically useful modification of natural religion. The content of every positive religion was 'equally true and equally false' because it served the 'unity of public religion' but also 'weakened and distorted the essentials'. (par. 9–10). Deistic rationalists treated the additions made by positive religion to natural religion with scant respect. On the other hand the so-called neology, the theology of revelation which scrupulously took into account the spirit of the Enlightenment, stressed the need for such a 'filling out' of natural religion and claimed the term 'positive religion' as an honourable title. This position continued until the discussion between 'positivists' and 'liberals' at the beginning of the twentieth century. [500]

According to K. G. Bretschneider, J. A. Ernesti was the first to 'call revealed teaching positive because in it God had complemented natural religion with a *cultum arbitrarium*.' [501]

---

[499] G. E. Lessing, *Werke* (ed. G. Hempel), vol. 14, p. 220 (§ 5). The fragment was not published until 1784, among Lessing's posthumous theological writings. See also K. Aner, *Die Theologie der Lessingszeit*, 1929, p. 347.

[500] See the article 'Positive Union', in RGG^3 V (1961), pp. 472–3.

[501] K. G. Bretschneider, *Systematische Entwicklung aller in der Dogmatik vorkommenden Begriffe* (1804), 3rd ed. 1825, p. 32, refers to Ernesti's *Opuscula*

Ernesti had tried to prove against Tindal and other deists that it was in no way unworthy of the divine perfection that some things in religion were arbitrary and that these were instituted by God in his wisdom for our own good.[502] Above all, perfect human happiness – especially in the case of fallen humanity – was impossible without such decrees of the divine will. In this way he defended revelation by analogy with positive lawgiving. Ernesti's pupil and disciple S. F. N. Morus also used the term 'positive' as a description of Christian theology. This was in commentaries on his *Epitome theologiae christianae* which first appeared in 1789. Although another pupil of Ernesti, C. F. Ammon, wrote in 1793 against calling Christianity a positive religion,[503] he agreed in his *Summa theologiae christianae* of 1803

theologica, first published in 1773, pp. 195–6. The same reference appears in C. F. Ammon, *Summa theologiae christianae*, 1803, Praefatio, p. V. In spite of this I have been unable to find the expression 'positive' in the place mentioned, or anywhere in the relevant article of Ernesti ('Vindicii arbitrii divini in religione constituenda').

[502] 'Vindicii arbitrii divini', *Opuscula theologica*, 2nd ed. 1793, p. 173: 'Nos contra dicimus, neque abhorrere a perfectione divina, aliquid esse in religione arbitrarium, neque negari posse, talia esse cum hominum salute sapienter a Deo constituta'; see also ibid., pp. 191ff.

[503] 'Ist das Christentum eine positive Religion?', *Neues theologisches Journal* I (1793), pp. 89–104 and 273–86. According to Bretschneider (*Systematische Entwicklung*, p. 32, n. 27), the anonymous article in this journal, of which Ammon was one of the editors, was by Ammon himself. Ammon says on p. 90 of the article that the dogmatic supernaturalist defends revelation 'as the only and complete source of his positive theology', and he describes it as 'inconceivable that reason, which seeks unity, could derive two directly contrary testimonies to the truth and untruth of the Christian religion from the term "positive", if it were agreed on the correct and precise sense of this word'.

The arguments of this article are part of the background to Hegel's work on the positive nature of Christianity, which appeared in 1795 (Nohl (ed.), *Hegels theologische Jugendschriften*, 1907, pp. 152ff). There are already references to the 'positive doctrines' of Christianity in a draft of Hegel's which includes notes from a reading of the *Theologisches Journal* (Nohl, pp. 362ff, esp 364; I owe this reference to Dr R. Leuze). Contrary to Ammon's intention, Hegel had extended the positive character to the doctrines of Christianity. There is evidence that this terminology was used previously in the school of C. Storr, of which Hegel had been a member: see F. G. Süskind, *Bemerkungen über den aus Prinzipien der praktischen Vernunft hergeleiteten Uberzeugungsgrund von der Möglichkeit und Wirklichkeit einer Offenbarung, in Beziehung auf Fichtes Versuch*

that Christian doctrine might be called positive provided that by positive was meant not merely the external authority of the lawgiver but also God's own special foreknowledge.[504] After this it became customary to emphasise the 'historico-positive foundations of Christianity'.[505]

e) When in 1799 in his *Speeches on Religion* Schleiermacher contrasted positive and natural religion and claimed that opposition to the positive and arbitrary was opposition to everything definite and real,[506] he was still following Ernesti's line of argument. Schleiermacher's justification of positive religion had a very powerful effect because he explained natural religion as a mere abstraction drawn from positive religion.[507] Schleiermacher's concept of positive religion also followed from the linguistic usage of the time. This makes it all the more surprising that in his famous and epoch-making description of theology as a positive science in the encyclopedic *Grundriss* of 1811, he used a quite different notion of positivity. This can be explained by the fact that here Schleiermacher was concerned with general considerations about scientific theory and not primarily with the difference between natural and positive religion.

In 1802, in his lectures on the methods of academic study,

---

einer Critik aller Offenbarung, printed as an appendix to Süskind's translation of Storr's *Bemerkungen über Kants philosophische Religionslehre,* Tübingen 1794. Süskind starts from the position that according to Fichte it is 'morally impossible for a revelation to give us such positive instruction' (p. 166). The word 'positive' does not occur in the relevant passage of Fichte (*Sämtliche Werke,* ed. J. H. Fichte, vol. V, p. 119), nor does it in Kant's books on religion. Süskind was evidently using it as a gloss, and did so repeatedly (pp. 174, 177–8, 196, 199). As the passages from Ernesti quoted above show, the term refers particularly to the gratuitous nature of God's provisions for salvation: 'all this . . . is *positive,* not originating in ourselves, but instituted by God' (p. 179).

[504] C. F. Ammon, *Summa theologiae christianae,* 1803, pp. VI–VII.

[505] The term occurs constantly in G. J. Planck, *Grundriss der theologischen Enzyklopädie,* 1813, but is not yet in use in his *Einleitung in die theologischen Wissenschaften,* Leipzig 1794–5.

[506] *Reden über die Religion,* 1799, p. 278; see pp. 242–3, 260–1, 263.

[507] *Reden über die Religion,* p. 277: 'The essence of natural religion consists in the strict sense in the negation of all that is positive and characteristic of a religion'; see p. 281, and also pp. 272ff.

Schelling had described the individual sciences, in contrast to philosophy, as 'positive sciences'. As well as theology and jurisprudence he mentioned natural science, but only in so far as the latter's knowledge was 'put to external and public use', which happened only in medicine. So Schelling spoke of 'three positive sciences' in all,[508] namely theology, jurisprudence and medicine. These were the three 'higher faculties' which, according to Kant, were devoted not to the pursuit of truth as such, like the faculty of philosophy, but to the pursuit of the 'natural ends' of the people: 'to be happy after death, to live among others in this life secure in one's property through public laws, and lastly to enjoy life itself in physical health and not to be cut off by early death.' [509] According to Kant, pursuit of these natural ends of the people was to be protected by the government, which therefore sanctioned the underlying statutes ('that is, the precepts laid down at a superior's discretion' 22) of the three 'higher faculties'. Thus according to Kant, the positive was associated with practical ends. Fichte also defined the 'three so-called higher faculties' on the basis of their 'practical indispensability and their validity in the eyes of the multitude'.[510]

Schleiermacher took over the term positive for the three higher faculties from Schelling, but like Kant and Fichte stressed their practical purposes. Thus in 1808 in his Memorandum on the setting up of the Berlin University he wrote: 'The positive faculties each arose from the need to establish an indispensable praxis securely on theory and the tradition of knowledge.' [511] In 1811 Schleiermacher gave a similar definition of a positive science at the beginning of his Brief Outline of the Study of

[508] F. W. J. Schelling, *Vorlesungen über die Methode des akademischen Studiums* (1802), 7th Lecture: 'On philosophy and positive sciences', quoted from E. Anrich (ed.), *Die Idee der deutschen Universität*, Darmstadt 1956, esp. pp. 62ff.
[509] I. Kant, *Der Streit der Fakultäten*, 1798. In the Akademie edition of Kant's works the quotation is in vol. 7, p. 30, and the next quotation in the text in vol. 7, p. 22.
[510] J. G. Fichte, *Deduzierter Plan einer zu Berlin zu errichtenden höheren Lehranstalt*, 1807, quoted from Anrich, *Die Idee der deutschen Universität*, p. 157 (§ 26).
[511] F. D. Schleiermacher, *Gelegentliche Gedanken über Universitäten in deutschem Sinn, nebst einem Anhang über eine neu zu errichtende*, quoted from Anrich, p. 258.

Theology: 'A positive science is one in which the elements belong together not as if they were necessary components of the organisation of science by virtue merely of the idea of science, but only in so far as they are required for the furtherance of practical ends.' [512] Theology's practical task, according to Schleiermacher, was to provide the necessary leadership for the Christian community, that is leadership of the church. Unlike Kant he held that theology was independent of the interests of the state (par. 3). By church leadership he meant that of properly trained clergy. Thus theology was a positive science because it grouped together 'those scientific facts and rules which must be known and used in order for a common leadership of the Christian Church, that is the government of the Church, to be possible' (par 5). Schleiermacher thereby reasserted the practical nature of 'positive theology' which Calixt had defended two hundred years before. [513] But whereas Calixt had held that positive theology was merely one of the theological disciplines, Schleiermacher used the term to describe theology as a whole. The theoretical reflections on theology as one of the three 'higher faculties', which were the background to Schleiermacher's position, were still a long way from Calixt. Schleiermacher, however, followed and complemented Calixt's initiative in associating theology's positivity with its practical orientation, even though the ultimate question of human salvation was thereby reduced to a matter of Christian praxis or rather – to be more specific – to ecclesial praxis (although to be fair the latter's purpose was the salvation of mankind as a whole).

4. Schleiermacher and the Thematic Unity of Theology

Schleiermacher and his disciple K. R. Hagenbach described theology as a positive science. [514] This was indeed an accurate

---

[512] Schleiermacher, *Kurze Darstellung des theologischen Studiums* (1811), 2nd ed. 1830, critical ed. by H. Scholz, 1935, 1 (§ 1). Paragraph references in the text are to this work.

[513] Wallmann (*Der Theologiebegriff bei Johann Gerhard und Georg Calixt*, pp. 144ff, esp. 147) has rightly drawn attention to this.

[514] K. R. Hagenbach (*Encyklopädie und Methodologie der Theologischen Wissenschaften*, 1833, 11th ed. 1884, p. 51) emphasised the 'positive' (in the

description of the function of theology – together with jurisprudence and medicine – in the nineteenth century university. At a time when the three classical faculties were losing their traditional primacy to the claims of philosophy and the sciences deriving from it, Schleiermacher succeeded in gaining a new place for theology in the university. He justified this in terms of idealist philosophy as well as in terms of the positive and practical nature of theology itself. However, theology's new position was more closely bound up with political considerations than Schleiermacher realised. Society and the state had an interest in the practical function of Christian theology. Schleiermacher neglected Kant's point that the three 'higher' faculties served not only the 'natural ends' of the people but also the interests of the government concerned with these natural ends. Given the position actually occupied by theology in the nineteenth century university, this was a big mistake. For the interest of the state in his definition of theology as a positive science, Schleiermacher substituted the church's interest in professional training, though in his own time the institutional form of the church's interest was by no means so independent of political involvements as to allow that of the state to be neglected. By idealising theology as a function of the church Schleiermacher forgot that it was not the church that gave theology a place in the university. Theology would continue as a university faculty only if society and the state also had reasons for wanting to keep it there. This would have meant a connection between church and state which Schleiermacher opposed.

On the other hand it is doubtful whether an independent church would wish to confine its interest in theology to the positive and practical side advocated by Schleiermacher. But this, of course, was not his point: he was concerned with the general

traditional sense) character of the three classical faculties: according to him, they had 'the source of their scientific status, not in themselves, like pure knowledge, but outside in a given area of life created by empirical conditions' and as a result of 'something supplied by an external authority'. Theology shared with the legal sciences a 'historical basis' and an institutional connection, in the one case with the church and in the other with the state, and with medicine the therapeutic character of the activity for which it was a preparation.

question of the position of the three 'higher' faculties in the university. But Schleiermacher's positive and practical theology must have an institutionally secure basis on which to operate. This basis could be either its secure position in society or its own power. Only a church which was a secure institution could be content with a theology concerned with the interests of the church as such an institution, a theology confined to the 'positive and practical'. As soon as its position as an institution was threatened – either by society or by a church which was suspicious of too many awkward questions about its own tradition – the positive and practical concept of theology was no longer sufficient.[515]

The ability of Schleiermacher's interpretation of theology as a positive science to prevent theology from disintegrating can be shown only by an application of his view to the material of the theological disciplines as Schleiermacher himself described them. We turn now, therefore, from a consideration of the basis of Schleiermacher's concept of theology, which he himself did not sufficiently examine, to the question of its internal consistency. This is the true test.

According to Schleiermacher, the internal unity of the theological disciplines and their subject-matter derives entirely from the practical connection of theology with the work of the church's leaders: 'Without this connection, the same items of knowledge cease to be theological and each become part of a different science' (par. 6, 1st ed.). Did Schleiermacher succeed in substantiating this view by his study of the individual theological disciplines and their relationship to each other? Do these disciplines really acquire their unity in Schleiermacher's account only from the demands of training for the ministry?

Schleiermacher distinguishes three chief theological disciplines. The first is philosophical theology. This is necessary to theology as a whole because there is no 'knowledge of Christianity' which does not see Christianity as one among other forms of religion

---

[515] G. Sauter (*Theologie als Wissenschaft*, 1971, p. 38) claims that the basis provided for the concept of theology by Schleiermacher and Hagenbach is 'still valid today, though it takes a different form' – the form they suggest is that of the slogan 'from text to sermon'. I can accept this view only in so far as it is a description of the existing situation.

and these 'in the context of other activities of the human mind'. (par. 21). Philosophical theology must therefore start by proving that the establishment of religious communities 'is a necessary element in the development of the human mind' (par. 22). Thence it must set out 'the essence of Christianity' as a 'particular form of belief' and the corresponding 'form of the Christian community' (par. 24).

Schleiermacher contrasts 'practical theology' with philosophical theology because it is concerned with the 'technique' of church or community leadership and can be divided into various branches (par. 25).

In the middle, between philosophical and practical theology, lies the 'main body of theological study' (par. 29), historical theology (par. 26). Historical theology is necessary because the business of church leadership requires a 'knowledge of the whole that is to be led'. This also involves knowledge of this whole at the various stages of its historical development. 'Because the whole is a historical whole' the present state of the church can be understood only 'as a result of what went before' (par. 26). For Schleiermacher the term historical theology covers a great deal. As well as church history it includes exegetical theology, dogmatics and 'ecclesiastical statistics' as a description of the present state of Christianity in so far as this is the result of its history.

'Historical theology' as the central element in the triad of theological disciplines is linked through practical theology to 'active Christian life' and through philosophical theology to 'true science' (par. 28).

After this brief look at Schleiermacher's division of theology into disciplines, we can enquire more closely into his concept of theology as a 'positive science'. If we take first the reason Schleiermacher gives for the need for the various disciplines and their relationship to one another, the question arises: is their unity the result merely of the practical educational need? Would it not follow from the essence of Christianity (the special object of philosophical theology) that Christianity is a 'historical whole' and that knowledge of it therefore requires historical theology? Could we not also derive practical theology from the essence of Christianity on the plea that Christianity is not a closed system from the past and that the question of its concrete realisation is still an open one? In this case practical theology would not be confined a priori to putting the responsibilities of 'church leadership' into effect.

It therefore seems that the unity of the theological disciplines can be derived not merely from the need for training clergy but also from the essence of Christianity, and this means that it is not primarily due to the practical need of future clergy to acquire knowledge. Schleiermacher himself suggests this when he says on the one hand that historical theology is the *foundation* of practical theology and on the other that it is the *proof* of philosophical theology (par. 27). In this schema there is an inner theological continuity from philosophical via historical to practical theology, based on the nature of Christianity rather than on external educational requirements. Schleiermacher's statement that the unity of the theological disciplines derives uniquely from the needs of training for the ministry is therefore unjustified because of the inner *theological* continuity of the various disciplines. Furthermore, his derivation of the need for historical theology from the requirements of church leadership is not convincing. He rightly says that church leadership requires a knowledge of 'the whole that is to be led in its various historical phases' (par. 26), including the present, and part of this is the knowledge of how this present situation arose. It is very revealing, however, that Schleiermacher must base the need for historical theology on the need to understand the church's present situation. If historical theology is the 'main body of theological study' (par. 28), its actual importance in relation to theology as a whole cannot be justified on these lines. Knowledge of the *present* state of Christianity would occupy a much more prominent position in the needs of church leadership if Christianity were not a *historical* religion. There is a need for such intensive exegetical study of the early documents only because Christianity proclaims as saviour of the world a figure from the past – Jesus of Nazareth. The further question therefore arises of the historical continuity of Christianity from its beginnings until the present – in other words, of the study of church history.

This makes it clear that the nature of the Christian religion determines the needs of education for 'church leadership', not vice versa. Schleiermacher himself in fact grouped the theological disciplines not according to educational needs but according to his idea of Christianity. The knowledge necessary for leaders of the Christian community is and must be determined by the nature of Christianity.

These considerations arise from the fact that theology has a clear unity of content – Christianity. Theology can be described, in a first approximation, as the science of Christianity. Schleiermacher's pragmatic conception of the unity of theology is true only inasmuch as the church with its educational needs is the historical reason why a science of Christianity is pursued in the universities, and in its own faculty. But the church's and society's interest in the science of Christianity does not *make* that science what it is. When these interests rule theology, theology is likely to become a corrupt science. Indeed theology is often reproached with neglecting the pure search for truth and becoming an ideology shoring up the churches or a prevailing social system. The history of theology shows that it must constantly reassert itself as a science devoted to the pursuit of truth against the pragmatic interest of the churches in the most effective form of theological training. If these educational interests become paramount then paradoxically theology might fail in its true service to the church, which lies in its duty to seek the truth.

The dangers of Schleiermacher's concept of theology showed particularly clearly in the confessional theologies of the nineteenth century, which accepted that the unity of theology could be justified by the needs of the church and its leaders in the sense of giving a confessional base to theology.[516] The consequence of Schleiermacher's theology based on the requirements of church leaders was that a confessional ecclesiality functioned as the unquestioned foundation of theology and could therefore acquire immunity from criticism. This, of course, was not Schleiermacher's intention, but it plainly shows the limitations of his concept of theology.

---

[516] See, for example, A. Harless, *Theologische Enzyklopädie vom Standpunkt der Kirche aus,* 1837.

5. Theology as the Science of Christianity?

Schleiermacher described the relation between the theological disciplines expressly in terms of a practical theology concerned with the responsibilities of church leaders, which thus made it a 'positive' science. But as we saw, he was at the same time making another assumption: that theology was in fact the science of Christianity. Theology could also be called a 'positive science' in this sense, although this was not what Schleiermacher meant. Christianity can be regarded as a historical phenomenon and thus as a positive object comparable with other objects of scientific enquiry. Such a science of Christianity would be 'positive' in the Enlightenment sense of the term, viz. that everything that happened in history counts as positive. Different notions of historicity produce variants in the concept of positive. In the theology of the Enlightenment Christianity was called positive because, in contrast to natural religion, it came from a positive revelation, or in supernaturalist terms, God *gave* Christianity by divine revelation. This theology of revelation as a version of theology as the science of Christianity is still held today. It prefers to be called the science of revelation or faith because it is not merely the secular study of a transitory historical phenomenon, but looks with the eyes of faith for God's action in Christianity.

In this section we shall be considering this idea of theology. At the same time we shall also consider Christianity as a cultural and historical phenomenon, the 'givenness' of Christianity as a particular religious community with a particular history. This offers us two alternatives. Either we can look at Christianity as one religion among many others in the context of the history of religion, and theology then comes under the general heading of science of religion. This is what Paul de Lagarde called for in 1873, and theologians of the history of religion school, especially E. Troeltsch, have taken over this line at least in theory, although in fact their theology is concerned mainly with research into Christianity, its historical conditions and environment. Or, if we single out Christianity from the rest of religious history because of its practical relevance to the present, Christianity itself becomes the object of theology. But in this case the practical interest in thus singling out Christianity becomes part of the definition of theology, even though Christianity as a historical phenomenon is still thought of as the subject of theological study. This view was held by G. Heinrici, who belonged to the school of A. Ritschl and explained the positive nature of theology in this manner. Heinrici mainly follows Schleiermacher but unlike him holds that the primary reason for the positive nature of theology is that 'its subject-matter is given in history'; its practical connection with the life of the church is a secondary consideration.[517] This historical side is more important for him than for Schleiermacher. Because of the contingency of history, this view of the positive nature of theology has a fluid attitude to the supernatural element. M. Kähler for example writes that theology is 'a historico-positive science' [518] and the 'science of Christianity' which 'cannot be severed from the science of history as a whole'.[519] Likewise M. Rade writes that theology is 'a particular science of religion and the church standing on the same ground as science as a whole.' [520] It becomes 'uprooted' if 'it can no longer justify its claim to be part of the science of history'. G. Wobbermin opposed this assignment of theology exclusively to history on the grounds that theology, like all other human sciences for which history was of fundamental importance, included systematic as well as historical disciplines, even though these systematic disciplines were still 'essentially characterised by

---

[517] G. Heinrici, *Theologische Encyklopädie*, 1893, pp. 4–5. However, according to Heinrici historical theology acquires its theological character only from its 'positive connection with the Church and its life' (p. 25). Theology differs from general religious studies in that in it the historical and practical elements combine in such a way that the historical reality of Christianity becomes its subject as 'the historical basis for the truth of the faith'.

[518] M. Kähler, *Wissenschaft der christlichen Lehre* (1883), 2nd ed. 1893, p. 12.

[519] Kähler, p. 6. Nevertheless, according to Kähler, Christianity, especially as a 'present force' in which its adherents 'have found the satisfaction of the deepest needs of their personal lives', presents an absolute challenge to intellectual enquiry' (p. 7), with the result that the non-Christian 'can neither recognise nor fully understand this object' (p. 8). We are unlikely to be far wrong in assuming that for Kähler it is the 'super-historical' element in Christianity (pp. 12ff), the living 'union of the permanently and universally valid and the historical in an immediate force' (p. 13), which is beyond the knowledge of the unbeliever.

[520] M. Rade, 'Die Bedeutung des geschichtlichen Sinnes im Protestantismus', *ZThK* 10 (1900), p. 79; the next quotation is from p. 80.

the historical method'.[521] But for Wobbermin too theology was 'the science of religion and in particular the Christian religion' (375). Theology studied religion both as a historical whole and also (in systematic theology) as 'the living present of a religious and moral consciousness' (414). Wobbermin defended the claim of theology to possess 'the character of a science in the strictest sense of the word' (423), and this included systematic theology whose job was to 'outline a whole view of the world' even though it could lay claim to no more than 'hypothetical validity'. Thus he differed from Troeltsch for whom ' (Christian) theology should be directed and subordinated to the science of religion', whereas Wobbermin held that 'the science of religion is an auxiliary discipline to (Christian) theology' (437). This constituted the positivity of theology in Wobbermin's conception, although he avoided the term because of its ambiguity in Schleiermacher (411).

Wobbermin's difference with Troeltsch also shows how the Protestant version of the conception of theology as a positive science had not completely cut itself off from the supernaturalist conceptions of the positive nature of theology, in which the delimitation of theology from the general history of religion requires a judgment of value or faith, particularly because it does not presuppose purely pragmatic points of view but, as in Wobbermin, is associated with the special claim to truth of the Christian religion made as a hermeneutical assumption.[522] But within the field thus marked out scientific methods should be applied as strictly as possible.[523]

[521] G. Wobbermin, 'Das Verhältnis der Theologie zur modernen Wissenschaft und ihre Stellung im Gesamtrahmen der Wissenschaften', *ZThK* 10 (1900), pp. 375–438, esp. 415, 418–19. The page references in the rest of this paragraph are to this article.

[522] On this, see Wobbermin's reasons for defending the view that Christianity is an absolute religion against Troeltsch, 'Das Verhältnis', pp. 384ff, esp. 391ff. This assumption was expressed even more clearly by F. Traub, 'Kirchliche und unkirchliche Theologie', *ZThK* 13 (1903), pp. 39ff, esp. 60ff. See also H. Eckert, *Einführung in die Prinzipien und Methoden der evangelischen Theologie*, 1909, and T. Steinmann, 'Kirche, Theologie, Wissenchaft', *ZThK* 21 (1911), pp. 315ff.

[523] As when Traub refers to the obligation of theology to 'test this assumption'. Testing a truth always means questioning it, 'at least hypothetically' (*ZThK* 13, p. 61).

Wobbermin's defence of the scientific status of systematic theology was opposed even in A. Ritschl's school by O. Ritschl. According to O. Ritschl theology was 'not a science at all in its original form of dogmatic theology interested mainly in apologetics', and only 'became more and more of a science in its historical branch after the eighteenth century.' [524] This ought to mean that O. Ritschl did not count systematic theology as a science at all but included it, together with practical theology, in 'ecclesiastical' theology as distinct from 'scientific' theology, as C. A. Bernoulli did. [525] But O. Ritschl did not wish to go this far. He stood by his explanation that 'I can recognise systematic theology as a science in so far as it is a special kind of psychological science.' [526] Schleiermacher had already prepared the way for this.

Behind these internal disputes lay the question of whether theology satisfied the conditions for scientific status, including the lack of presuppositions deemed necessary for this status. [527] The starting point for this discussion was Paul de Lagarde's demand (1873) that the theological faculties should be replaced by chairs in the general science of religion, because theology as it stood was not a science on account of its ecclesiastical tie. [528] Before this, Fichte had held in 1807 that there was room in the university only for a theology which renounced belief in positive revelation. Nobody took any notice then, but after Lagarde's attack, which F. Overbeck supported in the same year, [529] the

---

[524] O. Ritschl, 'Theologische Wissenschaft und religiöse Spekulation', *ZThK* 12 (1902), pp. 202ff, quotation from p. 205.

[525] C. A. Bernoulli, *Die wissenschaftliche und die kirchlihe Methode in der Theologie*, 1897. Of the systematic theologians of the period, only W. Herrmann allowed that the distinctness of systematic theology from the sphere of science might be a fact of positive significance, and even Herrmann, to the best of my knowledge, drew no conclusions from this about the position of theology in universities.

[526] O. Ritschl, 'Theologische Wissenschaft', p. 209. This view was criticised by Traub ('Kirchliche und unkirchliche Theologie', pp. 65ff).

[527] On this see E. L. Solte, *Theologie an der Universität. Staats- und Kirchenrechtliche Probleme der theologischen Fakultäten*, 1971, pp. 15ff, 24ff.

[528] P. de Lagarde, 'Über das Verhältnis des deutschen Staates zu Theologie, Kirche und Religion', *Deutsche Schriften*, 1920, pp. 40ff.

[529] F. Overbeck, *Über die Christlichkeit unserer heutigen Theologie* (1873), reprinted 1963, pp. IX–X and passim.

discussion spread. The Catholic side replied to the demand that theology should have no presuppositions by saying that there was no science without presuppositions.[530] The Protestants argued in a similar manner. F. Traub said that even 'unecclesiastical' theology had a presupposition, namely, 'the reality of religion'.[531] But the Protestants could also claim lack of presupposition in the sense that the scientific approach implied the readiness to question and test all presuppositions. Troeltsch entered the discussion with this suggestion in 1897. He agreed with Hertling that science in fact was 'always in some way connected with presuppositions'. But these presuppositions must 'always be hypothetically questioned'. 'The unavoidable presuppositions and axioms of true scientific thought must remain subject to revision and could be validated only by the results of clarification and interpretation, not by the church's say-so.'[532] Troeltsch thereby anticipated an important aspect of E. Spranger's remarks (in many ways conclusive) on presupposition in the sciences. In 1929 Spranger showed that the human sciences were always tied to the historical situation and the breadth and maturity of the researcher, as well as to the basic ideological attitudes from which understanding arises.[533] Today we are probably more inclined to agree that this is also true in principle of the natural sciences, even though in a different way. Spranger regarded the demand for no presuppositions as impossible – 'we can say no more about it' (20) – but he also stressed the connection of science with the idea of one truth accessible to the Logos (18f), which means that 'science, in contrast to simple credulous dogmatism, must always be prepared to subject its own

---

[530] G. von Hertling, *Das Princip des Katholizismus und die Wissenschaft*, 1899. A similar view is expressed by M. Schmaus, *Der Glaube der Kirche*, vol. I, 1969, pp. 224–5, and B. Welte, *Die Wesensstruktur der Theologie als Wissenschaft*, 1955, pp. 7–8. Further references in Solte, *Theologie an der Universität*, 1971, p. 25.

[531] Traub, 'Kirchliche und unkirchliche Theologie', p. 54.

[532] E. Troeltsch, 'Voraussetzungslose Wissenschaft', *Gesammelte Schriften*, vol. II, pp. 183–92, quotations from pp. 183–4, 186 and 188. Similarly O. Baumgarten, *Die Voraussetzungslosigkeit der protestantischen Theologie*, 1903.

[533] E. Spranger, *Der Sinn der Voraussetzungslosigkeit in den Geistes-wissenschaften*, 1929, pp. 13ff. The page references in the rest of this paragraph and in the next are to this essay.

presuppositions to criticism and perhaps to revise them. The virtue of science is not lack of presuppositions but *radical self-criticism*' (20).

Spranger believed that willingness to be criticised fundamentally and without stint was the opposite of 'simple credulous dogmatism' and this set the tone for attacks on theology even decades later by 'critical rationalism' (see above pp. 43ff). A Christian theology which is 'positive' in the sense that it holds the truth of the Christian faith to be indisputable in its 'core', which may be more or less narrowly defined,[534] cannot in fact be reconciled with this demand. The truth of the Christian tradition can function only as a hypothesis in any theology which proceeds scientifically.

Can theology be justified as the science of Christianity in this modified form, namely on the proviso that the truth of the Christian tradition must be treated as a hypothesis? The difficulty here is that a discipline concerned with a single general hypothesis cannot claim scientific status because there would be no possibility of ratification within such a discipline. Such ratification could come only from a wider field, in this case perhaps the science of religion in general. But Troeltsch's attempt to 'include religion in an independent and purely scientific philosophy of religion'[535] faced other difficulties. These difficulties arose in Troeltsch's passage from the psychological via the epistemological to the metaphysical answer to the question of

---

[534] In his essay 'Kirchliche und unkirchliche Theologie', Traub referred to an 'unavoidable presupposition' (pp. 60–1). Traub says that this 'basic presupposition' distinguishes theology from philosophy of religion, which considers 'the Christian faith merely as a mental fact' and makes no judgment on 'its objective truth'. Nevertheless he goes on: 'Theology also has an obligation to test this presupposition it makes', and testing a truth, according to Traub, means 'at least hypothetically questioning it' (p. 61). If this is seriously meant, the 'basic presupposition' of the truth of the Christian faith itself becomes a hypothesis, as Wobbermin claimed at the time (*ZThK* 10 (1900), p. 410). If this is so, it is misleading to talk about a 'basic presupposition' 'within' which all theological investigation must take place.
[535] E. Troeltsch, 'Die theologische und religiöse Lage der Gegenwart' (1903), *Gesammelte Schriften,* vol. II, p. 19; see in the same volume 'Rückblick auf ein halbes Jahrhundert der theologischen Wissenschaft' (1908), pp. 193ff, esp. 223ff.

the validity of religious experience. The problem is that in asking whether the Christian religion is true we cannot treat theology as a special science of Christianity or as a science of religion in the sense that its content can be properly distinguished from that of other disciplines.

Of course historically, under Christianity, the subject-matter of theology has in fact been mainly the Christian religion, its origins, nature and present relevance in its historical and modern forms. An indication that theology is not just a science of the Christian religion lies in the inclusion of the Old Testament and its exegesis in Christian theology. Of course the Old Testament can be regarded as a document concerned with the *pre-history* of Christianity in a theology defined as the science of Christianity. But then the question arises: why is Christian pre-history studied only in the Old Testament and not also in Greek philosophy and religion? The difficulty of including the Old Testament in teaching and research in a theology regarded as the 'science of the Christian religion' is shown by the fact that the Enlightenment and then Schleiermacher were inclined to regard the Old Testament as the source of another religion, the Jewish religion, and therefore to exclude it from Christian theology. On the other hand it is undeniable that the Old Testament is not only a document of Christian pre-history but also the only holy scripture of the early church and therefore itself a vehicle of Christian tradition. But then we immediately run into the difficulty of how to interpret the contents of the Old Testament if the Christian religion is not the same as the Jewish, regarding itself as independent from it and not just a Jewish sect. Furthermore the use of the Old Testament in Christian theology is not confined to its *interpretatio christiana* but is studied and researched for itself as part of theology. This suggests that it is not sufficient to call theology the science of the Christian religion. The interpretation of the Old Testament in the development of Christian theology has in fact been based on a science of God and his self-proclamation in his action (*oikonomia*) because this divine action began not with Christianity but with the creation of the world and, within the narrower confines of the history of divine election, with the choosing of Abraham. Consideration of the place of the Old Testament in theology makes the concept of theology as the science of Christianity untenable. It forces us towards a concept of theology as the science of God. The question of the truth of the Christian religion leads in the same direction. A theology which presupposes Christianity as its basis in the sense that it confines itself to the description and development of Christianity's historical data is not wide enough to enable the question of the truth of Christianity to be properly discussed. This is true both when the existence of Christianity or its origin in the figure of Jesus or in the apostolic kerygma is claimed to be divine revelation and when Christianity is studied as a datum of cultural or religious history. In the first case the truth of Christianity is something theology must presuppose. In the second case the truth of Christianity remains an open question because research into Christianity as a cultural and historical phenomenon and one religion among others is not in a position to answer the question. This question, as the path taken by Troeltsch shows, can finally be answered only by borrowing from 'metaphysics'. In both cases the question of the truth of Christianity goes beyond the scope of theology regarded as the positive science of Christianity. But in fact, of course, theology has repeatedly considered the question. Theological thinking and research has been devoted to it which shows clearly that the concept of theology as the science of Christianity is too narrow.

There exists the final possibility of saving the concept of theology as the positive science of Christianity if it is willing to leave the question of its truth to philosophy, at least in principle. Thus in a lecture given during 1927/8 Martin Heidegger defined theology as the positive science of Christianity, by which he meant a science of belief, because belief was the condition for the fact that 'there exists such a thing as Christianity as an event in world history'.[536] This leaves open the question of where this faith comes from, whether from experience, the authority of the church or a combination of the two. Heidegger excludes the grounds for belief from his concept of theology. He saw belief as an existentialist mode of self-understanding based on one's own existential decision, and so he did not need to consider the question. Because he presupposed this and therefore considered

[536] M. Heidegger, *Phänomenologie und Theologie*, 1970, pp. 17ff, quotation, p. 18.

belief not from the point of view of its content but as a way of understanding existence, Heidegger could fit theology into his system of sciences based on the analysis of existence. He related theology *negatively* to the other positive sciences. Accordingly philosophy did not claim to determine the subject of theology, as it did with the other positive sciences; it merely claimed the right of *correcting* because Christian faith as rebirth related only negatively to human existence (31). It is clear that even if the relationship is defined in this way philosophy assigns to faith its sphere of truth. And this would prejudge the claim made by theology for the Christian tradition, which it is theology's business to investigate, that the truth about reality is made known by this tradition. This claim made for the Christian tradition, which *mutatis mutandis* is also made by other religions, makes it impossible for theology to be included as a positive science in a system of the sciences defined by a philosophy independent of Christianity. Theology throughout its history has always resisted such an inclusion. This is not just because theology believes itself in the right but also because the claim it makes for the truth of the Christian tradition, although not necessarily fixed dogmatically in advance by theology, must at least be tested by theology itself.

Just as we saw earlier that the question of the truth of Christianity cannot be confined to the fact of its actual existence as a historical phenomenon, it has now become clear that it cannot be restricted to the truth of Christianity alone. Or rather, the question of the truth of Christianity cannot be enquired into without also enquiring into the question of the truth of all areas of human experience. This is because Christianity claims to be not just Christianity but God's revelation, or at least to be based on God's revelation. If this appeal to revelation is treated not just as a presupposition but as a theme of theological reflection, then theology must go beyond Christianity in its description and interpretation of Christianity. It must go beyond Christianity as a religion among and beside other non-religious areas of culture and also beyond Christianity as a revealed religion in contrast to natural human life. As soon as Christianity's appeal to God's revelation is taken seriously, then the subject of theology cannot be confined to a particular subject side by side with other subjects of other disciplines. Theology must then broach many other subjects as well as its particular concern with religious experience and Christianity. Thus theology traditionally speaks of the creation of the world by God. It must therefore take an interest in the way the natural sciences see the world, and not only from the point of view of whether the natural scientists are themselves Christian, but also from the point of view of whether the methods and findings of natural science are reconcilable with the understanding of the world implicit in the doctrine of creation.

The example of the doctrine of creation illustrates once more that theology cannot be only a science of Christianity. We may put it more strongly: theology cannot be the science of Christianity merely because as a 'positive science' it investigates Christianity as a phenomenon distinct from other limited areas of phenomena. Theology can do justice to Christianity only if it is not a science of Christianity but a science of God. As a science of God its subject matter is reality as a whole, even though as yet uncompleted whole of the semantic network of experience.

This is how theology in fact saw itself in the periods of its classical development at the time of the early church and in the middle ages. It was teaching about God and the things that happened through his divine ordinance (*oikonomia*). A 'science of Christianity' must also be concerned with this. Its task is to describe and interpret Christianity, and in order to do this it must constantly go *beyond* Christianity, if, at least hermeneutically, it wishes to repeat what the Old or New Testament and theological tradition says about God as something relevant to today. Theology which regards itself as the science of Christianity – and therefore as a 'positive' science – conceals the main problem, the problem of how it speaks about God and this leads unintentionally to the discrediting of talk about God.

6. Karl Barth and the Positivity of Revelation

Karl Barth with his own peculiar determination has impressed a whole generation with the idea that theology is about God and his revelation and not primarily the science of the Christian religion. But in turning to the theology of revelation Barth does not deny that he presupposes revelation.[537] A characteristic feature of his theology is that revelation cannot be 'justified'. In this theology as a science of God and his revelation Barth takes God and his word as the only possible *starting-point*. This is the only position God can hold in relation to the human enquirer. For God is 'never in any sense "object" but is always unchangeably subject'.[538] Theology is possible only as 'concrete obedience' the obedience of faith to 'the will of God in his revelation',[539] and so for Barth the datum is not man and his thinking and experiencing, but 'God himself in *his* word'. In Barth's words: 'Obviously this is no datum to be found in any sense on the level of our consciousness. It is not God as an assumption of our consciousness. It is God setting himself over against our consciousness and its assumptions.' [540] But the critical question by which to judge Barth's theological foundation is whether he has succeeded in making God and his revelation anything but the postulate of our (or his) consciousness. If it were possible, this would be the only proper way of conducting a theology as a science of God, with God himself and his revelation as the starting point.

Barth sees the difficulty: 'Theology should speak about God, but speaking about God in a valid way would mean speaking from revelation and from faith. Speaking about God would mean speaking God's word, the word that can come only from

---

[537] In his criticism of Herrmann's approach through an 'investigation of man's real self', Barth for once offered something like a defence of the opposite direction he had taken, by remarking that this enquiry is possible only if it already presupposes an image of man's self, against which man can see himself being measured. Ultimately, however this means, says Barth, that 'the revelation towards which, according to Herrmann, that question is to lead must be already understood as the presupposition of the question' ('The Principles of Dogmatics According to Wilhelm Herrman', *Theology and the Church*, London and New York, 1962, p. 258). In practice, this is an argument for and justification of the move towards a theology of revelation which Barth took. This is not at all the intention of his argument, however, which is designed rather to show the impossibility of any introduction or support for a theology of revelation.
[538] Barth, p. 260.
[539] Barth, p. 302.
[540] p. 260.

him.'[541] What does the phrase 'God's word' mean? It is often used casually by theologians as if there could be no doubt about what was involved. Barth says something about it in at least one place: 'Word is the revelation and self-communication of another person giving himself to us and if this person is God it is an expression of his lordship, not his power, but his lordship over us.' [542] But this also means that 'only God himself can speak about God'.[543] Theology can be only 'the service of God's will,' 'service of the word'. This is also true of ecclesiastical office and 'the special function of this office is to *watch* over the preservation or restoration of true doctrine throughout the inevitable ups and downs in the preaching of the kerygma, with the authority of the church and in the freedom of faith, which means looking towards the primary authority of the Lord'.[544] Barth's final answer to the question of the possibility of *human* speech about God and his revelation, according to early statements in Barth's 'dialectical' period,[545] therefore consists in saying that theology as a 'function of the Church' takes part, through the obedience of faith, in the movement of God's own revealing will, which presses for proclamation. It serves this proclamation by being 'the scientific test to which the Christian church puts herself', 'the task of criticising and revising her language about God'.[546] Human speech about God is possible only in this indirect manner: 'theology serves revelation by serving preaching'.[547]

Barth's idea of the scientific nature of theology to which he would like to hold in spite of his stress on the theology of revelation fits naturally into this conception. According to Barth, theology is scientific in its 'proper treatment of its object', its 'conformity with its object or its appropriate treatment of it'.[548] But the subject-matter of theology is God in his revelation, that is, the word of God (see above). Theology's proper

---

[541] 'Das Wort Gottes als Aufgabe der Theologie' (1922), quoted from the collection of essays, *Das Wort Gottes und die Theologie*, 1924, p. 167.

[542] *Die Theologie und die Kirche*, p. 352.

[543] *Das Wort Gottes und die Theologie*, p. 177.

[544] *Die Theologie und die Kirche*, 1928, p. 323.

[545] *Das Wort Gottes und die Theologie*, 1924, pp. 172ff.

[546] *Church Dogmatics*, Edinburgh 1936–62, vol. I/1, pp. 1–2.

[547] *Die Theologie und die Kirche*, p. 325.

[548] *Church Dogmatics*, loc. cit., p. 8.

treatment of its object is determined by whether it corresponds to the word of God through the obedience of faith.

Barth first put forward this view of the scientific nature of theology, viz. its appropriateness to its subject, in his *Christliche Dogmatik* of 1927. He was attacking the view of H. H. Wendt who, in accordance with the neo-Kantian tendencies of his time, tried to base scientific status on purely methodological considerations. 'The scientific character of a branch of knowledge depends not on its subject-matter but on its methical approach to it.' According to Wendt, scientific knowledge proves itself methodical by its context ('a complete and ordered knowledge of the whole tree to which the individual branch of knowledge belongs'), by 'critique', and finally by its 'proper proof' of what is asserted – a proof which 'may take very different forms according to the epistemological objects'.[549] This last condition is in a certain tension with Wendt's basic tenet that scientific knowledge does not depend on its subject-matter. Barth takes this up in making 'objectivity' the main criterion for scientific status. He does not say that in this he is propounding the view of M. Kähler. Among theologians in the previous generation it was Kähler who particularly stressed that scientific procedure must conform with the relevant subject-matter.[550] Kähler had, however, added that 'every particular subject requires its own form of scientific treatment within the general method of universal epistemological laws'. But at this point Barth diverges from Kähler. He severs the need for appropriateness to a particular subject from the 'universal epistemological laws'. He can thus agree with Wendt about the methodical nature of the procedure to be adopted with the reservation that 'the choice of means to establish the objective truth, the nature of the epistemological context, the critical

[549] H. H. Wendt, *System der christlichen Lehre,* 1906, pp. 2 and 3.

[550] M. Kähler, *Wissenschaft der christlichen Lehre von dem evangelischen Grundartikel aus* (1883), 2nd ed. 1893, p. 5: 'It is the object which determines the appropriate method . . .' That the only thing which could make theology a science was 'following a method of enquiry adequate to its object' was said even more clearly by Traub in his essay 'Kirchliche und unkirchliche Theologie', p. 65. The quotation which follows in the text is from Kähler, p. 14.

norms and the possibility of proof in any branch of knowledge must be determined by the particular subject, and this subject must not be forced to conform to a previously held idea of scientific method.'[551]

Unlike H. Diem,[552] Barth has not rejected outright the inclusion of theology in the 'encyclopedia of general scientific knowledge'.[553] He has allowed this as long as it does not endanger theology's appropriateness to its own subject. Barth holds that 'all the sciences at their acme might be theology' and then the 'separate existence of theology' would become superfluous.[554] In fact, of course, this is not the case, and Barth has no general theory of knowledge into which theology can comfortably fit. To describe theology as a science is to 'protest against what is conceded to be the "pagan" concept of science', and furthermore to assert that as a 'human striving for truth' theology has *only* science, not some kind of wisdom over and above all the sciences, to offer.[555]

Barth's basic idea that scientific status rests on appropriateness to the subject first and research method only in a secondary manner was rejected by H. Scholz in 1931. In a postscript to his lecture 'How can an evangelical theology be a science?'[556] Scholz gave his reason for this: 'I have not yet found a criterion by means of which any given idea can be judged appropriate to its subject, even in cases of serious disagreement' (52). At least such a verdict – and in this we must agree with Scholz – cannot be reached independently of formal criteria of scientific validity, in particular of the demand for control of its propositions. These demands make it possible to decide whether an assertion suits its subject-matter or not. This is the crux of the controversy between Barth and Scholz. We can only regret that Barth's

---

[551] *Christliche Dogmatik*, 1927, p. 115.
[552] See above, pp. 18ff.
[553] *Christliche Dogmatik*, p. 117.
[554] *Church Dogmatics*, I/1, p. 6.
[555] *Church Dogmatics*, I/1, p. 7.
[556] H. Scholz, 'Wie ist eine evangelische Theologie als Wissenschaft möglich?' *Zwischen den Zeiten* 9 (1931), pp. 8–53, esp. pp. 49ff. The quotation which follows is from p. 52.

argument for the scientific status of theology on grounds of
appropriateness to its object is sometimes used to justify
far-reaching assertions with no mention of Scholz's disagreement
with him and the problems it has raised.[557] If we presuppose the
reality of God and his revealing and saving action in Jesus Christ,
then we have said all that is necessary, and theology would speak
less about knowledge and more about recognition and 'pure
doctrine'. We would not hear much more about 'theological
science'.

Scholz laid down three formal postulates ('minimum
conditions') as fundamental criteria of scientific status:[558]
1. The Postulate of Propositions. 'In any science, besides
questions and definitions there can only be *propositions*' i.e.
'statements whose truth is asserted'. This concept of the
proposition corresponds to the concept of the assertion in use in
analytical philosophy. Scholz rightly holds that this postulate
includes the requirement of lack of contradiction (14). If
contradiction were not ruled out, all statements would be equally
allowable, so that seeking for truth would become meaningless
because the opposition between truth and untruth would
disappear.
2. The Postulate of Coherence. All propositions must be related
to a single field of study. 'We can speak of a science only if it
concentrates on one aspect of reality. All propositions belonging
to one and the same science must be capable of formulation as
statements about this aspect of reality' (20). Schleiermacher's
concept of theology (for example) does not conform to this
postulate because it denies that theology has a single subject and
the various theological disciplines are united only in a practical

---

[557] As in T. F. Torrance, *Theological Science*, London 1969. Torrance
employs the criterion of appropriateness: see pp. 26, 37, 112, 131,
144, 284–5, 288, 303. This criterion requires scientific statements to be based
on 'the given' (pp. 27ff, 37). In the case of theology this is God in his word:
'the given fact with which theology operates is God uttering his Word and
uttering Himself in His Word' (p. 32). In Torrance's view the 'scientific
theology' which bases itself on this datum is 'positive theology' (pp. 80, 281,
341) as opposed to 'natural theology' (p. 140).
[558] H. Scholz, 'Wie ist eine evanglische Theologie als Wissenschaft
möglich?', pp. 19ff. The subsequent page references in the text are to this
article.

purpose which lies outside theology (45).

3. The Postulate of Control. This concerns the requirement that the claim to truth made by theological statements should be subject to testing (21). However, this requirement is more general than the requirement of verification, which Scholz holds to be impossible in theology (48). His requirement is concerned only with intelligibility of formulation, with a declaration of the critical principle used, for example the 'evangelical' in evangelical dogmatics, so that 'the critical reader can form his own judgement on the propositions which are stated to be evangelical' (46). If the truth of theological assertions is not subject to control, then for Scholz theology fails as a science. All that remains is 'a personal confession of faith in the most decided sense of the word exempt from all earthly questioning' (48).

To these three necessary minimum conditions Scholz adds two further conditions, which are disputed: the independence postulate, which is concerned with the problem of lack of presuppositions, and the concord postulate, that the propositions of a discipline must agree with the true propositions of all other disciplines. The chief condition to be singled out from all these minimum conditions put together is, according to Scholz, that a science must be able to state its propositions as axioms (fundamental propositions) and as theorems deduced from these axioms (24).

In his *Church Dogmatics* in 1932 Barth rejected Scholz's conditions as 'unacceptable' for theology.[559] He did not go into the distinction between undisputed and disputed minimum conditions and their relationship to the chief condition of axiomatic presentation. According to Barth, even the requirement of lack of contradiction can be accepted only with reservations in theology. As for all the others, which include coherence and control, he says: 'We cannot give an inch without betraying theology, for every concession here would mean surrendering the theme of theology.' Barth's reaction justifies Scholz's sceptical suggestion that we cannot yet speak of theology as a science but only as 'a personal confession of faith exempt from all earthly questioning'.[560] Barth does not agree and

---

[559] *Church Dogmatics*, I/1, p. 8.
[560] H. Scholz, p. 48.

firmly maintains that theology as a human search for truth is a science investigating a 'definite object' by a 'self-consistent path'.[561] But it is impossible to see how Barth has any right to maintain this. What does a 'self-consistent path of knowledge' mean if the universal validity of the principle of non-contradiction is rejected? And what does the capacity to 'be accountable to everyone' mean when the control postulate is 'flatly' declared 'unacceptable'?

Barth's answer must have confirmed the opinion Scholz expressed in his lecture that theology 'interprets faith as such a radical venture that it is impossible to see how this venture can arrive at any propositions' of which 'truth is asserted'. A venture cannot to be judged as true or false.[562] Scholz made this remark about Barth's statements which referred to theology as free obedience, 'for in thinking about it we think for ourselves, but this thinking is obedience.' In this sense theology is a 'science of faith'.[563] It risks 'a wholly uninsured obedience.' (384) 'The theologian has no proof to offer himself or anyone else that he is not being merely fanciful but hears and accepts God's word. He can only feel certain. He can give neither himself nor anyone else the comfort of legitimation proving that he is acting under *orders*. He can only *act* under orders and so bear witness to the presence of the command . . .' (383).

When the foundation of theology is left to a venture in this way, not only is its scientific status endangered, but also the priority of God and his revelation over human beings, on which, for Barth, everything rests. Barth's unmediated starting from God and his revealing word turns out to be no more than an

[561] *Church Dogmatics*, I/1, p. 7.

[562] Scholz, p. 39.

[563] Barth, 'Die Theologie und der heutige Mensch', *Zwischen den Zeiten* 8 (1930), pp. 374–96, esp. 382ff. The concept of venture occurs on p. 384. In his late work, *Evangelical Theology: an Introduction* (London 1963), p. 100, Barth wrote, in apparent contradiction with his earlier remark: 'Faith is definitely no such venture as that which Satan, for instance, suggested to the Lord on the pinnacle of the Temple (Luke 4: 9–12). It is, instead, a sober as well as a brave appropriation of a firm and certain promise.' The contradiction, however, is only apparent, as the second quotation assumes that the promise is God's promise, and it is just this which the 1930 statement says cannot be demonstrated or proved, but only seized by a 'venture'.

unfounded postulate of theological consciousness. Barth rightly rejects the reduction of the subject-matter of theology to human religious consciousness, but his use of God and his revelation as an unmediated premise provides no escape from these problems. Barth's description of the obedience of faith as a venture shows, and his dispute with Scholz confirms, that a positive theory of revelation not only is not an alternative to subjectivism in theology, but is in fact the furthest extreme of subjectivism made into a theological position. Whereas other attempts to give theology a foundation in human terms sought support from common arguments, Barth's apparently so lofty objectivity about God and God's word turns out to rest on no more than the irrational subjectivity of a venture of faith with no justification outside itself.

The radical nature of Barth's position brings out very clearly a truth of more general relevance. The Enlightenment questioned anything held on authority which was not subject to proof by reason and experience. If we accept this as a valid stance, a 'positive' theology of revelation which does not depend on rational argument can rely only on a subjective act of will or an irrational venture of faith. For Barth's word of God – the church's preaching? scripture? Jesus himself? – demanding the obedience of faith cannot be unambiguous because it remains at least problematical whether it *is* God and divine revelation and not merely human convictions. If proof through rational enquiry is ruled out in advance, but for some reason or other we still want to hold the Christian tradition, nothing remains but the wholly uninsured venture of faith. We should not then conceal from ourselves that this risk is pre-eminently a 'postulate' of our consciousness, which must control its whole content. On the other hand this reduction of the positive nature of the tradition to the subjective leads to a plurality of positions with no rational means of comparing them. In other words, because of the subjectivisation of tradition's positivity theology has become 'positional'.[564] It is positional in so far as it closes its mind to the

---

[564] On this, see D. Rössler, 'Positionelle und kritische Theologie', *ZThK* 67 (1970), pp. 215–30. Nevertheless, it would be wrong to use the term 'positional' wherever a position was adopted, since this would not describe any specifically modern phenomenon. The term should be used only of

effort of intersubjective rationality in the clarification and demonstration of its principles.

Under these conditions how is any agreement in theology still possible and how can theology engage in public discussion?

A few years later Scholz continued his conversation with Barth in his contribution to Barth's *Festschrift* in 1936. Their earlier discussion could have left the impression that Scholz basically agreed with Barth that theology is not a science in the usual sense of the word, and that the difference between Barth and Scholz is merely that Barth calls what he does 'science' rather than a confession of faith exempt from proof. But now the difference has been brought out more sharply. Scholz has said plainly that no one – not even Barth – could formulate meaningful statements without subjecting them to criteria of truth or falsehood.[565] Scholz then admits that what a theological statement should be is a matter for 'definition' (267) or 'agreement' (269). Now according to Barth, a theological statement is a statement about God or a statement capable of being reformulated as a statement about God (271). Barth holds more exactly, however, that a statement about God is a theological statement only when it does not belong to a *rational* theology (274). But Scholz maintains that it is not clear what such a statement would be. If we say: 'A statement should be called *rational* only when it enlightens the natural man,' the question immediately arises as to what we are to understand by this 'natural man'. Scholz says we can successfully answer this question only if we accept that 'by natural man we mean a man who is not enlightened by a theological statement of the Karl Barth type'. He continues: 'This is as circular as you can get' (275). Thus his attempt to analyse the meaning of a theological statement ends in ironical despair. Scholz takes Barth's thesis that a theological statement is a statement about God which must not be rational to its absurd conclusion and thus answers implicitly Barth's rejection of his theories about science. He also issues a 'warning' which clearly

---

positions for which no attempt is made to offer a rational argument.

[565] H. Scholz, 'Was ist unter einer theologischen Aussage zu verstehen?', *Theologische Aufsätze Karl Barth zum 50. Geburtstag*, 1963, pp. 25–37, reprinted in G. Sauter, *Theologie als Wissenschaft*, 1971, pp. 265ff. The subsequent references in the text are to Sauter's book.

refers to Barth's restrictions on logic. He warns against the
non-rationality of a theology which rejects logical conclusions.
'It is', he says, 'always dangerous for a thinking being to
renounce logical argument' (277). 'We cannot meaningfully
deny even theological statements their logical consequences'
(277). If we are forbidden to draw any conclusions 'we are
denied the essential means which we possess as thinking beings of
getting clear what we are saying. We may regret that this is so.
But if we are created by God, we must conclude that he wanted
us to use the mind he gave us. Otherwise we would be bad or
unjust stewards of his gift' (278). This means, says Scholz, that
'the fact that a statement can be proved *cannot* be taken as a sign
this it is *not* a theological statement' (278). Scholz insists on the
need for logic and in so doing he also insists on the inescapability
of the minimum conditions of his theory of science. These merely
make explicit the requirements of logic. One of these
requirements is that every statement, because it must be asserting
something to be true, excludes its own contradiction because if
the statement is true this must be false. Otherwise it could not be
an assertion of anything. The logic of assertions also includes the
requirement that the assertions are made about something distinct
from the assertion itself. Thus a number of assertions can be made
about the same thing and can be known to be a description of the
same object because they do not contradict one another
(postulate of coherence). The postulate of control is also a
requirement of the logic of assertions because every assertion is a
hypothesis about something which may or may not correspond
to this thing and therefore may be true or false. The logical
positivist thesis correctly holds that a statement is meaningful
only if we can determine under what conditions it is true. This
implies that the statement can in principle be verified, but
without the restriction to a certain kind of verification (e.g.
through sense observations) or the requirement that such
verification is always possible.

Barth did not reply to Scholz the second time. If we consider
Scholz's arguments carefully, we must agree that even
theological statements cannot be exempt from logic. But if we
admit this, as Barth saw very clearly, we admit a great deal
including that a view of theology based on the positive nature of

revelation is untenable.

7. Positivity and History

The discussion of Karl Barth's concept of theology has shown how much the question of positivitism still dominates theology's self-reflection, particularly, curious though this may seem, where it is not expressly discussed but conveniently 'overlooked'. The significance of the various current positions on the question of theology's scientific status is perceptible only on the background of its history since the Enlightenment. In the problematic of positivity, the historical conditionality of the Christian religion is intertwined with the apparent irrationality of the revelation it proclaims. For the Enlightenment, the two actually coincided. For romanticism and idealism, on the other hand, the positivity of the historical dissolved in the historicalisation [*Historisierung*] of reason. The positivity of revelation theology obtruded itself on post-idealist historic consciousness precisely because its content was incommensurable with the historical shape of Christian history. At first, the elements of Christian dogma which were positive in this sense were still justified as an expression of the practical religious relevance of Christian history as opposed to that of a merely antiquarian history [*Historie*]. Is this practical relevance, however, in an assessment external to the historical, substantiated by a present-day judgment of faith, or is it rather a function of the significance proper to the historical content itself? The positivity problematic of Christianity in the theology of the twentieth century has come to a head on this question. Even dialectical theology has unwittingly helped to aggravate it by opposing, in the name of God and his revelation, history as the sphere of the relative and purely human. The attempt to make God and his revelation the great alternative to all that is purely human and therefore the proper theme of theology has turned out to be an extreme form of subjectivism in theology, and the latter's positivity, consequently, the decisionistic self-presentation of a subjectity which lacks its substantial ground and therefore

has to affirm itself in an act of despairing venture. Barth's aim —
to re-establish as the theme of theology, against those who
restricted theology to religious subjectivity, God and his
revelation and therefore the substantial ground of that
subjectivity — can be fulfilled only by elucidating the tradition
plexus pre-given to the theologian's subjectivity. Barth did this
in his *Church Dogmatics,* but only in the context of a previous
acceptance of revelation's positivity. If tradition is to speak for
itself and not merely reflect the self-understanding of an isolated,
autistic subjectivity, there must be an enquiry into the
significance proper to it in the historicity [*Historizität*] of its
origin and in the whole series of its forms. This question of the
significance proper to the historical prompts reflection on its
present relevance — a reflection which transcends the merely
historical but which is guided by the historical phenomenon
which became the object of a process of transmission because of
the significance seen in it.

Thus it is neither an unimportant accident nor the result of
external theological influences that with the passing of dialectical
theology the hermeneutical problem has become the centre of
theological discussion. A fundamental cause of this has been the
insight that the early Christian witnesses and the historical figure
of Jesus belong to an age which for us is past, and so their
relevance to the present can be assessed only by an act of
interpretation. The concept of God can have a decisive role in
this act of interpretation in so far as it mediates between the life
of Jesus and the present, points to what is identical in the process
of translating Jesus' message into the present experience of reality,
and above all substantiates both that message's claim to universal
validity and what is essential to interpretation, to mediation, in
the present. The solution of the hermeneutical problem must try
to show whether the primacy of God and his revelation over all
that is human and relative, which Barth restored as the theme of
theology, can, through reflection on its self-mediation in the
process of the Christian tradition, be stated in such a manner that,
although of course it still requires faith, it does not require the
positivity of basing theology on an arbitrary venture of faith on
the part of the theologian. Clarification is easier because in the
second half of this century the practical relevance of Christian

tradition can be regarded as less and less certain in itself. We can rely not on a Christian piety which sees it as self-evident but only on an interpretation proper to that tradition which makes unselfconscious personal piety possible, for those who learn from it, to see their lives in the context of a history [*Geschichte*] which is a divine history.

Bultmann has made the hermeneutical problem a subject of passionate theological interest, but it is Gerhard Ebeling who has used it to reformulate the concept of theology. Like Barth and Bultmann Ebeling regards theology as relating to the 'event of proclamation' without which theology would be 'blind'.[566] He expressly adopts the idea that theology is practical, not only because it helps to discover the goal of human life but because 'it relates to the praxis of the kerygma of the church.'[567] This is also where he looks for the specific 'proper object' of theology.[568] According to Ebeling it is 'the linguistic event of revelation in listening to the word of God' which gives theology this object, so that its interest is concentrated on the process, the occurrence of this linguistic event. This occurrence is not just, as in Bultmann, the existential occurrence of the believing self-understanding it brings, but it is the subject-matter of theology 'as the interpretation of a proclamation that has happened and is described in the Bible with a view to future proclamation in the church'. For Ebeling this is what makes theology 'scientific'. In his estimation 'scientific theology' is a tautology 'if one is not to narrow down the concept of science so far as to make it unusable'.[569]

In order to be more exact about the scientific nature of theology, Ebeling goes back to Schleiermacher's concept of

[566] G. Ebeling, *Theology and Proclamation*, London and Philadelphia 1966, p. 20.

[567] Ebeling, 'Theologie II', *Religion in Geschichte und Gegenwart*, 3rd ed., vol. VI, p. 770.

[568] 'Theologie II', p. 771. Ebeling associates himself in this article with Barth's rejection of Scholz's criteria for a science but does not discuss the problems this raises. In fact, as his more precise definition of the object of theology shows, his interest has moved away from Barth's. (All the quotations in the text are from the passage cited.)

[569] *Theology and Proclamation*, p. 21. Page references in the rest of the paragraph are to this book (translation emended).

theology as a 'positive science'. But he refers neither to the inclusion of theology in the 'higher faculties' of the university, nor to theology's reference to praxis. For Ebeling, unlike Schleiermacher whom he invokes, the positivity of theology lies in its relationship to a 'historical [*geschichtlich*] datum' (107). In the early paragraphs of his *Brief Outline,* Schleiermacher speaks not of historic data but of 'reference to a particular type of faith'. The latter, of course, for Schleiermacher is a historic datum, but he does not reflect on it in his attempt to determine the positivity of theology. In Schleiermacher's view a positive science is expressly concerned with the 'solution of a practical problem', which Ebeling does not mention in this connection. At least it is not omitted but subsumed into theology's 'responsibility' for the historical datum. Theology must not only accept this historical datum historically [*historisch*] but also be responsible for it 'in critical reflection and examination'. The historical datum 'forces' this on the theologian, says Ebeling, 'so long . . . as he refuses to commit himself blindly to mere chance events or to consider the historic datum as over and done with'.[570] This leads him to say. that 'because it is through and through related to history [*Geschichte*], (theology) is responsible science"; it bears 'responsibility for past history as for future history' (108).

Ebeling has introduced the relationship to the historic datum into Schleiermacher's definition of theology and thus *de facto* altered it. This hermeneutical step now allows him, however, to reformulate theology's relation to praxis, which was constitutive for Schleiermacher, by calling it 'responsible science'. This removes one of the weaknesses of Schleiermacher's conception: theology's hermeneutical 'responsibility' is fundamentally related to 'past history' [*Geschichte*]. The weight of the historical [*historisch*] in theology thus receives its due in Ebeling's scheme, whereas it could be included only with some awkwardness in Schleiermacher's concept of theology as a practical science. Having corrected Schleiermacher in this way, Ebeling follows the tendency visible in Kähler and Heinrici of associating the

---

[570] P. 107. One feels there should be some consideration here of the function of the idea of God as the basis of the compulsion to take responsibility for tradition, at least for the Christian tradition. The idea of God is naturally central to Ebeling's view of the word-event of tradition.

historical material of Christian theology with the practical relevance which distinguishes it. By means of his concept of the supra-historic, Kähler had tried to grasp the present significance of the 'historic facts' on which Christian tradition is founded as an effect of those facts themselves.[571] In another context Kähler had described the effect of these historic facts expressed in the witness of faith, in so far as this effect was caused by God's Spirit, as being also the word of God.[572] Thus Kähler became one of the fathers of dialectical theology. As we mentioned before, in Barth as also in Bultmann the word of God always stands in opposition to all that is human and historical. In connnecting theology's hermeneutical task with its relationship to the word of God which is its subject, Ebeling has been the first to connect, conversely, the theme of the word of God with the 'history of effects' of the history of Jesus and the preaching of the early church. Kähler prepared the way for this, but he did not get there himself: in the introductory section to his study of the supra-historic, the concept of the 'word of God' does not appear. Perhaps this was because for Kähler, as for W. Herrmann,[573]

[571] M. Kähler, *Wissenschaft der christlichen Lehre*, p. 13; see also his *Der sogenannte historische Jesus und der geschichtliche, biblische Christus*, 1892, p. 19. According to Kähler, it is a general rule that 'the truly historical aspect of a significant figure is the personal effect which can still be felt by posterity'. The effect left by Jesus is 'nothing other than the faith of the disciples', and in addition the 'preaching of his followers', which continues to take place down to the present (2nd ed. 1896, p. 109).

[572] *Wissenschaft der christlichen Lehre*, p. 369 (§ 451): 'The original word of God, that is the word which originates in the action of the Spirit, is present wherever the Gospel, through the action of the Spirit, is proclaimed in clear and believing witness.' This means that the word of God is not just the Bible. The Bible indeed is the word only by virtue of Christ, since Christ as 'the word of God made flesh forms the content of human speech and so makes it the word of God' (p. 368, § 447), and this 'active word of God . . . also lives in the Church outside the scriptures of the Old and New covenants' (p. 370, § 453).

[573] For Kähler see the first quotation in the previous note. For Herrmann, see the essay, 'Die Lage und Aufgabe der evangelischen Dogmatik in der Gegenwart' (1907), in W. Herrmann, *Schriften zur Grundlegung der Theologie*, ed. Fischer-Appelt, vol. II, 1967, p. 65: 'The moments in which the content of our experiences becomes God speaking to us directly are what gives religion its power'. Herrmann also gives a similar interpretation elsewhere to the concept 'word of God'.

'word of God' still signified the action of the divine Spirit in immediate experience, while the relationship of this action to the history of effects of the 'word made flesh' as a historic fact was as yet unclear. Barth and Bultmann, each in his own way, did some preparatory clarification: Bultmann described the word of God as the 'Christ-kerygma',[574] Barth described three forms of the word of God.[575] But for both of them it was precisely the word's relationship to the historical origin of the Christian tradition which remained problematic. Ebeling was the first to present the process of the transmission of Christian tradition as the history of effects of the word-event which took place in Jesus. His concept of theology as responsible science is related to this.

The description 'responsible science' is closely connected with the idea of hermeneutic. The task of the hermeneutical disciplines is to interpret the transmitted material from the past in relation to the future, to the extent that the latter forms the horizon of present understanding, so that the importance of the past for the present with regard to its future becomes intelligible. Furthermore, Ebeling's distinction between responsible and calculating sciences (108) essentially coincides with the traditional distinction between the (hermeneutical) human sciences and the natural sciences. Ebeling clarifies what sort of responsibility he has in mind in calling theology 'responsible science' when he says, against Bultmann, that he wishes to 'be responsible for the theology of the Word of God by taking up the quest for the historical Jesus in the right way . . . not to avoid the challenge of the Word of God, but so that one can truly hear the challenge . . .' (76). What he means by the challenge of the word of God is clearly 'the authority with which (Jesus) gave concrete utterance to God' (74), an authority which we should not desire to prove but which on its side 'legitimates' the Christian identity of the proclamation (57; cf. 74).

In comparison with Barth, Ebeling has historicalised [historisiert] the word of God, as Bultmann did up to a point. Bultmann had identified the early Christian preaching with the word of God and thus isolated this word as a datum of history

---

[574] R. Bultmann, 'The Concept of the Word of God in the New Testament', *Faith and Understanding,* London 1969, pp. 286–312, esp. pp. 297ff.

[575] Karl Barth, *Church Dogmatics,* I/1, § 4 (pp. 98–140).

[*Geschichte*] whose present-day relevance can be grasped only by translation and interpretation for the present with a view to the future. Ebeling goes beyond Bultmann by including the process of tradition as word-event in the concept of the word of God, thereby releasing the concept from the isolation from which it suffers in the theology of revelation. He thinks of the word of God simply as the essence of word inasmuch as the proper truth of word and language in general sees the light of day in the event that is communication and promise (see pp. 174–5 above). Because the word of God is interpreted as a history-of-effects extension of the history of Jesus on the one hand and as the truth of word and language in general on the other, this central concept of dialectical theology seems to lose its positivity.

Yet even in Ebeling's concept of word as word of God – which latter ultimately refers to the 'authority with which Jesus gave concrete utterance to God' – there is still an element of positivity in the sense of a revelatory authority which cannot be rationally proved.

We have already mentioned Ebeling's characteristic personalist approach to language (see pp. 174–5 above). Even if his rather narrow way of looking at language and its many dimensions were totally acceptable, it would still give rise to problems in thinking about God. What makes a particular word, in the strict sense, a word which God utters and in which God expresses himself so that it can properly be called 'God's Word'?[576] Ebeling's argument concerns first the concept of word, then the thought of God, and finally tries to bring the two together in the concept of God's word. His suggestion, however, that the word lets the Hidden be present (50ff) does not lead without further qualification to the 'experiential horizon of what we mean when we say God' (52), because the Hidden or Absent announced in language may be quite other. It may be true that the word 'God' has to do with the 'depth dimension' to which 'every word owes its existence' (58), but it must be explained more precisely in order to clarify the many levels of the phenomenon in question. Merely to suggest that the word is concerned with the truth of human being (82) is not sufficient: the suggestion simply

[576] This is the theme of Ebeling's book *Gott und Wort* (1966). The page references in the text are to this book.

represents an affirmation which still needs proof. More importantly, however, the claim of the word 'God' – as Ebeling himself stresses in other contexts – concerns the whole of reality, because speaking about God means speaking about the all-determining reality. Whether with regard to word and language we are truly speaking about God depends on whether we can show that we are speaking about the *all*-determining reality. If we could prove this, then we could show that the divine reality, with which the religions and philosophical enquiries about God are concerned, is present in the phenomenon of language in a quite specific way even though not exclusively, because as the all-determining reality it is to be thought of as present and active in every event. But we should still have to ask how God's reality active in language can turn human language into the word of *God*. Ebeling's argumentation lacks persuasive force precisely on this crucial point.

Ebeling merely reasserts the authority of Jesus and seeks to explain this by reference to human experience of self and to language in particular. In some places he succeeds only partially and in others fails altogether to justify his assertions. Thus his theology remains 'positive' to the extent that it presupposes the truth of the Christian faith, the authority of Jesus, without proof. All he does in support of this claim is to refer it to human experience of self and the phenomenon of language. But although these hermeneutical explanations lack the rigour of proof,[577] they are definitely moving in this direction. Ebeling's statements on human language take his theology beyond the confines of positivity. That theology goes further than a mere science of Christianity, because it does not see Christian faith merely as the expression of Christian piety, and it also goes further than the positivity of the theology of revelation by trying to show the reality of God and his word in the phenomena of language and in the linguistic process of Christian tradition. This clearly leads to a theology which is a science of God as communicated through the process of tradition. However, because Ebeling does not go the whole way but confines himself to partial explanations of the assumed authority of kerygma or of

---

[577] Ebeling attempts to provide such a proof (*Gott und Wort*, p. 54).

Jesus' authority as word of God, he does not exceed the bounds of positivity.

In present-day evangelical theology, the hermeneutical theme has been taken up by theologians of very different views following Bultmann and Ebeling. Ebeling's conception of a hermeneutic of the word-event is, however, regarded as too narrow. I myself, induced by H. G. Gadamer's hermeneutic, have tried to show that the task of interpretation as an attempt to fuse the horizons of the author and the interpreter presupposes the totality of history [Geschichte] as its ultimate frame of reference.[578] In pursuing this line,[579] I have emphasised Dilthey's point that every particular experience of meaning implies a semantic whole which, because experienced meaning is trapped in the historicality of the experiential situation, is accessible only in the anticipation of a future which has not yet appeared. This semantic whole implied in individual experiences of meaning and in the hermeneutical process has been taken as the standpoint in which the idea of God and the concerns of hermeneutics go together, in contrast to Ebeling's hermeneutic. Because discourse about God as the all-determining reality corresponds to the theme of the semantic whole, the network seems to appear here with less constraint and without the positivity inherent in Ebeling's invocation of the authority of Jesus. Moreover, the semantic whole implied in the hermeneutical experience can be described only as the totality of a history and thus remains within the radius of the reality revealed by the biblical God in its specific characteristic as history [Geschichte]. The hermeneutical problem of translating them into now consequently appears as a theme which is not external to the biblical transmission of faith but already incorporated into the biblical understanding of God and which is included in history's path towards the eschatological revelation of the biblical God.

Drawing on Dilthey's analysis of historical experience and in contrast to the narrower viewpoint of an existentialist hermeneutic, J. Moltmann has, in his essay 'Existenzgeschichte

---

[578] 'Hermeneutic and Universal History' (1963), W. Pannenberg, *Basic Questions in Theology*, vol. 1, pp. 96–136, esp. pp. 115ff.

[579] 'On Historical and Theological Hermeneutic', *Basic Questions*, vol. 1, pp. 137–81, esp. pp. 162ff.

und Weltgeschichte' (1968),[580] explained the consecutive significance of a 'horizon of total history' and of the 'future which
will definitively reveal the meaning of history' for all our present
experiences of meaning, and related the theological thematic of
faith as the 'anticipation and making present of the end of all
things which has not yet come' to the deliverance of the 'whole
expectant creation' (135). Because this anticipation of the end of
history, as an 'anticipation of the deliverance of all things,
discloses a future for our mortal bodies, for society and for
nature', it includes, as Moltmann rightly stresses, the political
idea of the 'liberation of every enslaved creature' (135) and
this becomes his starting-point for a 'political hermeneutic'
(139ff).

Catholic theology today also relates its self-understanding as
science of the faith to the questions of hermeneutics. We must
encounter 'the human witness to faith that we find in Scripture,
in the whole of tradition, in conciliar texts and so on'.[581]
According to E. Schillebeeckx, theology 'should be thought of as
a science of belief and thus (!) as a hermeneutical process'.[582] But
it is not always clear, as often in Schillebeeckx, whether the

---

[580] J. Moltmann, *Perspektiven der Theologie*, 1968, pp. 128–46, esp. pp. 130ff,
134–5. The immediately following page-references in the text are to this
book. (The essay here quoted is one not included in the E. T. of this work:
Hope and Planning, London 1971.)

[581] E. Schillebeeckx, 'Towards a Catholic Use of Hermeneutics', *God the
Future of Man*, London and New York, 1969, pp. 3–49, at p. 21.
Schillebeeckx's discussion uses hermeneutical techniques to revive an approach
to a theology of history which has a precedent in nineteenth-century Catholic
theology in the work of the Tübingen school. W. Kasper (*Glaube and
Geschichte*, 1970, p. 16) emphasises that the theology of history enabled the
Tübingen school to transcend the dichotomy of positive and speculative
theology.

[582] E. Schillebeeckx, *Glaubensinterpretation. Beiträge zu einer hermeneutischen
und kritischen Theologie*, 1971, p. 156. The concept of theology is described
more precisely here as 'that scientific method in which personal participation
in the faith handed on in the church is so effectively present that on the one
hand critical rationality with its scientific methods of research and reflection is
nowhere interrupted, supplemented or replaced from outside, and on the
other the history of the Christian interpretation of reality is continued and
made relevant to the present in creative loyalty by means of practical critical
interpretation'. Immediately following page references in the text are to this
book.

subjective presupposition of faith is to function as the indispensable positive starting-point for theological argumentation or merely provides the existential motivation for an objective semantic analysis of the Christian tradition without anticipating its results. At any rate Schillebeeckx holds that a critical theology must 'start with the question of meaning, understood as the question of the meaning of history' (170). The anthropological foundation for this is, according to Schillebeeckx, the 'negative dialectic' of the experienced 'threatenedness of human being' and resistance to it, both of which presuppose a horizon of meaning formed of hope (96ff) so that this 'negative dialectic is borne by a positive semantic horizon which directs our praxis, even though it can be expressed only pluralistically' (142). Clearly this is why, for Schillebeeckx, eschatology is the 'horizon on which themes such as redemption, the significance of Christ and the church must be articulated (170). The Christian reliance on an 'ultimate meaning' which cannot yet be defined, but the establishment of which by faith in Jesus Christ is 'promised as a redeeming possibility and as a mission', enters into competition with other views for the articulation of the positive horizon of meaning of hope which is implicit in the resistance to the experience of the threat to humanity.

B. Casper, in his remarks on 'The Significance of the Theory of Understanding for Theology',[583] has made a similar connection between the Christian message of revelation and the question of the meaning of human existence. Casper starts from the opposition between the 'hermeneutical confrontation with reality' and the knowledge obtained by the natural sciences (18ff) and then goes on to discuss language as the transcendental condition[584] for historic human existence (23ff). He stresses that human speech and understanding always operate in a 'totality of meaning' (24–5), which is given particular historical form as the 'totality of meaning' of a social environment (29). Casper, however, is interested only in the 'transcendental totality' which he claims is always given 'with man as man' (33).[585] He does not

---

[583] This is the title of the first essay in the volume published by Casper with K. Hemmerle and P. Hünermann, *Theologie als Wissenschaft*, Freiburg 1969.

[584] Casper actually says 'transcendental concretion' (p. 23).

[585] Attempts to provide a 'transcendental' basis for the experience of

undertake an analysis of the process of the historical changes in the experience of meaning. Instead, in a short-circuit which is typical of a whole style of theological argument, Casper immediately fits the Christian revelation into this general 'transcendental' structure as its only actual realisation. As a negative preliminary to this step, he stresses first that this total meaning is necessarily 'impossible to confirm in the openness and constantly changing movement of history' (38). Immediately after this comes the claim that it would be 'wrong to exclude the possibility that meaning might once in history address man *in a totally surpassing way*'. Why would it be wrong to exclude this possibility in view of the stress laid just now on the relativity and ambivalence of all history? And, if it is not to be excluded, how is it that it happens, if it happens at all, only once? Do not people in general – at least in religious contexts – live by the assumption that the meaning, the total meaning, of reality has been revealed to them in a 'totally surpassing way'? And if so, how can it be claimed that this really happens only in that 'eschatological communication' which Christians call 'the word of God and revelation' (39)?[586] And how can Casper maintain that in such a

---

meaning are also made in recent works on theological method. In B. Lonergan, *Method in Theology*, 1971, pp. 57ff, the investigation of the concept of meaning is a preparation for the particular area of the experience of religious meaning (pp. 101ff, see also p. 120). Lonergan, however, restricts 'meaning' to intentionality (p. 77; see also p. 103). A. Nygren's analysis of meaning (*Meaning and Method*, 1971, pp. 227ff) goes further than Lonergan's in that it takes account of the contextual nature of the experience of meaning (see also n. 432 above), but, like Lonergan, Nygren then distinguishes the area of religious meaning from other areas of meaning. The 'transcendental' approach expresses itself here in the examination of the different areas of meaning (including the religious area) to find their transcendental conditions of possibility ('presuppositions') (341ff, 351ff; see also pp. 160ff), whereas Lonergan simply applies to the specialised area of theology the general 'transcendental method' he has developed from his neo-Thomistic epistemology.

[586] It is noteworthy that for Schillebeeckx, unlike Casper, the idea of an ultimate eschatological meaning comes through the negativity of experience of the present threatenedness of human existence (*Glaubensinterpretation*, pp. 96ff, 142). Casper fails to notice this function of Schillebeeckx's 'negative dialectic' in his criticism of it ('Die Bedeutung der Lehre vom Verstehen', p. 52, n. 78), though it had been hinted at in *God the Future of Man*, pp. 154–5.

'unique' event meaning communicates 'itself' in a process by which 'the utterly surpassing eschatological fulness and salvaging of all meaning is given expression on the initiative of its guarantor' (38)? These are simply unproved assertions, and in their relation to the preceding considerations on language, knowledge and science simply articulate the positive character of 'supernatural' faith in its connection with the generality of an essence of human nature disguised, as so often today in Catholic theology, as 'transcendental'.

It must be mentioned as a distinct danger to theological reflection that a new topic – such as here the hermeneutical analysis of the meaning of historical experience – may be used as a means of dressing up old dichotomies (for example, here nature and supernature, in evangelical theology, law and Gospel) in new linguistic clothes. Such a course throws away the chance for theology to make real progress away from the difficulties of these traditional dichotomies.

Even in Schillebeeckx's work – as indeed in many of my own formulations – the problematic procedure of relating the Christian message as a historically specific form of the understanding of meaning in an isolated and unmediated way to a general anthropological structural description is not always avoided. As a simplified method for purposes of exposition, it may have some justification, but it is not adequate as a basis for theological statements. The universality of anthropological structural features can be matched only by the totality of their concrete realisation in the history of the human race. For this reason Schillebeeckx rightly includes the Christian tradition among a *plurality* of concretisations of the horizon of hope implicit in resistance to the experienced threatenedness of human existence. Nevertheless, instead of being an external juxtaposition of alternative solutions, this plurality must be seen as a struggle for verification which takes place within the process of historical experience, and the Christian belief in a history with an eschatological goal must be treated as itself a product of this process. Schillebeeckx takes an important step towards such an approach when he says that the 'thesis of faith' functions in theology as a 'hypothesis' which 'must be elucidated in the course of history itself', and, in other words, has no total meaning which is fixed in advance.[587] As a result, the promise's pointing beyond the present, the consequence of which is that 'interpretation becomes a "hermeneutic of practice" ',[588] leads 'from interpretation to action and then reinterpretation'.[589] This means that for the self-understanding of Christianity the dogmatic positivity of an untouchable premise of faith is absorbed into a critical and hermeneutical process concerned with a still open future. The scientific discussion of such a self-understanding as a 'hypothesis', however, requires a wider framework than that offered by the conception of theology as the science of Christianity or the science of faith, since for logical reasons the scope of a science cannot be co-extensive with that of a single hypothesis. Schillebeeckx's remarks can be seen as a preparation of the Christian self-understanding for such an expanded conception of theology.

Schillebeeckx's account clearly shows that hermeneutical analysis of tradition and in particular also of the eschatological category of 'ultimate meaning' has a critical function in relation to what is given here and now. None the less this critical impulse has its origin in the past, in so far as the past has 'a future-dimension of its own', 'an element which transcends facticity'.[590] In the movement from interpretation to practice and reinterpretation, tradition loses its positive character and is drawn into an open process, though one which is concerned with the tradition's future dimension. In his critique of the use in theology of the theory of the hermeneutic of history [historisch-hermeneutisch] and of the history of the transmission of tradition [Uberlieferungsgeschichte], G. Sauter[591] is apparently unable to see this connection. He therefore attempts to use the element of the new as a counter both to history and to the currently given.

---

[587] Schillebeeckx, *Glaubensinterpretation*, p. 169. See the earlier remarks of *God the Future of Man*, pp. 39–40. This presupposes that 'the question of meaning precedes the question of truth and validity' (*Glaubensinterpretation*, pp. 14, 36, 93).

[588] *God the Future of Man*, p. 37; see *Glaubensinterpretation*, pp. 46–7.

[589] *God the Future of Man*, p. 39.

[590] *God the Future of Man*, pp. 34–5.

[591] G. Sauter, *Vor einem neuen Methodenstreit in der Theologie?*, 1970. The subsequent page references in the text are to this book.

Sauter recognises, naturally, that theology must be classified not with the empirico-analytical but with the historico-hermeneutical sciences, but says that the crucial question is 'the mode of its hermeneutic' (67). He accepts Moltmann's 'political hermeneutic' in so far as it 'transfers the emphasis of hermeneutic to innovation' (68). For Sauter, however, this approach is in opposition to a concern with the continuity of history and tradition, since, says Sauter, the Reformation shows that questions of truth and legitimation cannot 'be answered by reference to the continuity of historical traditions' (28). [592] The emphasis on innovation in connection with the task of hermeneutic, however, should not remain a mere 'call to action', but must arouse 'a readiness for new learning processes' by 'creative perception of the present' in the light of the non-present (68), i.e., of the future of the eschaton opened up by the promise (42). This future should 'definitely not be treated as a historical extension of the effect of the past', but not as its 'cancellation' either, rather as 'the incorporation of origin' (54). [593] The 'not-present' of this future and the present 'must then be kept in close confrontation until the spark leaps and ignites the present, and so separates the passing from the coming' (68). Accordingly, theological theory is not measured 'by the degree of its correspondence with "reality" as an already pre-given reality, [594] but instead reality is challenged in a heuristic-prognostic way' (69). In this sense, Sauter too assigns a hypothetical character to theological statements. [595] Relating the 'not-present' of the promised future to the present becomes the task of a

[592] This view is obvious as regards the relationship of the Reformation to medieval theology and the medieval church, but not in the case of its relationship to the Bible, i.e., to primitive Christianity, which involves the question of Christian identity and so of historical continuity.

[593] Under the title 'incorporation of origin', Sauter himself in practice recommends a model of historical continuity (not, however, that of the history of effects) which I at one time, independently, attempted to describe as 'continuity backwards' or 'backward linking' ('Redemptive Event and History', *Basic Questions in Theology*, vol. 1, pp. 75–6).

[594] For this reason Sauter rejects Barth's criterion of 'appropriateness' (*Methodenstreit*, p. 65).

[595] Ibid., loc. cit. See also his essay, 'Die Aufgabe der Theorie in der Theologie', *Evangelische Theologie* 30 (1970), pp. 488–510, esp. p. 506.

pneumatology which is to 'understand reality as the sphere of God's action'.[596] As the counterpart of this, Sauter wants an anthropology to make 'human life visible in its movement and unrest' and so 'keep open the definition of man'.[597]

Sauter regards the procedure we have outlined as an alternative[598] to a theory of Christianity in terms of the history of the transmission of tradition, which he attacks in the shape of T. Rendtorff's concept of the history of Christianity. The *first* danger Sauter sees in this theory is that it is 'unlearnable' because it uses 'history' as a 'category for totality', that is, for 'the whole of reality in which everything has its place in advance and simply has to be arranged afterwards' (50), so that openness for the new and for the future is lost: 'real surprises, which not only disturb, but also bring progress, are practically excluded' (52). Sauter finds in my own work a concern with eschatology in the shape of a 'concentration of historical thought on the end of history which reveals the unity and totality of history' (54), but says that here too reality understood as this kind of 'historical totality' loses 'its openness and becomes in its turn a closed system'.[599] Sauter is here clearly imagining history as a compact and 'closed' unity, as it were present as a whole, rather than as the simultaneous growth of a plurality of processes which transcend themselves in their movement towards an open future and struggle with each other in an effort at unity, all in the context of that future and the contingencies it involves. He overlooks the fact that history envisaged as an open process contains within itself the contradictions between the future and the present and already at hand, and the contradictions between the various processes and subjects with their different anticipations of the still open future, in such a way that these contradictions are resolved in the process of history itself. It is, however, correct to say that an

---

[596] *Methodenstreit*, pp. 60ff; see also 'Die Aufgabe der Theorie in der Theologie', p. 508.

[597] 'Die Aufgabe der Theorie', pp. 508–9. Whether this complementary relationship of pneumatology and anthropology is meant to accommodate christology and its problem of 'definitive talk about God', or whether this is a third theory, is not clear.

[598] But not an exclusive alternative (*Methodenstreit*, p. 48).

[599] G. Sauter (ed.), *Theologie als Wissenschaft*, 1971, p. 66.

interpretation of the process of history exclusively in terms of effective history cannot do justice to these contradictions. In fact, Sauter is arguing for the replacement of this view by a more adequate understanding of history when he emphasises the opposition between the future and the unpredictable and any present or existing state but does not want to cancel the past so much as integrate it as an origin. Does this imply no attribution of meaning? And is not the process of history inevitably an attempt, albeit a provisional one which constantly fails, to find the total meaning of reality? Is it any more than a misunderstanding when Sauter sees even in Moltmann the danger of 'a total attribution of meaning',[600] as though the provisional character of human experience was to be made to disappear? Sauter's criticisms are directed at statements in which Moltmann, like me, refers to a 'horizon of meaning' revealed by eschatology which discloses 'the whole of reality', and to a 'final meaning which the future of history can give', though at present it is accessible only in the mode of expectation.[601] Is it possible to regard this as an attribution of meaning which sets an abrupt limit on the openness of human experience without refusing to consider the fact of the experience of meaning in general and the universal horizon of meaning which is always implicit in all individual experience of meaning?

The *second* danger Sauter sees in the 'conception of a total history of the transmission of tradition' is that 'the idea of an unbroken continuity' is expected 'to answer the open question of legitimation' (37). Sauter objects to this that 'a meaningful connection with the past' can be made only when the 'relevance of the contents of the tradition' can be taken for granted, that is, when 'the relevant origin is present' (40). This remark is justified: the relevance of the past and of contents of a tradition can never be secured just by 'unbroken continuity' down to the present. The discussions about the problematic of secularisation, for example, show that even the Christian background of a notion may not be very strong evidence for the present validity of its Christian inspiration when the relevance of ideas such as history,

---

[600] *Methodenstreit*, pp. 55–6.

[601] Quoted Sauter, *Methodenstreit*, p. 56. The page references in the text are again to this book.

personality, and openness to the future is secure in its own right. It is quite possible that their present plausibility may be independent of this Christian origin. The really decisive criterion of the truth or falsehood of assertions is not a demonstration of their historical continuity, but their ability to prove their worth in the context of present and future experience, though this always necessarily has a relation with the past. The process by which assertions prove themselves can certainly be described, in Sauter's terms, as a confrontation of the present with a 'not-present' hypothetically opposed to it. That can be accepted as a general description of hypothetical procedure in general. However, even in the natural sciences an individual hypothesis can usually be discussed only in a broader theoretical framework, which provides it with the basis of its plausibility. In this sense, the theologian must face the question of the context of justification'[602] of the non-present with which he is confronting the present. According to Sauter, the content of this is ultimately 'God's promise, which does not hand life over to its past, but bases it on the future and so produces hope'.[603] In order to explain the term 'God's promise', it is, of course, impossible to avoid reference to the Old and New Testaments, and so to the history out of which modern Christianity and its theology both come. Is this origin of the promise in the God we know of from the documents of the history of the faith of ancient Israel and primitive Christianity theoretically irrelevant, i.e., not normative for the context of justification in which theological theories are constructed? This could be so only if the probative context of theological statements depended exclusively on their present function as 'regulators of the discourse of the church', as Sauter in fact envisages.[604] The discovery and compilation of such 'rules

[602] In his essay 'Die Begründung theologischer Aussagen – wissenschaftstheoretisch gesehen' (*Zeitschrift für Evangelische Ethik* 15 (1971), pp. 299–308) Sauter develops the distinction between the context of justification [*Begründungszusammenhang*] and the heuristic context [*Entdeckungzusammenhang*] of scientific statements (see note 630 below).

[603] *Methodenstreit*, p. 54. In this sentence Sauter draws together the starting-point and conclusion of his *Zukunft und Verheissung* (1965).

[604] 'Die Begründung theologischer Aussagen', pp. 305–6. These 'rules for dialogue' are said to be not 'games rules for carrying on a conversation', but 'elements of a systematic linguistic structure, the elements of which reinforce

for dialogue' would presuppose a topic of 'church discourse', and would be comparable with the efforts of the twelfth-century theology which produced the *regulae theologicae* of Alan of Lille.[605] The price of this approach, however, would be an extreme ecclesiastical conventionalism. Sauter himself says such a systematic linguistic framework is 'constituted by the agreement of those who use it'.[606] But does not this mean making the positivity of existing church language the basis that theology presupposes, without regard for the fact that in the present pluralistic situation there is no such agreement capable of systematisation, and that even in the form of a conventionally unified language describable in rules for dialogue it would hardly be desirable? When Sauter wants to distinguish scientific and ordinary language in theology in the sense of the contrast between theological doctrine and Christian discourse (307–8), he raises the question of what criteria are to be used to construct the systematic framework of scientific theological language as opposed to the ordinary language. If its 'rules of dialogue' were to have the function of 'reducing biblical statements to a common denominator',[607] we should be thrown back from the positivity of the church's discourse to the positivity of biblical statements, and in addition the question of the relationship of biblical and ecclesial statements would bring back the whole problem of history, which Sauter wants to exclude from the discussion of the probative context of theological statements. This shows that the question of history as the subject-matter of theological theory construction cannot be avoided if the scientific language of theology attempts to retreat behind the positivity of

---

each other' (p. 306).

[605] See above, n. 441.

[606] 'Die Begründung theologischer Aussagen', p. 306. Sauter relies, as does Habermas in his consensus theory of truth (see above, n. 402), on Kamlah's 'interpersonal verification', and specifically on his statement that 'the truth of a statement is shown by homology' (*Logische Propädeutik*, 1967, p. 120). In this one-sided emphasis on the consensus aspect of truth Sauter overlooks the fact that Kamlah still presupposes 'competent judges' and 'experts' for the process of interpersonal verification (p. 119), and so does not exclude the factual aspect as the pure conventional theory does (see above pp. 219–20).

[607] Sauter's comment on an example of an ecclesial statement of doctrine, p. 305.

existing ecclesial discourse. Only the divergent reception of transmitted history can make sense of the actual plurality of present Christian awareness and present Christian language. It does this by allowing historical origins (whether the Reformation or primitive Christianity) to appear as common points of reference for the divergent views and so offer the possibility of communication, or at least meaningful dispute, between them while they still remain separate. Here again consideration of history brings freedom from the domination of present linguistic and cognitional conventions. But the investigation of the history of Christianity does not merely make the positivism of present-day Christian language relative; it also goes back behind the positivism of the origins of Christianity and places them in the context of general human history. This takes historical reflection to the level of universality at which the possible significance of the Christian tradition for the future of mankind can be formulated. This is now possible because its content can be related as a possible interpretation to the most diverse areas of present-day experience, in terms of which it must prove itself. These areas of experience include historical awareness. However, this is not the only reason why theological theory construction cannot escape the task of formulating the content of the Christian tradition in such a way that its own history is not alien to it. Any comprehensive theory today must be required to make its self-reflection part of its definition or at least compatible with it. Theology meets this requirement by making history itself a theme of theology as the mode in which reality is revealed in terms of the biblical understanding of God. To this extent the history of the transmission of tradition is far from being just the heuristic context within which theological statements arise;[608] as the subject-matter of a theory of Christianity it is also its theoretical frame of reference and probative context. At the same

---

[608] Sauter, 'Die Begründung theologischer Aussagen', p. 301. If the concept of the history of the transmission of tradition involves not only the heuristic context but also a summary designation of the theoretical context and therefore the probative context of theological statements, this does not mean that the heuristic context *as such* is defined as the probative context (a view Sauter rightly attacks, p. 300). The latter exists only in the concept of theory, which itself includes the heuristic context (see below, n. 630).

time, however, as the discussion of this chapter has shown, such a theory of Christianity in turn requires a wider frame of reference in order to be viable as theology.

Sauter's protest against theological historicism [*Historismus*] is justified to the extent that the crucial question of Christian theology is the present reality of the Christian faith. By this is meant not just the continued existence of Christianity in the present, even though its substance may have disappeared long ago, but the question whether the substance, the matter, on which the Christian faith ultimately depends, can prove to us that it has power in the present. And the reality on which the Christian faith ultimately depends is the reality of God. This is why theology, precisely as a theory of the history of the transmission of the Christian tradition, cannot be just a positive science of Christianity, either from a supernaturalist point of view or from that of the history of culture. Its real task is to examine the validity of the thesis of faith as a hypothesis. In doing this it cannot, as the science of God, have a field of investigation which can be separated or isolated from others. Though it considers everything it studies in particular relation to the reality of God, it is not a specialised positive science. The investigation of God as the all-determining reality involves all reality.

Chapter Five

THEOLOGY AS THE SCIENCE OF GOD

1. God as the Object of Theology

An examination of the various forms in which the self-understanding of theology has been embodied in the course of its history has led us to the conclusion that theology, as it appears in the history of Christian theology, can be adequately understood only as a science of God.

This presupposes that theology derives its unity from its object, and, further, that its object is unitary. This premise was doubted by William of Ockham and later by Schleiermacher, both of whom believed that theology was concerned with a variety of heterogeneous objects. In such a view the unity of theology must either be a unity of method or depend on the unity of a connnection with practical activity which is separate from its objects. However, it is clear that theology does not derive its unity as theology from its single method, since in its subsidiary disciplines it makes use of widely differing methods. Nor is the unity of theology dependent only on a practical connection external to its objects. This view of Schleiermacher's did not even survive his own application of it in his description of the interrelations between the theological disciplines, because yet another concept of theology made itself felt in his work, namely an implicit view of theology as the science of Christianity. This view of theology as a positive science of Christianity, which was only implicit in Schleiermacher's work, in the later part of the nineteenth century became predominant, but it led to a dilemma: in this process, either theology became a historical-antiquarian discipline, or it became entangled in the problems of a positivism which could be appropriated only decisionistically, a position irreconcilable with its claim to be a science. The question of the truth of Christianity can be discussed only within the framework of a science whose study includes not merely Christianity, but also the reality of God on which the Christian faith rests. We singled this out as the element of truth in dialectical theology's reaction to the direction taken by Protestant theology in the nineteenth century. In spite of this, dialectical theology too remained in practice a prisoner of nineteenth-century positivism because even Karl Barth could practise a science of God only as a science of faith. Partly because of the inadequacies of this approach, and partly because it did not allow the central truth of Barth's critique of 'the' theology of the nineteenth century to be fully felt, his critical position has to be reformulated.

That God is the true object of theology is sufficiently shown by the history of the concept of theology. We saw above that the term 'theology' originally had the narrow sense of the doctrine of God, as distinct from 'economy', the doctrine of God's plan of salvation and its accomplishment in saving history, from the creation to the eschatological fulfilment. The later extension of the concept of theology to cover the area of the divine economy was justified by the argument that everything studied within this comprehensive theology was studied from the point of view of its relation to God (*sub ratione Dei*). If the *concepts* of the objects with which theological investigation is concerned are not separated from the *relations* in which they stand, but the relations are seen as the expression of the reality of the objects, the examination of the various objects of theological study *sub ratione Dei* becomes not merely a subjective approach unrelated to their objectivity, but the approach which is appropriate to them and to the nature of theological objects as such. It is only this consideration *sub ratione Dei* which distinguishes the treatment of a wide range of topics in theology from their treatment in other disciplines which concern themselves with the same areas but from different points of view.

But, given the state of the question today, is not a definition of theology as the science of God just as much entangled with positivism as dialectical theology? Is not 'God' today under suspicion of being no more than a concept of faith, a religious

idea from a period of human history which we have now left
behind? If it were, theology would have to go behind the
concept of God and look for what was really meant by it, but
inadequately expressed. In the long run it would probably also
have to change its name for one which corresponded better to the
reality behind the idea of God. And yet, even among critics of
religion, where the God question is regarded as definitively
closed, there is no agreement about what it is that lies behind the
idea of God. Nor can the critique of the idea of God in terms of
one or other variant of the projection theory be today regarded
as by any means so securely established as to be immune to
criticism, and fundamental questioning of it is no longer
automatically regarded as a regression to an outmoded stage of
reflection. A sounder view would be that at least a knowledge of
the openness and inconclusive state of the question of God is
today necessary to anyone who professes an informed concern
with the legacy of the theological tradition. It is in this sense that
God can be regarded as the object of theology within the context
of the current discussion, i.e., first as a problem but equally as the
thematic point of reference for all its investigations. Here
theology's own decision to talk about God as a problem rather
than as a dogma is in fundamental agreement with the
knowledge of the mystery of the divine reality possessed by the
wisdom tradition of ancient Israel. In this tradition the divine
reality was regarded as the limit of all human wisdom,[609] even
when the mystery was revealed to it as divine wisdom. If
theology as the science of God decided to adopt a *dogmatic*
method, it would remain trapped in the difficulties of positivism
and also of religious subjectivism. By instead being concerned
with 'God' as a problem, it is able to break free of the
problematic of positivity and go on to challenge the limitations
of deliberately untheological views of reality with a new
credibility.

Here, however, a new problem immediately arises. If 'God' is
declared to be the object and theme of theology *as a problem,* the
idea of God in theology appears either as an object to be
explained in some other way or as a hypothesis. Both cases
produce difficulties for the premise that 'God' is the true object of

[609] G. von Rad, *Weisheit in Israel,* 1970, pp. 131ff.

theology. If the idea of God is explained by other data, for example by being reduced to anthropology as a projection, this process of explanation makes theology disappear into the perspective of a different discipline, for example philosophical anthropology, psychology or sociology. Alternatively, if the idea of God itself functions as a hypothesis, this seems to make it incapable of simultaneously defining the objects of a science, since to be verifiable hypotheses – as was stressed above – require to be related to a reality distinguishable from them. The boundaries of a scientific discipline therefore cannot coincide with those of a single hypothesis.

The second difficulty can be met by the argument that the idea of God is measured and verified *on its own implications*; in other words, the idea of God as, by definition, the reality which determines everything must be substantiated by the experienced reality of man and the world. If the substantiation succeeds, it does not depend on something external to the idea of God; rather, the successful method turns out to be identical in form with the ontological proof of the existence of God, the self-proof of the existence of God. However, while the result of the testing of the idea of God against empirical reality is still undetermined, which is the situation of finite knowledge, the idea of God as a mere idea in contrast with empirical reality remains a hypothesis. It is part of the finite nature of theological knowledge that even in theology the idea of God remains hypothetical and gives way to man's knowledge of the world and himself, by which it must be substantiated. On the other hand, as the *theme* of theology, God by definition includes the empirical reality by which the idea of God must be tested, and so defines the object of theology.

The way in which God is to be understood as the object of theology therefore corresponds exactly to the problematic position of the idea of God in our experience. This holds also of the circumstance that theology, being a finite search for knowledge, is constantly exposed to the possibility that its object, as a result of the process of being explained, may turn into a different one and that theology may therefore be absorbed into a different discipline. This difficulty too is an exact reflection of the fact that God is the object of theology only as a problem, not as established fact.

2. Theology, Anthropology and Science of Religion

God is not present to human experience as one object among others. 'No man has ever seen God' (1 Jn 4:12). How then can there be a science of God? Clearly, only on the assumption that the reality of God is *co-given* to experience in other objects, that it is therefore accessible to theological reflection not directly but only indirectly.

This is not to deny the possibility of direct experience of God. Such a denial would contradict the fact of religious experience, which is usually – however much it may be mediated by the whole relation of man to the world – a direct awareness of the divine reality, an 'encounter' with the reality of God. Unless we are to deny in advance the claim of religious experience to be an apprehension of divine reality, the possibility of direct experience of God must be accepted, however claims of this sort may be evaluated in individual cases. The immediacy of religious experience is an expression of the fact that man stands in constant relation to the fundamental mystery of his life, which transcends any immediate situation. The inescapability of this relation is still felt, when particular objects which make up religion have become uncertain, in the constancy of a basic trust which enables people to live their lives. This trust may remain obscure and unexplicit for those who struggle along in the unintelligible stream of life, busy only with its other, superficial phenomena. It can also, however, through the objects of religious awareness, reach the light of clear self-knowledge. Nevertheless the particular objects which give immediacy to direct religious experience still deprive it of intersubjective validity. Direct religious experience acquires intersubjective validity only by becoming relevant to men's understanding of the world and of themselves. It may do this either by being articulated in a conventional religious language or by deviating from linguistic tradition in a significant way which illuminates the present. Because theology, as an attempt to obtain knowledge, seeks intersubjectivity, it too must direct its attention to this indirect way in which the divine reality is co-given, to the 'traces' of the divine mystery in the things of the world and in our own lives.

We cannot undertake to describe here these traces of the divine mystery in human experience of the world and man or to discuss their importance as a basis for a doctrine of God. Nor can we go into the fact that traces of this sort appear only in the light of an acceptance of knowledge of God as possible. All this is part of the specialised task of theology in the narrow sense of the doctrine of God. The question which is important, however, to the development of our enquiry, which is concerned with the possibility of theology at all, is: *in what objects of experience* is God – as a problem – indirectly co-given, and what objects of experience can therefore be considered as possible traces of God? The only possible answer is: *all objects.* However, this answer is no more than a conjecture which requires proof and confirmation. As a conjecture – a uniquely compelling one – it follows from the definition of the word 'God' as the reality which determines all things. If 'God' is to be understood as the all-determining reality, everything must be shown to be determined by this reality and to be ultimately unintelligible without it.

The claim that God is the all-determining reality must be taken as a linguistic convention, a nominal definition and also as incomplete. In 1925 Bultmann was able to treat it as sufficiently generally accepted to be a suitable starting point for his essay 'What does it mean to speak of God?', *Faith and Understanding* I, 1969, 53–65). without further discussion. The definition presupposes a formal conception of the divine reality as 'power', without specifying what particular sort of power, whether of storms, death, law or love. The definition expands this conception by adding the proviso that the power is the power behind 'everything'. Implicit in this claim is the idea that this all-determining power is itself determined only by itself and not subject to determination by anything else, unless it determines that it should be determined by something else. The idea which lies behind the definition of God as the reality which determines all things is the result of the critique of the polytheistic conception of God in Greek thought, which moved towards the idea of the unity of the divine reality as the basis of the unity of the universe. Since the combination of Jewish monotheism with the philosophical idea of the unity of the divine nature in patristic theology,[610] western philosophy has never abandoned this concept. In this sense, then, the nominal definition of the concept of God as the all-determining reality is pre-given.

On the assumption, then, that the word 'God' is to be understood as referring to an all-determining reality, substantiation of talk about God requires that everything which exists should be shown to be a trace of the divine reality. This requirement applies, however, not to objects in abstract isolation, but to their unbroken continuity: 'all', as used in the concept of an all-determining reality, refers not to each individual thing on its own but to each in its continuity with all others. Theology as the science of God would then mean the study of the totality of the real from the point of view of the reality which ultimately determines it both as a whole and in its parts.

The close connection between theology and philosophy now becomes immediately apparent. Philosophical enquiry is not concerned with this or that being in its particularity, or with one area of reality which can be separated from others; it is concerned with the being of beings, or in other words with reality in general. This is clearest in the traditional fundamental philosophy of ontological metaphysics, which received its classical form from Aristotle. In addition, however, the epistemologically oriented systems of modern philosophy also always imply a theory of reality in general. This is true of sense empiricism, for which reality is given only in sense impressions, and in the final position of the *Critique of Pure Reason,* in which all our knowledge begins with experience, and therefore reality is given only in human experience, although it does not have to derive entirely from it, which enables Kant to conduct his enquiry into the conditions of possibility of experience. Transcendental philosophy, like ontological metaphysics, is always concerned with reality as a whole, which involves the double question of what the unity of existing things consists of, i.e., what is common to all existing things, and what it is that makes all that exists a unity as a single reality.[611] At this point, with the question of the unity which

---

[610] On this, see W. Pannenberg, 'The Appropriation of the Philosophical Concept of God as a Dogmatic Problem of Early Christian Theology' (1959), in *Basic Questions in Theology,* Vol. 2, London 1971, pp. 119–83.

[611] The ambiguity in the search for the unity of beings has been

unifies all existing things, philosophy reaches the question of God, the question of the nature of the reality which ultimately determines all things. For philosophy, however, the question of God is an ultimate question. The foreground of philosophy is occupied by other topics, such as the nature of reality as such, how it is accessible to us, the forms in which reality appears, and so on. It is therefore possible for philosophical enquiry to postpone the question of God, and even to avoid it if it refuses to formulate the question of reality as a whole. Philosophy cannot take the last course without contradicting itself, however, since the claims of its assertions about the nature of experience and reality in general always also imply assumptions about reality as a whole. Strict universality is unattainable without totality, and discussion of reality as a whole is inextricably connected with discussion of the possibility of such a totality, of the unity which unifies it. This question may not be explicitly discussed as the question of God, but inevitably it cannot be about anything else. The question can also be postponed, and in this case it may appear that philosophical discussion about reality as such can ignore the question of God. This, however, is merely a matter of the rigour of the discussion of the conditions implied in the philosophical question of experience and reality, even though fashion may present an approach which on principle stops at this

---

demonstrated by Heidegger in his studies in the onto-theological structure of metaphysics (*Identität und Differenz*, 1957, pp. 37–73). An alternative view is put forward by A. Nygren on the basis of his transcendental analysis of the categorial conditions of possibility of areas of meaning (*Meaning and Method*, 1971). Nygren makes no distinction between the One as what is common to all (i.e. the categories) and the One in the sense of the first, the thing that first establishes the unity of the particular area of meaning. Because of his one-sided attachment to Frege's distinction between 'reference' [*Bedeutung*] and 'sense' [*Sinn*], which makes him restrict context as a fundamental element in meaning to 'sense' and ignore it in 'reference', Nygren also fails to see the dependence of every particular meaning on its context of meaning and in turn on an ultimate totality of meaning which is the necessary presupposition of the experience of actual particular meanings. This allows Nygren to be satisfied with a number of different but equal areas of meaning, including the religious which is characterised by the category of the eternal. This makes no allowance for the fact that religious discourse includes the meaning of all other experience within itself, and is concerned, in the concept of the divine, with the total meaning of all experience.

point as a philosophical advance. Nevertheless, philosophy is still possible if the question of God is excluded. In theology, on the other hand, things as a whole are the object of study only in relation to the reality of God, that is, only because God is conceived of as the reality which determines everything.

Given, then, reality as a whole, what can we say about God as the all-determining reality? It is far from clear, if only because the idea of 'reality as a whole' is extremely difficult. How can we conceive of a totality without conceiving of something outside it? It seems that every totality is constituted as a specific whole only by being separated from something else that it leaves outside it. It seems that even an infinite totality must have at least its unifying unity outside itself, and in that case what is the relation of the totality of 'everything' that exists to the reality of the unity which unifies it, and what is its own reality? The totality which has its unifying unity outside itself cannot be the totality of everything that exists. Nor can it even be the totality of all finite reality as distinct from its ultimate unifying unity; to be this it would have to include its own reality as part of itself. What is shown here is the limitations of a concept of totality which defines a whole in opposition to its parts and then, necessarily, as determined by the parts. The problems raised by the concept of a totality of everything real – or even of everything finite – can be solved only by another category which transcends the opposition of whole and part. Nevertheless the question of the totality as opposed to the multiplicity of finite things forces itself upon us as a provisional expression of the unity we seek.

Greek philosophy conceived of reality as a whole as a cosmos or universe, with God as the origin or arche of this cosmos. The divine is what unites everything and holds it together, as Plato's Socrates says of the Good in the *Phaedo* (99 c 5 f). This attitude was given formal expression in the so-called 'proofs', which were supposed to reveal the nature of the divine by arguing from the world, and were later seen as demonstrating also the existence of God – as the first cause of movement, the first cause of existence and as final goal. Since Paul, classical Christian theology has always presupposed a knowledge of God based on the existence of the world. However Rm 1: 20 may be interpreted in detail, it definitely asserts a knowledge of God from the works of creation.

This knowledge about God as the author of the world was taken up by the Jewish tradition of God's saving action in history, which then presented itself as the tradition of the revelation of this God, and Jesus was thought of in the same way as the revelation of the identical God whose existence was known, or felt to be known, through the existence of the cosmos. Since the growth of modern science, however, this approach to God as the all-determining reality has been closed. Modern natural science provided a concept of nature which no longer needed the postulate of a first cause of the world. The crucial factor was less the exclusion of purpose from considerations of nature than the introduction of the principle of inertia. This made the idea of the tireless activity of the first cause of all events no longer necessary to explain the continuance of history or existence in general. Man, rather than the world, now became the basis for certainty about God.[612] Although the postulate of a first cause of the world was no longer needed, the idea of God remained necessary as the basis of man's understanding of himself in his relation to his world. Modern philosophy is totally dominated by the Augustinian idea that man cannot understand himself in his relation to the world without presupposing God as both his own origin and the origin of his world. This basic schema can be found in widely differing forms.[613] The starting point is Augustine's idea of *veritas* as presupposed in all human consciousness. An extreme example from the beginning of the modern period is Nicholas of Cusa's view of God as the basis for the agreement of human subjectivity with the pre-existing world. The more the autonomy of human subjectivity from the world was subsequently stressed, the greater was the need to postulate God as the common origin of mind and world in order to explain what was now a remarkable ability in subjectivity to coincide with a world which pre-existed it. This position was given classical formulation by Leibniz. According to Descartes

---

[612] I have discussed this development in a number of places, most recently in W. Pannenberg, 'Anthropologie und Gottesfrage' (1971), *Gottesgedanke und menschliche Freiheit*, 1972.

[613] The history of this development towards an anthropocentric concept of God in post-Renaissance philosophy has been described by W. Schulz, *Der Gott der neuzeitlichen Metaphysik*, 1957, who illustrates typical positions.

the existence of God was also the source of man's ability to form any idea of a perfect being. In Kant's view the existence of God was the basis for the harmony between man's moral constitution and the course of nature and man's needs as a natural being. Fichte in his late work reached the idea that God was the basis for the possibility of any reflective consciousness. Hegel regarded the infinite and absolute as necessary for the perception of anything as finite; by being aware of the finite we have already transcended the finite and reached the idea of the infinite. For Schelling and Schleiermacher, in a similar way to Nicholas of Cusa, God was again the source of the agreement between the subject and an objective reality.

The anthropological turn taken by post-Renaissance philo-sophical theology has a counterpart in the self-understanding of Christian theology. The Scotist concept of theology as a practical science, which later became normative among the Old Protestants, soon showed itself to be, unlike the Thomistic view of theology as a *scientia subalternata,* an anthropocentric interpretation of theology. The subject of theology is now man, and its theme is man's constitution, his goal as a member of the human species. This naturally involves a consideration of the place of religion in human life, and there are important connections between the definition of theology as a *scientia practica* and the fact that from the seventeenth century onwards, and especially in the nineteenth, religion became the fundamental theme of theology.[614] The concept of theology as a positive

[614] On the emergence of the concept of religion in the self-understanding of seventeenth-century Protestant theology, see J. Wallmann, *Der Theologiebegriff bei Johann Gerhard und Georg Calixt,* 1961, pp. 58ff. A. Calov was already using *religio* as a summary description of the subject-matter of theology (*Isagoge ad ss Theologiam,* Wittenberg 1652, pp. 299ff, in Wallmann, p. 57): 'Adaequate vox religionis . . . comprehendit omnia quae in theologia traduntur' (Calov, p. 310, Wallmann, pp. 57ff). An even earlier source for the definition of 'true religion' as the subject-matter of theology is M. F. Wendelin's *Christiana Theologia* (1634), mentioned by Karl Barth (*Church Dogmatics,* 1/2). Barth also (*Church Dogmatics,* 1/2) gives a very useful list of sources which show the progress of the concept of religion in early Protestant theology. Although the concept has its roots in classical ideas, especially Cicero and Augustine, its history really begins with Marsilio Ficino's *De Christiana Religione* (1474), as has been demonstrated by W. C. Smith, *The Meaning and End of Religion,* New York 1962 and 1964, pp. 34ff. Ficino was the

science had the effect of restricting the thematic thus defined. The development of theology's self-understanding can therefore be regarded as an independent, and originally much more far-reaching, counterpart to the development of an anthropocentric concept of God in post-Renaissance philosophical theology.

Corresponding to the firmly anthropocentric interpretation of the idea of God since the Renaissance is a specifically modern form of atheism. This was given classical formulation in Feuerbach's view that the idea of God is to be explained as a projection by man, who, because he is alienated from himself, worships his own nature as a separate, higher being. And it is true, if the term 'God' no longer has anything to do with anything outside man, if man is now aware of God only as the basis of his subjectivity, of the activity of his own human life, the question whether this is not an illusion cannot be avoided. However, this need not mean, as Feuerbach assumed, that 'God' was an illusion which men could at least in principle avoid, which, with sufficient progress in self-knowledge, they could simply discard. Even if the great post-Renaissance philosophers were right in their view that man could not adequately account

---

first to describe the instinct to worship God, which he referred to as *religio*, as a universal feature of human nature which fundamentally distinguished man from other creatures. In Ficino's view this instinct was exemplified in history in various degrees of purity and at its purest in the Christian religion. This concept of religion was then introduced into Protestant theology, not by Luther, but by Zwingli and Calvin, and taken over by Lutheran theology from the seventeenth century onwards. This enabled the seventeenth century, which was so concerned with doctrine, to see religion as primarily a system of doctrines: an early example is Hugo Grotius's work *De Veritate Christianae Religionis*, 1622 (see Smith, *The Meaning and End of Religion*, pp. 39ff). Smith (pp. 50ff and passim) describes this process as a 'reification' of the concept of religion which tends to prevent a more accurate description of the real process of religious life in terms of the appropriation of a religious tradition in faith. He therefore proposes that the concept of religion should be totally abandoned and replaced by those of tradition and faith (p. 141; see pp. 109–38). Even if we do not follow this suggestion (and Smith himself cannot avoid describing the peculiarity of the tradition in question by means of the adjective 'religious'), his criticisms should be accepted to the extent of describing religions not as different systems of beliefs and rites but as complexes of tradition and processes of tradition.

for himself in his subjectivity without the postulate of God, we might still be faced with a necessary, unavoidable and insuperable illusion, insuperable because constitutionally rooted in man's nature and yet an illusion if there were nothing outside us corresponding to the idea of God. Anthropological arguments from the problems raised by man's self-understanding do not alone provide us with a sufficiently firm idea of what is meant by postulating God as reality. Such a postulate carries conviction only if, and to the extent that, the *idea* of God derived from consideration of human self-understanding illuminates experience of the world. To this extent experience of the world and the search for the power that ultimately determines it is even today essential to any attempt to gain knowledge about the reality of God. Access to the idea of God, however, is no longer possible directly from the world, but only through man's self-understanding and his *relation* to the world.

But in what form does the *totality* of finite reality, and with it the correlative of the idea of God as the all-determining reality, [615] exist in man's experience of the world and himself? The totality of reality is not available to our experience in a complete state. It is still incomplete: the future is still open, the world and mankind itself are still in the process of development. Because reality, and our own lives and our experience of the world, are temporal and historic, they are necessarily incomplete. In such a situation, what source is there for a concept of totality?

We established earlier that every individual perception has specificity only within the context of a totality of significance. It follows from this that the idea of a totality of reality is necessary

[615] Though the idea of a correlation between the concept of God as the all-determining reality and that of the totality of finite reality which is determined by God has only limited validity because, while God may be thought of as the all-determining reality he must equally be thought of as independent of any correlates which might constrain his actions, that is, he is freedom itself, and himself the source of any constraints on his actions. Judged from this point of view, the idea of a correspondence between a totality of finite reality in general and the all-determining reality of the divine freedom is necessarily connected with the assumption that divine freedom constrains itself to self-communication through its actions. Without this assumption any knowledge of God through experience of the world and man's experience of himself would be totally impossible.

for any experience whatever, and certainly for experience of individual data. But this totality of reality itself is not yet given, since it does not exist anywhere complete. This is the most important of the criticisms against the ancient Greek metaphysics and its continued influence into modern times: in all its various forms Greek metaphysics regarded reality as existing complete in the cosmos, at least as regards the forms of reality. The idea of the completeness of reality in Greek philosophy may be bound up with its undervaluation of the individual in relation to the universal forms or ideas of things. However, the differential between the individual and the universal is not in a position to bring even the universal forms and laws and their perception by man to an end. The totality of reality does not exist anywhere complete. It is only anticipated as a totality of meaning. The totality which is an essential framework for any item of experience to have a determinate meaning does not exist at any point as a totality; rather, it can only be imagined by transcending what exists at any point. This anticipation, without which, as we said above, no experience is possible at all, always involves an element of hypothesis, of subjective conjecture, which must be confirmed − or refuted − by subsequent experience.

This has an important implication for the way in which within the context of human experience of reality God can become the theme of experience. *The reality of God is always present only in subjective anticipations of the totality of reality, in models of the totality of meaning presupposed in all particular experience. These models, however, are historic, which means that they are subject to confirmation or refutation by subsequent experience.* Anticipation therefore always involves hypothesis. On the other hand, this is the reason why the co-givenness or manifestation of the divine reality is historical. Even in this view, however, the revelation of the divine reality must always be thought of as a self-revelation, its being conditioned by the anticipatory character of human experience of meaning as a self-conditioning of God. The reason for this is that it would be a contradiction of the idea of God as the all-determining reality if he were to become accessible in any other way than by his own action. Nevertheless, this does not alter the fact that this anticipatory character of the experience of the totality of reality as a totality of meaning makes the historicality of the self-revelation of the divine reality intelligible. Seeing the totality of reality as a totality of meaning accessible only in particular anticipations also makes it possible to connect the historicness characteristic of the self-revelation of the divine reality in the biblical traditions with the problems raised by the totality of finite experience, which include the reality of God. In the theology of the early church and that of the middle ages, which were dominated by the Greek view of the 'cosmos', it was not possible to demonstrate in the same way a connection of this sort between the knowledge of God derivable from experience of the world and the historical self-revelation of God to Israel and through Jesus Christ to the whole of mankind. The question of God as the origin of reality as a whole did not lead, as a consequence of *its own logic,* to a recognition of the historic nature of divine self-revelation. As a result The Christian tradition on this point was forced to appear as 'supernatural', in contrast to the 'natural' theology of the philosophers. In consequence the historical character of divine self-revelation became merely an appendage to the definition of God as the origin of the world. A connection was made only as a result of hellenistic philosophy's inability to conceive of a divine origin, which enabled Christian theology to treat the historical self-revelation of God to Israel and in Jesus Christ as a declaration of identity by the previously unknowable origin of the world. This connection was, however, only external. In contrast, if the totality of reality itself is still incomplete and is at any time a totality only by anticipation in subjective models of meaning (because the experience of the meaning of the individual takes place only in the context of the whole), it follows not only that the particular experience of reality as a whole must be subjective, but also that it must be historical, and it further follows that the reality of God can make itself known only in the same way that reality as a whole as always been experienced, that is, historically [*geschichtlich*].

Following an important trend in the modern philosophy and sociology of religion,[616] we may regard 'religions' as including

[616] T. Luckmann, for example, follows Durkheim when he defines religions as 'specific historical institutionalisations of symbolic universes' (T.

any organisation of human life in which the prevailing experience of reality as a whole is given expression and which therefore also provides a basis for the order of society and the

Luckmann, *The Invisible Religion. The Problem of Religion in Modern Society*, New York and London 1967, p. 43). Luckmann describes 'symbolic universes' as 'systems of meaning that relate the experiences of everyday life to a transcendent layer of reality' (44), as opposed to other 'systems of meaning' which do not do this. According to Durkheim, society finds in religion 'les sentiments collectifs et les idées collectives qui font son unité et sa personnalité' (*Les formes élémentaires de la vie religieuse*, 5th ed., Paris 1968, p. 610). Religion is also assigned the role of integrating meanings in Talcott Parsons' 'cultural system'. More recent philosophy of religion is also aware of the unique role of religious belief in mediating a comprehensive horizon of meaning. W. T. Blackstone (*The Problem of Religious Knowledge*, Englewood Cliffs, New Jersey 1963, pp. 39ff), following Charles Morris and Erich Fromm, argues for a definition of religious belief as 'providing an object (or objects) of devotion and an *all pervasive* frame of orientation', The only defect in this definition is that it does not specify any connection between its two elements, although it might be presumed that 'objects of devotion' are in fact what provide the 'all pervasive frame of orientation'. F. Ferré (*Basic Modern Philosophy of Religion*, London 1968, p. 69) gives a similar definition, 'one's way of valuing most comprehensively and intensively', though again the relation between comprehensiveness and intensity is left undefined. Because of the problems connected with the notion of value introduced in this definition (see above, pp. 80ff., esp. pp. 98–9, 110ff.), that of meaning is to be preferred. As long ago as 1925 Tillich made meaning the basis of his analysis of the concept of religion in his *Religionsphilosophie* (1962, pp. 41ff), though because he takes it too much for granted, and does not go into the question of its structure, the relation between system of meaning and 'undetermined meaning' is left undefined in his account in much the same way as in Blackstone's and Ferré's definitions. W. Trillhaas (*Religionsphilosophie*, 1972, 31ff) has also stressed that religion is 'always a total aspect of existence' and an 'organisation of meaning', but he treats these as 'essential features of religion' among others, without examining their relations to each other and to the other features. The classical account of religion as an apprehension of a totality of meaning was given by Schleiermacher in the second of his *Speeches on Religion* in 1799. According to Schleiermacher the universe which is viewed and felt in religious experience is not to be confused with the cosmos, but has its highest manifestation in the historical continuity of the life of mankind, though this continuity, because it is a process, leads beyond mankind. In interpreting Schleiermacher's idea of the universe as a totality of meaning it is also necessary to remember the historical origin of Dilthey's hermeneutical concept of the complex of meaning in Schleiermacher's hermeneutic. This in turn corresponds to the concept of religion in the *Speeches* in that the use of the categories of whole and part is fundamental to both.

understanding which underlies it. Conversely, it will now be possible to talk about religious phenomena wherever an understanding of reality as a whole is articulated, even if there is no mention of God or gods. In the nature of things there is always a connection with the questions raised by the idea of God when an understanding of reality as a whole is articulated, since the question always arises of what the ultimate basis is for the unity of reality in any particular conception.

By defining religions as the place in which experience of the self-revelation of God or of divine reality in general is articulated in the totality of the reality of the world we do not mean that such a self-revelation of God is to be found only at the basis of the great historical religions and cannot occur in individual religious experience. However, individual experience is always related to a socially organised religion, even if only as a challenge to its norms and institutions. The different experiences and attitudes of individuals are elements in the history of a religion. Most importantly, only in the vital context of society do they acquire the status of intersubjectively valid truth in which the distinctness of the divine reality from individuals is expressed. In this sense, therefore, it is the historical religions rather than individual religious experiences alone which must be regarded as the expressions of the experience of divine reality within the totality of meaning of experienced reality.

Let us now combine this short discussion of the concept of religion with what was said previously about the historicality of the experience of reality as a whole through anticipation of the totality of meaning of the complex of experience. We have found that religions and their history are to be regarded as the locus of explicit perception of particular self-revelations of the divine reality in human experience. This means, however, that the historically of the experience God in religions is not just an addition to the conception of the idea of God as the basis of reality as a whole, but can itself be derived from this formal definition of the idea of God. The argument has therefore led to the inclusion of the formal as a whole into the historicness of positive religions. A definition of the uniqueness of Christian revelation among other religions is now sufficient to show that starting from the totality of reality as a particlar subjective anticipation of the totality of meaning enables us to go beyond the distinction between natural and supernatural-historic knowledge of God. While there is no room here for further discussion of the uniqueness of the biblical religions,[617] one feature may be mentioned. An important element in their uniqueness must be the fact that in the biblical tradition and in Christianity the history of religious experiences and their changing forms has itself become the theme of religion, the sphere of divine self-revelation. This is the source of the ability of the biblical religions to survive the experience of their own historical change. Whereas religions which are dominated by the idea of an allegedly unsurpassable mythical Golden Age and a corresponding world-order are swept away by the changes produced in them in the course of history, the Jewish and Christian religion, because it is a religion of history, can integrate changes in itself and see them as divine guidance.

What must we conclude from this discussion about the possibility of theology as a science of God? We started from the premise that theology as a science of God is possible only indirectly, in relation to reality as a whole. However, reality as a whole does not exist as a finished constituent of a cosmos but is part of a still unfinished process and is accessible as a whole only in the subjectivity of human experience in the form of an anticipated totality of meaning. In religious experience this becomes explicit as the revelation of divine reality, and the individual's religious experience is always in some way or other connected with the historical religions and derives its intersubjective relevance entirely from this connection. Theology as a science of God is therefore possible only as a science of religion, and not as the science of religion in general but of the historic religions. *Christian* theology, on this view, would be the study of the *Christian* religion, the science of Christianity. With this it seems that our discussion has returned to the concept of theology as the science of Christianity from which it tried to escape by exploring the possibility of a theology which would be a science of God.

---

[617] On this see also my essay, 'Toward a Theology of the History of Religions', *Basic Questions in Theology*, vol. 2, pp. 65–118.

It might be felt that this result could have been obtained more easily. However, we have returned to religion or Christianity as the theme of theology with a very specific purpose. Theology is now the science of religion and in particular the study of Christianity *in so far* as it is the science of God. The investigation of religions, and therefore of Christianity, has a theological character only when it examines religions to see to what extent their traditions provide evidence for the self-communication of a divine reality. Religions can be investigated from other points of view, from that of psychology or sociology or that of a phenomenology which compares and classifies the manifestations of religious experience, but the characteristic of theological investigation of religious traditions is that it looks at the specifically religious intention in religions and investigates the self-revelation of a divine reality in the various religions and their history. But to what extent is such an investigation feasible? Here again our previous line of enquiry has provided an answer in the connection of the idea of God with the totality of reality. A theological investigation of historically given religion operating on these principles would examine how far the conception of reality as a whole expressed in the religious tradition in fact takes account of all the currently accessible aspects of reality and is therefore able to identify the God described and worshipped in the religion as the all-determining reality. The traditional claims of a religion may therefore be regarded as hypotheses to be tested by the full range of currently accessible experience. They are to be judged by their ability to integrate the complexity of modern experience into the religion.

The same approach can be applied to the historical interpretation of religious traditions in relation to the situation in which the traditional texts were composed. Confrontation of a traditional understanding of God with the various aspects and constructions of present experience of reality is now replaced by a comparison of the content of the tradition with what the modern interpreter can reconstruct of the experiential situation of the author of a traditional text at the time of its composition. For each stage in the process of a religion's tradition the actual historical horizon of experience of the relevant group of worshippers in a given situation must be examined in the same way. Such a procedure provides information not just about the period studied, but also about the process of change itself. It makes the expressions of a particular religion in their characteristic institutions and literary evidence accessible to an interpretation which, because it is specifically theological, does not go beyond the experiential horizon of that religion in a given phase of its history. At the same time, however, it reveals the changes which the religion has in fact undergone under the pressure of its experience of reality and as a result of partial or general inadequacies in its resources for expressing changes in that experience.

Comparative procedures can similarly be used to examine the different ways in which different religions have been able to take account of the experience of reality to which their adherents have been exposed and the ability of the different religious traditions to cope with the experiential situation of mankind today. The theologian will then be able to meet these questions with hypotheses which will take account of the different statuses of the religions, of the superiority of the current state of one religion's tradition over that of others for obtaining an anticipatory grasp of reality as a totality and so being an expression of a self-communication of God.

These remarks about the relation between theology and the science of religion return to the discussion of this topic which took place at the turn of the twentieth century. On the ground that Christian theology did not satisfy the requirement of freedom from presuppositions, Paul de Lagarde and Franz Overbeck campaigned for the abolition of theological faculties and their replacement by chairs or faculties of general religious studies.[618] The history of religions school, and in particular its theorist Ernst Troeltsch, modified this demand into a call for Christian theology itself to 'return to a broader and more general base', namely to 'a general theory of religion and its historical development'.[619] On the other side, Harnack rejected the demand

---

[618] Details and bibliography are given in E.-L. Solte, *Theologie an der Universitat*, 1971, pp. 21ff.

[619] E. Troeltsch, 'Voraussetzungslose Wissenschaft' (1897), *Gesammelte Schriften*, II, pp. 190–1, 192. See also Troeltsch's discussion in 'Rückblick auf ein halbes Jahrhundert der theologischen Wissenschaft' (1908), *Ges. Schriften*,

for a general base for theology in the science of religion and the appropriate reorganisation of disciplines in his famous rectoral address delivered in 1901 at Berlin. Harnack felt able to base his answer not only on practical grounds but also on the claim that a concern with Christianity was fully sufficient for the study of religion because Christianity was 'not one religion among others ... but religion itself'.[620] Harnack's arguments also showed a Europe-centred outlook and a conviction of the superiority of Protestant culture.[621] On the other hand, Troeltsch only a year later proclaimed the superiority of Christianity to other religions an open question, to settle which the comparative science-of-religion investigation was essential,[622] and he became increasingly reluctant to give the question an affirmative answer.

The issue between Harnack and Troeltsch was simply the question whether theology could be a positive science restricted to the study of Christianity, or whether it needed a general base in comparative religion. There was no dispute over the status of Christianity as a religion. This assumption was first attacked by dialectical theology. It was attacked, and rejected, on the ground that the matter of theology was not human religion but God's revelation. In Karl Barth's eyes, 'the attempt to reconstitute theology as the "science of religion"' was 'a disloyal act which provokes revulsion and wrath. What else does it mean, but that theology is letting itself be seduced by a grossly misunderstood

---

II, pp. 223ff.

[620] A. von Harnack, 'Die Aufgabe der theologischen Fakultäten und die allgemeine Religionsgeschichte' (1901), p. 16. On the effects of this work see C. Colpe, 'Bemerkungen zu A. v. Harnacks Einschätzung der Disziplin "Allgemeine Religionsgeschichte"', Neue Zeitschrift für systematische Theologie 6 (1964), pp. 51ff.

[621] Compare Harnack's comments on the task of Christian mission, which he regards as 'more urgent' than 'for a thousand years' because '... it is certain that the nations which now divide the earth between them stand or fall with Christian civilisation, and that the future will tolerate no other alongside it' (Die Aufgabe der theol. Fakultäten, p. 9). Together with the confident assertion that 'historical knowledge' supports 'the claim of this religion to be the most precious possession of mankind' (p. 17), the remark clearly reveals the historical context, and consequent limitations, of Harnack's rejection of the proposal to broaden theology to include the philosophy of religion.

[622] E. Troeltsch, The Absoluteness of Christianity, Richmond, Va. 1971, London 1972 (German 1902).

instinct for self-preservation . . . into methodically subordinating the reality of God to the reality of religion?' [623] According to Barth, 'the borrowed term "religion", as used by recent theology, simply disguises a more or less shamefaced admission that as modern people (which is the main thing to be!) we no longer dare to talk about God openly and seriously' (303). In spite of a strong sympathy for Feuerbach, Barth regarded the phenomenon of religion as an essential part of man's nature,[624] and for that reason saw it as included in the unbelief of natural man, as being indeed the highest expression of such unbelief and so destined to experience God's revelation as judgment.[625]

It is no argument against this position to say that 'revelation must be received and . . . the name for the reception of revelation is "religion" '.[626] Barth too was quite firm on this. For him, revelation was 'an event which encounters man', and so 'a determination of man's existence', but as such it also seemed 'necessarily to be only a particular instance of the universal which is called religion'.[627] However, this general phenomenon of religion cannot be used as 'a norm and principle by which to explain the revelation of God . . . We have to interpret the Christian religion and all other religions by what we are told by God's revelation' (284). And what we are told is that as expressions of man's self-will they are 'unbelief' and fall under God's judgment. 'True religion' is obedience in faith to God's revelation. Barth's charge against neo-Protestantism was that it had reversed the relation between religion and revelation. For it

[623] Karl Barth, *Die christliche Dogmatik im Entwurf* (1927), p. 302. Barth based his assertion of the antitheological meaning of the concept of religion on Lagarde's statement that it followed from deism as opposed to the concept of faith (p. 303), but did not mention that the contrast was primarily with the principle of authority, not with the content of the Christian Gospel as such.

[624] *Die christliche Dogmatik*, p. 304: 'Another thing it should be possible to demonstrate in one way or another is that the occurrence of religion is based on a *structural necessity*, an a priori, of the human consciousness . . .'

[625] Barth, *Church Dogmatics*, I/2, pp. 299–325; see the earlier *Die christliche Dogmatik im Entwurf*, pp. 316ff.

[626] P. Tillich, *Biblical Religion and the Search for Ultimate Reality*, Chicago and London 1955, p. 3., quoted with approval by W. Trillhaas, *Religionsphilosophie* (1972), p. 40.

[627] *Church Dogmatics*, I/2, pp. 280–1.

'religion (had) not to be understood in the light of revelation, but revelation in that of religion' (291). As was said previously, his aim in this, that theology should not stop at a discussion of human experience and behaviour, but should concentrate on investigating the reality of God and its self-communication, must be fully accepted.[628] The question is only whether we have any knowledge of divine revelation in any other form than that in which it has already been received by men. This is different from Tillich's view that revelation must be experienced and that religion is simply the name for the experience of revelation. The point made here is that we can know of divine revelation only through human mediation, which means through the mediation of the religious form of human experience of revelation. This has the important implication, however, that it is impossible to look at divine revelation in advance on its own, in some way before all human religion, and compare it with religion. It follows that religious traditions, with the variety of their assertions about divine reality and divine activity, must first be allowed to appear as religions and therefore as an expression of human experience and its processing. Only then can they be tested for reliability and truth. The believer will of course come into contact with God's revelation in his religious tradition and not just with human religion. However, this subjective act of faith has intersubjective validity only to the extent that it combines either with emotions or conventional forms shared by others, or alternatively with grounds appreciable also by others. Only in this form can it be accepted in critical examination as an argument for the claim of a religious tradition to be true revelation. Only the positivity of a commitment in faith which isolates itself from critical thought can simply identify the revelation of God in its own religious tradition as opposed to others, and contrast it with all human religion, even within the same body of religious tradition. But by doing so, as we saw before, it takes the crucial step of making the irreducible subjectivity of a personal commitment in faith the basis of all claims about the content of revelation. There is no surer way of

---

[628] It is interesting to find that thinkers from other religions have also rejected the description of their traditions as 'religion' in the western sense. For details see W. C. Smith, *The Meaning and End of Religion*, p. 115.

abandoning the priority of the reality of God over the arbitrariness of pious subjectivity. This priority can be recognised, and used as a standard for the critical study of religious traditions, only in the form of the intention behind a tradition's statements of its faith, but then also as the intention behind all religious traditions. In this situation theology is operating as the science of religion in the sense described above. The method of a *theology* of religion and religions[629] is to test religious traditions by the standard of their own understanding of the divine reality. This is not the reduction of traditional statements of faith to anthropology which has been rightly objected to in the mere psychology, sociology or phenomenology of religion. Testing by the standard of the particular tradition's own understanding of divine reality does more than see how far the rest of the contents of the tradition agree with its understanding of God. In addition it tackles the more important question of whether the particular tradition has fulfilled in one historical situation, or now fulfils, the claim implicit in its talk of a God with power over reality. Does it, in other words, provide an interpretive approach to reality which gives insights into the way it is experienced in practice? We saw that this question is already inherent in the living out of a religious tradition. This means that it makes possible a critical examination of the specifically religious causes of the way the tradition changes through history, as well as an assessment of the truth it contains for a modern interpreter.

Just as in other scientific disciplines, the student does not approach such investigations with a mind which is *tabula rasa*. He brings with him an interest in the object of his study, and has preconceptions about it, which may also be connected with his own membership of a religious group. He may be a Christian. His Christian faith and the particular theological and devotional tradition to which he belongs may enable him to form questions and conjectures which prove productive for his investigation. On the other hand, they may also in one way or another deprive him of an impartial appreciation of his object, and even of his own

---

[629] Such a theology is the aim of H. R. Schlette, *Die Religionen als Thema der Theologie,* 1963, though he still attempts to fit religion into an existing Christian framework.

tradition. In either case, however, the theologian's private religious affiliation belongs to the heuristic, not the probative, context of theological statements.[630] Confusion between the two is most likely where a personal religious conviction is used as the basis for an argument for which intersubjective validity is simultaneously claimed.

The distinction of a Christian theology as something separate from the science of religion in general cannot therefore be justified by the claim that this allows for the role of the theologian's specifically Christian (and then Protestant or Catholic) religious convictions as the presupposition and basis of his study. If it is, it cannot avoid the difficulties connected with the positivity of a 'science of faith'. We found that the task of theology was the testing of religious traditions in general against their specifically religious claims, and it follows from this that a theology of the *Christian* tradition can be regarded as nothing

---

[630] I agree with G. Sauter (see note 602 above) in accepting as applicable to theology the distinction between heuristic and probative contexts. Nevertheless, there are still no firm criteria for its application to theology: the heuristic context can be provided only by the vital context of the individual researcher, not by theoretical concepts (for example, the history of the transmission of traditions) drawn up for purposes of *explanation*. Even the language commonly used in an ecclesial community, which Sauter (pp. 305ff) takes as the starting-point for his discussion of the construction of a theoretical probative context for theological statements, would be preferable as a heuristic context. Nevertheless, *reflection* on one's own vital context can make this latter itself the object of theoretical description and explanation. The distinction between the probative and heuristic contexts of scientific assertions, which we owe to H. Reichenbach (*Experience and Prediction. An Analysis of the Foundations and the Structure of Knowledge,* Chicago 1938, p. 7) has been critically qualified, with arguments of obvious cogency, by H. Albert (*Traktat über kritische Vernunft,* 2nd ed. 1969, pp. 38ff) on two accounts. Firstly, the concept of probative context suggests the illusion of a possible ultimate proof instead of the critical verification procedure developed by Popper. Secondly, the heuristic context is excluded from theory of science reflection and relegated to psychology, although the pragmatic situation in which scientific proof takes place must itself necessarily be included in theory of science reflection. This second point has a particular urgency for the hermeneutical disciplines, especially philosophy and theology, because here the vital context to which the researching subject belongs often itself becomes the object of investigation, which therefore includes elements of self-reflection. This is evident in the problems of relativity which particularly affect this group of disciplines.

more than a specialised branch of theology in general. Now it is clear that in the history of theology as it has developed in Christianity theology is for the most part identical with this specialised task of being a theology of the Christian tradition. This is true without qualification only of its subject-matter; from the formal point of view the statement must be qualified, since in the patristic and scholastic periods theology as a critical science in the sense here described was practised at best in rudimentary form. However, this method was always followed in rudimentary fashion where the contents of the tradition were brought into relation with the current understanding of reality and interpreted as illuminating current experience. This was normally accompanied by an independent reformulation of the tradition, though generally without critical awareness that this involved its truth. Nevertheless it is understandable that this critical awareness should be lacking as long as the Christian tradition of faith was not fundamentally called in question, inasmuch as compared with every failure of theological interpretation the prejudice in favour of the tradition's truth became an incentive for new attempts at interpretation. This is of course an extra-scientific inspiration, though one which was extremely influential in determining the direction of theological interpretation.

The restriction of theology in general to a theology of Christianity could be theoretically defended while the supremacy, 'truth' or 'absoluteness' of the Christian tradition could be taken as generally accepted at least within its own interpretive community. The only task then to be done, though it had to be constantly repeated, was to show that the tradition of the Christian faith was capable of integrating the totality of currently available experience into an overall understanding of reality, and also capable of supporting belief in the God of that tradition as the all-determining reality. In the past, while religious traditions were intact, such a presumption of truth could be taken for granted, not just theoretically, but also practically, i.e., recognised by society, especially in times when contact with other religions was slight. As a result, theology in the Christian tradition could be basically restricted to a hermeneutic of the Christian revelation. Since the contents of the

Christian revelation have become matters of dispute, however, it has been increasingly clear that Christian theology has two possible courses. It may hold on to its positivist position with an appeal to divine revelation. If it does, however, it will lose any hope of intellectual legitimation for its claim to general validity, since it will be assuming this claim rather than proving it in a situation in which it has been challenged by the claims of other religions and beliefs. Alternatively, the theology practised within the Christian tradition may see its role as Christian theology as to make the superiority of Christianity to other systems of belief the explicit object of investigation and proof in a theology of religions. Since the Renaissance, and in particular since Marsilio Ficino's work *De Christiana Religione* (1474), this has been regarded as the work of Christian apologetics and later of fundamental theology and has been pursued with varying energy and success.

Otherwise no basic objections can be made against the fact that theology within the Christian tradition concentrates on a theology of Christianity, provided that the assumption of the superiority of the Christian revelation to other religious traditions remains in principle open to discussion and is not isolated from criticism. Unfortunately isolation of this sort has often been the function of the concept of revelation in theology. Another effect of this isolation may be a restriction on the scope of theology; the 'absoluteness' or superior truth of the Christian or Judaeo-Christian tradition may be treated merely as a (heuristic) premise of theological work, and not as a problem and possible result of a comparative theology of religions. Even within such a wider framework, theology might well find that the biblical and Christian tradition was its central topic, at least in so far as it found the assumption of the truth of the Christian revelation confirmed by a confrontation with other systems of belief. In this situation, of course, the general science of religion would not lead its present shadowy existence on the edge of theology. And a theology which pursued in complete freedom its enquiry into the self-communication of a divine reality in human experience might also succeed in recognising Jesus Christ as the definitive revelation of God. Because it would be a theology of the *history* of religion, it would of course have to study the non-Christian religions on the horizon of the experience of reality which became the horizon of the experience of God first in Judaism and later in Christianity. This may make it appropriate to acknowledge the history of the Judaeo-Christian tradition as making a unique and crucial contribution to the history of human religion. However, theology could not start by making a decision on this matter the basis of its whole methodology and internal structure, but would have to allow scope within its own activity for comparative dialogue with other religious traditions and provide the methodological tools for this work.

Theology as it is organised today in German universities is always a branch of theology, restricted to a theology of Christianity. This situation can be explained only by reference to non-academic facts and interests. The first of these is the Christian church's interest in training its future leaders. The additional fact that this interest had such an overwhelming effect on the organisation of the discipline as to restrict the purely scientific thematic of theology to the field of a theology of Christianity may be explained by the influence which the churches possessed over the social life of societies influenced by Christianity at the time the European universities were founded. In some of these states, in a new, looser, pluralistic situation, and in different and less extensive form, the churches still possess such influence. A third factor, connected with the other two, is the overwhelming interest of students concerned with theological questions in learning more about their own faith through work with its basic sources, its history and the question of its present truth and possibilities of future development. All these motivations act within societies influenced by Christianity to produce a concentration on the specifically Christian within the general sphere of theology. A concentration of this sort may still remain plausible even when it is recognised that the scientific interest of theology in itself is wider than this. The crucial need is for an awareness of the implications of limiting theology to a hermeneutic of the Christian revelation. Doing this means treating as at least provisionally settled an issue which, in the broader methodological framework of theology in general, could be clearly seen as also a problem. The issue is the truth of the Christian revelation as compared with other religious traditions, a claim which is the constant basis of a hermeneutic of the Christian tradition. The enlargement of the field of scientific theology discussed here is not only theoretically possible, but could also be a practical possibility in the future through an intensification of exchange and competition between the different human cultures and religions and could have corresponding effects on the scientific organisation of theology even in the west. In the process the study of comparative religion would have to be given more room than at present, but this need not mean a sacrifice of the real theme of theology, provided that the science of religion were carried on in the way described, as a theology of religions. The only effect on theology would be to de-confessionalise it, which is in any case desirable in the interests of its status as a scientific discipline.

A theology which, because it is a theology of Christianity, is in our terms a branch of theology, would need at least to be based on a fundamental theology. This would attempt to define the particularity of the Christian revelation in the context of the general problematic of religion, in the same way that Schleiermacher envisaged his fundamental theology ('philosophical theology') as doing. Only the construction of such a concept of the specifically Christian can make it possible for the arguments of the specialised theology of Christianity to be reproduced and tested by others (provided that it makes use of a standard concept of Christianity). This is the same demand made of Barth by Scholz when he asked for a criterion for the evangelical element of evangelical theology. The content of such a criterion – irrespective of whether it is for what is Christian, evangelical or even specifically evangelical-Lutheran – will of course be open to discussion, but this does not diminish its value. It is sufficient if any proposal for a branch of theology attempts to formulate such a criterion as a way of making its arguments explicit and testable by others. Today it may be regarded as sufficient to provide a criterion to define Christianity in a specialised theology of Christianity. Just as Schleiermacher regarded the distinction between Lutheran and Reformed as bound to disappear and therefore did not formulate normative concepts for these distinctions within Protestantism, it is legitimate today to regard the denominational differences between the Christian churches in general as bound to disappear. In the present situation of Christianity and theology, it should be accepted that what is Christian should be regarded as being also at the same time evangelical and Catholic, that is, Christian without further qualification.

3. The Scientific Status of Theology

The previous sections of this chapter have attempted a provisional clarification of the concept of theology in terms of its object. The main question was how God can be the object of an investigation which claims scientific, and therefore intersubjective, validity. It remains to discuss in what sense scientific status can be claimed for such a study.

A convenient starting point is provided by the criteria formulated by Scholz in his discussion with Barth (see above, pp. 270f). While Scholz's minimum requirements for a science are today, after thirty years of intensive discussion in the philosophy of science, in need of supplementation and refinement, as minimum requirements they remain valid. Since they are based on abstraction from all the material differences between particular sciences, they should not be regarded as an expression of the now superseded ideal of a 'unitary science'. The classical statement of this concept was made by logical positivism, which attempted to impose as a standard of scientific procedure an ideal of logical form and empirical control which it claimed to derive from the natural sciences. Scholz's minimum requirements, in contrast, as was stressed previously, call simply for the explicit formulation of the implications of statements. It is this which, in spite of advances in the philosophy of science, has prevented it from losing its relevance to all disciplines which try to formulate and test statements about states of affairs.

The second of Scholz's three 'undisputed minimum requirements' is the 'postulate of coherence'. The ability of theology to meet this requirement has been shown in the previous paragraphs, where we saw that there exists a single area of investigation to which theological statements relate, as required by the postulate of coherence. This area is, in this view, the indirect self-communication of divine reality in the anticipatory experiences of the totality of meaning of reality with which the credal traditions of the historical religions are concerned. Theology examines the historical religions to determine how far the all-determining reality of God makes itself known in them as the unifying unity of all reality distinct from itself. Christian theology devotes itself to a similar examination of Christianity, though it must always take into account Christianity's connection with other religions in the process of the history of religions.

Scholz's first requirement, the proposition postulate, is met if it can be assumed that theological propositions have a cognitive character. This means that they are statements which typically say something about a state of affairs for which they claim truth, i.e. correspondence with the state of affairs which is the object of the statement. However, whether theological propositions are statements in this sense and thus have a cognitive character is less easy to decide thaan might be expected. Since the positivist criterion of meaning – verifiability through sense observations accessible to anyone at any time – cannot be applied to religious language, attempts have been made to interpret it as a purely 'expressive' language which does not intend to make statements about states of affairs (see above, pp. 33–4). It has been convincingly shown that such interpretations necessarily seriously distort the intention of religious language and cannot be regarded as a correct description of the statements of religion about itself.[631] There is no getting round the fact that people who express their religious convictions are in so doing referring to a specific – usually divine and divinely instituted – reality and intend to assert something as true of it. Even forms of religious language which have no direct propositional character, such as the language of prayer and the performative formulas which

---

[631] A particularly thorough demonstration is that by W. T. Blackstone, *The Problem of Religious Knowledge: The Impact of Philosophical Analysis on the Question of Religious Knowledge*, 1963, pp. 73–107. Blackstone for the most part follows the essay by J. A. Passmore, 'Christianity and Positivism', *Australasian Journal of Philosophy* 35 (1957). See also W. A. Christian, *Meaning and Truth in Religion*, Princeton 1964.

accompany liturgical acts, presuppose, in the linguistic expressions they use, other statements which contain assertions about divine and divinely instituted realities. [632] In their language they at least imply cognitive elements which, when considered in themselves, must be formulated in statements, unless the interpreter is willing to ignore what seems to be a clear feature of religious language. In the intention to assert something as true of divine and divinely instituted reality, therefore, there is no fundamental difference between the language of religious life and that of theological discussion, as has been claimed by many supporters of the view of religious language as expressive. [633] At most a distinction exists to the extent that theological discussion concentrates on the cognitive implications of religious language, though it cannot be denied that rhetorical or expressive elements may have some degree of importance in many theological utterances. In general, then, although it seems hard to deny the cognitive *intention* of religious or theological language, this is not enough to show that religious and theological propositions have also *in fact* a cognitive character, that they are to be taken seriously as statements about reality. [634] This is the real problem. Religious language can be regarded as cognitive in practice only if the reality it asserts is accessible independently of it. Only then is it distinguishable as a reality from the theological or religious statements about it, and the possibility of making such a

---

[632] On the last point see L. Bejerholm and G. Hornig, *Wort und Handlung. Untersuchungen zur analytischen Religionsphilosophie*, 1966. Bejerholm applies J. L. Austin's concept of a 'performative utterance' to liturgical formulas such as 'NN, I baptise you . . .' (For the notion of performative utterances see esp. J. L. Austin, *Philosophical Papers*, ed. J. O. Urmson and I. J. Warnock, Oxford 1961, pp. 220ff). One cannot ask of such formulas whether they are true or false, but only whether they are valid and effective or not. On the other hand, the statements of the creed cannot be reduced to performative acts, but form complex utterances which have a cognitive aspect even in the context of a liturgy (Bejerholm and Hornig, pp. 37ff). In addition, it must be noted that even a performative liturgical formula contains cognitive implications in the expressions it uses (e.g. 'baptism').

[633] On R. F. Holland (1956), see Blackstone, *The Problem of Religious Knowledge*, pp. 91ff.

[634] This distinction is rightly stressed by Blackstone, pp. 47ff.

distinction is a structural condition of statements; every statement distinguishes itself as a proposition from the state of affairs it asserts by the act of claiming to state truth of it. For a statement *intended as* an assertion to be meaningful as the statement *of* an assertion, there is no need to decide yet whether it is true or false. But it is necessary for the object or state of affairs of which something is asserted to be distinguishable from the assertion itself, since that, like the requirement of a claim of correspondence with the state of affairs, is implicit in the structure of assertions. The factors of identity and difference in the relation of an assertion to a state of affairs condition each other. The claim to correspond with the state of affairs automatically presupposes a difference between the assertion and the state of affairs, and conversely the distinction between the assertion and the state of affairs can be determined only by reference to the correspondence asserted.

It is at this point that the difficulty arises for religious and theological propositions which purport to be intelligible as cognitive statements, assertions. Today especially, the reality of God seems to be mentioned only in the utterances of believers and theologians. This is a result of the disintegration of the traditional metaphysical doctrine of God. However, if the reality of God cannot be distinguished from the assertions of believers and theologians about it, such assertions can no longer be taken seriously as assertions, but look like fictions created by believers and theologians.

The question whether theological propositions are assertions is at this point very closely connected with Scholz's two other minimum requirements, the requirement that scientific propositions must be verifiable and the requirement that their subject-matter should form a unified area. An assertion is clearly verifiable only if the state of affairs asserted can be distinguished from and so compared with the assertion. Equally the possibility of being distinguished from statements about it is a necessary condition for a single state of affairs or field of study to be regarded as the object of a number of statements (which must correspondingly be consistent with each other).

Out assumption that the unity of theology's field of study follows from the fact that it is concerned with all reality *sub ratione Dei* now turns out to be itself dependent on the possibility of distinguishing God as the object of theology from religious and theological statements about him. The only way in which this possibility can be established is if the reality of God (if it is to be asserted) is shown to be implicit, as the all-determining reality, in all finite reality, and in particular in the contexts of meaning of all events and states of affairs, which are made explicit in the anticipatory experiences of the totality of reality.

This formulation already indicates the way to investigate the applicability to theology of the third of Scholz's 'undisputed minimum requirements' for a discipline to be a science, the postulate of control. As Scholz saw, this presents very great difficulties for theology's traditional understanding of itself. The demand for control stands in opposition to the divine authority which theology has always recognised in Christian doctrine and especially in the Bible. It is also opposed to the dogmatic certainty which has been claimed for Christian doctrinal pronouncements on the basis of such authority. If it could be taken for granted from the start that Christian doctrine and the Bible embodied the authority of God, any claim to test these sources by human judgment could only be blatant arrogance and a refusal of the obedience due to God's majesty. But it is impossible to regard the question of the divine authority of the Bible and Christian doctrine as settled in advance. It is a disputed question and one which theology must treat as a problem. For this reason theology today must not avoid the demand for a means of testing its statements by criteria other than those of an authoritative doctrinal tradition. It can avoid it only at the price of allowing its statements not to be taken seriously as assertions about reality and letting religious and theological language be treated as merely expressive, as the expression of subjective attitudes. Also, since the existence of divine authority, for example in the form of scripture as the word of God, can no longer be treated as a generally accepted premise, this approach no longer offers corroboration of theological statements. The divine authority of scripture and reliance on the word of God in it or in the person of Jesus have themselves become assertions whose content must be subject to testing if the intended assertion is not to be regarded as an expressive linguistic gesture with no cognitive significance.

The requirement that theological statements must be verifiable is impossible to evade because verifiability is implicit in the logical structure of assertions. It implies that every utterance intended as an assertion must be subject to verification against the relevant state of affairs, and that, as explained, the state of affairs must be accessible as distinct from the assertion and capable of being compared with it, if the disputed utterance is to claim recognition as an assertion. It follows that every assertion necessarily has the logical structure of a hypothesis, though the person who supports it in argument need not necessarily be aware of this.

Assertions about states of affairs have to do with facts, but also with logic. The individual state of affairs does not become the object of an assertion in isolation, or, better, it is not distinguished from others in isolation and so related to the assertion. Form and content cannot be completely separated, and this entails that the testing of assertions must also extend to their logical form, to the conceptual connection between the propositions. The requirement that an argument must be free from contradiction can therefore once more be traced back to the logical structure of propositions in that they assert something and thereby exclude something else, i.e. claim to observe the principles of both contradiction and identity. This logical aspect of the verifiability of assertions and their conceptual context is also the basis of the requirement that the conceptual context of theological statements must also be capable of reproduction in logical terms. From this there follows the requirement of scientific honesty that the theologian too, when he formulates a proposition, must take responsibility for its logical implications and, in the interests of verifiability, make them explicit in all respects relevant to the particular theme. He must also see that his propositions are logically compatible, and by explicitly describing the logical relations between them he makes control of his argument easier.

The other, and more important, feature of assertions with which testing is concerned is the factual status of the asserted state of affairs. Here the problem for theology becomes more complicated because statements about God obviously cannot be verified on their object. There are two reasons for this. First,

God's reality itself is in dispute, and, second, it would contradict his status as God – as the all-determining reality – if he were readily available as a standard against which human assertions could be measured like any readily reproducible finite entity. God's Godhead – whatever may be the case with its reality – is certainly not accessible in this way, since that would contradict its definition. This is the truth in the slogan that God cannot be made an object because he is not at our command.

It follows that assertions about God and his actions or revelation cannot be directly verified against their object. This does not, however, mean that they cannot be verified at all. It is, after all, possible to test assertions by their implications. In many cases, both with the hypothetical laws of the natural sciences and with historical assertions, this is the only way in which the factual status of what is asserted can be verified. Even Popper's procedure for 'critical verification' is based on the testing of a theory by means of the conclusions derivable from it. The case with theological statements is similar: assertions about a divine reality and divine actions can be tested by their implications for the understanding of finite reality, to the extent that the object of the assertion is God *as the all-determining reality*. Here again the indirect approach shows itself to be the key to the scientific logic of theology.

In this respect theological statements belong, in precisely the same way as other scientific propositions, within a framework of theoretical networks, and can be verified only by reference to their function in the system of theoretical formulations. Theology is therefore subject to the requirement of scientific integrity which demands that theoretical models should be explicit and systematic. These, and the statements connected with them, then have the form of hypotheses. It has already been mentioned that the hypothesis form is part of the logical structure of a proposition in that the proposition distinguishes itself from the state of affairs to which it relates by the act of claiming to correspond with it, and this claim can always be rejected.

In the previous section (see above, pp. 315ff), a hypothetical element was shown to exist even in the prescientific way in which the experience of the total meaning of reality takes place in practice, and so in religious experience and the development of a religious sense. All experience of meaning is hypothetical in the sense of the Popperian principle of 'trial and error' to the extent that it is based on an *anticipation* of the totality of reality which is still *incomplete* in the process of reality. A closer examination of the connections between theological statements, religious experience and the formation of religious awareness, and of the ordinary perception of the meaning of individual data in all the various fields of experience shows that theological statements also possess a hypothetical structure with several levels.

In ordinary experience of meaning the totality of meaning is only *implicitly* anticipated, as the basis of the specificity of the particular meaning. In contrast, in religious experience there is already contained a form of *explicit* awareness of the total meaning of reality, even though it is only an indirect assumption within the awareness of the divine basis of all reality. It follows that if every experience of meaning, because it implicitly reaches out towards the totality of the process of experience which is not yet complete, proceeds hypothetically in relation to the context of meaning of all experience which is still undetermined and will emerge only from the as yet incomplete process of reality, religious awareness must have, again, a hypothetical relation to the totality of experiences of meaning available at any time because of the *implicitly* anticipated totality of meaning of reality which they contain. Therefore, if theological statements, as was previously shown, adopt a critical attitude to claims of a self-communication of divine reality in religious awareness, they must be third-order hypotheses: hypotheses about hypotheses about hypotheses. In more precise terms, theology statements are hypotheses about the truth and/or untruth of constructions of religious awareness: that is, they are about the *relation* of the implications about meaning contained in experience of reality in its most varied forms, which are also of relevance to religion, that is, to the understanding of life as whole. In this role theological statements are concerned both with the inadequacy of traditional and new religious assertions of meaning and with ascertaining the degree of their illuminative power. They must also decide what changes may be required in traditional assertions of meaning for the most successful integration of the present experience of meaning, and try to define their relation to other religious traditions. Models in theological theory, in which positive statements are made about God and divine a ctions, must take account of all these aspects.

We can now turn to the question whether, and if so how, the claim of theological assertions to truth in respect of their relation to fact is verifiable. It should be stressed again that the requirement of such testing must be recognised as appropriate because the logic of assertions itself provides the basis for testing by implying the distinction of assertion and state of affairs in the very act of asserting their correspondence. The thesis of logical positivism, that statements for which no verification conditions can be specified are to be regarded as meaningless, is partially correct. It would entail, for example, rightly, that if the assertion that Jesus is the bearer of God's revelation were accompanied by an insistence that this assertion was inherently incapable of being verified or legitimated, this would nullify the concept of an assertion. The only possible conclusion would then be that the proclaimed intention of making an assertion must involve a misunderstanding by the speaker of his own actions, and that he was in fact doing something other than making an assertion about a state of affairs. This is the truth in the positivist thesis of meaninglessness. Its errors lie in its lack of differentiation. An initial sign of this lack of differentiation is its treatment of statements as the only meaningful linguistic utterances. This restricted approach to language has now been corrected by the ordinary language philosophy of the later Wittgenstein and his pupils. The positivist criterion of meaning is, however, also undifferentiated in another way, namely in restricting verifiability to the possibility of tracing an assertion back to sense data or protocol sentences. Later work in philosophy of science has shown that the principle of verifiability must be given a broader meaning.

Karl Popper himself has shown that the verification principle in the sense of derivability from observations and protocol sentences is not applicable to the general statements of the natural sciences (see above, pp. 35ff). Verification in this strict sense is possible at best in the case of singular there-is sentences (see above, p. 51), and even then only on the assumption of a conventional acceptance that we share the same concepts, without which sentences of this sort (basic propositions) cannot be formulated. In other words, communicative understanding of meaning, with all the problems it involves about its semantic implications, is itself the basis of the verifiability of singular there-is statements. However, in many instances of a decision about singular there-is statements the general implications of communicative understanding of meaning and its disputed interpretations in explicit analysis can be ignored. This is not true of all cases, though, and in particular not of those in which the general element involved in a singular there-is statement is disputed.[635] The statement 'God is' is such a case. Additional problems also arise with this statement, since – because of the uniqueness of God and the connection of the concept of God with reality as a whole – singular and universal coincide.

If the verifiability of even singular there-is statements depends on a horizon of communicative understanding, this is certainly true of the testability of general statements. Popper denied that the proposed laws of natural science could be verified, on the ground that the universality of a rule could not be based on any finite series of particular cases. Even his own alternative criterion of falsification, however, is not schematically applicable even to the proposed laws of natural science. As T. S. Kuhn has shown, the decision whether a theory is falsified or not in a particular case depends on a more fundamental decision, namely on a decision between two competing paradigms of natural explanation (see above, pp. 55ff). The fundamental contribution of general statements within general theories is their ability 'to explain the evidence at hand' (see above, p. 57), and in this respect the theories of hermeneutic and those of natural science are completely comparable. The fact that the hypotheses of the natural sciences, as assertions of general rules, are also at least in principle falsifiable makes them unique only within the category which includes them as well as historical and hermeneutical

---

[635] Compare, for example, T. S. Kuhn's discussion of the problems involved in Lavoisier's discovery of oxygen in the face of the dominant phlogiston theory: *The Structure of Scientific Revolutions*, pp. 53ff, 69ff.

theories. This is why, in spite of Popper (see above, pp. 38–9), we may normally speak of a theory as 'proved' when it is able to explain the facts at hand. The possibility of deriving predictions from theories, in contrast, is the basis of a more specific approach, which, in a particular category of explanations, those which make use of hypothetical general laws, has a different function from the one it has in other categories of explanation. Hypothetical laws allow the prediction of events of the type they describe, whereas historical and hermeneutical hypotheses contain an element of prediction only to the extent that they exclude discoveries which contradict their assumptions and so may be refuted by the demonstration of such discoveries. However, the particular role of predictability in the case of hypothetical laws should not be made the norm of scientific explanation and theory construction. This follows from the fact that hypothetical laws, as assertions of general rules, are abstractions. They are related as abstractions to the contingent material of events, but these are said to satisfy certain general rules when their minor particular features are ignored. This means that statements of laws always presuppose assumptions about the contingent material in which instances of nomothetic behaviour are demonstrated. Alongside disciplines that study the abstract aspect of the construction of general rules there must be disciplines that investigate the interaction of individual and general structures in the occurrence of an event, and also disciplines which formulate the comprehensive horizons of meaning which function even in the process of investigation in the natural sciences as processes of paradigm refinement. This is true of theology as of philosophy, though in a different way. In theology, the totality of meaning in experienced reality, which is not itself an interpretation of meaning but has to be investigated before all interpretations of meaning as an implication of all concrete individual experiences, is formulated from the point of view of its unifying unity, the reality of God, and in the way in which awareness of it has appeared in the history of religious experience. Because the religious experience which theology studies is historical, theology is connected with history as philosophy, and in the rest of this section the particular way in which theological statements are verified will be compared with the procedures used in these two disciplines.

Like historical or hermeneutical hypotheses, theological statements relate to a body of data connected with their particular subject-matter which has to be given a coherent explanation in terms of that subject-matter. Theology is concerned with how the data have been mediated by the historic nature of religious experience.

In the case of historical hypotheses the data fall into two types. There are first all the kinds of evidence which permit conclusions to be drawn about the event being investigated (its effects and traces, such as texts, archaeological finds, etc.). It is impossible to say in detail in advance what is to be regarded as evidence for the event being studied, or what can be used as material for a hypothetical reconstruction of it. The documentary value of many currently available facts for the event under investigation is often recognisable only in terms of a particular theory – basically when the material is anything other than explicit references to the event in a language known to the investigator. Even explicit references, however, like all other traces of the event, reveal their full significance as evidence only through an interpretation of their implicit meaning, which can never be discovered except through a theoretical reconstruction of their past. Whatever has once been established to be evidence for the investigation of a historical situation, however, must always be taken into account in some way by every later reconstruction. This explains why the documentary evidence, while always conditioned by its use in a particular heuristic context, nevertheless retains a degree of autonomy and objectivity in relation to historical hypothetical reconstructions. At this point there is a close connection with the second type of data which a historical hypothesis must take into account. This is the previous attempts at explanation, and the problems revealed in them by subsequent discussion which made it necessary to go beyond them and look for new solutions. The problem situation created by the totality of previous attempts at explanation and their discussion, which constitutes the 'state of research', always includes agreement about the theories and evidence which any serious new attempt at a reconstruction of the events in question must take into account. We could speak here of 'rules of dialogue', though they are rules based solely on acquaintance with the issue, that is, prejudice no solutions, and their content is also constantly in flux, with the result that it is never possible to specify more than a current 'state of research' which every new contribution must take into account, whether it integrates the existing theories and evidence into a new model or demonstrates their irrelevance to the situation in question, as when the authenticity of a document is disputed.

Analogous considerations apply to the verification of theological statements. The analogy is limited, however, because theological assertions are concerned not with particular historical phenomena but with the way in which the all-determining reality, which includes not just the past but also the present and future, appears in them.

The presence of the all-determining reality in a historical phenomenon can be investigated only through an analysis of the totality of meaning implicit in the phenomenon. Such an analysis must distinguish between the way this totality of meaning is posited in the self-understanding of a historical figure or a text, whether explicitly or implicitly religious, and the way it is implicitly given in the historical situation of the person or text, which may often be in opposition to their self-understanding. A further distinction is required between the horizon of meaning of the historical phenomenon, which incorporates all these distinctions, and that of a present historical judgment on the phenomenon. Although the second is accessible only through the present historical judgment and in virtue of its own significance enters into the present and future of the present interpreter, this significance, which is what links the past with the present, is itself often truncated in the historical judgment's quest for historical facticity. Theological interpretation differs in not being primarily interested in establishing a past phenomenon as a fact. It takes this for granted, and then looks for the appearance in the phenomenon of the all-determining reality which also reveals itself as such in present experience. Establishing this requires a distance both from the traditional understanding or self-understanding of the historical phenomenon and from the process of historical judgment concerned mainly with fact. As a result, the understanding of the past appearance of the all-determining reality is transformed by comparison with the self-understanding of the traditional text or its author or of the historical person accessible through them, by being examined to see how far it can illuminate the interpreter's present experience of reality and so justify its past claim to be the all-determining reality.

From this point of view, from which the process of theological concept formation and theory construction is independent of the historical data with which it deals because its real interest is not in their mere historical occurrence but in what that contains, the all-determining reality of God, theology deals with the philosophical question of reality and must meet the criteria which apply to philosophical statements.

Because of the incompleteness of human experience, statements about the totality of reality are open to suspicion as being unwarranted dogmatism. Nevertheless they prove indispensable to a critical consciousness. Assumptions about reality are always inevitably presupposed in all actual experience, and it is necessary to bring them into the light of critical consciousness. It is possible to verify such assumptions because the totality of experience divides into areas, with the result that every assumption about reality must take account of the different areas of experience. The definition of these areas always represents a historical state of consciousness, and so must be hypothetical. The areas correspond largely to the areas of investigation of the different sciences, and so become fixed in consciousness, but they do not coincide because the areas of experience include in addition the areas of pre-scientific experience. For this reason a systematic account of areas of experience is a necessary basis for a systematic account of the sciences such as the classical one produced by German idealism and the different one more recently produced by critical theory in terms of the basic lines of human interests. Since the development of sciences at least makes a contribution to the definition of areas of experience, there is an interaction between pre-scientific experience and science in this process. It is therefore part of the task of philosophy to formulate the semantic relationships which are implicit in the sciences but extend beyond the boundaries of individual disciplines, as experience's totality of meaning; from this position it can then assign their significance to the various areas of experience and knowledge. To the extent that a philosophical model integrates the areas of experience already worked out in the sciences with each other and with the areas of prescientific experience, it substantiates its claim to describe the still open totality of meaning of experience.

Analysis of meaning, therefore, and reflection do not exhaust the activity of philosophy; there must also be a synthesis of meaning, or it will be impossible to formulate the results of the analysis. Hegel described this synthesis as speculative intuition which supplemented and transcended reflection,[636] and said that it was to be judged by its contribution to integrating the results of analytical reflection. Thus in Hegel's own practice speculative intuition had a hypothetical function, and it is therefore illegitimate, even within the Hegelian system, to treat it as established dogma. The process of verifying it – as with historical statements – must include two aspects. The areas of experience which are relied on as confirmation for philosophical statements (statements about total meaning) have themselves acquired philosophically relevant shape only from philosophical reflection. On the other hand, their objectivity – particularly where they have developed into areas of science – gives them an independence of philosophical interpretation (even though this helped to create them) and a distinctness of approach which enables them to be used as a check on philosophical statements. However, the construction of hypotheses in philosophy is also related to previous philosophical models and their problems, that is, to a particular state of the philosophical enquiry resulting from discussion. Because philosophy is not restricted to any particular area of investigation, these two aspects are so closely connected in it that every new philosophical system also includes a new interpretation of the previous history of philosophy.

Like philosophical statements, theological statements are

[636] Hegel, 'Differenz des Fichteschen und Schellingschen Systems der Philosophie' (1801), *Philosophische Bibliothek* 62a, 1962, p. 31; cf. pp. 17ff. The hypothetical character of speculative intuition, already obscured in the above article by Hegel's use of Schelling's term 'transcendental' to describe it, later disappears completely when Hegel combines reflection and intuition as the 'negativity' of the self-explicitating concept (*Wissenschaft der Logik,* II (1816), *Philosophische Bibliothek* 57, 1934, pp. 496–7).

offered as hypotheses about the total meaning of experience, but *firstly* from the point of view of the reality which ultimately determines everything given in its still incomplete totality, and *secondly* with reference to the way in which this divine reality has made itself known in religious consciousness.

From the first point of view theological theories imply philosophical hypotheses about reality as a whole and are therefore to be tested by the criteria which apply to philosophical hypotheses.

From the second point of view theological theories always combine a philosophical approach with the religious embodiment of human experience in a particular historical form, in order to describe and verify the consequences of the self-communication of divine reality revealed in it. For this purpose the theological statements must show that they are revealing the implied meanings of the relevant form of historical conciousness, and to do so must satisfy the criteria for historical and hermeneutical hypotheses. This means that the process of the transmission of the historical forms of religious experience must be constantly brought into the analysis, because in the act of the transmission and reception of religious material what was at stake at every stage of the tradition was that material's implications on a changed horizon of experience and therefore the same theme which it is theology's business to consider methodically on the experiential horizon of the present. For this reason the concept of, for example, the Christian religion already includes a whole complex of tradition of this sort, and must therefore be studied as a process of transmission and not as a system of doctrines and rites.

Systematic and historical considerations can never be completely separated in theological study. The former are clearly involved when the implications of meaning contained in some historical element of religious expression – a myth or a rite – are formulated in order to see how far divine reality makes itself known in them. At the same time, however, what is being investigated is not only the reality which determined the totality of the past experience, but also the reality which determines the totality of our experience, since this too is included in the intention of the traditional rite or myth to express truth.

Conversely, the religious experience which was given expression in particular traditional ideas and the implications of which are defined by theological theories constitutes a critical principle for the adoption and modification of existing philosophical hypotheses or philosophical implications of the sciences.

In addition to these philosophical and historical criteria which have to be met by a theological hypothesis, a second group of criteria is formed by the history of theological theory construction and state of the enquiry reached in this. In particular, the *conceptuality* of new theological theories is never directly derived by verbal agreement from their subject-matter, for example, from the biblical writings, but depends for its formulation on the current state of discussion in theological theory.[637]

The interplay of tradition and present under the guidance of tradition's claim to show the way to knowledge of the all-determining reality results in a combination of interpretation and criticism in the development of theological, as of philosophical, theory. The critical element in theology concerns not just the tradition, to assert its content even against its own temporally conditioned self-understanding, but also the practical and intellectual customs of its own time which it confronts with the all-determining reality that reveals the present truth of tradition for the present in order to call it to its own truth.[638] In

[637] For example, the description of Jesus as the revelation or the revealer of God is not justified merely by the appearance of the notion of revelation in the biblical texts, but depends also on the discussion of the concept of revelation in subsequent theology, though this interpretation of revelation must fit the semantic implications of the biblical texts. The interpretation must also be related to current philosophical discussion, as for example when the category 'revelation' is assigned to a prior knowledge of the whole of history in spite of the incompleteness of the historical process. Finally it must enable the various areas of experience to be combined from its particular point of view, by, for example, enabling the totality of reality to be treated as the still incomplete process of a history.

[638] In this connection, note how G. Sauter, in his essay in theological theory construction, postulates a pneumatology as a counterpart to anthropology (*Evangelische Theologie* 30 (1970), 508–9). Note, however, that this opposition too needs to be formulated in historic terms, i.e., for Christian theology, in christological terms, if it is to escape the mere conventionalism of theological

such a procedure, however, any tension between tradition and present reality must still be legitimated by the disclosure of that reality's deeper truth which it is its vocation to acknowledge.

It is therefore quite possible to verify theological statements, even in relation to their claim to truth. It is quite a different question, however, whether such verification can ever be brought to a final conclusion, negative or positive. We saw earlier how difficult such a decision can be even in the case of the hypotheses of natural science. The peculiar difficulty of making a final judgment in the case of philosophical and theological statements arises from the fact that such statements have to do with reality as a whole, and not just with its general structural features, but with the totality of its temporal process. Because of this a final judgment is impossible for someone who stands within this still open process, and not at its end. For such reasons John Hick and I. M. Crombie believe that while religious and theological statements are verifiable in principle, only the eschatological future can settle their verification.[639] An important part of this view is that it is only the end of all history which can bring a final decision about all claims about reality as a whole and therefore in relation to the reality of God and the destiny of man. Nevertheless, since assumptions about reality as a whole are unavoidable for the lives of men in the present, it is necessary here and now to work out criteria which will make possible at least a provisional decision between them. Such a decision can be based only on the success or failure of assumptions about reality as a whole, such as are made explicit in religious traditions and philosophical models, to prove themselves in the various areas of our actual experience. Traditional statements or modern re-formulations prove themselves when they give the complex of meaning of all experience of reality a more subtle and more convincing interpretation than others. When Ebeling says that

---

'linguistic rules' (see above, pp. 293–4). Sauter seems mainly interested in its use as a basis for ethical statements as hypotheses about what can be achieved by human actions.

[639] J. Hick, *Philosophy of Religion*, Englewood Cliffs, NJ 1963, pp. 100ff (bibliog.); cf. Id., *Faith and Knowledge*, (London 1967²) pp. 169ff; I. M. Crombie, 'Theology and Falsification', in A. Flew and A. MacIntyre (ed.), *New Essays in Philosophical Theology*, pp. 109–130.

God verifies himself by verifying us, that is, by bringing our lives into his truth,[640] he must have something similar in mind. Of course the substantiation of the concept of God by the insights it provides into our own lives must extend to all the dimensions of experience accessible at any particular time. It cannot be a mere existential certainty which is incapable of adducing any premises or arguments in its support. Equally, on the other hand, it cannot compel by force of logic the assent of anyone who remains closed to its premises; and because reality and its systems of meaning are still incomplete, different anticipations of the final truth are always possible, however improbable they may appear from any one position. For these reasons the theological testing and reformulation of traditional religious statements can never attain theoretical certainty, but at most can form judgments only on their substantiation or non-substantiation and give reasons for saying how far a given religious assertion is to be regarded as substantiated or not. Theological statements about the relation between religious assertions and the all-determining reality of God whose existence they assert are similarly to be judged as substantiated or not substantiated, irrespective of whether they retain the form of the statements of the religious tradition or distance themselves from them. Theological statements, and the theological models to which the individual statements belong, are also to be evaluated by their success in giving a coherent interpretation of the data of the religious tradition and the systems of meaning of present experience. In particular cases a judgment on this point will rarely be undisputed. Nevertheless, on the basis of the discussion of this section it is possible to define criteria for the conditions under which a (Christian) theological hypothesis is to be judged as not substantiated. For the theological examination of other religious traditions appropriate alterations would need to be made in the first criterion.

Theological hypotheses are to be judged not substantiated if and only if:

    1. they are intended as hypotheses about the implications of
    the Israelite-Christian faith but cannot be shown to

---

[640] G. Ebeling, *Gott und Wort*, 1966, p. 83 (= *Wort und Glaube*, II, 1969, p. 429); also *Wort und Glaube*, II, pp. 186ff; and *Einführung in theologische Sprachlehre*, 1971, pp. 213ff.

express implications of biblical traditions (even when changes in experience are allowed for);

2. they have no connection with reality as a whole which is cashable in terms of present experience and can be shown to be so by its relation to the current state of philosophical enquiry (in this case theological statements are transferred to the critical categories of mythical, legendary and ideological);

3. they are incapable of being integrated with the appropriate area of experience or no attempt is made to integrate them (e.g. in the doctrine of the church as it relates to the church's role in society)

4. their explanatory force is inadequate to the stage reached in theological discussion, i.e. when it does not equal the interpretive force of existing hypotheses and does not overcome limitations of these which emerge in discussion.

Chapter Six

THE INTERNAL ORGANISATION OF THEOLOGY

1. The Relationship of the Systematic and Historical Tasks of Theology

We found theology to be the science of God, but a science which can approach its subject-matter only indirectly, through the study of religions. This is because while God's reality is not accessible to any direct observation, it has always been the central topic of religions in the form of the powerful ground of man's world and the source of power to overcome the experiences of evil and suffering which occur in that world. Consideration of the divine reality in this way always has a particular historically conditioned form. Even direct religious experience in the present proves, on analysis, to be determined and mediated by its historical situation and related in some way or other to an existing religious tradition. The matter of theology – and not just of Christian theology or of the theology of Christianity – [641] always bears the marks of history. For the theology of Christianity this state of affairs is further intensified because Christianity is one of the religions in which the historicness of experience of God has itself been made the object of enquiry. In Christianity this has taken the specific form of the definition of a historic event as the final, eschatological act of God and so the reference-point for all later Christian awareness.

[641] In this chapter I use the term 'Christian theology' in the sense of 'theology of Christianity'. The second description is more precise. It makes it quite clear that the concept of theology being used is defined by its particular object. The phrase 'Christian theology', on the other hand, is hard to free from its associations with an inherently denominational approach which may not be examined; in this context 'Christian theology' would consist simply in the working out of a position assumed without discussion in advance.

The historic conditioning of the matter of theology makes it necessary to ask what relation there is between the historical and the systematic elements in theology. Theology cannot be just historical, because it is concerned not just with religious experiences, convictions and institutions of former ages, but also with deciding about their truth,[642] deciding, that is to say, about the reality of God. In the case of a tradition like the Christian one, which, in spite of many splits, has an unbroken existence from its origins to the present, a decision on its truth has particular urgency at present, and this is particularly true within the area of the tradition's cultural influence, the societies which have grown out of the Christian tradition.

Investigation of truth is systematic by its nature, since it necessarily investigates the agreement of the various contents of the tradition with each other and with the particular experience of reality in its own time. An investigation which seeks truth must be systematic in order to correspond to the unity of truth, the mutual correspondence of everything that is true. Theology must proceed systematically in so far as it is investigating the truth of the religious content of a religious tradition, and this investigation must be the task of all theological disciplines to the extent that they are practised as *theological* disciplines and are intended to be taken as such. In this sense it can be said that 'theology' is synonymous with systematic theology. The history of Christian theology is therefore essentially the history of the systematic interpretations of Christianity. On the other hand, it is no less true, particularly of Christianity, that theology developed only as the interpretation of historically mediated materials, as the interpretation of a historic datum. This is connected with the previously mentioned peculiarity of Christianity among religions, namely that Christianity is based in a totally unique way on a historical event and a historical figure, the interpretation of which is therefore the central function of the

---

[642] In this sense Ebeling is right to say, 'If there were now only historical theology, there would be no theology any more' ('Discussion Theses for a Course of Introductory Lectures on the Study of Theology', *Word and Faith,* London and Richmond, Va. 1966, p. 431). See also E. Jüngel, 'Das Verhältnis der theologischen Disziplinen untereinander', Jüngel, Rahner and Seitz, *Die Praktische Theologie zwischen Wissenschaft und Praxis,* Munich 1968, pp. 34–35.

Christian tradition. However, theology in the broader sense is also concerned with historical patterns of life. Historical knowledge is therefore needed to carry out the systematic function of theology, even where this knowledge is not known to be historical. Historical knowledge of this sort can also be acquired for its own sake within general history and the philological disciplines, and this is also true of Old Testament and early Christian literature and church history. The fact that these specialised fields can also be valued for the investigation of their historical detail with theology excluded makes it all the more important to emphasise that in the context of theology the investigation of historical detail can never be an end in itself. All investigation within theology must be subordinated to the investigation of the extent to which the particular historical data under investigation represent a self-communication of the all-determining divine reality. In practice the contexts in which this question is put are very restricted. The identification of the scientific approach in the historical disciplines with the use of general historical methods encourages the tendency of students of these disciplines to restrict themselves to the historical and leave all questions about the meaning or truth the phenomena may have for the present to systematic theology, which they then eagerly criticise for paying insufficient attention to historical-exegetical problems and research. In reaction to this restricted view of history in the exegetico-historical disciplines, a tendency developed in the most recent period of the history of theology dominated by dialectical theology, particularly among exegetes, to carry out the systematic function of theology as part of biblical exegesis, under the title 'theological hermeneutic'. In the process the systematic work was often very incompletely done, sometimes grotesquely so, when exegetical findings were applied directly to the present without an adequate philosophical or theological examination of the principles of interpretation being used. Instead, the intellectual history of modern life and thought, and the complex relation of that history to its Christian origins, was completely ignored. It is no accident that in such enterprises church history was largely passed over. Procedures of this sort took particularly questionable forms when, for the sake of a direct 'application' of biblical sayings to the present, the historical evidence itself was distorted. This was not an infrequent occurrence, particularly in the field of New Testament interpretation, where it was encouraged by the normative status of the biblical writings in the Christian tradition. This process, as it culminated in the German theology of the last twenty years, has enabled the historicist restriction to the merely historical to present itself in reaction, even in the exegesis of biblical texts, as a model of scientific restraint. Nevertheless, the truth in the demand for *theological* exegesis must be observed, or there is a risk that the problems of historicism will draw theology into a new 'kerygmatic' counter-position. There can be no theological interpretation, on the other hand, at the expense of historical accuracy; rather theological interpretation must reveal the theological dimension of a historical phenomenon *as a historical phenomenon*. It must show how the all-determining reality makes itself known in the relevant phenomenon and how this is given only limited expression in, for example, a text referring to the phenomenon. It is possible to show the existence of attitudes of this sort in the historical phenomena by assigning them their place in the history of the transmission of tradition because the history of the transmission of religious phenomena is itself a process brought about by changes in the experience of reality in general and in the understanding of the all-determining reality in particular. The field of investigation must therefore be extended beyond, for example, the immediate circle of New Testament texts to include the Old Testament and Judaism, church history and the development of the history of theology, and in addition the systematic problems of the present. Only such a procedure makes it possible to examine and justify the categories used in the theological interpretation of phenomena from religious history, such as the biblical texts, in their contexts, and to avoid using too narrow a frame of reference in interpreting, for example, the history of the primitive Christian tradition.

Discussion of this sort about the interrelatedness of the systematic-philosophical and the exegetical-historical aspects of theology reveals the problems involved in any division of theology into disciplines. The appearance of real independence presented by the individual disciplines rests largely on illusion. In each case the distinction of disciplines within theology separates out coherent areas, and this may make it appear that the distinction rests simply on pragmatic considerations of a division of effort. This may indeed be largely true of the present situation. If it were, it would remain to say only that such a division of effort in the interests of the unity of the subject-matter must be accompanied by a particularly high degree of interdisciplinary co-operation. In the case of theology this co-operation consists not only in the fact that thematically autonomous areas of research come into contact on their fringes, but much more because strict independence can be claimed only with great difficulty, if at all, for the individual disciplines within Christian theology as theological disciplines.

Nor is the pragmatic consideration of the division of effort in fact a sufficient explanation for the organisation of theology into its present subsidiary disciplines. Theoretical considerations were involved in all the stages which have led to the distinction of autonomous disciplines with separate fields. These were not, however, on the whole the same criteria as those employed to produce the later encyclopedist schemas. These were attempts, by means of constructive deduction from an abstract and general concept of theology, to justify *post factum* a division into disciplines which had been made on quite different grounds, which were often later no longer clearly understood. The modern list of disciplines in Christian theology can be made intelligible only by the discovery, independently for each individual discipline, of the motives which historically have led to its acquiring independent status. Attempts to derive the present list of disciplines from a general concept of theology without going through this process can produce only an ideological justification of the existing academic organisation of theology. Only when the motives which were historically important in the setting up of the independent individual disciplines are clarified can there be a reasonable discussion of the question whether these motives are to be regarded as valid today. And only at this point will the understanding of theology which will emerge from the present discussion have any role, whether critical or constructive. This must not just mean the substitution of new justifications for the now untenable reasons of the past; where the old reasons are

no longer convincing, changes and alternatives in the
organisation of the discipline must be considered.

Even today the process by which the subsidiary theological
disciplines gained autonomy is largely unexplored, but it is clear
that – apart from the separation of canon law – the fundamental
distinction was that between biblical interpretation and
systematic theology. The beginnings of this distinction go back
to the middle ages, though the development into autonomous
disciplines did not reach any completion before the late
eighteenth century. All the other theological disciplines have
acquired their autonomy in modern times.

In the theology of the early church the systematic and
historical functions of theology were not separate. What we
today call theology was in the early Church centred on the
interpretation of scripture.[643] Only at the end of the second
century was the (typological) interpretation of the Old
Testament with reference to Christ followed by interpretation of
the New Testament writings and commentaries on them.[644]
Other theological writing had a more occasional character
(apologias, polemical writings, treatises on particular
controversial topics such as the resurrection of the dead and,
later, the Trinity), or must be seen as introductory or summary
accounts for use in instruction. None of this led to a distinction
between the systematic and historical interpretation of scripture.
The nearest thing to this is perhaps the Alexandrian distinction
between various levels of meaning in the text of scripture, the
lowest of which was the literal or historical meaning.[645] In spite
of this, however, Origen laid great emphasis on the fact that he
was a biblical theologian and devoted most of his life's work to

---

[643] On this, see M. Elze, 'Schriftauslegung', IV A, *RGG,* 3rd ed., V, 1520–8.
[644] The turning-point was Irenaeus's theological appeal to the apostolic
writings against the Gnostics (see H. von Campenhausen, *Die Entstehung der
christlichen Bibel* 1968, pp. 213ff). Irenaeus's pupil Hippolytus of Rome
subsequently was 'the first theologian of a major church to produce biblical
commentaries regularly' (Campenhausen, p. 314), but his work was still
devoted mainly to the Old Testament.
[645] On the theory of the fourfold sense of scripture, see H. de Lubac, *Histoire
et esprit. L'intelligence de l'Ecriture d'après Origène,* Paris 1950, and the short
account in E. von Dobschütz, 'Vom vierfachen Schriftsinn. Die Geschichte
einer Theorie', in Harnack-Ehrung, 1921, pp. 1–13.

producing commentaries on scripture.[646] The different levels of meaning in Alexandrian scriptural interpretation did not become the starting-point of different lines of research or disciplines in theology.

In medieval theology there appeared alongside scriptural commentaries not only didactic and occasional writings of various sorts, but also collections of sayings of the Fathers. The origin of these goes back to late antiquity, but in the twelfth century they were attracting interest for a new reason, the real or apparent contradictions in the statements of the Fathers (Abelard's *Sic et Non*). They now lost their connection with the exposition of scripture, and were collected by topic and compared for compatibility by the dialectical method. This practice was the origin of the scholastic method, and in particular of the *quaestio* form, and this new dialectical approach was later extended to commentary on scripture. In the medieval universities there appeared, besides the *magister,* who interpreted scripture, the interpreter of the sentences, the *baccalaureus sententiarius.* His task was to comment on Peter Lombard's collection of Sentences by formulating *quaestiones* on the sayings of the Fathers and on the previous discussion of them. The future teacher of theology had to prove himself in this role before he was allowed to interpret scripture as a *magister.* [647] Work on the *sententiae* was not the concern of an autonomous discipline, but a preparatory stage on the way to the theologian's highest task, and to this extent it remained subordinated to the task of interpreting scripture. Nevertheless from the middle of the thirteenth century the status of the interpreter of the *sententiae* grew steadily. As early as 1230 Roger Bacon complained in his *Opus Minus* that the biblical texts were becoming obscured in the teaching of theology by the proliferation of *quaestiones.* [648] In fact, however, the shift of interest towards the systematic relevance of the material contained in scripture and the patristic tradition as a

[646] H. v. Campenhausen, *Die Entstehung der christichen Bibel,* pp. 361ff, and esp. Id., *Griechische Kirchenväter* 1955, pp. 50ff.

[647] M.-D. Chenu, *Introduction à l'Etude de Saint-Thomas d'Aquin,* Montreal-Paris, 2nd. ed. 1954, pp. 71ff, 113ff, 226ff (German trans. 1960, pp. 84ff, 266ff).

[648] Chenu, pp. 227, 231 (GT pp. 304ff).

result of the *sententiae*, their interpretation and the discussion of the questions raised by this was only 'the normal consequence of the constitution of theology into an organised science'.[649] There can be no doubt that systematic theology's growth into an autonomous discipline begins here.[650] However, there was still a long way to go before the goal implicit in this tendency was reached, particularly in biblical interpretation and its self-understanding. In the middle ages, as in early Protestantism, exegesis was 'enclosed within the frontiers fixed by systematic theology. Hence theology in the strict sense was the total explication of Christian doctrine, proceeding by systematic methods and normative for exegesis'.[651] This explains why there was no incentive for systematic theology to seek independence from scriptural interpretation, but it is more surprising that the Reformers' attack on scholastic theology, which was based on biblical interpretation, also did not yet lead to the establishment of biblical theology as an autonomous discipline.[652] Instead, the Reformers' criticisms appeared as a general theological demand for reform, and their only immediate effect was to make the systematic treatment of Christian doctrine keep closer to the content of the biblical texts. Melanchthon's theological *Loci* were intended as a summary account of the content of scripture. It was only the development of a 'positive' theology *alongside* 'scholastic' theology in Catholic theological thinking of the

---

[649] Chenu, pp. 227–8 (GT p. 300).

[650] M. Elze (*RGG* V, 1525) puts the beginning of systematic theology's growth into an independent discipline back to the beginnings of the scholastic method in the twelfth century.

[651] G. Ebeling, 'The Meaning of "Biblical Theology" ' (1955), *Word and Faith*, pp. 79–97. The quotation is from pp. 82–3.

[652] As late as Andreas Hyperius (*De Theologo seu de ratione studii theologici*, Basle 1572), no distinction was made between systematic theology (or dogmatics) and exegetical theology as disciplines. After a discussion of general premises of the study of theology (Book 1), Hyperius's book deals with the study of scripture as the foundation of theology (Book 2). This, however, is mainly a set of hints for private scripture reading (pp. 91ff), and only towards the end of the book is there a recommendation to listen to public interpreters of scripture in addition to private study (pp. 389ff). Then, in Book 3, the discussion immediately switches to the study of the books 'in quibus praecipui universae Theologiae loci explicantur'.

sixteenth century,[653] and the Protestant rehabilitation of a scholastic or academic theology – therefore of the systematic function of theology – *alongside* scriptural interpretation after the beginning of the seventeenth century, which allowed biblical-exegetical and systematic theology to co-exist as disciplines. This development took place in parallel with the gradual victory of the analytical method in early Protestant (systematic) theology. It is characteristic of this that no distinction was made at first between scripture and its interpretation, although the systematic presentation of Christian doctrine was felt as something on its own and distinct from scripture. To express this J. H. Alsted in 1623 took over the Catholic distinction between *theologia positiva* and *theologia scholastica,* identifying *theologia positiva* with scripture itself. [654] A few years later Georg Calixt, in his *Apparatus theologicus* of 1628, reinterpreted the concept of *theologia positiva* in the perverse but influential way described earlier (see above, pp. 238–9), to mean a summarising 'positive' presentation of Christian doctrine. Calixt nevertheless retained the distinction between scripture and the theology of the schools, which he preferred to call 'academic' rather than 'scholastic', but replaced Alsted's use of 'positive theology' in this distinction by the term 'exegetical theology'. [655] This formulation of Calixt's may be the origin of this term.

[653] See above, pp. 243ff.

[654] For references see no. 498. Of the Catholic writers of the period with whom I am familiar, the closest to Alsted is C. Gill. In 1610, citing Durandus, Marsilius von Inghen and Pierre d'Ailly, Gill subdivided the theology which dealt with revelation 'in eam (1) qua assentimur principiis revelatis, (2) eam qua eadem explicantur, defenduntur et probantur, (3) eam qua ex iisdem principiis conclusiones aliae colliguntur' (*Commentationum theologicarum de sacra doctrina, et essentia atque unitate Dei libri duo,* Cologne 1610, p. 3). For Gill (1) is identical with *fides* or *doctrina a Deo revelata,* and the corresponding term in Alsted, in a Reformation context, is an identification of *theologia positiva* and scripture. However, Alsted combines the functions distinguished by Gill as (2) and (3) in his term *theologia scholastica,* and describes the first by another term not used by Gill, *theologia positiva.*

[655] *Apparatus theologici . . . ed. altera,* Helmstedt 1661, pp. 176ff (see note 487 above). See also A. Calov, *Isagoges ad ss Theologiam libri duo de natura theologiae et methodo studii theologici,* Wittenberg 1652, p. 330; J. F. Buddeus, *Isagoge historico-theologica ad universam theologiam singulasque eius partes,* Leipzig 1727, p. 302.

The distinction between exegetical and systematic[656] (academic) theology was not given sharper definition until the development of the concept of a 'biblical theology' distinct from scholastic or dogmatic theology.[657] This term, which goes back to the first half of the seventeenth century and was taken up by P. J. Spener in 1675, is first used, in a similar way to Luther's attack on scholastic theology, as 'the slogan of a programme of theological reform'.[658] In this case, however, unlike Luther's, the contrast with early Protestant scholasticism referred only to the form of its presentation,[659] since the systematic and therefore also philosophical form of this theology had been repeatedly recognised as having a legitimate place of its own since the beginning of the seventeenth century. The ultimate result, therefore, was only a sharpening of the distinction between biblical exegesis and systematic theology. The proposal for a biblical dogmatics as distinct from the scholastic form (A. F. Büsching, 1758)[660] was now soon superseded by the distinction

[656] The concept of system was introduced in connection with the analytic method in theology, notably by B. Keckermann (*Systema logicae*, Hanover 1600; *Systema ss theologiae*, Hanover 1602). Keckermann's concept of system was taken over for use in philosophy by C. Timpler (*Metaphysicae systema methodicum*, Hanover 1606). Among Keckermann's successors the term systematic theology became established as the name for the analytic treatment of theology in the schools. See O. Ritschl, 'System und systematische Methode in der Geschichte des wissenschaftlichen Sprachgebrauchs und der philosophischen Methodologie' (Göttinger gelehrte Anzeigen, 1907, pp. 9ff); Id., *Dogmengeschichte des Protestantismus*, III, 1926, pp. 271ff and also A. von der Stein 'Der Systembegriff in seiner geschichtlichen Entwicklung' (H. Diemer, ed., *System und Klassifikation in Wissenschaft und Dokumentation*, 1968 (= *Studien zur Wissenschaftstheorie* 2), pp. 1–13, esp. 8–9.
[657] See Ebeling, 'The Meaning of "Biblical Theology"'; also the articles by V. Hamp and H. Schlier under this entry in *LThK*, 2nd ed., I, pp. 439–49.
[658] Ebeling, 'The Meaning of "Biblical Theology"', p. 84.
[659] Ebeling, 'Biblical Theology', p. 85.
[660] Ebeling (p. 87) says that Büsching was responsible for 'the decisive change' which turned 'Biblical Theology' from an auxiliary discipline into 'a competitor with the sovereign dogmatics'. According to K. G. Bretschneider, Büsching insisted in his dissertation (*diss. inaug. exhibens epitomen theologiae e solis litteris sacris concinnatae*, Göttingen 1756), 'amid the massive disapproval of his contemporaries, on a distinction between pure biblical doctrine and theological system' (*Systematische Entwicklung aller in der Dogmatik vorkommenden Begriffe* (1804), 3rd ed. Leipzig 1825, p. 74).

between biblical studies, which increasingly saw their work as historical, and dogmatics of any sort. J. A. Ernesti gave this distinction a theological basis. In his essay on the necessary connection between historical and dogmatic theology (1773), he explained that while history [*Historie*] also required conceptual clarity and rigour, it was particularly important for dogmatic theology to be based on historical theology, because the task of theology was to argue on the basis not of human reason but of faith and the authority of God, which had made itself known in the facts recorded in holy scripture. Everything now depended on a correct understanding of the biblical words and the events they reported (*vera intelligentia verborum et historiarum*).[661] Without this theology would be robbed of its certainty, and therefore Luther and Melanchthon had returned to the study of historical (!) theology.[662] With Ernesti biblical exegesis is therefore already absorbed into the concept of historical theology. Conversely, J. P. Gabler stressed the historical character of biblical theology in his famous inaugural lecture at Altdorf in 1787.[663]

The separation of the systematic and historical elements in theology to form distinct disciplines is a relatively recent event. Similarly, the other theological disciplines acquired autonomy only at various times since the Renaissance. Church history began to develop into an independent discipline at the end of the sixteenth century, after it had acquired increased relevance through the denominational disputes about the relationship of the church of the papacy and Christian antiquity. The first lectures on church history were given in 1583 at Frankfurt-on-Oder by A. Wenzel. Church history became a separate course a little later at Helmstedt, with Georg Calixt as professor, the same Calixt who had already made a theoretical case for the need for a historical theology alongside biblical exegesis as a preparation for polemical theology and dogmatics.[664] Within biblical theology

---

[661] J. A. Ernesti, 'De theologiae historicae et dogmaticae conjungendae necessitate et modo universo', *Opuscula theologica* (1773), 2nd ed. Leipzig 1792, pp. 511–34, at p. 528.

[662] Ernesti, p. 530.

[663] J. P. Gabler, *Oratio de justo discrimine theologiae biblicae et dogmaticae regundisque utriusque finibus*, Altdorf 1789.

[664] G. Calixt, *Apparatus theologicus*, pp. 165, 182–272.

the Enlightenment led subsequently to a separation between Old Testament and New Testament studies, as it became the custom to regard the two parts of the biblical canon as the documents of two different religions, Judaism and Christianity.[665] The movement in this direction had already begun with J. A. Ernesti's proposal, in his 'Guide for the Interpreter of the New Testament' (1761), that the two parts of the canon should be treated separately. This proposal was followed in the publication of a separate *Biblical Theology of the New Testament* by L. Bauer (1800–2).

Practical theology too did not become an independent course until the end of the eighteenth century, even though lectures on pastoral theology had already by that time a history of two hundred years. The recognition of practical theology as an academic discipline was particularly encouraged by Schleiermacher, but even so remained controversial down to quite recent times. Closely associated with practical theology was the youngest theological discipline, missionary studies, which came into being during the nineteenth century. It made its appearance in 1897 at Halle with a special chair of Protestant Missiology, held by G. Warneck, and subsequently spread rapidly, with the establishment of chairs in both Protestant and Catholic theology faculties. In German theology missionary studies usually included science of religion, which similarly developed around the turn of the nineteenth century. Science of religion failed to win a place as an autonomous discipline in theology faculties in Germany, unlike other countries, even though the history of religions school started in Germany, notably at Göttingen. C. Colpe has explained this situation as the result of Harnack's intervention in the discussion about the transformation of theology faculties into faculties of history of religion and the setting up of chairs of history of religion in theology faculties.[666] Harnack's action may have something to do with the fact that the chairs of history of religion set up at Berlin

---

[665] See G. Hornig, *Die Anfänge der historisch-kritischen Theologie. Joh. Sal. Semlers Schriftverständnis und seine Stellung zu Luther*, 1961, pp. 89ff.

[666] C. Colpe, 'Bemerkungen zu Adolf v. Harnacks Einschätzung der Disziplin "Allgemeine Religionsgeschichte" ', *Neue Zeitschrift für systematische Theologie* 6 (1964), pp. 51–69 (see above, p. 316–7 and esp. note 621).

and Bonn in 1910 and 1912 were soon moved to the philosophy faculties. The chair founded at Leipzig in 1912 went the same way, but not until 1946. With the chair at Erlangen also part of the philosophy faculty, there is only one Chair of Comparative Religious History and Philosophy of Religion in a German theology faculty, that at Marburg, which has been in existence since 1920.[667] In the Protestant theology faculties of Halle, Tübingen, Mainz, Hamburg, Heidelberg and Munich religious and missionary studies are combined. The failure of science of religion to become established as an autonomous discipline in German theology must inevitably be seen as a problem, both in comparison with the situation in other countries, especially now the USA, and in the context of the concept of theology outlined in the last chapter. In terms of the view of theology put forward in this book, as a science of God and as such concerned with religions, science of religion must be seen as the discipline which is basic to all theology. The only qualification necessary is that it should not exclude investigation of the divine reality experienced in religions but, as a 'theology of religions', make it an object of study. The support of a general theology of religion would also confer practical benefits on a theology overwhelmingly devoted to the study and description of the Christian religion. Accordingly, although this does not correspond to the present organisation of theology as an academic discipline, particularly in Germany, this function of science of religion will be the first topic in the following discussion of theology's subsidiary disciplines.

2. Science of Religion as Theology of Religion

The beginnings of the critical and comparative study of religion go back to antiquity. With the Renaissance it received a new and important impetus.[668] It was also considerably extended by the reports of Christian missionaries and the work of philosophers, classical scholars and especially orientalists in the eighteenth and

[667] Colpe, p. 53.

[668] See O. Gruppe, *Geschichte der klassischen Mythologie und Religionsgeschichte*, 1921; H. Pinard de la Boullaye, *L'étude comparée des religions*, I, Paris 1922.

nineteenth centuries. Even so, at the first International Congress of the History of Religions in Paris in 1900 J. Réville could say that the science of religion was still a young discipline which had begun to become established as an independent university subject only a quarter of a century before.[669] In 1873 a chair of the history of religions was set up at the university of Geneva, and lectures on the subject had been given regularly at Basle since 1834. Before the other Swiss universities followed the example of Geneva, chairs of the history of religions were founded in all the theology faculties in Holland starting in 1876. In France a chair was created in 1879 at the Collège de France, its first holder being the Protestant theologian Albert Réville, and in 1886 a whole section for religious studies was founded at the Ecole des Hautes Etudes. During this period the science of religion similarly became firmly established in universities in England, the United States and Scandinavia. Of all the countries in which important progress was made during the nineteenth century in science of religion, only Germany lagged behind in this development. Réville explained this fact as the result of the existence in Germany of theology faculties with denominational ties,[670] and called for theology to subordinate its denominational features to its character as science by including general science of religion.[671] He regarded the attachment of the discipline to philosophy faculties as no more than a temporary emergency solution. When demands were made for the transformation of theology faculties into faculties of the history of religion, or at least for the inclusion of religious studies as one of the disciplines within theology faculties, Harnack had objected that the forcible separation of the history of religions from the study of languages and history would mean condemning the theology faculties to 'incurable dilettantism', and claimed that the study of the Christian religion as a model was sufficient for the knowledge of

[669] For this section, see J. Réville, 'La situation actuelle de l'enseignement de l'histoire des religions', *Revue de l'histoire des religions* 43 (1901), pp. 58–74.

[670] 'La situation actuelle', p. 71.

[671] pp. 72–3: 'Assurément, partout où il existe des Facultés de théologie universitaires, la place de l'enseignement de l'histoire des religions paraît marquée dans ces Facultés, à mesure surtout qu'elles se dépouillent du caractère confessionel qui doit nécessairement être subordonné au caractère scientifique, le seul qui soit universitaire.'

religion in general.[672] Réville replied that, on the other hand, knowledge of other religions was essential for a knowledge of the religion of the bible, and that the alternative: either restricted specialisation or dilettantism, was not convincing.[673] In fact this alternative, which was Harnack's main argument, would strictly make it completely impossible for the religious concerns and their history ever again to be the object of scientific investigation as a single phenomenon. This left the claim that Christianity was sufficient for a knowledge of religion in general as the only argument of Harnack's which had any real force. This argument too, however, presupposed not only a claim for the absoluteness of Christianity in advance of any discussion,[674] but in addition the claim that Christianity possessed a monopoly of political validity. It is this latter claim which shows how far Harnack was from regarding the absoluteness of Christianity as something requiring examination within a framework of investigation into the history of religions. According to Harnack, it was 'certain that the nations which now divide the earth between them stand or fall with Christian civilisation, and that the future will tolerate no other alongside it'.[675] It is true that Harnack put forward this view in connection with his demand for Christian mission, as evidence that this now appeared 'more urgent than for a thousand years', and as a reason for paying more attention to non-Christian religions in theology. Nevertheless it is clear that his own position deviates from this attitude only in its conclusions, and only this attitude gives any plausibility to his claim that the study of Christianity is sufficient to provide a knowledge of religion in general. It is also no less clear today that this political attitude has proved to be an illusion, and that today a sense of its Christian responsibility makes Christian theology unable to distance itself too emphatically from such an imperialist

[672] A. von Harnack, *Die Aufgabe der theologischen Fakultäten und die allgemeine Religionsgeschichte*, 1901, pp. 9ff.

[673] J. Réville, *Revue de l'histoire des religions* 44 (1902), pp. 423–4. The first of these two views was also argued very forcibly against Harnack by A. Deissmann (*Der Lehrstuhl für Religionsgeschichte*, 1914, p. 15), who also emphasised the importance of religions as forces in the present which the missionary in particular had to face.

[674] A. v. Harnack, *Die Aufgabe der theol. Fakultäten*, p. 16.

[675] ibid., p. 9.

and colonialist obsession with Europe. The need today is for it to engage in a dialogue with other religions, [676] which is impossible if the premise that the Christian religion possesses sole validity is declared in advance to be not open to discussion.

It is to be feared that this association of the science of religion with missiology, which has since become characteristic of the form in which the former has entered theological faculties, [677] particularly in Germany, has taken place in the perspective suggested by Harnack. The association means that the study of non-Christian religions is narrowed down to what is required for Christian missionary activity, which needs some knowledge of these religions to do its work. This results in an undue emphasis on religions still in existence and their present state of development. Investigation of the world of religions for its own sake must break through such restrictions. It must concern itself with the whole range of the religious life of mankind. The importance of a single religion and its particular stage of development can be fully seen only within the framework of a history of world religions. The sciences of religion therefore form the appropriate framework for the practice of Christian theology and all its disciplines. They are not only of theological interest from the particular point of view of missionary work, but also relevant to the study of the origin, history and systematic self-understanding of Christianity itself. Only a dogmatic view of Christianity, which separates the Christian faith as knowledge of revelation from the world of religions, which it dismisses as merely human projections, could treat religions as a phenomenon

[676] Such a dialogue is indeed 'in terms of a theology of religions not an ultimate goal, but a *transitional situation*' (K. Goldammer, 'Die Gedankenwelt der Religionswissenschaft und die Theologie der Religionen', *Kerygma und Dogma* 5 (1969), pp. 105–35, quoted from p. 130), but nevertheless this sort of dialogue works seriously for understanding and even possible 'agreement' (Goldammer), and should be more than a tactical truce. See also K. Goldammer, 'Die Idee des Dialogs und des dialogischen Denkens in den interkonfessionellen und interreligiösen Beziehungen und Erwägungen', *Erneuerung der Kirche. Festschrift H. Bornkamm*, 1966, pp. 127–39.

[677] See O. G. Myklebust, *The Study of Missions in Theological Education*, Oslo 1955; additional material in G. Rosenkranz, 'Missionswissenschaft als Wissenschaft', *Zeitschrift für Theologie und Kirche* 53 (1956), pp. 103–27; A. Lehmann, 'Die Religions- und Missionswissenschaft im theologischen Studium', *Wissenschaftliche Zeitschrift der Universität Halle* 6 (1957), pp. 767–72.

so external to Christianity as not to require consideration until missionary work makes Christianity look outwards.

The science of religion as the fundamental theological discipline should be separated from the study of the missionary aspects. One result of this, however, would be to make the treatment of such aspects in an independent theological discipline dubious. The missionary element is so closely connected with the uniqueness of the Christian religion and the Christian church that it must be studied in all the disciplines belonging to Christian theology, historical as well as systematic. This fact also makes its separation from the other aspects of a Christian theology open to serious objections.[678] The needs of missionary training alone cannot justify the isolation of missiology as an autonomous and uniform academic discipline, and on the other hand this concern with practical training requires an introduction to Christian theology as a whole, not just within a specialised branch. Missionary subjects constitutes an independent study less from a historical and systematic point of view than in relation to the present understanding of the church's missionary activity. Such a study, however, belongs to practical theology. It does not justify the need for a fundamentally autonomous theological discipline; it was only the association of the work of science of religion with missiology which raised the latter to the status of an independent theological discipline. If the need for a science of religion as an independent discipline in theological faculties were accepted, this discipline would become responsible for providing a basis for

[678] See also C. Colpe's remark that missionary studies 'may very well become the victim of the realisation that all theology should be related to mission' ('Die Funktion religionsgeschichtlicher Studien in der evangelischen Theologie', *Verkündigung und Forschung* 13 (1968), pp. 1ff, esp. p. 11). However, Colpe treats 'the science of mission and ecumenism' as a unit, although the relationship between denominational studies, ecumenics, and missiology certainly cannot today be regarded as clear in this context, as Colpe assumes, presumably with the situation in the Hamburg Faculty in mind. According to Colpe, a division of the discipline described as 'the science of mission and ecumenism' should 'not be contemplated ... because we should at least keep open minds about changes in the substance of Christianity such as can occur in missionary work and in the emergence of younger churches'. On the other hand, there seems to be no reason why this possibility could not be allowed for equally well within the other theological disciplines.

theology in general, while missiology could be accommodated as a branch of practical theology.

There is, however, one condition to be met before the science of religion can acquire the status of a fundamental theological discipline, and in its present state of development it does not meet it. This is that the science of religion should not restrict itself to describing human religious experiences, their connections with other sorts of experience and their institutional embodiment in the life of society, but must also investigate the reality experienced in religious life and its history. Such an approach is closed in advance if the Enlightenment view that the religious domain is private is maintained and the truth of religious convictions is declared to be subject only to the individual's subjective decision. This would mean that the psychology, phenomenology, sociology and history of religion would be concerned exclusively with the human side of religious life. Particularly under the influence of the phenomenology of religion, this sort of suspension of judgment about the existence of an object of religious experience has become common: '. . . science can describe only man's actions in relation to God, not God's actions.' [679] A sharp distinction is then made between theology and the science of religion. [680] K. Goldammer, for example, maintains that 'the object of the science of religion' is not identical with 'the object of religion'. The 'object of religion' is a 'sacred power', but the 'objective reality' of this is 'not the concern of the science of religion'. [681] Goldammer hopes, by suspending judgment in this way, to avoid either admitting or denying the truth of religious assertions and to be able to keep free of either 'illusionism' or 'realism'. In this he is clearly deceiving himself, since suspension of judgment is itself a prejudice in favour of an immanent or anthropological interpretation of religion. The greater the apparent success of

[679] G. van der Leeuw, *Phänomenologie der Religion* (1933), 2nd ed. 1956, p. 3.

[680] H. W. Gensichen has described this as the 'minor solution' to the problem of the relationship between theology and the science of religion, and the one overwhelmingly adopted today ('Tendenzen der Religionswissenschaft', *Theologie als Wissenschaft in der Gesellschaft*, Göttingen 1970, pp. 28–40, esp. 33–4.)

[681] K. Goldammer, 'Die Gedankenwelt der Religionswissenschaft', pp. 115–16.

interpretations of religion as expressions of spiritual attitudes and social factors, the more unnecessary it becomes to postulate a transcendental reality as the object of religious experience. F. Heiler has seen this much more clearly when he describes the modern science of religion as 'for the most part making religion a human concept and eliminating the divine'.[682] This is, of course, not a negative result of the investigation of the science of religion, but simply the result of its deliberate exclusion of a specific object of religious conduct. A mere phenomenology, psychology or sociology of religions cannot get to grips with religion's specific object, and the claims of such investigations to be sciences of religion and religions must consequently be described as problematic. Any physical science is expected to investigate its particular object without prejudice and not to exclude on principle its typical features. Heiler has rightly demanded that the study of religious phenomena should 'take seriously religion's claim to truth'.[683] Taking this claim seriously need not mean – and in a scientific investigation cannot mean – accepting such truth-claims unexamined. A scientific investigation can admit assertions only to the extent of treating them as problematic and trying to test their claims. This testing must keep to the implications of the assertions themselves. In the case of religious traditions, this means that assertions of communications from a 'sacred power' have to be tested for the character of power thus claimed, first in regard to the experiences undergone by the bearers of the traditions and secondly in regard to the experience of reality available in the present. Assertions of the reality of divine powers thus have to be tested for their power to illuminate reality. This is no more than the systematic and conscious performance of what actually happens in the history of every religious tradition when the gods of a religion prove themselves in the sight of the members of the religious group to be capable of mighty acts or not. In this sense we can accept Heiler's view that 'all science of religion is ultimately *theology* because it is concerned not only with psychological and historical phenomena but also with the experience of other-worldly

---

[682] F. Heiler, *Erscheinungsformen und Wesen der Religion*, 1961, pp. 4–5.
[683] ibid., p. 17.

realities'.[684] It should be noted that Heiler has in mind the postulated mystical core of all religious experience, which he regards as self-evident. In contrast, our concern is with the power of a particular religious tradition to illuminate the vital experience of its adherents, or with its failure to show such power. This attitude is better expressed in Troeltsch's description of the science of religion as theoanthropic than in Heiler's unhistorical vision of a single source for the multiplicity of religious traditions.

The real thematic of religions – the communication of divine reality experienced in them – can be made the object of scientific investigation only in a *theology* of religions, not in a mere psychology, sociology or phenomenology of religions. These can be no more than auxiliary disciplines of a genuine science of religion. This science would examine the communications of the all-determining reality reported by religious traditions, communications from the 'sacred power' worshipped in the religion in question, to see how far they actually prove themselves to be such in the experiences of the people who belong to such religious traditions. We have seen that such a theology of religions is perfectly capable of subjecting the assertions of religious traditions to critical examination. Such a *critical* theology of religions does not produce an interpretation of religions on the basis of a previous religious position. It is therefore distinct from the attempts at a *dogmatic* theology of religions which have been made in the recent past particularly by Catholic theologians.[686] A critical theology of religions would be

[684] ibid., loc. cit.

[685] E. Troeltsch, 'Die Selbständigkeit der Religion', *ZThK*, 6 (1896), pp. 79ff., 94ff.; 'Geschichte und Metaphysik', *ZThK*, 8 (1898), pp. 29–30).

[686] So Karl Rahner explicitly describes his essay 'Christianity and the Non-Christian Religions' (*Theological Investigations*, vol. 5, London and Baltimore 1966 pp. 115–34) as 'basic traits of a Catholic dogmatic interpretation of the non-Christian religions' (p. 117), and H. R. Schlette makes a sharp distinction between the theology of religions, which he regards as 'a specialised area of theologico-dogmatic systematics' (p. 138) and a systematic approach to the science of religion (*Die Religionen als Thema der Theologie*, 1963, p. 63). In his definition of the relationship between the science of religion and the theology of religion, Schlette stresses the neutrality of the former on the question of the truth of religion (*Die Religionen*, pp. 43ff, esp. p. 46). See also E. Fahlbusch, 'Theologie der Religionen. Überblick zu einem

theology in virtue of its attempt to examine the specifically religious theme of religious traditions and ways of life, the divine reality which appeared in them, and not some other psychological or sociological aspects. This does not mean anything like an *interpretatio christiana* of non-Christian religions assumed in advance in accordance with an existing position.[687] It is of course inevitable that every investigator should bring a subjective position to his work, nor would it be desirable to eliminate this, since the different interests and approaches can open up different aspects of the subject. The science of religion is no different from any other discipline in this respect. On the other hand, a dogmatic 'premise' which was the starting-point of the whole argument but at the same time was not open to critical examination would be neither necessary nor permissable in the methodology we have outlined for a critical theology of religions. The basis of this methodology is acceptance of the fact that the question of the 'true' religion is historically disputed, and that the dispute is concerned with the ability of the various religious traditions both to accommodate a changing experience of reality by the use of symbols from its own stock and at the same time to assimilate the elements of truth which appear in other religious traditions. This does not involve the assumption either that only the Israelite and Christian religion has shown such a power of accommodation or that all forms of religion are inherently open to the future and converge in this openness.[688] It

---

Thema römisch-katholischer Theologie' (*Kerygma und Dogma* 15, 1969, pp. 73–86), and the works listed there.

[687] In his sympathetic discussion of my 'Towards a Theology of the History of Religions', *Basic Questions in Theology,* vol. II, pp. 65–118, H. W. Gensichen has misinterpreted my views in one respect when he suggests that it is 'a view of the history of religion based on premises specific to Christian theology' ('Tendenzen der Religionswissenschaft', in *Theologie als Wissenschaft in der Gesellschaft,* ed. H. Siemers and H. R. Reuter, 1970, p. 38). My point is rather different. Because of its historical and eschatological outlook, the Christian faith makes it possible to claim the history of religions as the history of the manifestation of the God revealed in Jesus Christ, and so to test its eschatological consciousness against religious history treated as the history of the manifestation of the reality of God as disputed in this process.

[688] This is my answer to the questions asked by P. Beyerhaus ('Zur Theologie der Religionen im Protestantismus', *Kerygma und Dogma* 15 (1969),

is of course true that the Israelite-Christian tradition has in fact
shown an unusual degree of assimilating and accommodating
power, and its historical sense and openness to the future have
enabled it not to expel from consciousness the historic changes
which have taken place in its religious awareness, but to take
account of it to a much greater degree than, for example,
mythical religions can. These, however, are not dogmatic but
empirical statements about the uniqueness of the Judaeo-Christian
tradition as compared with other systems of religious tradition. It
was of course this particular religious tradition which first made
possible a historical understanding of reality in general, and
through it the historical study of itself and other religious
traditions, but it is hardly possible now to regard this by itself as a
dogmatic prejudice which might interfere with the unprejudiced
evaluation of phenomena.

A theology of religions in the sense described would include
first a philosophy of religion which would have the task of

---

pp. 87–104) in reply to the essay of mine mentioned in the previous note. I did
not claim that 'theological openness to the future' was 'the feature in which all
religions come together' (Beyerhaus, p. 96). On the contrary, it is typical of
mythical religions that they are closed to the possibility of future changes in
themselves. This is what brings their actual history into a contradiction with
their self-understanding which undermines the truth of mythical
consciousness. Nor did I claim that as a result of their interaction in history
'the religions' are 'necessarily moving towards a future unity which can
already be discerned' (Beyerhaus, p. 97). In the first place such a moving
together is in no sense 'necessary', but is something which can be detected
only in the actual process of the history of religions, even though it may be
explicable in terms of the universality which characterises the great gods of
religions. Secondly, there is nothing in my arguments which contradicts
Beyerhaus's correct statement that 'parallel to this process of amalgamation
there is also a process of fission' (p. 97). Nevertheless in the actual history of
religion from the beginnings of Israel to the present, the integration of the
most diverse religious traditions which Christianity has brought about, and
the tendency originating in it and in Islam (and intensified by their rivalry) to
develop a complete religious world, is unmistakable. Of course in a Christian
interpretation of the relation of one religion to others it is necessary to bear in
mind 'not only the confirmation, but also the condemnation, of man in his
religion' (Beyerhaus, p. 97), and the 'daemonic' element in religion. A basis
for this may he found in the critique of mythical consciousness implicit in the
actual course of history, which I expressed in the essay referred to earlier (pp.
287–8).

constructing the general concept of religion and of introducing in the context of that the idea of God as the all-determining reality.[689] In the state of the problem resulting from the work of post-Renaissance philosophy, such a philosophy of religion would require a general anthropology as a basis. An example of the work such a philosophy of religion would do is the construction of the concept of religion in connection with the objects of human experience of meaning, that is, so as to take account of the totality of meaning implicit in all experience of meaning, a totality which in turn implies the existence of an all-determining reality as its unifying unity. Discussions of this sort can be seen as a development of Schleiermacher's analysis of religion as the 'contemplation and intuition of the universe'. This approach means that the analysis of the experience of meaning, in addition to its base in anthropology, makes use of assumptions about the reality pre-given to human experience and about the possibility of apprehending that reality in experience. The specific areas with which philosophy of religion is concerned are therefore, first, basic forms of religious conceptions of the 'sacred power' of the divine reality, second, the corresponding understanding of the world and man and, thirdly, the forms of the religious relationship, i.e., of worship. To do this, philosophy of religion makes use of the work of the auxiliary disciplines of the psychology, phenomenology and sociology of religion in organising the source material. Through their position midway

---

[689] C. Colpe describes the relationship of the philosophy of religion and theology differently when he assigns the question of the 'validity' of religious experience, in the sense of the assumption of a religious a priori, to the former, and reserves the 'question of truth' to theology ('Die Funktion religionsgeschichtlicher Studien in der evangelischen Theologie', *Verkündigung und Forschung* 13 (1968), p. 8; cf. p. 7, n. 16). My account, on the other hand, uses 'theology' as a category which bridges the gap between the philosophy of religion and the history of religions. In view of the philosophical origin of the concept of theology, it would be wrong to challenge its legitimacy in philosophy in principle, though not every philosophy of religion also includes a theology of religion. Philosophy of religion frequently limits itself to the anthropological aspects of religious experience, as also do transcendental theories of a religious a priori. In such a case the philosophical discussion of the phenomenon of religion remains incomplete. Even more frequently the history of religion has been described not as a 'divine-human' process (Troeltsch) and therefore theologically, but as a purely human occurrence.

between empirical investigation and conceptual systematisation these auxiliary disciplines link the two major disciplines of the science of religion, philosophy of religion and the history of religion.

Theory construction in the history of religion translates the general and therefore abstract concept of religion produced by philosophy of religion into the historic reality of religious life. The history of religions does not just organise the source material of religion into a temporal sequence, but also has to sketch models of the development of particular religions and ultimately of world religion in general, without, however, forcing the diversity and incompleteness of the history of individual religions into a single schema.[690] Within such a history of world religion or religions it will then be possible to assign the religion of Israel and Christianity its proper place. In this way a theology of religion provides a frame of reference for the theological disciplines concerned with the investigation and interpretation of Christianity.

Until religious studies develop into a theology of religions in the sense described here, and so become the basic discipline of theology in general, this basic theological work must be accommodated provisionally within systematic theology. Historically in modern theology the topics we mentioned have been studied by Protestant theology usually in the prolegomena to dogmatics, and in Catholic theology they have been included

---

Another approach is that of Hegelian philosophy of religion, which presents the history of religions as the realisation of their general concept understood in a 'theological' sense. The attitude adopted here differs from these in distinguishing between understanding of the general concept of religion in philosophy of religion and a theology of the history of religions (including that of Christianity). In the former the concept of God remains problematic, but the latter examines the extent to which the gods asserted to exist by the traditions have proved themselves in the historical experience of the religions. This approach takes into account the fact that a general concept of religion always remains abstract, while the actual historical reality of religion can be grasped only in a description of this history and not in terms of general concepts.

[690] In my essay, 'Towards a Theology of the History of Religions', (*Basic Questions*, vol. II, pp. 65–118) as focuses I have emphasised the importance for the unification of the history of religion of the processes of integration which develop in the course of the history of religion as a result of the universality of the divine figures.

in fundamental theology. The second solution could be regarded as appropriate if fundamental theology could hand over the functions of Christian apologetics, from which it developed,[691] to another discipline and treat the theology of religion and religions as its true activity. The latter subject cannot be part of a Christian apologetics because it is much more concerned with providing a more general frame of reference for a theology of Christianity. The association of theology of religion with apologetics is an expression of a narrow denominational view of the function of theology as a scientific discipline. The inclusion of the theme in the prolegomena to dogmatics may have a similar implication, though in practice the work of providing a theoretical basis for a specialised Christian theology can find a place here just as in a fundamental theology associated with apologetics. Both treatments of the subject-matter of religion must, however, be described as emergency measures, since the universality of the subject bursts the bounds of these more specialised disciplines. Such an emergency solution is justified as long as, and only as long as, no true fundamental theology, that is, a theology of religion and religions, is available.

The function of a theology of religion as described here takes up Schleiermacher's call for a 'philosophical theology' to provide a basis for theology as a whole.[692] In Schleiermacher's view, however, the task of philosophical theology would be 'to describe the essence of Christianity, what makes it a unique religious system'.[693] Schleiermacher himself, like Catholic fundamental theology later, associates this tasks with that of Christian apologetics, and distinguishes it from the function of philosophy of religion, which deals with the diversity of religious bodies in a general way (§ 23). Nevertheless, since Schleiermacher describes philosophical theology as having to

---

[691] See below, pp. 415–6.

[692] Troeltsch already treated the work of a 'general science or philosophy of religion' (*Gesammelte Schriften*, II, 1913, p. 224) in providing a basis for theology as performing the function of the 'philosophical theology' (p. 225) which Schleiermacher called for but did not produce, though Troeltsch wanted to give extra emphasis to 'freedom from presuppositions' by calling it 'philosophy of religion'.

[693] F. Schleiermacher, *Kurze Darstellung des theologischen Studiums*, par. 24. The subsequent references in the text are to this work.

start 'outside Christianity', that is, 'in the general concept of the religious or believing community' (§ 33), philosophical theology cannot be concerned, as it might first appear, with defining the typically Christian from the point of view of Christian faith and in distinction from other religious systems, but only with a specialised form of philosophy of religion. Schleiermacher says that the basis of philosophy of religion is ethics, which considers 'the essence of religion and of religious groups' in general, 'in connection with the other activities of the human spirit' (§ 21; cf. §§ 33, 35). Our account has instead described anthropology as the basis of philosophy of religion, because ethics, in the broad sense in which Schleiermacher understands the term, itself presupposes a basis in anthropology, and because the religious outlook is not mediated by ethics as a general theory of action but rooted *directly* in the constitution of human being.

The separation of 'philosophical theology' (with apologetics as a main element) from the general philosophy of religion created a state in Schleiermacher's theory in which the only function of philosophical theology was to isolate theoretically the typical features which distinguished Christianity from other 'religious systems', and it does not study Christianity in connection with the history of religions. This function is assigned to the philosophy of religion.[694] The result is that Schleiermacher does not give full recognition to the importance of history for religions and for Christianity in particular. The main limitation of Schleiermacher's position, however, is that he studies religion or piety only as an organisation of subjective experience, not as the self-manifestation of divine reality. In both these respects the 1799 *Speeches on Religion* contain elements of a more comprehensive approach, but its developed form appears in Hegel's philosophy of religion rather than in Schleiermacher himself.

3. Biblical Exegesis and Historical Theology

If the modern subjects of biblical exegesis and church history are

[694] On this see the propositions borrowed from the 'philosophy of religion' in Schleiermacher's dogmatics (*The Christian Faith*, trans. H. R. Mackintosh

taken as together forming historical theology, a fundamental decision about the character of this discipline is already taken. The history of theology must be concerned with the differences between the functions of these subjects and with the reasons for their development as independent subjects. In contrast to the interpretation of scripture, which was the origin of all Christian theology, church history did not emerge as an independent theological discipline until late – after the end of the sixteenth century – and was at first merely an auxiliary discipline, a status to which it has been repeatedly relegated in our own time by Karl Barth.[695]

The term 'historical theology'[696] was used as early as the first half of the seventeenth century by H. Alting, in lectures published under that title in 1664, twenty years after his death. The lectures dealt with the development of Christian doctrines in historical order, starting with the Old Testament. In 1759 J. A. Ernesti contrasted this concept of theology, as including, or even mainly consisting of, biblical theology, with dogmatic, scholastic or academic theology (Alting had made a similar contrast – see note 751 below).[697] Gabler's distinction, nearly thirty years later, between biblical and dogmatic theology is in the same line, though Gabler connects the distinction with the different idea of a biblical dogmatics, as opposed to that of the schools (see above, p. 355–6). Ernesti, however, had gone further than the mere contrasting of history [*Historie*] and dogmatics. He mentioned in passing that dogmatic theology too ought to be a part of historical theology, since it dealt with the judgments and opinions of theologians, their *dogmata*.[698] In Ernesti's own work,

---

and J. S. Stewart, Edinburgh, 1928, p. 31).

[695] Karl Barth, *Church Dogmatics*, I/1, p. 3.

[696] J. Pelihan's *Historical Theology* (London 1970, Philadelphia 1971) was unfortunately not available to me at the time of writing.

[697] J. A. Ernesti, 'De theologiae historicae et dogmaticae conjungendae necessitate et modo universo', *Opuscula theologica* (1773), 2nd ed., Leipzig 1792, pp. 514–15. See also note 662.

[698] Ibid., p. 514: 'Nam dogmatica proprie est illius ipsius historicae Theologiae pars, de placitis et opinionibus Theologorum, quae sunt proprie dogmata, nostraque demum aetate, a nostratibus quibusdam, ita appellari coepit ea quae olim scholastica, post, proper invidiam verbi, acroamatica dicebatur.' O. Ritschl (*Dogmengeschichte des Protestantismus*, I, 1908, p. 27)

however, this remark led no further. It was Schleiermacher who first included dogmatic theology in historical theology alongside scriptural exegesis and dogmatics.[699] His action had little influence because the systematic and historical elements seemed so clearly to embody distinct principles. Even Richard Rothe, who accepted the inclusion of dogmatics in historical theology, was able to follow Schleiermacher only at the cost of separating the function of speculative – and therefore properly speaking systematic – theology from dogmatics and making it, with the speculative theologians, the crown of the theological system.[700] A. Dorner, who also followed Schleiermacher's inclusion of

stresses the importance of the change which can be seen taking place here in the meaning of 'dogma', from divinely revealed doctrines of the Bible or the church to the opinions of theologians.

[699] Schleiermacher, *Brief Outline*, §§ 69ff., esp. § 97; cf. also §§ 26–28. O. Ritschl (*Die Dogmengeschichte des Protestantismus*, I) refers to earlier versions of this view which were put forward by K. T. Tittmann (1775) and J. C. Döderlein (1780) who took up Ernesti's suggestions. On Schleiermacher, see the interesting and stimulating remarks of E. Jüngel, 'Das Verhältnis der theologischen Disziplinen untereinander', *Unterwegs zur Sache. Theologische Bemerkungen*, 1972, pp. 34–95, esp. 49ff. According to Jüngel, Schleiermacher's inclusion of dogmatics in historical theology should be regarded as an answer to Fichte's demand for the abolition of theological faculties by transferring the philological and historical branches into general philology and history. It is possible that Fichte made this demand, which occurs in his 1807 *Deduzierter Plan einer zu Berlin zu errichtenden höheren Lehranstalt* (esp. § 26) as a result of the discussion on the opposition between historical and dogmatic theology stimulated by Ernesti and Gabler, though he himself did not make this distinction, but contrasted the 'scientific' and the 'practical' parts of theology. Nor does he make any explicit reference to dogmatics. There is, however, a problem about interpreting Schleiermacher's encyclopedic conception of historical theology as a reply to Fichte on the ground that it 'removes the basis of Fichte's criticisms' (Jüngel, p. 49). Fichte's *Deduzierter Plan,* though written in 1807, was not published until 1817, whereas Schleiermacher's encyclopedic view originated in his Halle period, and the first edition of the *Brief Outline* (1811) already contains the main lines of the later edition. It is, of course, possible that Schleiermacher had heard of Fichte's work in draft as a result of his work on the Berlin university commission, though this has not yet been demonstrated. For the present it seems better to interpret Schleiermacher's extension of the concept of historical theology to dogmatics as in fact a reaction to the intra-theological discussion on the distinction between biblical-historical and dogmatic theology.

[700] R. Rothe, *Theologische Ethik*, I (1845), 2nd ed. 1867, pp. 48–9 (§ 8), also

dogmatics in historical theology in his *Encyklopedia*, differed from Rothe on this point only in basing speculative theology on historical theology.[701] Not even with his association of exegesis and church history in historical theology, however, did Schleiermacher win general acceptance. The reasons which made even his pupil Hagenbach feel unable to follow Schleiermacher on this point are significant. According to Hagenbach, while it could not be denied that 'essentially *historic* matters, no less than the primitive history of Christianity itself', were 'revealed by exegesis', 'historical knowledge in itself is not the main concern of exegetical theology'. The reason, said Hagenbach, was that the holy scriptures 'are not of historical importance to us merely in the same way as the other monuments of Christian antiquity: as the deeds of our foundation, the deeds of revelation, they make a quite different and much wider claim on our study than other historical sources'.[702] For these and similar reasons, the separation of biblical theology and church history often seemed, and still seems, so natural that no effort is made to justify it against the alternative of classifying the two fields together as historical theology.[703] On the other hand the combination has been

---

pp. 53ff (§ 12). On the description of 'speculative theology' as the crown of the theological system, see K. Rosenkranz, *Encyklopädie der theologischen Wissenschaften*, 1831, XXXIV. Rosenkranz in fact makes dogmatics the first section of this speculative theology (pp. 4ff), followed by ethics as the second (pp. 57ff).

[701] A. Dorner, *Grundriss der Encyklopädie der Theologie*, 1901, pp. 102ff. Dorner's justification of the need for a speculative theology alongside historical theology also shows why speculative should follow, rather than precede, historical theology. According to him, 'mere historical knowledge of Christianity would give us no guidance about its significance' (p. 21), and ascertaining the historical facts 'also requires a scientifically based judgment of the value of the Christian religion' (p. 106). For Rosenkranz, on the other hand, the speculative description of the general idea of the Christian religion necessarily precedes the examination of the various forms in which it appears in history [*Historie*]. Connecting these with their speculative truth is the task of practical theology.

[702] R. K. Hagenbach, *Encyklopädie und Methodologie der Theologischen Wissenschaften* (1833), 11th ed. 1884, p. 121.

[703] Examples are H. Diem, *Theologie als kirchliche Wissenschaft*, 1951, and Diem's pupil F. Mildenberger (*Theorie der Theologie, Enzyklopädie als Methodenlehre*, 1972).

vigorously championed under the influence of the historical school, for example by G. Heinrici and especially A. Dorner.[704]

The answer given to this question has direct consequences for the scope of the exegetical disciplines. If they are separated from historical theology because of the normative status of the biblical texts in Christian faith, the question of the canon is fundamental for the self-understanding of these disciplines: they would then have to be understood as interpreting the scriptures recognised as of canonical validity in the Christian church. A withdrawal of biblical from historical theology for these reasons has been called 'a dogmatic prejudice'.[705] On the other hand, if the exegetical disciplines are treated as part of historical theology, the question of the canon has no more than secondary importance. There is a much greater awareness of the connection between the religion of Israel and the rest of the Middle East and of the importance for primitive Christianity of Jewish history in the 'inter-testamental' period, and similarly the boundaries between primitive Christianity and the history of the early church become fluid. In this approach the formation of the canon is seen as a moment *within* the history of Christianity. This is not to deny that the formation of the canon reveals structural peculiarities of Christianity and the Christian tradition. This can be seen in the two stages of the process. The first was the acceptance of the Alexandrian canon of the Old Testament, which was followed considerably later by the growth of a second canon of primitive Christian writings. The two features which emerge from this are the identity of the Christian God with the God of the Jews and the normative status of the initial period of Christianity, which derives ultimately from the eschatological character of the ministry and life of Jesus himself. The study of the biblical documents and the history of their acceptance does therefore have particular importance, but within historical theology. It is important because of this unique structure of the process of the Christian tradition, which means that a 'historical understanding', not only of the present, but of any later period of Christianity, 'must be based primarily on its relation to its

---

[704] G. Heinrici, *Theologische Enzyklopädie*, 1893, pp. 25ff; A. Dorner, *Grundriss der Encyklopädie der Theologie*, 1901, 33ff.

[705] Dorner, p. 34.

beginnings'.[706]

Nevertheless, the function of biblical studies in theology as a whole is not simply analogous to the authority of the biblical documents for the faith of later periods. The initial impulses which led to the development of a biblical theology were certainly directed towards the goal of replacing the traditional school dogmatics by biblical dogmatics (see above, pp. 355–6), but a more accurate appreciation of the *peculiarities* of the biblical writings and their statements quickly resulted in the realisation that the individual documents and their peculiarities were rooted in their period. As a result even Gabler in 1787 was no longer calling for the simple replacement of school dogmatics by biblical dogmatics. It was necessary to distinguish, he said, 'between what in the words of the apostles is truly divine and what is accidental and purely human'. Because of this, biblical theology provided only the basis on which to build a dogmatics 'appropriate to our age'.[707] However, it proved much more difficult than Gabler assumed to separate 'a truly divine form of the faith' from the temporal husk. The result of this was that the actual function of biblical exegesis in theology as a whole, and especially in systematic theology, was mainly 'to prevent systematic theology from isolating itself dogmatically'. Consequently, and paradoxically, it was biblical theology which made the most important contribution to the emergence, in the Christianity of the modern period, instead of a restrictive and monolithic authoritarian structure, of a tendency towards authoritarian Christian life and a correspondingly critical attitude towards tradition'.[708] This observation is indisputable, though it should

[706] *Heinrici,* p. 26 (referring to present-day Christianity). On the other hand, Dorner (*Grundriss,* pp. 34–5) underestimates the normative value of the initial period *within* the history of Christianity. In the authority of the twofold canon of scripture Heinrici sees no more than an example of a general principle of religious history ('the beginnings of an effective religious movement constitute the beginning of the new age,' p. 26), and does not recognise the uniqueness of the Christian process of tradition which is displayed in the formation of the canon.

[707] J. P. Gabler, *De justo discrimine theologiae biblicae et dogmaticae* . . . (1789), quoted from the excerpts translated in W. G. Kümmel, *Das Neue Testament. Geschichte der Erforschung seiner Probleme,* 1958, p. 118.

[708] T. Rendtorff, 'Historische Bibelwissenschaft und Theologie' (1968), in

not be allowed to obscure the tension which exists between this result and the original aims of biblical theology. This tension constantly reappears because, as T. Rendtorff has emphasised, the specific and authoritative significance of the Bible for church and theology — therefore also for the existence of Christianity in the present — is the reason for the emergence and continued existence of the historical study of scripture (47). This is of course connected with the fact that the historical study of scripture is 'no less than the only scientifically respectable context in which the formulation of questions and insights which are in conflict with the tradition seems not merely possible but also an inescapable duty' (46). Biblical studies are relevant to theology as a whole not simply as a means of critical liberation from the weight of tradition. This liberation itself is only a by-product of the search for the biblical norm and can be achieved only by an appeal to the norm. It is the combination of these two opposite aspects which constitutes the difficulty of the historical study of the bible. This also explains the 'higher order biblicism' which enables historical study of the bible to become 'an authoritative source of information for theology in general', although this means exposing it to 'demands for answers and proposals for its application which are not, and cannot be, a consequence of its own scientific work' (55). At the same time, such demands for answers have their source in the material on which biblical exegesis works. Jesus, the Old Testament traditions in the light of which the first Christians understood the meaning of Jesus, and the apostolic message started the process of the Christian tradition and constantly restart it, because the faith of every later age as faith in Jesus Christ is constantly referred back to them. However, the historical study of the Bible cannot by itself satisfy these demands for answers because the historical study of scripture by itself is unable to provide a basis for Gabler's distinction between the truly divine and what is time-conditioned in the apostolic writings. This is a task for theology as a whole because it involves a distinction which can be made only on the horizon of the experience available at any particular

---

Theorie des Christentums. Historisch-theologische Studien zu seiner neuzeitlichen Verfassung, 1972, pp. 41ff, quotation from p. 43. The following page references in this paragraph are to this book.

time, against which the tradition has constantly to prove its power in new and different ways.

The two commonest answers to the question about the specifically theological character of the historical study of the Bible can now be seen to form a false alternative.

When the function of biblical studies is understood in terms of the normative function of the double canon of scripture, it is natural to look for the specifically theological significance of both biblical studies and the biblical writings in the immediate relevance of their statements to the present. This imputes to the biblical data a truth-claim which purports to make direct contact with the present at any period and whose relevance to the presence can be simply described by appropriate methods, though these may have to clear away what is time-conditioned in the statements and background of the Bible. Such an approach, however, must lead to unhistorical and forced interpretations, as can be seen in great detail from the existentialist interpretation of the New Testament, which disregards the history which lies between the primitive Christian writings and the situation of the interpreter, and the changes this history has produced in the content of religion. Not least among the failings of this approach is that it ultimately does not do justice to the present because it does not consider it in relation to its origins.

The apparent alternative is to treat the biblical texts strictly and exclusively as sources for the religious history of Israel and primitive Christianity. In this case, however, the exegetical disciplines seem to lose their theological character because they now seem to be concerned only with historical phenomena in the study of which consideration of their present force is inadmissible. Such connection as can then be made with theology seems to derive from the role of the disciplines in investigating the origin of Christianity.[709] Paradoxically, the loss of a theological concern resulting from such a strictly historical interpretation of biblical exegesis has often encouraged it to seek an almost violent liberation from the merely historical, which easily produces a blurring of the outlines of rigorous historical research.

[709] The still unsolved problems created by this interpretation with regard to the Old Testament have been discussed above (p. 262).

The same problem of a consistent historicalisation also occurs with church history, though in this case it is usually felt to be less constricting in Protestant theology because church history is not regarded as involving normative claims comparable with the canonical authority of the biblical writings.

The dilemma of a historicalisation of biblical exegesis at the cost of losing its theological character on the one hand and retaining the normative character and present relevance of its material at the cost of losing historical cogency in its interpretation on the other cannot be solved by purely hermeneutical considerations. The attempt to solve it in this way tends rather to reveal the difficulties of any hermeneutical technique, since hermeneutic tries to interpret what is historically distinct as a variant of present-day life or as a possible mode of the present-day understanding of existence. Such a direct connection of religious history with the present may be tolerated in religious practice, but not in reflective analysis whose aim is to find out the basis of the treatment of the tradition in religious practice.

The dilemma between a historicalising elimination of theological content and a 'theological' interpretation which does violence to the historical can be resolved only if the historical procedure of scriptural exegesis is set within a *theologically* oriented history of religions which would be a theology of religions. In this context it is not just application to the present which gives the biblical texts their theological dimension. It is now the phenomena of the history of the Judaeo-Christian religion themselves and their own context in that history which requires them to be interpreted as the self-manifestation of the divine power over everything, i.e. of the all-determining reality. The situation of the texts themselves raises the question whether and how far the religious conceptions documented in these texts were adequate to the experience of reality of their period, how far therefore they were able to describe the divine activity they claimed to have taken place as a manifestation of the all-determining reality. The question whether, and if so how, what appeared at the time a convincing self-manifestation of divine reality can also be accepted by later generations as an expression of the all-determining power cannot be settled in the same enquiry, because this question involves a consideration of the whole process of change in the understanding of reality. In the historical interpretation of scripture this question can and must remain open. It can be left open with the assurance that the enquiry into the relevance of the biblical texts in the context of present experience of reality does not begin by attaching some sort of theological interpretation to a previously historically neutral substance, but merely applies in relation to the present experience of reality the same procedure followed by the historian in relation to the past experience of reality in which the texts themselves were produced. In both cases the enquiry is about the ability of the texts to show, on the horizon of human experience of reality at a particular period, that the content of their religious message is the all-determining reality. To this extent the enquiry in both cases is theological.

The theological study of biblical texts must not, then, be confused with the search for their relevance to the present. On the other hand, the two questions cannot be simply separated either. The question whether we, with our views, should say that God really revealed himself in the phenomena reported in these texts can be answered only in connection with the question whether this God shows himself to be the all-determining reality, and so God, on the horizon of present experience. Nevertheless, whatever the answer given to this question at a particular time, the religious traditions of the past (like existing non-Christian religions) retain their autonomy. Even if their claim to truth is not obvious, they remain as a challenge to the contrary experiences of the present and their protest has a chance of being proved right in a future perspective.

Apart from their historical meaning, the biblical texts also have a specific connection with the present through the fact that all present-day Christian piety depends on a reference back to these texts. Conversely, modern Christianity's relationship with the Bible depends on the complex of experience of the modern world and on the present-day confrontation with other forms of piety and Christian conviction. In the Christian tradition the authority of the Bible represents the definitive claims of Jesus himself and his history. This is why each new generation of Christians always looks back to the apostlic message and the knowledge of Jesus himself which it contains. The form of this relationship, however, is determined by the context in which reality is experienced at the particular time. This means that its investigation and criticism cannot be a matter for biblical studies but are a matter for church history, the more recent history of theology or systematic theology. Within such a framework the correspondence of the later appropriation of the biblical texts to their original meaning can be only one point of view among others, but it is given due importance by the normative status which the appropriation itself attributes to the texts. This normative status holds not for the original experiental context, but only for this later one, in relation to which the God to whom the texts bear witness proves himself to be God when the witness of the texts is believed. Because of the authority of the Bible in the history of Christian's reception, especially in its explicit ecclesial form, knowledge gained about the history of theology through biblical studies also becomes important in the present process of the reception of the Christian tradition. The assessment of this importance, however, is not the business of the historico-critical interpretation of scripture as such, but the function of work in systematic and practical theology, using the results of historical theology.

4. Biblical Theology

Any discussion of the position of biblical theology in the encyclopedia of theological disciplines must deal with the correctness or incorrectness of its further subdivision into Old Testament and New Testament theology. If this subdivision is treated as natural, it becomes impossible to see the problems which the existence of these disciplines in their separate state creates for theology's understanding of its work.

As already mentioned (above, p. 355), biblical theology did not become separate from dogmatic theology until the late seventeenth century. Initially its development into an autonomous study represented the pietistic victory of 'simple' biblical faith over the 'scholastic' dogmatics of early Protestant orthodoxy. Later it was consolidated as a result of the increasingly clear recognition of the historical gap between the period of primitive Christianity and the contemporary situation of Christianity. Since then the independence of biblical from dogmatic theology has been justified by its role in giving expression and constant support in the organisation of study to the normative status of the first period of Christianity (including its origin in Old Testament Judaism) and modern Christianity. Although in recent decades, as a result of the tendency to 'theological exegesis', it has been common within the exegetical disciplines to deny this formal basis of their distinctness from dogmatic theology, it has always been reinforced by the inescapable realisation of the historical character of their material, the biblical documents.

No such technical justification can be given for the division of biblical theology into exegetical theology of the Old Testament and exegetical theology of the New Testament. A realisation of this in one form or another exists today in many quarters. For example, the ultimate aim of Rad's work, in support of which he cites R. de Vaux, H. Schlier and G. Ebeling, is 'a "biblical theology" in which the dualism of an Old Testament and a New Testament theology each convinced of its own distinctness might be overcome'.[710] P. Stuhlmacher has also described this 'binary division of scriptural interpretation' as 'extremely dubious' theologically.[711] When, however, Stuhlmacher goes on to say that the division is 'the same sort of emergency measure as the strict separation between exegesis and church history, dogmatics and

---

[710] G. von Rad, *Theologie des Alten Testaments,* vol. II, 4th ed. 1965, p. 447. The current English edition of this work (*Old Testament Theology,* vol. II, Edinburgh and London 1965) is based on an earlier German edition and does not include this passage.

[711] P. Stuhlmacher, 'Neues Testament und Hermeneutik', *Zeitschrift für Theologie und Kirche* 68 (1971), pp. 127–61 (quotation from p. 155). Stuhlmacher's view (like that of H. Gese, see note 717) depends on a recognition of the documents of primitive Christianity and those of the Old Testament as belonging to the history of the same tradition, whereas F. Mildenberger is led to call for the 'abolition of this distinction' between the two branches of exegesis by considerations of the unity of the canon (*Theorie der Theologie,* 1972, p. 77).

practical theology' it must be pointed out that the separation of
the exegetical disciplines raises much more serious objections
because of the historical reasons underlying it.

After J. A. Ernesti had begun the independent exegetical
treatment of the New Testament in his *Anweisung für den Ausleger
des Neuen Testaments,* of 1761, the theoretical justification for this
step was presented with full force ten years later by J. S. Semler
in his study on the liberal investigation of the canon. Semler
regarded the Old Testament as the book of a different religion,
the Jewish religion, the national particularism and externality of
which had in essence been superseded by the univeralism and
interiority of Christianity, although the very beginnings of
Christianity were still disfigured by the dross of its Jewish
origin.[712] The books of the Old Testament, in his view, 'belong
to the history and truth of *the Jewish religion,* but they have no
connection with the Christian religion; they are neither the basis
nor the content of Christianity'.[713] The significance in the history
of theology of these judgments of Semler's, which on many
points recall Spinoza's *Tractatus theologico-politicus* (1670) [714], is, in

[712] On this see E. Hirsch, *Geschichte der neueren evangelischen Theologie,* IV,
1952, pp. 61ff, and also the rather anachronistic attack on Semler's position as a
modern 'gnosis' by H. J. Kraus in his *Geschichte der historisch-kritischen
Erforschung des Alten Testaments* (1965), 2nd ed. 1969, pp. 109–10. Particularly
illuminating is the sentence from Semler's *Versuch einer freiern theologischen
Lehrart* (1777, p. 105) quoted by Hirsch (p. 65) which says that the death of
Jesus was ordained by God 'to be the means of the foundation and extension of
a general superior religion which would supersede Judaism and paganism
simultaneously by spiritual knowledge and effects'. In his *Abhandlung zu freier
Untersuchung des Canon,* I, Halle 1771, p. 63 (§ 13), Semler describes it as the
purpose of his book to promote 'the general acceptance and proper exercise of
the *Christian,* the truly divine religion, which is, and should be, very different
from the Jewish mentality'.

[713] J. S. Semler, *Versuch einer freiern theologischen Lehrart,* Halle 1777, p. 109 (§
37).

[714] Among the latter are the view of Christianity as an independent religion
from that taught by Moses (chap. 29, 348-9; cf. Preface 7, 31), the belief that,
unlike the divine law, which was identical with the natural law (chap. 4,
82–3), the 'ceremonies' of the Old Testament were instituted only for the
Hebrews (chap. 5, 93, 12ff), whereas Christ was 'sent for the instruction of all
mankind' (chap. 4, 86, 36ff), and brought knowledge in the Spirit (4, 87, 9).
Others are Spinoza's connection of the validity of the 'ceremonies' with the
continued political existence of the Jewish state (chap. 5, 97, 15ff) and his

the estimation of J. Kraus, that the 'impetus for the use of historical criticism in the study of the Old Testament has been, curious though it may seem, the contribution of rationalism'.[715]

The conception of Judaism and Christianity as two different and independent religions each of which has produced its own sacred book and must consequently be the subject of a special exegetical discipline is no longer convincing as a justification for the separate existence of these two disciplines. Firstly, Christianity is not a religion that is independent of Judaism even though it came into existence in the womb of Judaism. Rather, incipient Christianity appealed to the truth of the *Jewish* belief in God. It was to this that Jesus had called his contemporaries and this which made the first Christians see Jesus as the Messiah, the Son of Man and the servant of God. Christianity in its beginnings was much more a Jewish sect than a religious principle independent of Judaism. This can be seen secondly in the fact that the Jewish canon (in its Alexandrian form) was until the end of the second century simply 'the Bible' for Christians too.[716] Until this time faith in Christ was simply the point of view from which the Christians interpreted the Jewish Bible. It was not until a later stage that this interpretive standpoint was given substance by the

---

belief that they had been diverted to the promotion of 'physical and temporal happiness and assurance of the kingdom' (chap. 5, 92, 27). Lastly there is the distinction between the word of God and scripture, which is also generally regarded as characteristic of Semler's position (Hirsch, p. 58; Kraus, p. 111, both on Semler's *Abhandlung* I, p. 75). The page and line references to Spinoza are to the German translation of the *Tractatus* by L. Gebhardt in vol. 93 of the Philosophische Bibliothek. I am indebted to Prof. Dr A. Altmann for pointing out that the contrast between Jewish and Christian religion goes back to Spinoza.

[715] Kraus, *Geschichte*, p. 110.

[716] H. von Campenhausen insists that, although Christianity is not a religion of the letter but 'the religion of the spirit and of the living Christ', there is a fact, 'at first sight paradoxical', which 'must not be evaded': 'The old Jewish Bible was and at first remained the only written norm of the church, and was – with different degrees of emphasis – everywhere recognised as such' (*Die Entstehung der christlichen Bibel*, 1968, p. 77, with a reference to the same author's essay 'Das Alte Testament als Bibel der Kirche vom Ausgang des Urchristentums bis zur Entstehung des Neuen Testaments', in *Aus der Frühzeit des Christentums. Studien zur Kirchengeschichte des ersten und zweiten Jahrhunderts*, 1973, pp. 152–96).

canonical collection of the apostolic writings. Thirdly, historical scripture scholarship has established the unity of the transmission process which links primitive Christianity with ancient Israel and post-exilic Judaism, and which resulted in the canonical – and non-canonical – writings of the 'inter-testamental' period. H. Gese has recently stressed the importance of this factor in his 'Reflections on the Unity of Biblical Theology'.[717] According to Gese, what first brought the process of the formation of an Old Testament canon to a conclusion was the eschatological consciousness of primitive Christianity and the Jewish reaction it produced. Primitive Christianity, says Gese, did not take over an already complete Old Testament canon; 'rather, the Old Testament comes into being as a result of the New Testament; the New Testament forms the end of a process of tradition which is essentially a unity, a continuum' (420). This is to explain the end of the formation of the Jewish tradition by an internal cause, by the eschatological character of the history of Jesus, which is also the final reason for the formation of a New Testament canon distinct from the subsequent history of the church. We recognised previously that this was the basis for the independence of biblical theology from dogmatics, and it now proves to be the factor which welds together the processes of tradition within Judaism and within Christianity. This must make the division between Old Testament and New Testament exegesis, particularly in view of its origin in a division between Christian and Jewish religion, appear dubious. In its effect on scholarship it has done most damage to New Testament studies. Without the division between the two exegetical disciplines, exaggerated interpretations of primitive Christianity in hellenistic categories would almost certainly have received less emphasis, and the need for a single history of the religion of Israel and Judaism, including primitive Christianity, in the sense of a theology of this process of tradition, would have been felt more strongly much sooner.

There are of course considerations of a practical sort[718] which give some support to the retention of the division of disciplines made on other grounds. The principal one is the great mass and

---

[717] *ZThK* 67 (1970), pp. 417–36; see esp. Gese's criticism of the Reformers' attachment to the Masoretic canon of the Old Testament, pp. 422–3.

[718] See also P. Stuhlmacher, *ZThK* 68 (1971), p. 155.

diversity of the material. The interpretation of the Old
Testament today calls for specialised knowledge of the general
and religious history of the ancient Near East and of the relevant
languages, and New Testament studies require knowledge of
rabbinic and apocalyptic Judaism and also of the complex
hellenistic world. It is now hardly possible for a single scholar to
meet simultaneously the demands which have grown up in these
fields under the influence of the separation of the two disciplines.
It can also be argued that the evidence of the origin of
Christianity requires particularly detailed examination and
assessment within the framework of a Christian theology.
However it is possible to take account of both requirements
within a single discipline through specialisation on the part of the
individual scholar. The conflicting demands do not make a
separation of the disciplines necessary when it is not justified by
the nature of the study.

What, now, are the fundamental tasks to be performed within
a biblical theology envisaged as a unity? In a biblical theology
dominated by the idea of the canon, the main task would
inevitably be to provide a unified interpretation of the individual
biblical documents. Historical methods had in the beginning, and
may still have, no more than a subsidiary function in the work of
textual interpretation. On the other hand, if biblical theology is
seen within the broader framework of a historical theology of
Christianity, which in turn describes one segment of the history
of world religion, the history of the religion of Israel, of Judaism
and of primitive Christianity must be at the centre of biblical
theology. In this view the exegesis of the biblical writings
functions as a theology of the formation of the Judaeo-Christian
tradition and is not an end in itself. Finding the present meaning
of biblical statements will now mean looking at their dependence
on the meaning of the individual statement in the context of the
history of the religion of Israel and Judaism and cannot be an
isolated activity. The implications of this affect even homiletics.
The meaning of many biblical statements makes an immediate
impact when they are connected with fundamental questions
arising out of human existence as such. This immediacy,
however, is in its turn mediated and must be examined in
scientific reflection in its mediation. In addition, most biblical

statements explicitly depend on a historical context, and not even their general human significance can be separated from this. Man himself is a historical being, and in addition the general human relevance of biblical texts often cannot be seen without a historical interpretation, or depends on an attitude towards Israel's election and eschatological hope. This last reason in particular makes the immediacy of the effect of biblical statements impossible to compare with the immediacy possessed by aesthetic works from earlier periods. As religious documents, the holy scriptures of the Jews and Christians are tied to history in a different way. They can of course also be judged from literary and aesthetic points of view, and this has relevance for homiletics, but this approach does not capture their specifically religious essence.

The history of religion in Israel, Judaism and primitive Christianity must be treated as a single process of tradition in which the spread of Christianity into the world of hellenism appears as only the last phase of a chain of receptions of non-Israelite religious traditions into Israel's religious consciousness. Starting with the world of Canaanite religion, through the contacts with Egypt and Babylonia to the symbiosis of the Jewish community with the Persian Empire and the tedious arguments about its attitude to hellenistic culture, comparable events constantly recurred. In this process the Jewish faith and the Jewish religious tradition constantly reasserted themselves in a new world of experience whose structure and images had been fixed by these very religions. They did this usually not by isolating themselves from that world, but by adapting it to the characteristics of the Jewish faith. It is not enough to describe this process as part of the history of ideas; it was totally bound up with the political and social history of Israel, the ancient Near East and the Mediterranean world. Conversely, in theology the political history of Israel, Judaism or the primitive Christian community is of no interest in itself, but only for its relevance to religion and religious history. An account of the political history of Israel in isolation from its religious history therefore appears as an abstraction, with little to offer theological research or teaching. The same applies to the summary accounts of the doctrinal contents of the biblical documents which usually go by the titles of 'theologies' of the Old and New Testaments. This literature is usually influenced by the tradition which thinks of 'biblical theology' as in competition with dogmatic theology and as presenting the simple biblical message as an alternative to the school theology with its load of superfluous scholasticism. There are two common approaches in this school. In one the doctrinal contents are detached from the historical sequence of the biblical writings and assembled by topic, which leaves considerable scope for the interpreter's personal taste. Alternatively – as in the works of Bultmann and von Rad – the theological outlooks of the most important contributors to the tradition are dealt with separately in historical sequence.[719] The one-sidedness of an approach based on an abstract history of ideas has already been partly avoided in the more recent accounts of this type. Bultmann and Rad describe the theological outlooks of the biblical documents against the background of the history of the institutions of Israel and primitive Christianity. Nevertheless in these accounts it is the religious outlooks themselves, with their differing contents, which occupy the centre of interest, with the result that the institutions and their development remain no more than a background. If the religious outlooks as they developed and changed were the real theme, the significance of political and institutional history, and of foreign cultures and religions, would have to receive much more discussion, since both of these were involved in the modification of the experiential reality in terms of which the various biblical writers tried to define the God of their tradition as the all-determining reality. If this process of development and change in the religious outlooks of the biblical writers or their sources were the real topic of description and analysis in biblical studies, the appearance of irreducible subjectivity in the religious outlooks described would disappear. This has come to be seen, particularly by von Rad, as a problem because of the difference between the historic-theological perspectives of the Old Testament writers and the secular

[719] Rudolf Bultmann, *Theology of the New Testament*, trans. K. Grobel, London and New York, 2 vols, 1952 and 1955 (original 1948–53); Gerhard von Rad, *Old Testament Theology*, London and Edinburgh, vol. I 1962, vol. II 1965 (original 1957 and 1960).

approach of modern history. Of course it would be no more of a solution to treat the religious outlooks as a mere expression of the secular history of their period. A purely political, social or cultural view of the history of Israel and Christianity would remain just as abstract as the isolation of religious attitudes which made them seem merely subjective in comparison with the other events. The two abstractions are in complete mutual dependence. The real task is to work out the influence of the political, social and cultural changes on the experience of reality as a whole, and *so* on religion. It would then be possible to understand how these changes were handled in the religious tradition in which the contributors to the biblical tradition were rooted. We should then have achieved an examination and description of the process of tradition in Israel, Judaism and primitive Christianity which had left behind the complementary abstractions of a merely politically or institutionally oriented history of Israel or primitive Christianity on the one hand and the subjective religious attitudes of the representatives of these traditions on the other.

Even today, however, a double interest stands in the way of such a treatment of the development of tradition in Israel and primitive Christianity. There is first the desire that faith should remain subjective and not explicable in terms of more basic factors, and second the pathos of a positivistic view of science in the use of historical methods, as a result of which the specific concerns of theology is excluded. The dichotomy between the general historical analysis of, for example, a history of the politics and institutions of Israel and primitive Christianity on the one hand, and that of the subjectivity of the religious outlooks of the representatives of the biblical traditions isolated from those events on the other reflects the modern dichotomy of an isolated religious subjectivity and the objectivity of science. This dichotomy reaches a peak in the contrast between a descriptive *history* of the religion of Israel or primitive Christianity, with no theological basis, and a *theology* of the Old and New Testaments. It is not generally realised that the fundamental problems of biblical theology in this area derive from the dilemmas of modern social existence and the connected problems of modern Christianity. Projecting the dualism of modern Christianity on to the technical problems of biblical theology makes it appear there in reified form as an apparently insuperable dichotomy of religious contents and historical states of affairs. When this dichotomy is reified into a 'datum' and used as an argument against any injection of systematic-theological considerations, it obscures the fact that it is precisely such considerations which are the basis of this picture of biblical data.

The task of providing a unified account of the history of the transmission of the tradition of Israel and primitive Christianity which includes both political and institutional history and a description of religious outlooks must be the goal of biblical theology and be at the centre of both research and teaching. In addition to an assessment of the textual tradition and the other tools of historical reconstruction in relation to this aim, this requires a critical discussion and interpretation of the present state of development of historical methodology. This includes a critical history of historical methods and their application in biblical theology. Such a history would have to describe the specialist interests which led to the development of these methods in the biblical sciences and the specialist implications which resulted from their use. This is the only way to achieve a critical methodological consciousness which is aware of the inconclusive nature of historical methods and of the detailed problems of their current state of development, and which will make possible the necessary developments to meet the needs of a biblical theology.

5. Church History

The writing of church history is said to start with Eusebius of Caesarea, or even with Luke's Acts of the Apostles,[720] but church history as a theological discipline does not begin until the sixteenth century. The denominational disputes of the period made Flacius Illyricus produce his *Magdeburg Centuries* to show how long ago and how far the Roman church had departed from

[720] F. C. Baur, in his *Epochen der kichlichen Geschichtsschreibung*, Tübingen 1852, pp. 7ff, began with Eusebius, though he did mention the possibility of tracing his subject back to its 'earliest beginnings' in the gospels and Luke's Acts of the Apostles.

the origins of Christianity, and Baronius attempted to defend it against his charges. The relevance of this subject for the period is indicated by Andreas Hyperius's inclusion of church history, in 1572, as the most important topic of practical theology.[721] Later, in 1628, Georg Calixt treated church history as an independent discipline and placed it between exegetical and polemical theology.[722] On the other hand, Abraham Calov included the study of church history only in the *secundaria studia theologica*, outside the sequence of the major disciplines, after exegesis, didactic theology, polemic, moral theology and homiletics.[723] G. J. Planck also thought it necessary to say in the course of his remarks on the study of theology that 'it can certainly do no harm', if, between the study of exegesis and dogmatics, 'some attention is also given to church history'.[724] It was only the nineteenth-century awareness of history which finally confirmed church history as one of the theological disciplines and gave it a place in the structure of the theology course. The increasing awareness of the difference between the historical present and not only previous periods of the church but also primitive Christianity created a growing need to trace the developmental context which supplied the continuity within which the various periods nevertheless retained – if not created – their Christian identity.[725] It was only the neo-orthodoxy of our own century, which regarded the whole period of modern Christianity as a falling-away from the Gospel, which suppressed these questions in an attempt to make direct contact with the Reformation and

---

[721] A. Hyperius, *De Theologo seu de ratione studii theologici*, Basle 1572, pp. 562, 567ff.

[722] Calixt, *Apparatus theologici . . .*, p. 165: 'porro ulterius tendentibus (i.e. for those who want to go beyond the study of scripture and explain and defend its truth) . . . necessaria est Historia ecclesiastica.' Cf. pp. 182ff.

[723] A. Calov, *Isagoges ad ss Theologiam libri duo*, pp. 355ff.

[724] G. J. Planck, *Einleitung in die theologischen Wissenschaften*, vol. II, p. 528.

[725] In his study of Albrecht Ritschl, *Faith and the Vitalities of History* (New York 1966), P. Hefner showed that the search for the continuity of Christianity through its history was the central problem of Ritschl's theology. Ritschl's assessment of hellenism and early Catholicism, which embodies the attitudes of bourgeois Protestantism at the end of the nineteenth century, affected Protestant views of history far beyond its immediate sphere of influence thanks to its influence on Harnack's work on the history of dogma.

scripture. However, this claimed directness has been revealed increasingly clearly as a fiction, with the result that the problem of the relevance of church history as a link between the origins of Christianity and its present has once more become inescapable in theology.

Church history is not just a particular theological discipline, as biblical theology can be said to be. It embraces the whole of theology, whereas biblical theology as a discipline can only *per nefas,* and the individual exegete only by exercising considerable courage, transcend the limits of their own discipline in order to consider its contribution to theology as a whole. The matter of biblical exegesis requires it to do this, but only in so far as that matter cannot be the concern uniquely of historico-critical biblical science. In contrast it is the field of church history as church history which stretches beyond its formal boundaries into biblical theology on the one side and dogmatics and practical theology on the other. Unless a fundamental distinction is made between the canonical scriptures (as in early Protestantism) or the whole apostolic age (as by Karl Barth) and the age of the church and its history,[726] there is no reason for denying the discipline responsible for investigating the history of Christianity competence to study the beginnings of Christianity, and indeed its prehistory,[727] even though it is valuable to draw attention to a contrast, based on the uniqueness of the Christian faith, between the apostolic church and the apostolic writings *as a significant constituent of the history of Christianity* on the one hand and all later ages of the church on the other. For the same reasons Schleiermacher's inclusion of dogmatics in historical theology is based on sound arguments; the present formulation of the Christian doctrinal tradition on the one hand consists of the present acceptance of its historical development and on the other effects the same synthesis of tradition and awareness of the lapse of time which can be found generation after generation in the history of the church. It is impossible therefore just to deny the competence of church history to say how this task is to be accomplished under present conditions when the discipline studies so many examples of the performance of the task in past

[726] Barth, *Church Dogmatics,* I/1, pp. 164–70.

[727] F. C. Baur, *Die Epochen der kirchlichen Geschichtsschreibung,* pp. 262–3.

situations. Similar arguments hold in the case of Christian ethics and, as we shall see in more detail later, for practical theology.

The function of systematics in the narrow sense, the investigation of the present truth of Christianity, is certainly not simply identifiable with a historical account of its development. In a positivist view of history, or one which equates history with recording facts, this appears self-evident. History itself, however, can be studied and described with a systematic (and practical) intention. In this approach the problems and tasks of the present are illuminated by the long legacy of their past and by an awareness of the undeveloped possibilities that past holds for the future. Church history practised in this way would leave the systematic theologian with only the analysis of philosophical and theological principles as his particular field, and in theory this work could be accommodated as well or better as part of a theological philosophy of religion which functioned as the basic discipline of a theology of religions. This is the only theological discipline which has broader functions than church history. Church history has a similar position as a branch of the theology of religions to that of biblical theology within church history. Church history is the treatment of Christianity from the point of view of the history of religion.[728] This statement raises the question of the relation between the history of the church and secular history. Anyone who studies this question in detail soon

---

[728] H. Karpp has objected to the nomination of Christianity as the object of church history on the ground that 'Christianity' is not a single phenomenon ('Kirchengeschichte als theologische Disziplin', in E. Wolf (ed.), *Festschrift R. Bultmann,* Stuttgart 1949, pp. 149–67, esp. pp. 152ff). On the other hand, nor is 'the church'. The existence of a number of churches itself makes it necessary, when describing the empirical material of church history, to introduce as a cover term the concept of a Christianity which has been institutionalised in a number of competing churches. Karpp's alternative description of this material as 'the many-branched church' (see below, note 731) involves two implications. First, it assumes that the multiplicity of churches is ultimately only one church, although there is no simple way of demonstrating the existence of this church in institutional terms. Second, to describe the division of Christianity into mutually exclusive churches as a 'many-branched' unity involves a prior harmonising interpretation. This may be the goal of church history in its ecumenical form, but nevertheless the data of church history on the whole show a different picture, and one which historical investigation cannot simply ignore.

makes the remarkable discovery that there is no such thing as a secular history of the Christian cultural sphere. There are attempts at a world history. On the other hand there are national histories, and in between there are accounts of the history of Europe (for example). But the cultural area of Christianity – if this term may be used here without geographical or demographic restriction for the dynamic process of the history of Christianity – begins in the fourth century, when Christianity ceased to be one factor among others in the hellenistic world and became the formative influence on the Constantinian empire, and its history continues even after the loss of its original territories to Islam with the transfer of its centre of gravity to Europe. Its frontiers reach far beyond Europe, especially since the Christianisation of the two Americas. It is even questionable whether it makes sense to talk about frontiers at all, in view of the existence of Christian churches in all parts of the world and in every nation. On the other hand, there can be no doubt that the history of Europe and America is particularly closely bound up with the history of Christianity, and it is questionable whether the history of Europe can ever escape from this all-enfolding mould without doing violence to itself. It was Christianity which passed on to Europe the legacy of the ancient world and so made European history up to the fifteenth and even the eighteenth centuries a series of renaissances of antiquity. It was again Christianity which made Europe the 'expansive west' (A. Weber) which pushed out beyond its own frontiers to bring the whole of mankind into the area of the European spirit and European civilisation. This expansion was of course connected with the European nations' desire for power, with their greed for the wealth of the rest of the world, and later with the search for markets for European industry. Nevertheless the initial spark, and a constant series of new impulses, came from the Christian missionary spirit, however perverted by association with the aims of colonial exploitation. The history of Christianity is the framework from which the history of Europe can be separated only by force. These remarks show the extent to which history in general is the history of religion, right down to all the processes of secularisation and emancipation, because the concern of religion involves no less than the whole of reality and human destiny.

Church history is therefore not a branch of history, naturally subordinate to general history. On the contrary, it unites in itself what in secular history is divided into specialised areas, ancient history, medieval and modern history, the history of the Mediterranean world, of Europe and America, and in addition all the tendencies and elements of world history which lead beyond a Europe-centred outlook, all of which originated in Christianity.

When one considers this feature of church history as compared with the various branches of secular history it is clear that, apart from the attempts at universal history, no branch of history is under such pressure from its particular subject-matter to consider the whole of history as church history.[729] This feature is inherent in Christianity on the one hand because of the range and dynamism of its history, which cannot be properly assessed except in relation to the whole history of mankind in the world, and on the other because of the universality of the search for salvation. In the form of what Habermas has called the 'anticipation of achieved living' at any period, this determines the course of history,[730] but to a particular degree in Christianity, because here the nature of history as the scene of man's realisation and God's revelation has been made explicit.

The question of the relationship of church history to universal history includes the question of the theological character of church history. Should church history be regarded and treated as a theological discipline at all? The question has often been found difficult, and particularly in recent times. It certainly seems clear that church history differs from branches of secular history not in its methods but (if at all) in its subject-matter.[731] It is even important for church history to be able to claim that the methods

[729] A similar view has been expressed by G. Kretschmar in an unpublished paper, 'Kirchengeschichte als Wissenschaft', written as part of the study group of the evangelical theology faculty of Munich in the summer of 1972 (pp. 3f of the MS).

[730] Kretschmar, p. 4.

[731] Karpp has rightly insisted that church history differs from profane history not in any special method but simply in its object, in that church history, as the history of the preaching of the Gospel, is concerned with 'the many-branched church in its dialectical relationship to the kingdom of God' ('Kirchengeschichte als theologische Disziplin', pp. 149ff, esp. pp. 154, 155).

it uses in its field are no different from those generally held to be valid in historical research. While this may be true, it still does not exclude the possibility that the particular theme of church history may be the source of a correction of the general approach to historical method which claims general validity. Church history faces in a way no other branch of history does the question of the relevance of the religious concern to the understanding of history because it deals with the history of a religion the essence of which is belief in a God who acts in history. And Christianity is concerned not just with the history of God's dealings with a particular people but with the whole of mankind. In this situation if the history of this religion is told with no reference to the question of the action of its God in its history, that history is itself a denial of the belief in the God who acts in history.[732] In this context one ought to be able to expect that this question should be regarded as open rather than as settled in advance. It is settled in advance, however, when church history is guided by an approach derived from secular history and based on the exclusion of the religious element, in which religious events are treated as an expression of human ideas and study of them concentrates on looking for the other aspects of human life from which they must derive. Church history approached in this way will inevitably become an argument for atheism. Its overall picture will show that the events of history, as they are generally accessible to men, show no trace of divine activity. The work of the church historian will therefore result in an impression of the impotence and consequently of the unreality of the Christian God. From this point of view also, the biblical assertions of divine action in history must inevitably appear as assertions based on no more than subjective faith, with no claim to general validity. The way is then of course open for a similar interpretation of church history. The denial in advance of its general relevance deprives it of any claim to any other status than that of arbitrarily chosen personal values. It is only against this

[732] W. Nigg spoke in similar terms of a gradual draining of content from the concept of the church as a result of the work of church historians: 'It is as though the church ceased to exist with the work of the last church historian' (*Die Kirchengeschichtsschreibung. Grundzüge ihrer historischen Entwicklung*, Munich 1934, p. 247).

background that the question whether church history is a theological discipline can be seen in its full starkness.

It is therefore clear, above all in church history, that an approach to history based on the exclusion of the possibility of God and his action constitutes a prejudice against the reality of the biblical God. It is thoroughly understandable that such a view of history should have arisen out of the Enlightenment's confrontation with the conflicting claims of the Christian denominations to possess the truth. It must have seemed that only by ignoring the contradictions of the mutually exclusive doctrinal systems was there any hope of looking at historical reality without prejudice, purely 'pragmatically', in the vocabulary of the period. Inevitably, however, the Enlightenment attack on authority led to the exclusion of the theological element because in the past the overwhelming tendency, in spite of some counter-currents, had been to identify God's action in Christian history with the prosperity of the church, and the church was now split into hostile denominations with opposed and mutually exclusive positions. Just as after the period of the wars of religion which filled the seventeenth and eighteenth centuries, people were tired of denominational bickering and worked to set the state, law and the sciences on a basis which was independent of denominational disputes, the understanding of history also had to be freed from the spirit of partisanship.

This sealed the fate of the old *historia sacra*. Today not even those who want to see more attention paid to the theological character of church history want to return to this dogmatic view of history. H. Jedin, for example, who, following A. Erhard, would like to see church history regarded as historical theology,[733] and regards salvation history as the only adequate concept of it,[734] nevertheless also opposes the merging of the subject of church history into a treatment of salvation history by

---

[733] H. Jedin, 'Kirchengeschichte ist Theologie und Geschichte', in R. Kottje (ed.), *Kirchengeschichte heute*, Trier 1970, pp. 33–74, esp. p. 43. See also A. Ehrhard, 'Die historische Theologie und ihre Methoden', in W. Schellberg (ed.), *Festschrift Sebastian Merkle*, Düsseldorf 1922, pp. 117–36.

[734] H. Jedin, 'Kirchengeschichte als Heilsgeschichte?', in Id., *Kirche des Glaubens – Kirche der Geschichte. Ausgewählte Aufsätze und Vorträge*, I, 1966, pp. 37–48.

a theology of history on the ground that 'church history is a science and follows strict historical principles'.[735] This twofold concern with methodological rigour on the one hand and the theological character of church history on the other is generally resolved by a distinction of different levels of treatment. P. Meinhold has distinguished the perspective of church history from profane or secular history on the one hand and from the history of salvation with its theological interpretations on the other. Meinhold's picture of the three levels as concentric circles with the history of salvation as the innermost[736] seems to H. Lutz, however, too much like a 'rigid hierarchical progression', and Lutz advocates instead 'a free, mutually complementary relation between the three perspectives'.[737] All such distinctions and arrangements of perspectives or levels of treatment are inevitably unsatisfactory, however, because they do not produce a generally applicable systematic, but make purely external and subjective links between disparate elements. General validity, as ever, attaches only to the historical method, which the church historian uses in the same way as any other historian, but which, as a result of its association with an insistence on eliminating theology from church history, has aroused this uneasiness in those who would like to do church history as part of theology.

The next stage is a call for an additional dogmatic interpretation of church history,[738] in spite of the fact that any

[735] 'Kirchengeschichte ist Theologie und Geschichte', p. 44.

[736] P. Meinhold, 'Weltgeschichte – Kirchengeschichte – Heilsgeschichte', *Saeculum* 9 (1958), p. 288.

[737] H. Lutz, 'Profangeschichte – Kirchengeschichte – Heilsgeschichte', in R. Kottje, *Kirchengeschichte heute,* pp. 75–94, esp. p. 94.

[738] E. Iserloh, for example, calls for 'church history to be practised as theology', not just with regard to its material object, but in the sense that the church historian should look at 'the progress of the church through history with the eyes of faith', with a *credo ecclesiam* (E. Iserloh, 'Was ist Kirchengeschichte?', in *Kirchengeschichte heute,* pp. 10–32, at p. 29). This statement fails to distinguish church history from a deliberately partisan account. Apart from this, it is in itself questionable whether the theological character of research and description in church history can or should take the form of a partisan *credo ecclesiam*. The reason for this is that the church and the kingdom of God do not coincide, and the church must therefore, in its history as in other respects, be seen in 'its dialectical relationship to the kingdom of God' (H. Karpp, note 728, p. 155).

such intrusion of dogmatic interpretation into the historian's analysis can only limit the rigour of his historical method. The theological character of church history is compatible with the historical rigour in its practice only on condition that it is not introduced as a dogmatic perspective. Such perspective would also inevitably arouse suspicion if it were regarded as a subjective attitude of the church historian distinct from the principles of his methodology. Conversely, we find that such a dogmatic attitude is not at all essential to historical theology – indeed for a theology of history it would be just as much a limitation and distortion. Today a theology of history can no longer start from a dogmatic assertion of the reality of God in one sense or another and go on to interpret the course of history on that basis. Compared with such interpretations, the secularity of the prevailing understanding of historical method is fully justified. Religious ideas can be recovered for history only when they are studied as a disputed theme in history itself. It is in such an approach that the modern theology of history holds out prospects of success, prospects which would be cut short in advance by a rigidly dogmatic outlook. Although the reality of the God asserted in the Christian tradition is disputed, church history might be expected, without sacrificing its methodological rigour, to examine and describe the history of Christianity[739] in a way that would involve, for each period, an investigation of the relation between its experience of reality and the Christian view of reality handed down to it by tradition. It would then have to consider the related problem of how far in this historic experiential situation the God of the Christian tradition had manifested himself to the participants as the all-determining reality, as indicated by the actual changes undergone by the attitudes and way of life of Christians. Self-manifestations of this God which met these criteria could then be described, in the language of tradition, as 'the action of God', and the associated changes in Christian life and attitudes could be critically compared with the current traditional self-understanding of Christianity.[740] However, the concept of 'the action of God' to

[739] See above n. 728.

[740] In this respect church history presents exactly the same problems for theological study as the history of Israel, though P. Stockmeier

refer to the experience of the self-manifestation of the God of tradition as the all-determining reality could be introduced only on the admission that the divinity of this God, and equally all talk of his 'action' in the past, has always been disputed in the course of history and has still constantly to prove itself as the all-determining reality against new forms of the experience of the world and of man.[741] This sort of theology of church history could perfectly well operate with descriptive and undogmatic methods. This position would justify it in offering a generally applicable corrective to the historical view of reality which underlies the present state of historical attitudes to method. The corrective would consist in reintroducing into the concept of history the religious element which was excluded for understandable reasons in the eighteenth century.

The possibility of treating church history as a theological discipline which has been discussed here connects at various points with Ebeling's definition of church history as the history of the interpretation of scripture.[742] Ebeling's position is by far the most impressive modern attempt to describe church history as

---

('Kirchengeschichte und Geschichtlichkeit der Kirche', *Zeitschrift für Kirchengeschichte* 81 (1970), pp. 145–62) thinks there is a difference. According to Stockmeier: 'While an interpretation of the Old Testament in terms of salvation history seems possible from the position of the New Testament, "salvation history" gives the church historian no criteria for validly assessing facts and events' (p. 160). In fact, the only difference seems to be that for the interpretation of the Old Testament Stockmeier allows a dogmatic perspective based on the 'position' (which one?) of the New Testament, but for church history he does not. A rigid dogmatic perspective would be just as suspect in either case, but this does not mean that the historian must ignore the fact that the material of his history is itself theological in character and has a bearing on the question of salvation, as Stockmeier inevitably shows in his own discussion. In such a situation even historical investigation, when dealing with material of this type, must critically examine those features of it which go with such a consciousness.

[741] I myself in my previous work did not see sufficiently clearly the theological significance of the continuing dispute surrounding the reality of God in history (see W. Pannenberg, *Basic Questions in Theology*, Vol. I, pp. 66ff, 90f, but cf. Vol. II, pp. 85ff). In particular I failed to see that taking this fact into account makes it possible to substantiate a claim for general rational validity on behalf of a theology of history.

[742] G. Ebeling, *Kirchengeschichte als Geschichte der Auslegung der heiligen Schrift*, 1947.

a theological discipline. The remarks made above coincide with Ebeling's views on the one hand in recognising that Christians' self-understanding has always been formed and renewed in the context of the interpretation of scripture, and on the other in seeing the interpretation of scripture as the paradigm case of the confrontation of the current state of experience of reality with the Christian tradition. The only difficulty in this approach is that it requires the interpretation of scripture to be defined very broadly, in fact as equivalent to the process of tradition itself. If the term is used in its narrower sense, there is no escape from G. Kretschmar's objection that 'the hermeneutical conception of the science of history now receives a final intensification, but at the same time the *church* as the subject of history completely disappears, and ultimately also history itself. In practice it cannot be seen . . . as more than what comes in between revelation and the present and must always be overcome in the act of faithful listening'.[743] In other words, the interpretation of scripture should be regarded as only one typical structural element in the process of the Christian tradition. There is one other aspect of Ebeling's view which requires correction, or perhaps expansion. His definition of church history as the history of the interpretation of scripture in fact – contrary to its intention – provides no answer to the question of the character of church history as a theological discipline. It is after all possible for scriptural interpretation to be studied without reference to the self-manifestation of the all-determining reality in the experience of the interpreter, simply as a succession of different interpretations. Does this mean that the question whether divine reality is involved must be left once more to the irrationality of a 'decision of faith'? What it does show, is that the study and description of church history as the interpretation of scripture is not by itself a *theology* of church history. Whether or not it leads to one can be decided only by the way it describes the process of tradition and reception which is characterised by the authority and constantly repeated interpretation of scripture. Church history as a theological discipline in the specific sense of the word exists only when the reception of tradition, which takes place through the medium of

<hr>

[743] See above, note 729, pp. 5f of the unpublished MS.

scriptural interpretation, but not only in its explicit practice, is regarded as a coming to terms with the changing experience of the all-determining reality about which the biblical writings talk in their own way. Paying attention to the transformations which take place in the experience of the all-determining reality in the context of all the experience of a particular period and in relation to the traditional ways of talking about God enable us to talk about the action of God in history even in a purely descriptive and hypothetical sense. The fundamental issue here is simply the application of the general principles of a theology of religion and its history to the history of Christianity.

In this approach the tensions in Christian history between Christianity and the church must constantly be borne in mind.[744] In one sense this is a problem of modern Christianity resulting from the divisions between the denominational churches, though even before the Reformation church and Christianity were never simply identical. Only in the church does Christianity acquire an institutional expression of its existence. In particular, without the Church no Christian tradition and no sense of Christian identity through the process of this tradition is possible. And above all, every individual Christian lives his Christian life in the church in which he received baptism and in whose liturgical life he participates in one way or another. 'Church' means the totality of believers, but it also refers to one of the many institutions in Christians' environment. This is why tensions can arise between Christianity and the church. Changes in the experience of reality are often the cause of such tensions. Because of this situation a theology of church history cannot restrict itself to a biography of the church as a particular institution in the life of Christianity, but must extend its treatment to include every aspect of that life.

For this purpose a fundamental concept is that of the people of God, which the church adopted as a description of itself from an early period as part of its continuation and extension of the ancient Israelite belief in election. The church is in another sense only one of the institutions in the life of the Christian people of God, but precisely for that reason the all-embracing term 'people

---

[744] In recent years the need for this distinction has been argued particularly by T. Rendtorff (*Christentum ausserhalb der Kirche. Konkretionen der Aufklärung*, Hamburg 1966).

of God' is particularly suited to a descriptive and critical theology of the church. There is also inherent in it right 'from the origin of the church an involvement with the data of history',[745] an element of the uniqueness of the matter of church history which itself calls for the theology of history to examine critically the extent to which the claim contained in this consciousness is substantiated. The theological meaning of this claim and its testing is made fully clear by the connection of the idea of the people of God with belief in election, which can be traced through the history of Christianity from the collapse of its imperial vision to the development of modern nationalism. An investigation of this sort shows Christianity and the church to be inherently historically structured phenomena, whose nature can therefore be grasped only by a theology of history. What makes the historical character a reality in the mind of the church and Christianity themselves is the constant reference back to the 'fundamental and unique happening', the Christ-event.[746] The Christ-event is also the touchstone for all particular historical realisations of the church; by keeping in memory the past history of Jesus Christianity and the church are made to look beyond these to their future fulfilment, which has not yet appeared but which nevertheless enables them to confront their present.

It seems that a church history which examines its subject in its theological essence and also operates as a reflection of the historicality of Christianity and the church is itself a systematic account of Christianity. If Christianity and the church are related to history of their very nature, this nature can be understood only as it exists in their actual history, a history which derives its impetus from the search for substantiation of their self-understanding and sense of God and for that reason makes possible a critical discussion of their truth claims in relation to the actual course of that history.

---

[745] P. Stockmeier, 'Kirchengeschichte und Geschichtlichkeit der Kirche', p. 156. Stockmeier does not explicitly emphasise the connection with the idea of election.

[746] Stockmeier, p. 157, who, however, does not mention that the Christian faith's historic reference *back* to the Christ-event is also a constant stimulus to its reference *forward* to the future.

6. Systematic Theology

1

The concept of systematic theology came into theology in the seventeenth century after the introduction of the concept of system into theology (see above, n. 656) to describe the theology known as 'scholastic', 'academic' or 'acroamatic'. J. F. Buddeus, writing in 1727, regarded the term as already common.[747] Buddeus also said that the identification of systematic theology with thetic or dogmatic theology was common, though he himself argued for an extension of the term dogmatics to cover not only systematic theology but the contrasted field of exoteric or catechetical theology.[748] Buddeus was also in favour of including ethics or moral theology in systematic theology.[749]

The first use of the term *theologia dogmatica* in a book title by L. F. Reinhart in 1659 is well known, but the term had already been used by G. Calixt in 1634 and a year later by H. Alting.[750] In

[747] J. F. Buddeus, *Isagoge historico-theologica ad theologiam singulasque eius partes,* Leipzig 1727, pp. 303–4: 'Acroamatica theologia, uti diximus, systematicae etiam nomine venit, idque licet generatim de omnibus compendiis, adcuratiori methodo conscriptis, adhiberi queat; subinde tamen speciatim de istis rerum theologicarum commentariis, in quibus cuncta fusius, et magno adparatu, edisseruntur, et non tantum doctrinae sacrae veritas adstruitur ... sed et dissentientium errores refutantur, usurpatur. Duo autem cum primis requiruntur, ut tractatio quaedem systematicae theologiae nomen promereatur, primo ut omnia cognitu ad salutem necessaria plene, deinde et iusto ordine et apta quaedem connexione, exhibeat; neque exhibeat modo, sed et explicet, probet, atque confirmet.'

[748] Ibid., p. 304: 'Acroamatica haecce atque systematica theologia etiam thetica vocari solet; nec tamen quidquam obstat, quo minus hocce, uti et dogmaticae theologiae nomine, tum catecheticam, tum systematicam, complectamur.' According to K. G. Bretschneider (*Systematischer Entwicklung aller in der Dogmatik vorkommenden Begriffe* (1804), 3rd ed. 1825, p. 72), the identification of acroamatic theology with dogmatics goes back to the turn of the eighteenth century. Among predecessors and contemporaries of Buddeus Bretschneider mentions Hildebrand (1692), Niemeyer (1702) and Pfaff.

[749] J. F. Buddeus, *Institutio theologiae moralis,* Leipzig 1711, p. 16 (§ 21). Buddeus draws on J. M. Lange, J. F. Mayer and on the moral theology of J. G. Dorscheus (1685).

[750] O. Ritschl, 'Das Wort *dogmaticus* in der Geschichte des Sprachgebrauchs

Alting's use the meaning of the term was fixed by the contrast with *theologia historica,* though the contrast related not to content but merely to the form of presentation.[751] In this Alting departed from the previous view of the distinction. In 1550 Melanchthon had described the dogmatic or didactic as a part of the content of the Bible and other ecclesial literature,[752] and J. Gerhard, in the first volume of his *Loci theologici* (1610), had also made a similar division of the content of scripture into *historica* and *dogmatica.*[753] The view of the distinction between historical and dogmatic as relating to the mode of presentation rather than to content may derive from the Roman Catholic terminology of the sixteenth century.[754] What is the point of the distinction? According to Gerhard Ebeling, the dogmatic approach in Alting's sense would have meant 'the responsible reflection on the dogmatic, assertive, linguistic event which furthers and makes possible the cause of theology'.[755] For Alting, however, scriptural exegesis, and therefore historical theology in his sense, must also have had a definite 'assertive' character. A more probable interpretation of the distinction is that dogmatics provided a unified discussion and summary of the content of scripture, a similar idea to the one contained in the later view of dogmatics as systematic theology. G. J. Planck wrote in 1794: 'Systematic theology is the essence of the very same truths of religion which are contained in the Bible, but with their premises and implications made explicit and placed in the context appropriate to their mutual relations, or – in other words – set out in an arrangement in which one either supports

---

bis zum Aufkommen des Ausdrucks *theologia dogmatica*', in *Festgabe für Julius Kaftan,* 1920, pp. 260–72, esp. p. 263.

[751] H. Alting, *Theologia historica sive systematis historici loci quatuor,* Amsterdam 1664, p. 4: 'Opposita utique sunt dogmatica et historica; at non subjecto, sed modo; non re considerata, sed forma considerandi' (quoted O. Ritschl, *Dogmengeschichte des Protestantismus,* I, 1908, p. 31, n. 1.).

[752] *Corpus Reformatorum* (=CR) 14, 94: 'Pars aliqua in scriptis ecclesiae est *dogmatike* seu doctrina'; 14, 147–8: 'In sacris literis alia dicta sunt legalia, alia evangelica, alia dogmatica, alia consolatoria, alia simpliciter narrationes de eventibus seu bonis seu malis' (quoted Ritschl, 'Das Wort *dogmaticus*', p. 267).

[753] J. Gerhard, *Loci theologici,* ed. Cotta, I. p. 110; II, p. 49a.

[754] See the works by F. Turrianus mentioned by Ritschl, 'Das Wort *dogmaticus*', p. 266.

[755] G. Ebeling, *Theology and Proclamation,* London 1966, p. 112f.

and explains another or limits and more precisely defines another.'[756]

Planck went on to explain that the 'systematic treatment of the biblical material gives rise to the system of dogmatics on the one hand and that of Christian moral teaching on the other'. He regarded the division of systematic theology into these two branches, however, as 'merely arbitrary'.[757] In fact, however, the development of this classification was the result not of a division of an earlier unity but of the discussion about whether ethics, which in the sixteenth century was treated separately from *sacra doctrina,* should be regarded as a theological or merely a philosophical discipline.[758] J. Wallmann is almost certainly right to regard this as the real point of the innovation Georg Calixt introduced with his *Epitome theologiae moralis* of 1634. 'The novelty of Calixt's work is not that he set up *"agenda"* as a separate ethical field alongside *"credenda"* and made it the object of an independent presentation – Melanchthon had already done that by producing an *Epitome philosophiae moralis* and *Elementa doctrinae ethicae* alongside his *Loci.* No, the novelty of Calixt is that he raised the field of ethics to the status of a theological theme, and by labelling it *"theologia moralis"* brought it into the concept of theology.'[759] Wallmann suggests that Calixt's reason for this was not so much a specific interest in ethics as his association of the concept of theology with the practical tasks of

[756] G. J. Planck, *Einleitung in die theologischen Wissenschaften,* vol. I, Leipzig 1794, p. 113. Planck also remarks explicitly that systematic theology does not deal with, 'and cannot deal with, any other material than that of the Bible' (p. 114). At the same time, anyone who 'does not also have a systematic knowlege' of the truth of religion 'does not yet fully know it' (p. 116), because 'only a systematic treatment' gives all our knowledge 'its highest possible degree of clarity, precision and distinctness' (p. 115).

[757] G. J. Planck, *Grundriss der theologischen Encyklopädie,* 1813, p. 222 (§ 172). For a different view, see Ebeling's suggestion that the distinction between the 'dogmatic' and the 'ethical' may go back ultimately to the Aristotelian distinction between dianoetic and ethical virtues (*Theology and Proclamation,* p. 112, referring to Aristotle, *Nic. Eth.,* 1103 a 5).

[758] See, for example, B. Keckermann's classification of theology as a whole as a 'practical science' alongside ethics (P. Althaus, *Die Prinzipien der deutschen reformierten Dogmatik im Zeitalter der aristotelischen Scholastik,* 1914, p. 27).

[759] J. Wallmann, *Der Theologiebegriff bei Johann Gerhard und Georg Calixt,* 1961, p. 153.

the church's ministry. Certainly there is no reason on the evidence for crediting Calixt with a desire to make ethics independent of dogmatics. The view of ethics as the general theme of the Christian world, in comparison with which dogmatics was concerned only with the particular forms of faith in history, belongs to a later period. Moreover, to the extent that this tendency became dominant at the Enlightenment it involved an ethical interpretation of theology as a whole on the basis of a general *philosophical* ethics more than a specifically *theological* moral doctrine.

This can be demonstrated in the theological influence of John Locke's philosophy or Kant's basing of religion on ethics, and also from Schleiermacher's attempt to provide a philosophical foundation for theology. As is well known, Schleiermacher claimed that theology was based on ethics as 'the science of the principles of history'.[760] Only ethics, the science of the action of reason on nature,[761] could show the concept of the religious or believing community (§ 33) to be 'a necessary element for the development of the human spirit' (§ 22) and a prerequisite for a definition of the unique features of the Christian religion. Schleiermacher, however, assigned this function of providing a general basis for theology to philosophical ethics, not to the specifically theological variety, Christian moral doctrine. He treated this latter as belonging rather to dogmatic theology, the task of which he described as 'the systematic presentation of the concept of doctrine at present prevailing in the church' (§ 3 of the 1st ed.). Schleiermacher even said explicitly of the division into religious and moral teaching that 'this separation cannot be regarded as essential' (§ 223), and that it was therefore 'desirable' for 'the undivided treatment to reappear from time to time' (§ 231). The subject-matter of Christian ethics, he argued, was 'the understanding of morality given with the Christian faith', the principles of which at least are found in the teaching of doctrine.[762] This enabled even Karl Barth, in his attack on what

[760] F. D. Schleiermacher, *Kurze Darstellung des theologischen Studiums,* 2nd ed., 1830, § 29 (cf. p. 9, § 37 of the 1st ed.). The page references in the text are to this work.

[761] Schleiermacher, *Grundriss der philosophischen Ethik,* ed. A. Twesten, Berlin 1841, § 75 (p. 22), § 95 (p. 28).

[762] H. J. Birkner, *Schleiermachers christliche Sittenlehre im Zusammenhang seines*

had become an established division between dogmatics and ethics, to say that Schleiermacher must be 'credited' with having had, 'from his own particular standpoint . . . a nice understanding of the inner nexus and ultimate unity of dogmatics and ethics'.[763]

The tendency which grew up in the eighteenth and nineteenth centuries to base theology on a *philosophical* ethics had nothing to do with the distinction between *theological* ethics and dogmatics within systematic theology. It is not true to say, as Rothe did, that 'an independent ethics has always shown at once a tendency to reverse the roles, replacing dogmatics as the basic theological discipline'.[764] This tendency was much more characteristic of the philosophical ethics which was the expression of a general awareness of truth independent of denominational presuppositions. Consequently Calixt, with his directly contrary aim of including ethics in theology, cannot be held responsible for this tendency. Rothe already misunderstood Calixt when he treated him as a predecessor of his own attempts to base theology as a whole on an ethics derived from speculative *theology*,[765] though he was quite clear that his own work was not a continuation of Schleiermacher's efforts to base theology on a *philosophical* ethics.[766] It was left to Barth to obliterate this distinction and interpret Calixt as seen by Rothe as the starting-point of a historical development which led directly via Schleiermacher to Rothe, who, according to Barth, 'was merely taking Schleiermacher's presuppositions seriously'.[767]

The attempt to base theology in general, and systematic theology in particular, on a philosophical ethics, which was begun by Schleiermacher, was revived in a different form, in Kantian terms, in the school of Ritschl and its main representative today is Gerhard Ebeling. From having seemed solidly

philosophisch-theologischen Systems, 1964, pp. 73ff. On Schleiermacher's definition of the relationship between dogmatics and ethics, see the discussion in Birkner, pp. 66ff and Schleiermacher's own remarks in the introduction to *Die christliche Sitte,* ed. L. Jonas, 2nd ed. Berlin 1884 (= *Werke,* vol. 12, pp. 12–13).

[763] Karl Barth, *Church Dogmatics* I/2, p. 785.
[764] Barth, pp. 782–3.
[765] R. Rothe, *Theologische Ethik,* vol. I, 2nd ed. 1867, p. 68.
[766] Ibid., pp. 63ff.
[767] *Church Dogmatics,* I/2, p. 786.

established, however, it has now become extremely insecure. [768] Whereas the Enlightenment regarded the self-evident principles of ethics as belonging to the sphere of human nature, as compared with the historically determined 'positive' forms of religious belief, in the interval the history-conditioned nature of enlightened reason itself, and also of its theory of the self-evidence of ethics, has become clear. Particularly important in weakening the conviction that moral norms were prior to any arbitrary human desires was Nietzsche's attack on moral theory, which derived all moral norms from a human will which set up its own values. [769] The impact on the moral sense of the sociological critique of ideology and of psychoanalysis is thus the same. The result is that today the theology of Christianity can no longer treat ethics as an independently secure foundation, but instead ethics itself must build on the religious meanings given to human existence and their historical form in Christianity provided that these are not identical with their outmoded denominational expressions but can undergo a renewal in order to meet the modern sense of truth.

This situation has the consequence that theological ethics can treat its dependence on the historic tradition of the Christian religion, and therefore too on the dogmatic reconstruction of the complex of meaning of the Christian tradition, as an advantage. It does this when it exposes all abstractly general approaches to the basis of ethics − whether transcendental, phenomenological or anthropological − as abstractions. Having done this it can show that ethical awareness is historically conditioned, and

[768] On this see my discussion with Gerhard Ebeling: Ebeling, *Die Evidenz des Ethischen und die Theologie* (1960, reprinted in Ebeling, *Wort und Glaube,* vol. II, 1969, pp. 1–41); W. Pannenberg, 'Die Krise des Ethischen und die Theologie' *Theol. Literaturzeitung* 87 (1962), pp. 7–16. Ebeling published a reply under the same title in *Wort und Glaube,* vol. II, pp. 42–55, and there followed a correspondence, since published: *ZThK,* 1973, pp. 448–730.
[769] On the connection between atheism and the attack on morality in Nietzsche, see G. Rohrmoser, *Nietzsche und das Ende der Emanzipation,* 1971. Rohrmoser describes the attack on morality as a consequence of the atheism (see esp p. 55), but it seems better to regard the attack on morality as Nietzsche's chosen instrument for undermining the idea of God. Nietzsche's psychological analysis of morality would, on this view, be a development of Feuerbach's psychological attack on religion, comparable in many respects with Marx's development of it in his theory of economic alienation.

depends on the underlying religious or quasi-religious assumptions about meaning.[770]

2

In the eighteenth century the term 'systematic theology' included only dogmatics and moral theology. Even Schleiermacher knew of no third discipline which had ever been included in systematic theology.[771] K. Rosenkranz also subdivided systematic theology (which he called 'speculative' theology) into only dogmatics and ethics, although he did attach polemics and apologetics, which Schleiermacher had assigned to his proposed discipline of 'philosophical theology', to speculative theology, if only as 'elements of the whole' which were not capable of being 'complete sciences in themselves'.[772] Later, K. R. Hagenbach, claiming the support of Nösselt and Tholuck, also assigned apologetics and polemics to systematic theology, this time as subsidiary branches of dogmatics.[773] For Heinrici, apologetics and philosophy of religion together comprised 'philosophical theology', but as a part of systematic, and in

[770] Rothe took the opposite approach, and found it necessary to preface dogmatics, which he regarded as a branch of historical theology, with a speculative and purely systematic treatment in the shape of his 'theological ethics'. Because he was unable to reconcile the historical and speculative (or systematic) elements, he regarded 'speculative dogmatics' as an empty phrase (*Theol. Ethik*, I, 2nd ed. 1867, p. 62). Nevertheless the fact that his own theological ethics shows the influence of historical factors on every page indicates the inadequacy of this solution.

[771] Schleiermacher, *Die christliche Sitte* (*Schleiermachers sämtliche Werke*, Section 1, vol. 12), p. 3: 'But if we ask whether a third [area] has ever been included in systematic theology, the answer is negative.' Schleiermacher also deliberately avoided the term 'systematic theology' (*Die chr. Sitte*, p. 4 note), using instead the term dogmatics as a comprehensive lable for dogmatic and moral theology, on the ground that the name 'systematic theology' encouraged a neglect of the fact that Christian doctrine was historicly conditioned, although even as historicly conditioned it still had to be systematic (Schleiermacher, p. 7).

[772] K. Rosenkranz, *Encyklopädie der theologischen Wissenschaften*, Halle 1831, p. 365.

[773] K. R. Hagenbach, *Encyklopädie und Methodologie der theologischen Wissenschaften*, 11th ed. 1884, pp. 362–3, esp. p. 363 n. 4.

particular dogmatic, theology, while dogmatic 'polemics' was no longer treated as an independent discipline.[774] Later again, A. Dorner included dogmatics and polemics in historical theology, apologetics and ethics in systematic theology.[775]

With no other theological discipline as much as with polemics does the very description of the discipline give such a vivid indication of its roots in particular periods and events in the history of the church, and also significant are the changes of name the discipline has had in the course of history. According to Hagenbach, polemics in the strict sense of a particular theological discipline 'begins with the separation of the churches at the Reformation'.[776] As early as 1623 J. H. Alsted mentioned a particular theological discipline by the name of *theologia controversa*,[777] corresponding to the prolific writings about the *controversiae* between the denominational parties since the end of the sixteenth century. In 1652 Calov described the same discipline as polemics.[778] The raising of polemics to the status of an independent theological discipline, with the function of expounding the doctrinal issues which divided the denominational parties from the point of view of one's own theory and in opposition to the other side's, reflects the peak period of denominational disputes. This golden age of polemics began to pass away with the beginning of the eighteenth century. By 1893 Heinrici could announce: 'This discipline has been dead for over a hundred years,' and accordingly he denied it the value of an independent discipline (which Hagenbach still supported) and included polemical argument among the general functions of systematic theology.[779] On the whole Heinrici's view was proved right, although 'in the reawakening of denominational fervour in the nineteenth century' polemics was revived by K. von Hase (1862) and T. Tschackert (1885). From the eighteenth century

---

[774] G. Heinrici, *Theologische Encyklopädie*, 1873, pp. 232ff, see also p. 229.

[775] A. Dorner, *Grundriss der Encyklopädie der Theologie*, 1901, pp. 87ff, 107ff.

[776] Hagenbach, p. 373.

[777] J. H. Alsted, *Methodus ss theologiae*, Hanover 1623. The discipline called by this name 'tractat de controversiis religionis. Verum haec est pars theologiae Scholasticae.'

[778] A. Calov, *Isagoges ad ss Theologiam libri duo de natura Theologiae et methodo studii theologici*, Wittenberg 1652, vol. I, p. 330, vol. II, pp. 252ff.

[779] Heinrici, pp. 229, 180 n. 3.

onwards the old polemics was more and more replaced by a comparative symbolics and the study of denominations. The name *theologia symbolica* appears as early as 1688 as a description of the exposition of one's own confessional documents,[780] which were also known as symbolic books. In this early form symbolics was auxiliary to polemics, 'its historical documentation',[781] and in S. Mursinna's work of 1754 symbolics and polemics stood side by side.[782] As the disputes between the denominations became a matter of history [*Historie*], polemics began to be replaced from the middle of the eighteenth century by comparative accounts of the 'symbolic' doctrinal foundations or doctrinal concepts of the different Christian denominations. G. J. Planck, in his *Abriss einer historischen und vergleichenden Darstellung der dogmatischen Systeme der christlichen Hauptparteien* of 1796, still concentrated almost exclusively on doctrinal differences, but P. Marheinecke, in his *Christliche Symbolik* of 1810, brought spirituality, worship and church order into his account. Marheinecke's book had made the decisive step towards an extension of symbolics into a study of denominations which compared the whole life of the churches, and the process was completed in 1892 by F. Kattenbusch with his *Lehrbuch der vergleichenden Konfessionskunde*.[783] There was, however, one basic point on which comparative symbolics and denominational studies were agreed, and this was the conviction that Christianity had found its final form in separated churches. As late as 1927 H. Mulert could express, as a totally sincere opinion, the view 'that the organisation of Christianity always remains something earthly, and that external unity is not required to make the ideas and energies of Christianity effective'.[784] Since then the ecumenical movement has brought about a change of consciousness. Today we no longer regard denominational divisions as insuperable, or external unity as a dispensable part of

[780] B. von Sanden, *Theologia symbolica lutherana*, 1688, quoted from Heinrici, p. 182.

[781] Hagenbach, p. 337.

[782] According to A. F. L. Pelt, *Theologische Encyklopädie als System, im Zusammenhang mit der Geschichte der theologischen Wissenschaft und ihrer einzelnen Zweige*, Hamburg 1843, p. 57.

[783] On this development see also H. Mulert, *Konfessionskunde*, Giessen 1927, pp. 1–21.

[784] p. 37.

the Christian faith. Correspondingly, the old denominational studies have been replaced by a new ecumenical theology which inherits the legacy of polemics and irenics, symbolics and denominational studies, in so far as they were 'earlier forms of denominational encounter and dispute',[785] but, unlike them, feels an obligation to the process of Christian unification which characterises the present period of church history through the ecumenical movement. This development has still left it undecided, however, whether ecumenical theology should continue to be included in systematic theology rather than treated as part of missiology, and so as a branch of practical theology. Relations between the churches are not a field which can be subordinated to the study of mission, but an additional one, though it is connected with mission to the extent that missionary territories turn into young churches, and relations with them turn into normal inter-church relations. However, inter-church relations also include relations with the other, 'old', but separated denominational churches, relations burdened by the inherited differences which were once dealt with in the discipline of 'polemics'. Only as the doctrinal disputes between the churches retreat into the background will ecumenical theology be able to move from the field of systematic theology into that of practical theology.

The transformation of polemics via symbolics and denominational studies into modern ecumenical theology affects the area where systematic and practical theology overlap. Consideration of the problems of apologetics leads at first sight into quite different areas.

The term 'apologetics' as a description of a theological discipline did not emerge before the end of the eighteenth century, according to Ebeling.[786] It was used in 1794 by G. J. Planck as the name of the first and fundamental branch of exegetical theology.[787] This use is characteristic of the Protestant view that the authority of scripture settled the question of the

[785] J. Brosseder, *Oekumenische Theologie – Geschichte und Probleme,* 1967, p. 11.
[786] G. Ebeling, '*Erwägung zu einer evangelischen Fundamentaltheologie*', ZThK 67 (1970), pp. 479–524. The quotation is from p. 489.
[787] G. J. Planck, *Einleitung in die theologischen Wissenschaften,* vol. I, Leipzig 1794, pp. 271–362.

whole truth of Christianity. Planck himself regarded this as the main concern of apologetics, as can be seen from his later remarks about the previous history of the discipline: he regarded it as the successor to the literature on the truth of the Christian religion, which he described as beginning with Marsilio Ficino (*De religione christiana,* 1474) and Juan Luis Vives (*De veritate religionis christianae,* 1543).[788] This literature too, especially in its later examples, was already largely concerned with the reliability of scripture, particularly as regards the biblical miracles. This connection with the literature on the truth of the Christian religion also explains how Schleiermacher could detach apologetics from its association with exegetical theology and include it in his proposed philosophical theology, which would have the task of determining, within the existing framework of philosophy of religion, not now the truth but the uniqueness of the Christian religion.[789] In Schleiermacher's view a decision about the truth of Christianity could be made not by theology, but only by personal Christian conviction, which Schleiermacher regarded as an essential prerequisite for theological investigation: 'We entirely renounce all attempt to prove the truth or necessity of Christianity; and we presuppose, on the contrary, that every Christian, before he enters at all on inquiries of this kind, has already the inward certainty that his religion cannot take any other form than this.'[790] Planck, in 1794, had expressed the opposite view in these words: 'It may be that only the few are capable of understanding and feeling that the assertion of the existence of a divine revelation requires the strongest possible proofs because it assumes the greatest of all miracles; one thing, however, everyone must feel, namely that the whole benefit that he expects from religion and knowledge of religion depends entirely on whether this assertion is justified or not. This should therefore be sufficient inducement to everyone to consider

---

[788] Planck, *Grundriss der theologischen Encyklopädie,* 1813, p. 56 (§ 53).

[789] F. D. Schleiermacher, *Kurze Darstellung des theologischen Studiums,* 2nd ed., § 39.

[790] F. D. Schleiermacher, *The Christian Faith,* trans. H. R. Mackintosh and J. S. Stewart, Edinburgh 1928, p. 60 (§ 11, 5: one of the 'propositions borrowed from apologetics'). See also H.-J. Birkner, *Schleiermachers christliche Sittenlehre,* 1964, pp. 59–60.

whether and how it may be proved. Even the layman should really not take this on the word of the theologian alone, but insist on hearing from him at least the main arguments on which the proof may be built. If the layman cannot examine them for himself, it will be even more necessary, a more sacred duty, for the theologian to acquaint himself with them, not just in general terms, but by his own careful examination.'[791]

In itself it is not to be regarded as a false development that apologetics in its subsequent stages did not remain under the influence of Schleiermacher's religious subjectivism, but as well as the unique *nature* of Christianity investigated the question of its *truth*. This development took place in spite of the appointment to the first Protestant chair of apologetics in Bonn in 1819 of Schleiermacher's pupil H. Sack, an appointment simultaneous with that of the Catholic S. Drey to a chair at Tübingen. It was the result of growing interest in two topics, on the one hand the confrontation with the outlook of modern science, particularly natural science, and on the other the study of religion as a possible framework within which to define the place of Christianity. Troeltsch too later struggled to combine these two tasks in an effort to provide a general foundation for theology, but his efforts were frustrated by two aspects of the contemporary treatment of apologetics, its rivalry with the study of the principles of dogma and the name apologetics itself. In the role of a mere 'specialised topic alongside the study of theological principles' apologetics came to acquire 'the fatal reputation of being a tendentious undertaking with either a reactionary or a progressive colour',[792] a process which eventually produced the 'anti-apologetic bias of early dialectical theology'.[793] On the other side it should be stressed that the dogmatic theory of principles performed, in its treatment of the subject of religion as a general frame of reference for a systematic account of the Christian faith, a task which required more thorough treatment on its own. This task is the one which has been discussed in this book under the name 'theology of religions', seen as a basic discipline of theology.

[791] G. J. Planck, *Einleitung in die theologischen Wissenschaften*, vol. I, p. 93.
[792] G. Ebeling, art. cit. (note 786), p. 495.
[793] Ibid., p. 497, n. 40.

This need was taken into account in Scandinavia by the setting up of chairs of the philosophy of religion and apologetics alongside those of dogmatics and ethics. This connection with the philosophy of religion made it clearer than in German Protestant theology that the real task to be performed in 'apologetics' was that of providing a basis for Christian theology in general. This point was also given more adequate attention in Catholic theology as a result of the development of apologetics into fundamental theology.[794] This gave the fundamental importance of the religious thematic in particular for theology as a whole more recognition in the organisation of study than it received in German evangelical theology. Nevertheless a suitable treatment of this thematic would have to include the history of religion, rather than relate a Christianity previously defined as a revealed religion externally to a general concept of religion. This would mean that the question of the truth of Christianity cannot be decided a priori either by the theologian's personal religious decision or by fundamental theology but is involved in the whole of the science of theology, which studies Christianity as a historic religion in the unfolding of its history.

3

Our discussion of the questions associated with apologetics and fundamental theology have brought us back to the demand that

[794] The origin of fundamental theology with J. N. Ehrlich (1859/62) and Ehrlich's dependence on F. A. Staudenmaier's *Encyklopädie* have been discussed in detail by Ebeling on pp. 498 ff of the article cited above, n. 786. Ebeling (p. 501) mentions that as early as 1843 A. F. L. Pelt, in his *Theologische Encyklopädie,* had used the term 'fundamental theology' for the most important of the three subordinate disciplines he distinguished in systematic theology. Pelt in turn mentions J. F. Kleuker as having been the first to use the term 'fundamental theology', in his *Grundriss einer Encyklopädie der Theologie* (1800/01), though in a different sense from Pelt himself, 'as a single term for the written sources of revelation which provide Christian theology with its foundation or source of knowledge' (quoted Ebeling, p. 502). This description recalls on the one hand Planck, and in particular his view of apologetics, which was similarly connected with the teaching of scripture (see above, n. 760), but on the other also the discipline of 'positive theology' argued for by Melchior Cano, which had the task of defining the sources of evidence for

Christian theology should be given a foundation in a general theology of religion. It cannot be the function of this fundamental theology to determine the truth of Christianity; all it can do is provide a provisional location of Christianity within the historical world of religions. To this extent Schleiermacher was right in limiting the function of philosophical theology to the investigation of the distinctive nature of Christianity. However the question of truth lies outside the competence of philosophical or fundamental theology not because it has to be settled in advance of all theology in the subjectivity of the theologian, but on the contrary because the question constantly reappears in Christianity as a historical phenomenon, that is, in the process of the history of its tradition, from each step in the tradition to the next, nor can it be answered conclusively even in the present. It is therefore inadequate for theology to regard itself as the unfolding of a truth entrusted to it in advance as complete. In view of this the question whether its prior completeness is guaranteed by the authority of revelation or by the subjective certainty of an experience of faith sinks into insignificance. The truth of the faith is not given to theology in advance for the simple reason that it is still in dispute in the history of Christianity and so is the *object* of Christian theology. The function of theology is to study and describe Christianity understood as the history which receives its impetus from the investigation of the truth of the Christian faith, or of the reality of the kingdom of God made present in Jesus. Theology would

---

theological statements, which turned out to coincide with the documents of revelation (see above, pp. 243f). Petrus Annatus, in his *Apparatus ad positivam theologiam Methodicus* (1700), does in fact report the widespread use of the term 'fundamental theology' to describe positive theology: 'Nam sicut nequit esse sine fundamento domus, ita nec sine positiva stare potest scholastica, in positiva siquidem fundatur scholastica; unde positiva fundamentalis theologia a nonnulllis vulgo vocatur, et merito' (p. 8 of the 1727 Erfurt edition). If this is correct, fundamental theology was first the doctrine of the sources of revelation and evidence for theology. Planck's idea of apologetics as the presentation of the truth of scripture is still in this line, though in his work a change appears. The old, narrow approach, dominated by authority, now begins to pass over into the more general enquiry into the truth of the Christian religion. This already had a tradition of its own, but as a result of the Enlightenment it acquired a new relevance to fundamental theology.

not do justice to the historical reality either of Jesus or of the
Christian church if it did not pick out the open question of the
truth first of Jesus's Gospel and then of the first Christians' Gospel
of Christ as the driving force which creates the historicality of
Christianity out of the gap between the truth which has already
appeared and the truth that has not yet emerged in its
universality. This brings back the question of the relation
between the systematic and historical elements in theology, this
time from the point of view of theological systematics itself. The
remark that dogmatics and ethics, the Christian teaching on faith
and morals, can be very well presented within a historical
theology[795] derives its force from the historical nature of
Chrisitianity and its truth. Even the *distinctive nature* of
Christianity, the definition of which Schleiermacher made the
task of apologetics, can be suitably described only as the working
out of the historical consequences which have flowed from the
basic tension of Jesus' proclamation of the kingdom of God and
are constantly rekindled by it. Christianity is not the result of this
process produced at some point in the period of primitive
Christianity, nor is it identical with the message of Jesus with
which the process starts; it is simply the process itself, which
derives its impetus from the basic tension in the message of Jesus
and its definitive embodiment in the event of the cross and
resurrection of Jesus. There is no 'essence of Christianity' which
can be separated from this process, the dynamism of which
continues to this day; or, if an essence is separated it must become
a pale abstraction. The essence of Christianity is this history from
the advent of God's future in Jesus to the future of the kingdom
of God to be inaugurated by the returning Christ.[796] This
historicality characterises not only the fact of Christianity but
also the content of Christian teaching. Consequently a
christology which does not in its full historical reality present the
tension between the incarnation of Christ and his future remains

[795] Naturally this means not that these subjects are only of antiquarian
interest, but, on the contrary, that their present relevance, if it is not to bend to
every passing fashion, must draw on history.

[796] As far as I know, the only attempt to describe the history of Christianity
from this point of view was made by F. C. Baur in his *Geschichte der christlichen
Kirche*, 5 vols, 1853–63. Baur sets out to describe 'the movement of the idea of
the Church' in which 'the historic material is so permeated by the idea

abstract, and an ecclesiology which elaborates a concept of the essence of the church in isolation from its actual historical foundation and mission becomes ideology.

The tasks involved in describing the essence and truth of Christianity do not therefore, in principle, go beyond the limits of a historical theology. They could indeed be performed only in a historical theology, provided always that, while remaining historical, it adopted a systematic approach. A historical theology of this sort would mean the end of the opposition between historical and systematic theology. On the other hand, as long as systematic treatment has not fully affected the historical material in the historical disciplines of theology, or is only in its beginnings, a *special* systematic theology will be necessary in addition and as a supplement to them. It will be responsible for the *provisional treatment* of the themes which historical theology, in the fully elaborated form of a theology of Christianity, could accommodate within itself. Such a universal theory of Christianity which would absorb all the disciplines of Christian theology which are now separate would certainly also require a preliminary terminological clarification of such concepts as religion, God, man, history, creation, society and science. Such conceptual clarification would count, however, not as an aim in itself but only as a preliminary treatment or summary of the real task; the proper investigation and exposition of this would have to be dealt with by the historic concreteness and dynamism of its object.

Even with a theology of religions, the general philosophy of religion can accordingly claim only the status of a propaedeutic. In the detailed treatment of the phenomenon of religion the abstraction of the general concept of religion, which is unavoidable as a starting point, must be subsumed in the complexity of the historical reality of religions. The process will

---

(according to the standard of the particular moments to which it assigns itself) that the overriding power of the general can be seen in the particular' (*Die Epochen der kirchlichen Geschichtsschreibung,* Tübingen 1852, pp. 249, 268). For Baur, however, as this quotation shows, the idea takes precedence over history, whereas in the view we are considering it is not a pre-existing idea of Christianity which unfolds in history, but the progress of history itself which decides on the essence, idea and truth of Christianity.

show that this complexity does not disintegrate into an amorphous multiplicity. The reason is that religions are concerned with the *one* truth of the divine. For the same reason opposition and hostility between them is unavoidable, and this also explains why the history of religions finally results in a unity which is based in the unity of its theme, which is revealed in the battles of history. This is also the reason why the history of religions, with all its complexity, can nevertheless provide a unified account which, like religions themselves, is supported by the anticipation of the unity of its theme.

Even a theology of Christianity cannot avoid starting from abstract concepts and conceptual relations, that is, from general discussions of religion, God, man, revelation, faith and tradition. At a stage in the development of theology in which the theology of Christianity was fully integrated into a general theology of religions, this preparatory task could be left to general philosophy of religion. However, as long as the position of Christianity in the world of religions is in dispute and while the general science of religion has not yet become an examination of its object *as* religion and so a *theology* of religions, this preliminary task will have to be performed within Christian theology itself. Within Christian theology it will be the function of systematic theology, until such time as historical theology is fully developed. Traditional dogmatics, by treating God, election, creation, man, redemption, church and sacraments as items of doctrine, has all too often lost sight of the fact that these concepts are real only in the movement of a history in which both their nature and their truth are still being determined. A systematic theology of Christianity must express the historicalness nature of Christianity and its truth in order to match its material. This is made all the more urgent by the fact that in Christian consciousness history as the history of revelation and salvation is already explicitly thematic. The basis of this Christian sense of history, which is the incarnation, the anticipated present and abiding *perfectum* of what is definitive, includes the specific form of Christianity itself as an anticipation of the totality of its content, and not just the form of faith but also, through it, that of Christian love.

The redefinition of the relationship between concepts and

history — which means also that between the systematic and historical elements — in theology makes possible new solutions for three fundamental problems, the relationship between theology and philosophy, that between the pluralism and unity of truth and that between theory and practice.

1. The opposition between theology and philosophy is seen to be unfounded in that, because of its universality, the philosophical concept can give only a *provisional* grasp of a history which transcends every concept that can be formulated in history, just as we may *therefore* say the same of religious descriptions of life.

2. In a perspective based on the superiority of history over concept (concept in the sense of the theme of man's attempt to understand history), the plurality of viewpoints in the struggle for the one truth — a plurality that is insuperable within the historic process — becomes intelligible because of the openness of history. When we conceive of history as the cause of this plurality, we have thereby made the most comprehensive claim to truth that is justifiable in view of relativity and pluralism: only to the extent that a viewpoint has assimilated the conditions of the plurality in which it appears as one among many is it not merely subject to this plurality but also able to transcend it.

3. In an acceptance of the superiority of history to concepts the relationship of theory and practice is changed. Practice is both based on the concept (of Christianity) and also released from previous conceptualisations so that it in its turn can exert an influence on the understanding of the nature and truth of Christianity.

Before the relationship between systematic and practical theology outlined in the last sentence is discussed, we must give a final description of the work of systematic theology in terms of its contents.

In the present organisation of theology, the systematic aspect of theology in general becomes the specialised function of systematic theology. Systematic theology becomes more adequate to its task the more it realises that the investigation of the nature and truth of Christianity is not a specialised *area,* but the shared responsibility of Christian theology as a whole, and the more it combines the systematic and the historical in its own activity. And conversely, the less willingness the systematic theologian shows to penetrate the *historical* phenomenon of Christianity in systematic terms, the more subjectively contingent and arbitrary elements his models will contain.

In the present state of theology and science of religion the *theology* of religion must be done in forced and temporary association with systematic theology, even though the subject is also dealt with from more specialised points of view in missiology and the science of religion. Because of this the concepts of religion have the central position in the internal structure of systematic theology, since otherwise theology as the science of God can study its true object only indirectly as the object of religion. This new importance of the religious element in modern theology goes parallel to the anthropocentric tendency of post-Renaissance thought, which is also particularly clear in its philosophical theology. The study of religion presupposes as its basis a general anthropology to provide a frame of reference for all discussions about the status of religious concepts in the weft of the human world, and in particular for meeting the arguments of modern atheism.

The most general foundations of systematic theology will therefore have to come from anthropology. Moreover, theology broaches the anthropological phenomena with a view to their religious and theological implications.[797] Other implications of anthropology include the questions of man's relationship to the non-human world, questions of natural philosophy or ontology on the one hand and of epistemology on the other. Finally, anthropology itself is concerned with the relationship of the more abstract, and for that very reason more fundamental, questions of biological anthropology and sociological analysis of the social forms of human behaviour to the historical concreteness of the living-out of human life into which the philosophy and theology of history translates the *abstract* levels of anthropological enquiry.

[797] In this connection see the discussion on the relationship between theology and philosophy above, pp, 303ff.

On the basis of general anthropology the theology of religion first elaborates, by way of introduction, the concept of religion (philosophy of religion) and then subsumes it in the actual movement of the history of religion. Because it is a *theology* of religion it is concerned in the history of religion with the history of the apparition of the reality of God as well as of that of man. It therefore includes the topics contained in the traditional doctrine of God as well as christology, ecclesiology and ethics. All four of these groups of themes, however, can also be treated independently, the question of God in connection with the problem of mind in the immediate context of the theme of religion, christology in its connection with general anthropology, which is indicated by the doctrine of the incarnation, and ecclesiology in connection with the need for a philosophy and theology of human society: ethics, finally, can be studied both as a general science of action with a basis in anthropology and with regard to the dependence of the objectives of action on the context of the experience of meaning and ultimately on the religious understanding of meaning in its concrete historical form at any given time. Because of the dependence of moral attitudes on a sense of meaning, theological ethics, as Schleiermacher saw, presupposes what he called 'religious doctrine' and is quite incapable of replacing this. For this reason ethics is, of all the subject areas of systematic theology, the least suited to providing a basis for it. Inevitably, this task can be performed only by the doctrine of God as the systematic presentation of the all-determining reality – if such a task, which seems to be required by the meaning of the concept of God, can be performed without abstraction from the indirectness of human knowledge of God and its dependence on the process of the history of religion. On the other hand ethics connects systematic theology with practical theology, which can also be understood as a specialised branch of ethics, the ethics of action *in the church*.

7. Practical Theology

A concern with the praxis of life is the basis not merely of a particular theological discipline but of theology as a whole. Theology's concern with the divine *as* all-determining reality *as a matter of dispute* is connected with the fact that reality as a whole is still incomplete. This means that questions about the all-determining reality and the coherence of meaning in life go beyond the immediate and theoretically determinable and involve what is not yet present, which includes what can be brought about by the practical activity of man.

The practical character of theology as a whole has been brought out only in a limited way in theology's view of itself as a 'practical science' (see above, pp.231ff). The concern with God as the ultimate goal and highest good of man which in this view was fundamental to theology was generally restricted to a matter of the conditions and means of *individual* salvation. Even Calvin included the church among the external means of salvation. The fact that in the hoped-for salvation individual and society belong together – because the perfection of society as the precondition of the individual's salvation is what the Christian hope for the kingdom of God means – was pushed into the background by the emphasis on individual salvation in the formation of the concept of theology as a practical science. Nevertheless the idea of the kingdom of God has had considerable effect on the modern history of Christianity. Puritanism and the English revolution of the seventeenth century are inconceivable without it. In the German Enlightenment from Leibniz on, it was given an ethical twist and became the guiding concept of man's moral nature. In Kant's philosophy of religion the implications of the idea of the kingdom of God for social ethics were given clear expression, although its political relevance was neutralised by Kant's distinction between law and morality.[798] These ideas continued to be influential in nineteenth century theology, for example in Ritschl, and even later in the religious socialism of the twentieth

[798] On this, see P. Cornehl, *Die Zukunft der Versöhnung. Eschatologie und Emanzipation in der Aufklärung, bei Hegel und in der Hegelschen Schule*, Göttingen 1971, pp. 67–72. By setting a morality based on individual intention above mere legality Kant set limits to the enthusiasm for the future which accepts social emancipation at the expense of the individual, and these have been shown by the history of the French Revolution and later developments to be both realistic and necessary. At the same time, however, he made the idea of the kingdom of God relative to the moral actions of the individual.

century, though the basis was always the social obligation of *individual* moral self-fulfilment. In this view the church could be seen as the institutional form of the moral kingdom of God which Ritschl claimed Jesus had founded, or it could equally, as in the views of Rothe, disappear into the moral state. In both cases ethical individualism was the basis. Because the effect of the idea of the kingdom of God was to pose and simultaneously neutralise the dialectic of individual and society, the relationship between church and state, and the history of that relationship since the Reformation, were hardly considered. The fact that ethical individualism remained a one-sided basis for the ethical interpretation of the idea of the kingdom of God may go some way to explain why it did not produce any development beyond the narrowly individualistic concept of theology as a practical science, but at most led to a secondary extension of it to deal with the moral practice of Christianity. In addition, the concept of theology as a whole as a practical science was so closely connected in Protestantism with the analytical method of orthodox dogmatics that it lost influence when this declined in the eighteenth century. In its place a different view of 'practical theology' developed.

In his *Institutio theologiae moralis* of 1711, J. F. Buddeus described moral theology as 'practical' theology in the strict sense because it was concerned with *agenda* as opposed to *credenda*. Indeed with regard to its aim, the whole of theology could, according to Buddeus, be called a *scientia practica,* though for that part of it which investigated action the name was in use in a more specialised and strict sense, as a description of the subject-matter of the disciplines involved.[799] The name 'practical theology' for moral theology goes back to an older, narrower usage, in which it was a comprehensive term for the theory of pastoral work and

[799] J. F. Buddeus, *Institutio theologiae moralis,* Leipzig 1711, prol. § 4 (p. 6): 'Ea vero theologiae pars . . . quae agenda seorsim considerat, practica vocari solet, ab objecto scilicet, non a fine. Ratione finis enim omnia theologia practica est. Dicitur et moralis, voce ista latius accepta.' The last qualification is explained in § 10 (p. 9) as meaning that in addition to moral theology in the narrow sense *iurisprudentia divina* and *prudentia christiana* have to be regarded as disciplines concerned with *agenda.* Cf. also Id., *Isagoge historico-theologica ad theologiam universam singulasque eius partes,* Leipzig 1727, p. 545: 'Quae circa agenda versatur theologia, practica vocari solet, itemque moralis, voce hac in

penitential practice. Since the fourth Lateran Council of 1215, every metropolitan church had been required to appoint a *magister* for this subject. He was to be responsible for teaching, in addition to holy scripture, what was relevant to pastoral work (*quae ad curam animarum spectare noscuntur*). The relevant literature was described as practical theology as distinct from speculative theology.[800] The synod of Dordrecht referred similarly to a *theologia practica* concerned with various questions of conscience.[801] According to J. H. Alsted in 1623, the term *theologia practica* was used 'in the schools' for the *theologia casuum*.[802] This subject could also be developed into a Christian ethics or moral theology, as by Calixt and (under the name 'practical theology') by H. Nyssen.[803] In his *Disputatio de theologia practica*, of 1646, Gisbert Voetius combined moral theology, ascetical theology and 'church policy', the last of which comprised liturgical studies, church discipline and homiletics.[804] This book places the particular tasks of the pastor in the general framework of a theological science of action based on moral theology. In the following period, however, the identification of practical theology with moral theology, which was already visible in Buddeus,[805] became complete, with the result that

---

latiori significatione accepta. In strictiori enim si sumitur, theologia moralis eam theologiae practicae partem denotat, quae docet, quo pacto homo regenitus in vitae sanctae studio rite progredi atque proficere debeat.'

[800] E. C. Achelis, (*Lehrbuch der praktischen Theologie*, vol. I (1890), 3rd ed. 1911, pp. 9–10) mentions especially J. Molanus, *Theologiae practicae compendium* Cologne 1590, and also refers to J. F. von Schulte, *Die Geschichte der Quellen und Literatur des Canonischen Rechts von Gratian bis auf die Gegenwart* vol. II, 1877, pp. 521–2. The relationship between this sense of the notion 'practical theology' and that of a 'theory of pious living' (Achelis, pp 5ff.) seems to me fluid.

[801] Achelis, p. 12.

[802] J. H. Alsted, *Methodus ss theologiae*, Hanover 1623, pp. 121–2: 'Usitata est in Scholis distinctio Theologiae in positivam, scholasticam et in controversam . . . Theologia practica illis specialiter dicitur theologia casuum.'

[803] Achelis, pp. 5ff. Achelis traces the contrast between theoretical and practical theology back beyond G. J. Planck to Marheineke and M. Kähler.

[804] G. Voetius, *Selectae disputationes theologicae pars III*, 1646, quoted from Achelis, p. 12.

[805] Note how, in the quotation reproduced in n. 799 above, Buddeus distinguished a narrower and a broader meaning of moral theology, only the

pastoral theology[806] became a separate field restricted to the study of the pastor's professional tasks.

Accordingly, in 1795, G. J. Planck treated moral theology and practical theology as interchangeable terms, while he excluded pastoral theology from the concept of theological science as 'applied' theology.[807] The exclusion is logical if the discipline does no more than match the various professional requirements of the pastoral clergy without trying to develop from that into a necessary element in theology, but remaining content with the status of an 'applied science'.[808]

In this state of the question it is easy to see how Schleiermacher's conception of a 'practical theology' as part of his theological encyclopedia could have provided a new justification for a discipline which about this time had become an

second of which coincides with the idea of practical theology.

[806] On the literature of pastoral theology since Erasmus Sarcerius (*Pastorale oder Hirtenbuch vom Ampt, Wesen und Disziplin der Pastoren und Kirchendiener*, etc., 1550), see C. F. Stäudlin, *Lehrbuch der Encyklopädie, Methodologie und Geschichte der theologischen Wissenschaften*, Hanover 1821, p. 341.

[807] G. J. Planck, (*Einleitung in die theologischen Wissenschaften*, vol. II, p. 543) treats the terms moral theology and practical theology as identical. At the same time he relegates 'those theological studies which belong to applied theology' to an appendix (pp. 593ff). His reason is that 'for the theologian they may be indispensable – though even then not for all – but to theology itself they cannot be!' (p. 598). They make no contribution 'to a clearer, more developed and more solid knowledge of the truths of religion themselves' (pp. 598–9). Nor do they deserve the title of independent sciences (p. 599), since they do no more than apply rhetoric and paedagogics to the material of theology: 'In other words, these allegedly independent sciences have no objects which would support independent scientific work' (p. 600).

[808] The view of practical theology as an 'applied' science was subsequently supported by Hagenbach (*Encyklopädie*, 11th ed. 1884, pp. 422–3) and Heinrici (*Theologische Encyklopädie*, 1893, pp. 283–4), and also recently by H. Schröer ('Der praktische Bezug der theologischen Wissenschaft auf Kirche und Gesellschaft', in H. Siemers and H.-R. Reuter (ed.), *Theologie als Wissenschaft in der Gesellschaft*, 1970, pp. 156ff, esp. 164). In taking this position, however, these writers do not seem to realise that, as Planck's criticisms showed, its result is to deny practical theology the status of a necessary element in the science of theology. The treatment of practical theology as an applied science was attacked in the nineteenth century by C. D. F. Palmer ('Zur practischen Theologie', *Jahrbuch für deutsche Theologie* (1856), I, pp. 317–61, quoted Hagenbach, p. 422), and in the current discussion by G. Otto (G. Otto (ed.), *Praktischtheologisches Handbuch*, 1970, p. 24).

autonomous university subject,[809] though one which, as Schleiermacher said, had 'previously been treated as a theory more in connection with minor details than with questions of importance'.[810] In his *Brief Outline of the Study of Theology*, published in 1811, Schleiermacher assigned the description of the 'craft' of church government to practical as opposed to philosophical and historical theology.[811] However, Schleiermacher believed that the function of theology as a whole was to serve the needs of church government, and that only this practical aim provided the theological disciplines with their unity (§§ 5f). Accordingly, his whole concept of theology was in fact designed to lead up to practical theology, but conversely, in spite of the rather bleak description of its theme as the craft of church management, practical theology was derived from the concept of theology itself as the completion and 'crown of theological study'.[812] The difficulties of this solution cannot be separated from the formalism of Schleiermacher's concept of theology, which was criticised above (pp. 253–5). That discussion showed that for Schleiermacher too the unity of theology was *in fact* by no means dependent exclusively on the connection of the various disciplines with the work of church government, but was also firmly based on a necessary connection with the essence of

---

[809] On the Catholic side, pastoral theology became an autonomous university discipline at Vienna in 1777 as a result of the reform of studies by the Empress Maria Theresa in 1774 (see H. Schuster, *Hundbuch der Pastoraltheologie. Praktische Theologie der Kirche in ihrer Gegenwart,* vol. I, 1964, pp. 40–92). On the Protestant side the call of Hyperius's pupil W. Zepper in 1595 for the appointment of a *professor practicus* (Achelis, *Lehrbuch,* vol. I, 3rd ed. 1911, p. 12) was not acted upon until 1794, when a chair was created at Tübingen (D. Rössler, 'Prolegomena zur praktischen Theologie', *ZThK* 64 (1967), p. 357).

[810] F. D. Schleiermacher, *Kurze Darstellung des theologischen Studiums,* 1st ed., p. 8, § 32 (p. 10 of Scholz's ed.).

[811] *Kurze Darstellung,* 2nd ed., § 25 (Scholz, p. 100): 'It is not the purpose of practical theology to teach a proper understanding of this task. It presupposes this and is concerned only with the proper performance of all the tasks which must be included in the concept of church government . . . theory has nothing more to contribute' to a proper understanding of the task 'once philosophical and historical theology have been drawn on clearly and in the proper measure' (ibid).

[812] *Kurze Darstellung,* 1st ed., p. 8, § 31 (Scholz, p. 100).

Christianity, although this actual basis did not appear in his explicit concept of theology. But if, in spite of Schleiermacher's assertions, the real basis of the unity of theology in his thinking is not its connection with the work of church government but the essence of Christianity, the derivation of practical theology as no more than the craft of church management turns out to be no more than an apparent solution to the problem of demonstrating the necessary connection of practical theology with the concept of theology as such. The formalism of Schleiermacher's encyclopedic justification of practical theology may also explain why, in his detailed exposition, he accepted the existing institutional framework of parochial life without question and made it the basis of his account, to such an extent that W. Jetter could describe his model as 'a blueprint for the clerical church, and almost its apologia'.[813]

A genuine solution to the problem of providing a basis for the discipline of practical theology in the concept of theology as such must, unlike Schleiermacher's, start from the essence of Christianity itself. It is no accident that the discussion on the foundations of practical theology after Schleiermacher developed along these lines.

Schleiermacher's Berlin rival, P. K. Marheinecke, was not the only one to put forward alternatives to Schleiermacher's definition of practical theology as a mere 'craft'. In 1837, in his *Entwurf der praktischen Theologie,* Marheinecke attempted to demonstrate its necessary connection with the essence of the Christian church, and on this question he was followed by Schleiermacher's pupil, C. J. Nitzsch.[814] The reason Nitzsch gives for his position is interesting. Schleiermacher's definition of the theme of practical theology as the simple 'craft' of church management would be unobjectionable, he says, 'if the practical theologian could simply take for granted a theoretical and systematic science of Christianity which was totally complete and autonomous, and a precise historical description of the present

---

[813] W. Jetter, 'Die Praktische Theologie', *ZThK* 64 (1967), pp. 451ff (quotation from p. 463). See also Schleiermacher's *Kurze Darstellung,* 2nd ed., §§ 277ff.
[814] See D. Rössler, 'Prolegomena zur Praktischen Theologie', *ZThK* 64 (1967), pp. 357ff, esp. 360ff.

moment in the activity and life of the church'. But since 'particularly at present the practical theologian can take for granted very little agreement on theoretical questions and historico-critical principles, and certainly has no complete and recognised body of fundamental theology available to him',[815] he must, says Nitzsch, take upon himself the task 'of understanding and evaluating the existing situation in relation to the idea of the Christian church and Christian life in order to discover the guiding principle of all ministerial activity in the church'.[816] In other words, it was no special fondness for the association of practical theology with a particular dogmatic ecclesiology which prompted Nitzsch to agree with Marheinecke on this topic. On the contrary, the decisive consideration for him was the realisation that no unanimity can be taken for granted on this question, though he regarded it as obvious that any consistent theory of church activity must be based on a particular concept of the church.

It is easy to understand why practical theologians were unhappy with such a dependence on a concept of the church which was either taken over from dogmatics or had to be provided by practical theology itself as a dogmatic foundation. The situation meant that the development of theory in their discipline could all too easily become a mere reflection of the changing trends of a different discipline, namely dogmatics. In particular their experiences with the effects of dialectical theology, which directly opposed its dogmatic concepts of the church, which it presented as revealed norms, not only to what it called 'the world', but also to the existing church,[817] made it seem desirable to make practical theology once and for all independent of the pretensions of dogmatics. This feeling was reinforced by the fact that in the actual treatment of practical theology the dogmatic foundations frequently proved to be a mere ideological veneer and made no difference to the division of the discipline into homiletics, catechetics and pastoralia because these fields

---

[815] C. J. Nitzsch, *Praktische Theologie I: Allgemeine Theorie des kirchlichen Lebens,* Bonn 1847, pp. 32–3.

[816] Nitzsch, pp. 31–2.

[817] See T. Rendtorff, *Kirche und Theologie. Die systematische Funktion des Kirchenbegriffs in der neueren Theologie,* 1966, pp. 173ff, esp. 175ff, 191ff.

were required by the church's existing practice as embodied in the traditional duties of the parish clergy. Instead of leading to an appreciation of the real nature of these fields as a reflection of existing conditions, the derivation of practical theology from a dogmatic concept of the church all too easily resulted in their being surrounded with a false prestige as 'the establishment of the kingdom of God in the church and through the church in the world' (A.D. Müller).

In an attempt to escape from these difficulties, D. Rössler appealed to what he called the 'legacy' of Christoph Palmer, that is, the suggestion made by Palmer in 1856 that practical theology should be based not on dogmatics but on ethics. According to Palmer, whereas dogmatics had the task of 'making the deeds of God transparent' in their necessity, alongside that necessity there existed 'what is not yet done, but will be done, not by any divine necessity but through human freedom'.[818] Human freedom, according to Palmer, was the concern of both ethics and practical theology. Ethics was concerned with Christian life and practical theology with the ecclesiastical form of this, life in the church. Palmer's position was in essence a restatement of the view arrived at by Voetius in the seventeenth century, though he did not make Palmer's theoretical distinction between dogmatics and ethics. Palmer insisted, against Marheinecke, that Christianity was in the first place to do with life, and only secondarily with concepts, and accordingly he saw the practical disciplines as closely related to history, but opposed to dogmatics. In this view Palmer was very close to Schleiermacher's overall position, though he did not follow him in his narrow definition of practical theology as a 'craft' of church management, since Schleiermacher too regarded ethics and history as closely related. The relation between the two was reversed in Palmer's account, but the thesis that practical theology must be based, with ethics, in historical theology reads like a development of elements of Schleiermacher's position in the direction of Dilthey's later reformulation of their basis. Certainly, while Schleiermacher did not make ethics a subdivision of history, he definitely did so with dogmatics, which

---

[818] C. D. F. Palmer, 'Zur praktischen Theologie', *Jahrbuch für deutsche Theologie* 1856/I, pp. 317–61, at p. 331, quoted D. Rössler, 'Prolegomena . . .' (note 814 above), p. 367.

Palmer now contrasted with both ethics and history in support of his isolation of speculative theology.

The difficulties inherent in Palmer's position are revealed by the fact that he himself was unable to avoid drawing on dogmatics. Palmer himself could not do without the concept of the church and the ideas of redemption and reconciliation through Christ. The explanation that the relevant statements are not borrowings from dogmatics but the result of an independent approach to the same themes is not very convincing.[819] It makes sense at all only against the background of Palmer's exceptionally stringent requirement that dogmatics should demonstrate divine *necessity* in the facts of revelation history. It is certainly true that there are other, historical-empirical means of access to the reality of the church and the experience of redemption and reconciliation in Christ. On the other hand, dogmatic reflection too has always been rooted in this vital context. On this point Schleiermacher saw more clearly. The historical-factual cannot be reduced to the necessary, and consequently such reduction cannot be the function of dogmatics. It is equally inadequate to define human freedom merely in terms of its distinctness from necessity. A theory of concrete freedom, and the historical forms it has taken in Christian religious consciousness, would dissipate the illusion of an abstract opposition between dogmatics and ethics.[820] An outline of such a theory was produced by Hegel.[821]

---

[819] Rössler, 'Prolegomena', p. 370.

[820] The fact that such oppositions were set up can be understood as the reaction of the emancipatory tendencies of the Enlightenment against the Christian religious tradition. Emancipation itself, however, is not yet freedom (see G. Rohrmoser, *Emanzipation und Freiheit*, 1970). As Hegel saw, when he recognised the contradiction in the Enlightenment attack on tradition, it can destroy the basis of the consciousness of freedom when this is transmitted by the tradition from which one is seeking to escape.

[821] See my paper 'Die Bedeutung des Christentums in der Philosophie Hegels', in *Gottesgedanke und menschliche Freiheit*, 1972, pp. 78–113. I agree with T. Rendtorff in the view that 'the problem of the constitution of freedom' is the 'central problem' of theology in the situation created by the Enlightenment (Rendtorff, 'Theologie als Kritik und Konstruktion', in *Theorie des Christentums*, 1972, pp. 182–200, at p. 197). However, in my view 'the attempt at a pure apprehension of personal consciousness as the subject of its conditions' (p. 194) implies a dubious answer to this question, namely the thesis of the self-constitution of the subject, which led Fichte into difficulties

Palmer's attempt is particularly instructive today in view of the widespread demand for an empirico-critical rather than a historico-critical theology, and in particular for the scientific status of practical theology to be defined in terms of the sciences of social action.[822] These tendencies could result simply in a repetition of Palmer's work with different emphases. Just as Palmer can be shown to have ignored the inseparability of Christian ethics from dogmatic presuppositions, so attempts to establish a science of action with an independent theoretical basis can be shown to neglect the dependence of such a discipline on the experience of meaning which is prior to any particular action and makes it possible for action to take place at all.[823] Meaning in this context should not be thought of primarily as the conferral of meaning postulated by intentional theories of meaning. Meaning does not come in the first place from definitions or systems of meaning (which are 'closed').[824] The experience of meaning arises rather out of the context which is implicit in every particular experience. This context is what first gives the particular experience significance. It can be secondarily constructed and reconstructed in definitions or systems of

(D. Henrich, *Fichtes ursprüngliche Einsicht*, Frankfurt, 1967). The constitution of freedom (and so of the subject itself) becomes a problem only because it cannot be conceived of as the self-positing of the subject and so not simply as autonomy.

[822] A similar demand can now be heard from various quarters, e.g. on the one hand H.-D. Bastian ('Vom Wort zu den Wörtern. Karl Barth und die Aufgaben der praktischen Theologie', *Evangelische Theologie* 28 (1968), pp. 22–55, esp. pp. 40ff, drawing on G. Krause, *ZThK* 64 (1967), p. 484), and on the other H. Schröer (see n. 808, p. 160). Schröer's use of Habermas's concept of 'knowlege-constitutive interests' to support his case, however, on the ground that faith is the knowledge-constitutive interest of theology (pp. 166–7) is no more than the metaphorical adaptation of a catchy phrase. On pp. 187–8 of the same book H. R. Reuter has tellingly shown the incompatibility of Habermas's ideas with the use made of them by Schröer.

[823] See above, pp. 80–103, esp. 94ff, 102–3.

[824] See K.-W. Dahm, 'Religiöse Kommunikation und kirchliche Institution', Dahm, Luhmann and Stoodt, *Religion – System und Sozialisation,* Darmstadt/Neuwied 1972, pp. 133–88, esp. pp. 174 and 182. These statements are intelligible in the context of N. Luhmann's intentional theory of meaning, but Dahm evidently wants to go beyond this (pp. 175–6, 182) to find a prior access to the experience of meaning.

meaning as the context of meaning of particular experienced meanings, but this does not exhaust it or make it no more than such 'closed' models of meaning. The vital context within which this historic experience of meaning takes place is the basis of both the dogmatic and the ethical reflection of Christian consciousness, and also of the theories of practical theology about the activity of the church. For this reason neither ethics nor practical theology can be regarded as no more than the statement of the implications of dogmatic axioms. With regard to their *heuristic context*, all these disciplines have an independent source in the historical life-world of the Christian tradition.[825] As regards its *probative context*, of course, a theory of action in the church necessarily requires the general framework of a theory of Christian action in general, that is, of a Christian ethic, and this, as a *Christian* ethic, in turn presupposes a science of the 'life-world of Christianity'.[826] This science cannot be just a science of action, and therefore must go beyond the boundaries of ethics, if it deals with the sense of meaning which underlies action in the context of the Christian life-world (including the conflicts which arise in its articulation). Nor can such a science of the historical life-world of Christianity be limited to *modern* Christianity, even though in practice this will be the immediate context for reflection on the determinants of present action within Christianity and the church. The world of present Christianity – in so far as it can be isolated in the historic context of the 'modern age' and grasped as a uniform quantum – is constituted by the use of the Bible and faith's reference back to Jesus of Nazareth but also, therefore, implicitly or explicitly exposed to examination of its continuity with the beginnings of Christianity. This means that the world of modern or present-day Christianity itself can be understood only in the context of a general theory of Christianity. Such a theory of

[825] H. Schröer, 'Der praktische Bezug', pp. 164–5 rightly urges the adoption by practical theology of the idea of life-world which was fundamental to Husserl's late work. It should be noted, however, that the Christian life-world is constituted by its historic origins and mediated by processes of tradition.

[826] T. Rendtorff, for example, calls for a 'reconstitution of theology as a science . . . as a theory of the present-day practical life-world of Christianity' ('Theologie in der Welt des Christentums' (1969), reprinted in *Theorie des Christentums,* 1972, pp. 150–60, quotation p. 157) or 'of the practical life-world of Christianity in the conditions of the modern age' (p. 160).

Christianity has generally taken the form of a systematic account of Christian doctrine and has been called dogmatics. There can be no doubt that the reduction of Christianity to doctrinal content detached from the process of Christian history has sadly impoverished the theory of Christianity, and there can be no doubt that the only adequate form for such a theory today is that of a theory of the history of Christianity. However, this makes no difference to the fact that this task is the one traditionally performed by dogmatics.

In all this it is still necessary to avoid basing a Christian ethic or a theory of the action of the church on dogmatic norms constrasted directly with the historical reality of Christianity and the church. This does not mean that there is no need for any dogmatic reflection on the Christian religious consciousness, but merely accepts the validity of the criticisms made of a narrow and one-sided dogmatics. If practical theology is rooted in the historical reality of Christianity and the church, it must necessarily be led to co-operate with dogmatics. And in the framework of historical theology dogmatics too reveals itself as a theology of Christianity as a single historical phenomenon, with the additional characteristic of a systematic method.

Making the history of Christianity and the church the common basis[827] of dogmatics, ethics and practical theology does not make theology historical in the sense of absorbing it into antiquarianism. The only historical approach which ends in this blind alley is one which is stuck in detail and no longer considers the totality of history. A study of historical themes which is aware of the totality of history as something still incomplete constantly returns to the present and to practical life. Its attempts to grapple with history give a richness to its understanding of the present which cannot be acquired in any other way and enables it to steer its practice in the light of the implications of a history it has understood.

Any fundamental consideration of the meaning and function of practical theology must clarify the concept of practice which gives the discipline its name. The meaning of 'practice' is not self-evident, and it is therefore right that the question of the

[827] See H.-D. Bastian's remarks ('Vom Wort zu den Wörtern', p. 32) on history as 'the link which unites the human and the natural sciences'.

relation between theory and practice should have come into the centre of the discussion about practical theology's understanding of its task.[828] That these questions are about much more than the refinement of terminology will be clear when it is realised that the derivation of practical theology from dogmatics which we have just rejected rests on a very specific definition of the relationship between theory and practice. In this definition theory stands over against reality as a postulate, and praxis is the external realisation of the theoretical imperative. Such a view corresponds more closely to Aristotle's *poiesis* than to his *praxis,* which was not the realisation of a model through productive activity but the active pursuit of a chosen way of life.[829]

According to Aristotle, theoretical knowledge is distinct both from practical and from poetic knowledge. At the same time, theoretical contemplation is a form of activity, in fact the highest form, the attribute of the gods and essence of their blessedness.[830] This is why Aristotle can say that the theoretical life, which has its *telos* within itself, is also, because of its *eupraxia,* practical in the highest sense.[831]

The self-sufficiency of theoretical contemplation, which simply in itself represents the highest form of practice, is in this respect, as M. Theunissen has acutely observed,[832] 'very closely connected with the fact that the being to the self-sufficiency of which contemplation owes its own self-sufficiency is already complete; nothing more is wanting to it'. There is a fundamental difference between this Greek *theoria* and a theory whose goal is realisation and which describes the immediate as history in relation to an open future, as the Frankfurt School's 'critical

[828] As in Bastian's article, pp. 25–55 en passim, and in G. Otto's introduction to his *Praktisch-theologisches Handbuch,* p. 23.

[829] On the distinction between *poiesis* and *praxis,* see Aristotle, *Metaphysics,* 1025 b 21ff.

[830] Aristotle, *Nic. Eth.,* 1078 b 21ff. On the origin of this view of the blessedness of the theoretical life in Plato, see B. Snell, 'Theorie und Praxis', *Die Entdechung des Geistes,* 3rd ed., Hamburg, 1955, pp. 401–22, esp. 406ff. (The English edition of the book, *The Discovery of the Mind* (Oxford 1953) is from an earlier German edition and does not include this essay).

[831] Aristotle, *Politics,* 1325 b 21. See F. Dirlmeier in his commentary on the Nicomachean Ethics (Berlin 1964, pp. 594–5).

[832] M. Theunissen, *Gesellschaft und Geschichte. Zur Kritik der kritischen Theorie,* Berlin 1969, p. 7.

theory' does in opposition to traditional theory.[833] In this, the reality described by the theory is assumed to be still incomplete. Theunissen has suggested that the basis of such a view of reality and its corresponding connection of theory and praxis may have 'a Judaeo-Christian origin'.[834] The ability of thought to see itself as theory at all, of course, is here again a Greek legacy, but it is modified in that theory is not simply brought into relation with the still open future of a historically grasped world and so with practice, but is 'itself immersed in the current of a praxis by which it too is permeated'.[835] Admittedly, Christianity cannot regard the final fulfilment as simply a lack in the present world, as though all that was needed to bring it about was to convict the present world by argument of its inhumanity and call for its radical transformation. Christian faith sees the final state as already present in this existing world because of Jesus Christ, in spite of injustice, suffering and death, and maintains that the fulfilment which is still wanting in it can only be the historic working out of the reconciliation which is already present and active in the world as a result of Jesus Christ.[836]

The only practical theology which corresponds to this definition of the relationship of theory and practice, one which is present in outline in the Christian faith itself, is one which expresses the practical bias which the Christian faith derives from the history of Jesus Christ and which continues to operate in the history of Christianity, though at times impeded. The theology will analyse the present practice of the churches in relation to the whole of the history of Christian reconciliation and offer critical interpretations of it in an attempt to produce

[833] M. Horkheimer, 'Traditionelle und kritische Theorie' (1937), in *Kritische Theorie*, vol. II, pp. 160ff.

[834] M. Theunissen, *Die Verwirklichung der Vernunft. Zur Theorie-Praxis Diskussion im Anschluss an Hegel* (*Philosophische Rundschau*, Beiheft 6), Tübingen 1970, p. 87.

[835] Theunissen, *Verwirklichung der Vernunft*, p. 84.

[836] So, as Theunissen (*Verwirklichung der Vernunft*, p. 87) points out, Hegel assigned philosophy the threefold task of understanding the reconciliation objectively achieved in the incarnation and set in motion in the history of individuals and of mankind, of understanding itself as an element in this process and so thirdly working for 'the secular reconciliation which has not yet taken place in history'.

models of present-day church practice. The practice of the *church* will have to remain the specific field of practical theology unless it attemps to develop into a general Christian ethic, in which case the social nature of Christian action, which is characterised by the forming of a church and acting in a church, will be a particular sub-division. Even if the practice of the church remains its specialised study, however, there is no need for practical theology to be no more than pastoral theology, the sort of introduction into the traditional activities of the parish clergy which it became through its subdivision into homiletics, cathechetics and pastoral and liturgical studies. But this pastoral theology will not simmply measure the present reality of the church against some dogmatic norm of the church; following the practical bias inherent in Christian history, it will see itself as an element in a process of historic practice in which it too is included. With this approach it will not be able simply to ignore the existing office of the parish clergy with its various areas of activity which were reflected in the traditional disciplines of pastoral theology. What it will be able to do is to set the existing office in a wider context of church practice within the social life-world of Christianity, and so contribute to its proper development.

Practical theology's concern with the social and therefore church-forming nature of Christian practice guarantees it an independent access to the church and its history alongside its inevitable involvement with the dogmatic doctrine of the church and with church history. As a theory of the church's activity which includes the history of the church, practical theology will have to recognise the fundamental importance of missiology to its general theme.[837] The mission directed to all mankind is not

---

[837] Schleiermacher himself (*Kurze Darstellung des theologischen Studiums*, 2nd ed., § 298) called for a 'theory of mission . . . which is so far almost totally lacking' as part of practical theology, though only as a function of an existing community. This 'local community' (§ 277) is the basis of his exposition of practical theology as a separate discipline. C. J. Nitzsch similarly included mission in practical theology, simply as a subsidiary element (*Praktische Theologie*, I, pp. 479ff; see also p. 133), but E. C. Achelis, citing notably Ehrenfeuchter, wrote that 'practical theology will be unable to do without the theory of mission because missionary activity is one of the necessary activities in the life of the church and is required by the concept of the church' (*Lehrbuch*

simply the practice which originally created the church, but also the ultimate horizon on which the whole life of the church must be understood. By its origin in mission the individual community is drawn into a history of divine election which looks towards a future in the kingdom of God; it is inserted into a Christian life-world which transcends its own particularity. Only within the vital historic context of the church which has grown up out of mission is it possible to define the position of the individual community in the life of Christianity, on the one hand in relation to the regional and universal organisational structures of church life, on the other with regard to the relationship between the church and Christianity. This perspective would also make it possible to overcome the differences between the Protestant presentation of practical theology, which is based on the individual community, and the Roman Catholic one, which is based on the central authority. That the point of view of an approach from mission also makes the relationship between the church and Christianity intelligible will be seen when it is realised that the gap between the church and the kingdom of God is connected with the fact that mission means that the church is founded for a future in the kingdom of God and so for all mankind. C. J. Nitzsch saw clearly that the idea of the kingdom of God was essential to a definition of the relationship between the church and Christianity: 'In virtue of this distinction [sc. between the church and the kingdom of God] the life of the church is one which brings about the advance and perfection of the Christian and moral life,' [838] The idea of the kingdom of God as something distinct from the church operates at every level of the church to prevent it from regarding itself as an ultimate goal. It can also give it a theological justification for seeing itself, even within Christianity, as one institution among others, and so understanding its activity as a service to a society which is not inherently ecclesial and which is today overwhelmingly pluralistic

---

der praktischen Theologie, I, 1890, 3rd ed. 1911, p. 29).

[838] C. J. Nitzsch, *Praktische Theologie,* vol. I, 1837, p. 14. In this context Nitzsch's ethicising interpretation of the kingdom of God is less of a limitation than his failure to see the connection of mission with the church and the kingdom of God, which alone reveals the historic nature of the relationship between the latter.

in religion. This applies in particular to its relationship with the state. It is one of the limitations of Nitzch's model of practical theology that he did not see that the original political meaning of the idea of the kingdom of God enables it to transcend the distinction between church and state in the same way as that between church and Christianity,[839] and that this was why the relationship between church and state could become a problem within the 'new people of God' which was Christendom. To overlook this in a concentration on the internal life of the church is as inadequate as the opposite thesis of Rothe that in Protestantism the church was destined to disappear into the moral state. A practical theology aware of its obligation to explore the general truth of the unity of God and man in Jesus of Nazareth and of the presence of the coming kingdom in him, as a hope for mankind and the basis of the church's practice, will have to re-analyse in the modern period the relationship between state and church in order to define correctly the church's responsibilities in the tasks facing society at present. This analysis must take account of the religious implications of the political structures and revolutionary movements of the modern period as well as the corresponding consequences of the split in the church for the libration of the state from explicit religious ties. It must also consider the possible contribution which might be made by the ecumenical movement of our times to the general problem of unity without uniformity as it affects both state and church. The reasons for the necessity of dealing explicity with religious matters in ecclesial institutions distinct from the state must be given equal weight with the responsibility the churches share for society. All these themes converge in the problem of the meaning and possibility of freedom, which is, for good reasons, both religious and political in nature. Practical theology must include all this if its traditional pastoral divisions are to acquire new relevance from a clearer connection with the problem of the practice of Christianity as a whole.

[839] Nitzsch (pp. 266ff) regards the state as a 'divine protection' (p. 271), with a positive relation to the church.

INDEX OF NAMES

INDEX OF SUBJECTS